WELFARE, PLANNING, AND EMPLOYMENT

WELFARE, PLANNING, AND EMPLOYMENT
Selected Essays in Economic Theory

Abram Bergson

The MIT Press
Cambridge, Massachusetts
London, England

This book was printed and bound in the United States of America.

Library of Congress Cataloging in Publication Data

Bergson, Abram, 1914–
Welfare, planning, and employment.

Includes index.
1. Welfare economics—Addresses, essays, lectures. 2. Employment (Economic theory)—Addresses, essays, lectures. 3. Public welfare—Planning—Addresses, essays, lectures. 4. Manpower policy—Addresses, essays, lectures. I. Title.
HB846.B47   330.15'5   81-23679
ISBN 0-262-02175-7   AACR2

CONTENTS

PREFACE

Written over a period of more than four decades, the essays in this volume cannot really be said to have a single, common theme, but all fall in the realm of economic theory, and the various topics touched on are often closely related to each other. Thus, an initial group of writings, dealing with the concept of social welfare and the conditions for an economic optimum, falls squarely in the field of welfare economics. Essentially that is also true of the group that follows, comprised of essays relating to problems of measuring welfare and efficiency. A third category of writings focuses on rather different themes, socialist economics and public enterprise, but all these essays could be viewed as representing applications of welfare economics. The final group of essays on income and employment theory, however, is clearly positive rather than normative in character and so represents something of a break with the balance of the writings included.

The essays are said to have been selected. In fact, I include all but a few minor items among the writings in theory that I have published since the appearance, in 1966, of my *Essays in Normative Economics*. On the other hand, given the technique of reproduction that is used in the present volume, the marginal cost of incorporating additional materials, I understand, is relatively modest. In the circumstances, there seemed to be a case to include here three widely cited articles that were reprinted in the 1966 collection but are closely related to those published more recently. I refer to essays 1, 4, and 9. I have also taken the opportunity to reproduce now two early pieces—essays 14 and 15—that were not included in the 1966 collection. Although these two articles have received only modest attention since they were published, I allow myself to imagine that that may have been due to some extent to their appearance during World War II and the resultant professional absorption in more applied pursuits. The articles may retain interest as an early attempt to grapple with what has lately come to be a major concern in economic theory: integration of macro- and microeconomics.

Abram Bergson

Cambridge, Massachusetts
July 1981

I
SOCIAL WELFARE AND THE ECONOMIC OPTIMUM

REPRINTED FROM
QUARTERLY JOURNAL OF ECONOMICS
FEBRUARY, 1938

A REFORMULATION OF CERTAIN ASPECTS OF WELFARE ECONOMICS[1]

SUMMARY

Assumptions, 310.— I. General conditions for maximum welfare, 311.— II. The Lerner conditions, 316; the Pareto-Barone-Cambridge conditions, 318; the Cambridge conditions, 320. III. Review and comparison of the relevant points of the various expositions, 323.—IV. The sign of dE, 330.

The object of the present paper is to state in a precise form the value judgments required for the derivation of the conditions of maximum economic welfare which have been advanced in the studies of the Cambridge economists,[2] Pareto and Barone, and Mr. Lerner.[3] Such a formulation, I hope, will clarify certain aspects of the contribution of these writers, and at the same time provide a basis for a more proper understanding of the principles of welfare.

I shall develop my analysis under a set of assumptions which in certain respects differ from those introduced in the welfare studies. It will be assumed throughout the discussion that the amounts of all the factors of production, other than labor, are fixed and, for convenience, non-depreciating. While a variable capital supply is included in some of the

1. I am very grateful to Mr. Paul Samuelson for suggestions on many points.

2. I use this caption to designate those economists whose names are directly attached to the Cambridge School — Marshall, Professor Pigou, Mr. Kahn — as well as others, such as Edgeworth, whose welfare analysis is in all essentials the same as that of the Cambridge group. But in the course of my discussion I shall refer mainly to the studies of the first group of economists. This will ease my task considerably, and, I believe, will involve no loss of generality.

3. The studies referred to are Marshall, Principles (all references to the Third — 1895 — Edition); Pigou, Economics of Welfare (all references to the Fourth — 1932 — Edition); Kahn, Economic Journal, March, 1935; Pareto, Cours d'Economie Politique (all references to the Lausanne — 1897 — Edition); Barone, The Ministry of Production in a Socialist State (Translated from the Italian article of the same title in Giornale degli Economisti, 1908; the translation appearing in Hayek, Collectivist Economic Planning); and Lerner, Review of Economic Studies, June and October, 1934.

welfare studies, this is not a well developed part of the analysis, and for our present purposes it will be desirable to confine to the simpler case the discussion of the evaluations required.[4] I shall assume, also, that the variables involved in the analysis — the amounts of the various commodities consumed and services performed — are infinitesimally divisible. This assumption will be interpreted more strictly than is usually done. Otherwise it is the postulate of the welfare writers, and its introduction here will involve no significant departure from their analysis. Finally, I shall assume that there are only two kinds of consumers' goods, two kinds of labor, and two factors of production other than labor in the community, and that each commodity is produced, with labor and the other factors, in a single production unit. This assumption is introduced only to simplify the notation employed. The discussion will apply, with no modification, to the many commodity, many factor, and many production unit case.[5]

I

Among the elements affecting the wefare of the community during any given period of time are the amounts of each of the factors of production, other than labor, employed in the different production units, the amounts of the various commodities consumed, the amounts of the different kinds of work done, and the production unit for which this work is performed by each individual in the community during that period of time. If we use A and B to denote the two kinds of labor; C and D to denote the two factors

4. On a simple model, similar to that of Barone, the analysis may be extended to the case of a variable capital supply.

5. The assumption that each commodity is produced in one production unit, it is true, excludes an element of "external economies" from the analysis. But in the present essay I am interested only in the maximum conditions for the community's welfare, and not in the departures from the maximum under a given institutional set-up. To the extent that, in the many production unit case, there are external economies, these will require no modification in the maximum conditions I shall present, for these conditions relate only to marginal *social* value productivities.

of production other than labor; and X and Y to denote the two consumers' goods; we may express this relationship in the form

(1.1) $W = W(x_1, y_1, a_1^x, b_1^x, a_1^y, b_1^y, \cdots,$

$x_n, y_n, a_n^x, b_n^x, a_n^y, b_n^y, C^x, D^x, C^y, D^y, r, s, t, \cdots).$

Here C^x and D^x are the amounts of the non-labor factors of production C and D employed in the production unit producing the consumers' good X; C^y and D^y are the amounts of these factors employed in the production unit producing the consumers' good Y; x_i and y_i are the amounts of X and Y consumed by the ith individual; and a_i^x, b_i^x, a_i^y, and b_i^y are the amounts of each kind of work performed by him for each production unit during the given period of time.[6] The symbols r, s, t, $\cdots$, denote elements other than the amounts of commodities, the amounts of work of each type, and the amounts of the non-labor factors in each of the production units, affecting the welfare of the community.

Some of the elements r, s, t, $\cdots$, may affect welfare, not only directly, but indirectly through their effect on (say) the amounts of X and Y produced with any given amount of resources, e.g., the effects of a change in the weather. On the other hand, it is conceivable that variations in the amounts of commodities, the amounts of work of each type, and the amounts of non-labor factors in each of the production units also will have a direct and indirect effect on welfare; e.g., a sufficient diminution of x_i and y_i may be accompanied by an overturn of the government. But for relatively small changes in these variables, other elements in welfare, I believe, will not be significantly affected. To the extent that this is so a partial analysis is feasible.

I shall designate the function,

(1.2) $E = E(x_1, y_1, a_1^x, b_1^x, a_1^y, b_1^y, \cdots,$

$x_n, y_n, a_n^x, b_n^x, a_n^y, b_n^y, C^x, D^x, C^y, D^y),$

which is obtained by taking r, s, t, $\cdots$, in (1.1) as given, the Economic Welfare Function.[7]

6. I am assuming that an individual's labor time may be divided among the different types of work in any desired proportions.

7. It should be emphasized that in (1.2) other factors affecting wel-

Let us write the amounts of X and Y produced respectively by the X and Y production units as functions,

(1.3) $X = X(A^x, B^x, C^x, D^x)$; $Y = Y(A^y, B^y, C^y, D^y)$,

where A^x and B^x are the amounts of the two kinds of labor and C^x and D^x are the amounts of the other two factors of production employed in the X production unit; and A^y, B^y, C^y, D^y are defined similarly for the Y production unit.

If we assume that E varies continuously with $x_1, y_1, \cdots$, we may write as a general condition for a position of maximum economic welfare that, subject to the limitations of the given technique of production and the given amounts of resources,

(1.4) $dE = 0.$

Equation (1.4) requires that in the neighborhood of the maximum position any small adjustment will leave the welfare of the community unchanged. By use of (1.3) and (1.4) it is possible immediately to state in general terms the conditions for a maximum welfare.[8]

One group of maximum conditions relates to the consumption and supply of services by each individual in the community. They require that the marginal economic welfare of each commodity and the marginal economic diswelfare of each type of work be the same with respect to each individual in the community.[9] If we denote the marginal economic welfare of commodity X with respect to the

i^{th} individual, $\dfrac{\partial E}{\partial x_i}$, and of Y, $\dfrac{\partial E}{\partial y_i}$, the first group of these con-

fare are taken as given. I do *not* assume that economic welfare ıs an independent element which may be added to other welfare to get total welfare.

8. The conditions I shall develop in this section are a group of necessary conditions for a maximum. They are also the conditions for any critical point, and are sufficient in number to determine the location of such a point (or points) if there is one. In section IV below I shall consider the problem of determining whether a given critical point is a maximum or not.

9. This rather awkward terminology is adopted instead of, say, the phrase marginal economic welfare *of* the ith individual in order to include the possibility that an increment of X or Y given to the ith individual will affect the welfare of others.

ditions requires that, for all i, and for some p, q, and ω,

(1.5)
$$\frac{\partial E}{\partial x_i} = \omega p$$

and

(1.6)
$$\frac{\partial E}{\partial y_i} = \omega q.$$

Similarly if we denote the marginal economic diswelfare of the various types of work with respect to the ith individual $\dfrac{\partial E}{\partial a_i^x}$, $\dfrac{\partial E}{\partial b_i^x}$, $\dfrac{\partial E}{\partial a_i^y}$, $\dfrac{\partial E}{\partial b_i^y}$, the second group of these conditions requires that, for all i and for some g^x, h^x, g^y, h^y, and for the ω already chosen,

(1.7) $-\dfrac{\partial E}{\partial a_i^x} = \omega g^x,$ (1.8) $-\dfrac{\partial E}{\partial b_i^x} = \omega h^x,$

(1.9) $-\dfrac{\partial E}{\partial a_i^y} = \omega g^y,$ (1.10) $-\dfrac{\partial E}{\partial b_i^y} = \omega h^y.$

The minus signs and the multiplicative factor ω are inserted in these equations for convenience.

The remaining maximum conditions relate to production. They require that the economic welfare of the consumers' goods produced by a marginal increment of each type of work should equal the negative of the diswelfare of that increment of work, and that the increment of economic welfare due to the shift of a marginal unit of factors C and D from one production unit to another should equal the negative of the diswelfare caused by this adjustment. Using the notation $\dfrac{\partial X}{\partial A^x}$ for the marginal productivity of A^x, and a similar notation for the other marginal productivities, we may write these conditions in the form,

(1.11) $p\dfrac{\partial X}{\partial A^x} = g^x,$ (1.12) $p\dfrac{\partial X}{\partial B^x} = h^x,$

(1.13) $q\dfrac{\partial Y}{\partial A^y} = g^y,$ (1.14) $q\dfrac{\partial Y}{\partial B^y} = h^y,$

and,[1]

$$(1.15) \quad \omega\left(p\frac{\partial X}{\partial C^x} - q\frac{\partial Y}{\partial C^y}\right) = -\left(\frac{\partial E}{\partial C^x} - \frac{\partial E}{\partial C^y}\right),$$

$$(1.16) \quad \omega\left(p\frac{\partial X}{\partial D^x} - q\frac{\partial Y}{\partial D^y}\right) = -\left(\frac{\partial E}{\partial D^x} - \frac{\partial E}{\partial D^y}\right).$$

In equations (1.11) through (1.14), ω, which was present in all terms, has been divided out.[2]

It will be convenient to designate p the *price* of X, q the *price* of Y, and g^x, g^y, h^x, h^y, the *wage* of the types of work A^x, A^y, B^x, B^y. Equations (1.5) and (1.6) thus require that the marginal economic welfare per "dollar's worth" of each

commodity, $\dfrac{\partial E}{\partial x_i} \cdot \dfrac{1}{p}$ and $\dfrac{\partial E}{\partial y_i} \cdot \dfrac{1}{q}$, be the same for each com-

modity and for all individuals in the community. Similarly equations (1.7) through (1.10) require that the marginal economic diswelfare per "dollar's worth" of each kind of work be the same with respect to each kind of work and each individual in the community; equations (1.11) through (1.14) require that the wages of each type of labor should equal the marginal value productivity of that type of labor;[3] and with an analogous interpretation, equations (1.15) and (1.16) require that the marginal value productivity equal the cost due to a shift in C or D from one use to another.

II

The maximum conditions presented in section I are the general conditions for a position of maximum economic

1. The derivatives on the right hand sides of (1.15) and (1.16) indicate the effect on welfare of an adjustment in C or D for which all other elements — x^i, y^i, etc.— in welfare are constant. Such an effect would arise, for example, through a positive or negative evaluation of the relative amounts and kinds of "factory smoke" emitted in the two production units for varying amounts of one or the other factors employed in each unit.

2. Strictly speaking this procedure assumes a value proposition, which we shall introduce later, to the effect that ω is unequal to zero.

3. In the present essay it will be understood that all value productivities are *social* value productivities. Compare footnote 5, p. 311, supra.

welfare for any Economic Welfare Function. The maximum conditions presented in the welfare studies relate to a particular family of welfare functions. Their derivation thus requires the introduction of restrictions on the shape of the Economic Welfare Function I have presented. Three groups of value propositions suffice for this purpose.

I shall designate the various maximum conditions derived by the names of those writers, or groups of writers, who have been especially responsible for their elucidation. For reasons which will appear I have altered somewhat the content of the conditions, and there are differences in the analyses of the various writers which must also be noted. The latter differences will be pointed out in this section and in the one following.

The Lerner Conditions

The First Group of Value Propositions: *a shift in a unit of any factor of production, other than labor, from one production unit to another would leave economic welfare unchanged, provided the amounts of all the other elements in welfare were constant.*

The First Group of Value Propositions enables us to state certain of the maximum conditions in terms of the production functions alone. From these evaluations the right hand side of (1.15) and of (1.16) must equal zero.[4] The two equations thus may be written,

$$(2.1) \qquad p\,\frac{\partial X}{\partial C^x} = q\,\frac{\partial Y}{\partial C^y},$$

$$(2.2) \qquad p\,\frac{\partial X}{\partial D^x} = q\,\frac{\partial Y}{\partial D^y},$$

and they now impose the condition that the marginal value productivity of factors other than labor be the same in every use.

Equations (2.1) and (2.2) still contain the variables p

4. The net effect on the community's welfare of the "factory smoke" arising from a shift of the non-labor factors from one use to another is zero. (Cf. footnote 1, p. 315.)

and q, which involve derivatives of the Economic Welfare Function. If we combine (2.1) and (2.2), however, we have two equations,

$$(2.3) \qquad \frac{q}{p} = \frac{\partial X}{\partial C^x} \Big/ \frac{\partial Y}{\partial C^y} = \frac{\partial X}{\partial D^x} \Big/ \frac{\partial Y}{\partial D^y} ,$$

the second of which involves only the derivatives of the production functions. It requires that in the maximum position the ratio of the marginal productivity of a factor in one use to its marginal productivity in any other use be the same for all factors of production, other than labor. The first equation of (2.3) requires that all these ratios equal the price ratio.

The significance of (2.3) for the determination of maximum welfare may be expressed in the following manner: whatever the relative evaluations of commodity X and commodity Y, that is, in Barone's terminology, whatever their ratio of equivalence, (2.3) requires that in the maximum position given that one factor C is so distributed that a small shift from one production unit to another would alter the amounts of X and Y in such a manner as to leave welfare unchanged, i.e., given that C is so distributed that $\dfrac{\partial X}{\partial C^x} \Big/ \dfrac{\partial Y}{\partial C^y}$ equals the ratio of equivalence of the two commodities, then the other factors in order to be so distributed must have a ratio of marginal productivities equal to $\dfrac{\partial X}{\partial C^x} \Big/ \dfrac{\partial Y}{\partial C^y}$.

The condition (2.3) can be interpreted in another manner, which however does not bring out as directly the significance of the condition for a position of maximum *welfare*. The equality of the marginal productivity ratios implies that there is no possible further adjustment for which the amount of one commodity will be increased without that of another being reduced. A shift in one factor from X to Y can at best be just compensated by a shift of another from Y to X, if (2.3) is satisfied.[5]

5. Mr. Lerner, as far as I am aware, is the only economist to present

The Pareto-Barone-Cambridge Conditions

The Fundamental Value Propositions of Individual Preference: *if the amounts of the various commodities and types of work were constant for all individuals in the community except any i^{th} individual, and if the ith individual consumed the various commodities and performed the various types of work in combinations which were indifferent to him, economic welfare would be constant.*

The First Group of Value Propositions implies that under the assumption that the amounts of the factors of production other than labor are constant, the Economic Welfare Function may be written as

$$(2.4)\quad E = E(x_1, y_1, a_1^x, b_1^x, a_1^y, b_1^y, \cdots ,$$
$$x_n, y_n, a_n^x, b_n^x, a_n^y, b_n^y).$$

For from these propositions a shift in C or D from one production unit to another would have no effect on welfare, if all the other elements were constant. The Fundamental Value Propositions require that E be some function of the form,

$$(2.5)\quad E = E[S^1(x_1, y_1, a_1^x, b_1^x, a_1^y, b_1^y), \cdots ,$$
$$S^n(x_n, y_n, a_n^x, b_n^x, a_n^y, b_n^y)],$$

where the function,

$$(2.6)\qquad\qquad S^i = S^i(x_i, y_i, a_i^x, b_i^x, a_i^y, b_i^y),$$

and interpret (2.1) and (2.2) in the form of (2.3), his interpretation being the second of the two alternatives I have noted. In the studies of Pareto, Barone, and Marshall the conditions (2.1) and (2.2) are presented with the price ratios already equated to the individual marginal rates of substitution (cf. infra). In the studies of Professor Pigou and Mr. Kahn the procedure is the same as that of Pareto, Barone, and Marshall except that these two writers include in their analysis the possibility of departures from (2.1) and (2.2) due to such effects as are discussed above in footnote 1, p. 315.

Mr. Lerner advances the conditions (2.3) for all factors of production, labor as well as non-labor (Review of Economic Studies, October, 1934, p. 57). On the face of the matter this formulation is inconsistent with Mr. Lerner's own advocacy of the supremacy of individual tastes in the sphere of consumption, and I have therefore taken the liberty to modify his conditions accordingly. The other economists also do not allow for individual preferences as between production units in their analysis.

expresses the loci of combinations of commodities consumed and work performed which are indifferent to the ith individual.

The Fundamental Value Propositions enable us to state all the consumption and labor supply conditions in terms of the individual indifference functions, S^i, as ratios of (1.5), or of any other of their number. For consider the equation,

$$(2.7) \qquad \frac{\partial E}{\partial x_i} \Big/ \frac{\partial E}{\partial y_i} = \frac{p}{q},$$

obtained from (1.5) and (1.6) by division. Using the Fundamental Value Propositions,

$$(2.8) \qquad \frac{\partial E}{\partial x_i} \Big/ \frac{\partial E}{\partial y_i} = \frac{\partial E}{\partial S^i} \frac{\partial S^i}{\partial x_i} \Big/ \frac{\partial E}{\partial S^i} \frac{\partial S^i}{\partial y^i} = \frac{\partial S^i}{\partial x_i} \Big/ \frac{\partial S^i}{\partial y_i}.$$

The last ratio in (2.8) is one of the slopes of the indifference locus of the ith individual, or in the Hicks and Allen terminology, the marginal rate of substitution of commodity Y for commodity X.[6] Thus (2.7) requires that the marginal rate of substitution of the two commodities be the same for all individuals. By successively combining (1.5) with equations (1.7) through (1.10), the same result is obtained with respect to the other elements of welfare.

All the production conditions may now be stated in terms of the indifference functions and the production functions. For equations (1.11) through (1.14), the statement that the wage of each type of work should equal the marginal value productivity of that type of work may be interpreted to mean that the marginal product of a given type of work employed in producing a given commodity should equal the marginal rate of substitution of that commodity for that type of work. In the same manner conditions (2.2) not only require that the ratios of marginal productivities of the various factors other than labor be equal, but that these ratios should equal the marginal rate of substitution of the two commodities.

The Fundamental Value Propositions thus require that,

6. Cf. *Economica*, February, 1934.

whatever the ratios of equivalence between the various commodities and types of work, given that the types of work performed and commodities consumed by one individual are so fixed that for any small adjustment among them economic welfare is unchanged, i.e., given that the marginal rates of substitution and marginal productivities for this individual equal the respective ratios of equivalence, then for all other individuals to be similarly situated, their marginal rates of substitution must be the same as those of this individual. Under our implicit assumption of homogeneous factors, the respective marginal productivities of course must in any case be equal for all individuals.

Again the Fundamental Value Propositions may be interpreted also to mean that in the maximum position it is impossible to improve the situation of any one individual without rendering another worse off.[7]

The Cambridge Conditions

Let us designate

$$(2.9) \qquad m_i = px_i + qy_i - g^x a_i^x - h^x b_i^x - g^y a_i^y - h^y b_i^y,$$

7. The Pareto-Barone-Cambridge Conditions are developed by Marshall in the Principles (pp. 413–415, 526–527; Append. XIV), but the derivation of the production conditions is based upon the very simple illustrative assumption of a producer-consumer expending his capital and labor in such a manner as to maximize his utility. Under more general assumptions the conditions are developed, without the utility calculus used by Marshall, by Pareto (Cours, Vol. I, pp. 20ff., Vol. II, pp. 90ff.) and Barone (Ministry of Production), and with the utility calculus, by Professor Pigou (Economics of Welfare, particularly pp. 131–143) and Mr. Kahn (Economic Journal, March, 1935). All of these writers either develop the consumption conditions independently of their formulation of the production conditions (Marshall, Pareto) or assume the consumption conditions *ab initio* (Barone, Pigou, Kahn); and, as we shall indicate, the interpretations vary. Mr. Lerner in his study in the Review of Economic Studies, June, 1934, presents all the conditions together, and interprets them most lucidly in the second of the two senses we have pointed out.

As I have noted elsewhere (footnote 5, p. 317) none of these writers includes in his analysis individual preferences between production units. Also, Professor Pigou and Mr. Kahn include the possibility of departures from (2.3), and perhaps from (1.11), (1.12), (1.13), (1.14), for the direct effects on welfare of shifts of the factors of production from one use to another.

the Share of the ith individual. In (2.9), p, q, etc. are taken proportional to the respective marginal rates of substitution. Thus m^i is defined, aside from a proportionality factor. The sum of m^i for the community as a whole is equal to the difference between the total wages and the total value of consumers' goods in the community.

The Propositions of Equal Shares: *If the Shares of any i^{th} and k^{th} individuals were equal, and if the prices and wage rates were fixed, the transfer of a small amount of the Share of i to k would leave welfare unchanged.*

The Propositions of Equal Shares enable us to state in terms of the distribution of Shares the remaining condition (1.5). According to these evaluations, if the Shares of i and k are equal, then for the price-wage situation given,

$$(2.10) \qquad dE = \frac{\partial E}{\partial m_i} dm_i + \frac{\partial E}{\partial m_k} dm_k = 0,$$

for $dm_i = -dm_k$. Equation (2.10) is equivalent to the condition imposed by (1.5) that the marginal economic welfare per "dollar's worth" of X is the same for i and k.[8] Thus if the Shares of all individuals are equal, the condition (1.5) is satisfied.[9]

8. The proof is as follows:
$$\frac{\partial E}{\partial m_i} = \frac{\partial E}{\partial x_i}\frac{\partial x_i}{\partial m_i} + \frac{\partial E}{\partial y_i}\frac{\partial y_i}{\partial m_i} + \frac{\partial E}{\partial a_i^x}\frac{da_i^x}{\partial m_i} + \frac{\partial E}{\partial b_i^x}\frac{\partial b_i^x}{\partial m_i} + \frac{\partial E}{\partial a_i^y}\frac{\partial a_i^y}{\partial m_i} + \frac{\partial E}{\partial b_i^y}\frac{\partial b_i^y}{\partial m_i}$$
By (2.9)
$$1 = p\frac{\partial x_i}{\partial m_i} + q\frac{\partial y_i}{\partial m_i} - g^x\frac{da_i^x}{\partial m_i} - h^x\frac{\partial b_i^x}{\partial m_i} - g^y\frac{\partial a_i^y}{\partial m_i} - h^y\frac{\partial b_i^y}{\partial m_i}.$$
Using this equation (2.7), and similar equations for the commodities and services,
$$\frac{\partial E}{\partial m_i} = \frac{\partial E}{\partial x_i}\cdot\frac{1}{P}.$$

9. Among the welfare studies the Cambridge Conditions are the distinctive characteristic of the writings of the members of the Cambridge School. They are advanced in the works of all the Cambridge economists, and in none of the other welfare studies we have considered. But certain qualifications must be noted.

The Cambridge economists require an equal distribution of incomes, $(px_i + qy_i)$, rather than of Shares as the condition for equality of the marginal economic welfare per "dollar" for all individuals (with quali-

The three groups of value propositions are not only sufficient for the derivation of the maximum conditions presented in the welfare studies. They are necessary for this procedure. For it is possible, and I shall leave the development of the argument to the reader, to deduce from the maximum conditions presented the restriction imposed upon the Economic Welfare Function by the value judgments introduced.

But it should be noted that the particular value judgments I have stated are not necessary to the welfare analysis. They are essential only for the establishment of a particular group of maximum conditions. If the production functions and individual indifference functions are known, they provide sufficient information concerning the Economic Welfare Function for the determination of the maximum position,

fications which we shall note directly, cf. Kahn, Economic Journal, March, 1935, pp. 1, 2; Pigou, Economics of Welfare, pp. 82ff.; Marshall, Principles, p. 795). If it is assumed that the amounts of the various types of labor performed by each individual in the community are given, this condition is of course the same as ours. But otherwise for a requirement of equal incomes there is unlikely to be any position which satisfied all the conditions for a maximum. For it would be necessary that in the neighborhood of the maximum position the marginal productivity and marginal diswelfare of each type of work be zero.

[The condition of equal incomes is not necessarily inconsistent with the other postulates. There might be some indifference functions and production functions such that all the maximum conditions are satisfied. But it may be noted here, in general, as a minimum requirement that the various conditions must be consistent with each other. Compare Lange, Review of Economic Studies, October, 1936, pp. 64, 65, and Lerner, ibid., p. 73.]

For convenience I have presented the Cambridge Conditions in a rather simple form. In a more elaborate exposition of the conditions advanced by the Cambridge economists I should have to introduce — and on *a priori* grounds I believe it desirable to introduce — modifications in the distribution of Shares for changes in the price-wage situation which might affect different individuals differently — some moving to a more preferable position, and others to a less preferable one — and for other special differences between individuals. (Cf. Marshall's reference to the distribution of *wealth*, op. cit., pp. 527, 595, and Pigou's reference to the distribution of the *Dividend*, op. cit., p. 89; but cf. also Kahn's reference to the distribution of *money incomes*, p. cit., pp. 1, 2.)

if it exists.[1] In general, any set of value propositions which is sufficient for the evaluation of all alternatives may be introduced, and for each of these sets of propositions there corresponds a maximum position. The number of sets is infinite, and in any particular case the selection of one of them must be determined by its compatibility with the values prevailing in the community the welfare of which is being studied. For only if the welfare principles are based upon prevailing values, can they be relevant to the activity of the community in question. But the determination of prevailing values for a given community, while I regard it as both a proper and necessary task for the economist, and of the same general character as the investigation of the indifference functions for individuals, is a project which I shall not undertake here. For the present I do not attempt more than the presentation of the values current in economic literature in a form for which empirical investigation is feasible.[2]

III

The formulation I have used to derive the maximum conditions of economic welfare differs in several respects from that of the welfare studies. It will be desirable to review briefly the relevant points of the various expositions, and the departures of the present essay from them. I shall continue to use the set of assumptions stated on page 310.

1. Cf. footnote 8, p. 313
2. This conception of the basis for the welfare principles should meet Professor Robbins' requirement that the economist take the values of the community as data. But in so far as I urge that the economist also *study* these data it represents perhaps a more positive attitude than might be inferred as desirable from his essays. (The Nature and Significance of Economics, London, 1932, particularly chapter VI.) Whether the approach will prove a fruitful one remains to be seen.

It may be noted that tho Professor Robbins is averse to the study of indifference curves (pp. 96ff.) his own analysis requires an assumption that a movement of labor from one use to another is indifferent to the laborer and that a shift of other factors of production is indifferent to the community. Without these assumptions, for which I can see no *a priori* justification, his whole discussion of alternative *indifferent* uses, and his references to the most adequate satisfaction of demand from a given amount of means are without basis.

In the Cambridge analysis[3] the welfare of the community, stated symbolically,[4] is an aggregate of the form,[5]

(3.1) $$\bar{E} = \Sigma U^i(x_i,\, y_i,\, a_i^x,\, b_i^x,\, a_i^y,\, b_i^y).$$

In this expression U^i is some function of the indifference function, S^i, and measures the satisfactions derived by the ith individual from $x_i,\, y_i,\, a_i^x,\, b_i^x,\, a_i^y,\, b_i^y$. If individual temperaments are about the same, that is, if individuals are capable of equal satisfactions, the marginal utilities or derivatives of the utility functions of different individuals, it is assumed, will be equal for an equal distribution of Shares.[6]

It is possible to derive all the maximum conditions, in specific terms, from the equation

(3.2) $$\Sigma dU^i = 0.$$

The technique used by the Cambridge economists is less direct and varies in certain respects. For our present purposes these procedural differences are of little special interest, but it will facilitate our discussion of the analysis of Pareto and Barone if we append the following notes.

Marshall develops the Pareto-Barone-Cambridge consumption and labor supply conditions separately from the rest of his analysis.[7] These conditions are that for some price-wage situation $p,\, q,\, g^x,\, h^x,\, g^y,\, h^y$, and for all i,

(3.3) $$w^i = \frac{U_1^i}{p} = \frac{U_2^i}{q} = \frac{-U_3^i}{g^x} = \frac{-U_4^i}{h^x} = \frac{-U_5^i}{g^y} = \frac{-U_6^i}{h^y}$$

3. The passages in the Cambridge studies which are particularly informative as to the Cambridge concept of welfare are Marshall, op. cit., pp. 80ff., 200ff., 527, 804; Pigou, op. cit., pp. 10–11, 87, 97; Kahn, op. cit., pp. 1, 2, 19; and also Edgeworth, Papers Relating to Political Economy, Vol. II, p. 102 (from the Economic Journal, 1897).

4. Aside from Marshall's appendices, the exposition of Marshall, Professor Pigou, and Mr. Kahn is non-mathematical, but the few relationships we discuss here may be presented most conveniently in a mathematical form. This will also facilitate comparison with the studies of Pareto and Barone.

5. In the analyses of Professor Pigou and Mr. Kahn some modification of (3.1) would be introduced to take care of the direct effects on aggregate welfare of shifts of factors of production from one use to another (cf. footnote 1, p. 315).

6. With the qualifications of footnote 9, p. 321.

7. Cf. the references in footnote 7, p. 320.

In (3.3), w^i is the marginal utility of money to the ith individual and U_1^i, U_2^i, U_3^i, etc., are the marginal utilities of the various commodities and disutilities of the various types of work. In Marshall's exposition it is shown that, for any given amounts of X, Y, A^x, B^x, A^y, B^y, if the conditions (3.3) are not satisfied some U^i can be increased without any other being decreased. Thus for (3.2) to hold, (3.3) must be satisfied. Professor Pigou and Mr. Kahn do not develop the conditions (3.3), but assume them *ab initio* in their analysis.

If the conditions (3.3) are satisfied, (3.2) may be written in the form

$$(3.4) \qquad\qquad \Sigma w^i \Delta_i = 0,$$

where

$$(3.5) \quad \Delta_i = p \, dx_i + q \, dy_i - g^x \, da_i^x - h^x \, db_i^x - g^y \, da_i^y - h^y \, db_i^y.$$

The remaining conditions again may be derived from (3.4). However, in Mr. Kahn's reformulation of Professor Pigou's analysis,[8] it is assumed also that the Shares are distributed equally, and the remaining conditions are developed from the requirement that

$$(3.6) \qquad\qquad \Sigma \Delta_i = 0.$$

The summation in (3.6), with certain qualifications, is Professor Pigou's index of the National Dividend.[9] The procedures of Professor Pigou and Marshall differ from this, but the variances need not be elaborated here.[1]

Pareto and Barone also assume initially that conditions (3.3) are satisfied, but Pareto like Marshall shows in an early section of his work that, otherwise, it is possible to increase the *ophélimité* of some individuals without that of any others being decreased.[2] To develop the remaining con-

8. Economic Journal, March, 1935.
9. Professor Pigou's index does not include cost elements; it relates to large adjustments — whence the problem of backward and forward comparisons; and it is expressed as a percentage of the total value product at the initial position. Cf. Economics of Welfare, Chap. VI.
1. But cf. section IV, infra.
2. Cours, Vol. I, pp. 20ff.

ditions, aside from the Cambridge Conditions, Pareto expressedly avoids the use of (3.2) on the ground that

nous ne pouvons ni comparer ni sommer celles-ci [dU^1, dU^2, etc.], car nous ignorons le rapport des unités en lesquelles elles sont exprimées.[3]

Instead Pareto proceeds directly to (3.6) and deduces the maximum conditions for production from it. In this, evidently for the same reason, Barone follows.[4] Neither Pareto nor Barone introduces the Cambridge Conditions into his analysis. Pareto merely assumes that the shares are distributed "suivant la régle qu'il plaira d'adopter," or in a "manière convenable,"[5] and Barone that they are distributed according to some "ethical criteria."[6]

The basis for developing production conditions directly from (3.6), for Pareto, is that this equation will assure that if the quantities of products

étaient convenablement distribuées, il en resulterait un maximum d'ophélimité pour chaque individu dont se compose la société.[7]

Barone adopts the requirement that the sum be zero because this

means that every other series of equivalents different from that which accords with this definition would make that sum negative. That is to say, either it causes a decline in the welfare of all, or if some decline while others are raised, the gain of the latter is less than the loss of the former (so that even taking all their gain from those who gained in the change, reducing them to their former position, to give it completely to those who lost, the latter would always remain in a worse position than their preceding one without the situation of others being improved).[8]

Mr. Lerner, in the first of his two studies on welfare, advances as a criterion for a maximum position the condition that it should be impossible in this position to increase the welfare of one individual without decreasing that of another. From this criterion he develops graphically the

---

3. Ibid., Vol. II, p. 93.
4. Cf. Ministry of Production, p. 246.
5. Cours, Vol. II, pp. 91, 93, 94.
6. Op. cit., p. 265.
7. Op. cit., pp. 93, 94.
8. Op. cit., p. 271.

first two groups of maximum conditions. Like Pareto and Barone he does not introduce the Cambridge Conditions into his analysis but, as he indicates, ignores the problem of distribution.[9] In his later paper Mr. Lerner presents the first group of maximum conditions alone, on the basis of the criterion for a maximum that it should be impossible to increase the production of one commodity without decreasing that of another.[1]

In my opinion the utility calculus introduced by the Cambridge economists is not a useful tool for welfare economics. The approach does not provide an alternative to the introduction of value judgments. First of all, the comparison of the utilities of different individuals must involve an evaluation of the relative economic positions of these individuals. No extension of the methods of measuring utilities will dispense with the necessity for the introduction of value propositions to give these utilities a common dimension. Secondly, the evaluation of the different commodities cannot be avoided, even tho this evaluation may consist only in a decision to accept the evaluations of the individual members of the community. And finally, whether the direct effects on aggregate utility of a shift of factors of production from one use to another are given a zero value, as in Marshall's analysis, or a significant one, as in the analyses of Professor Pigou and Mr. Kahn,[2] alternatives are involved, and accordingly value judgments must be introduced.

While the utility calculus does not dispense with value judgments, the manner in which these value judgments are introduced is a misleading one. Statements as to the aggregative character of total welfare, or as to the equality of marginal utilities when there is an equal distribution of Shares, provided temperaments are about the same, do have the ring of *factual* propositions, and are likely to obscure the

9. Review of Economic Studies, June, 1934.
1. Ibid., October, 1934.
2. Cf. footnote 1, p. 315 and footnote 3, p. 324.

evaluations implied. The note by Mr. Kahn, in reference to his own formulation of the maximum conditions for economic welfare, that

many will share Mr. Dobbs' suspicion "that to strive after such a maximum is very much like looking in a dark room for a black hat which may be entirely subjective after all." [3]

is not one to reassure the reader as to the nature of the welfare principles derived in this manner. To the extent that the utility calculus does conceal the rôle of value judgments in the derivation of welfare principles, the criticism directed against the Cambridge procedure by Professor Robbins and other students of economics[4] is not without justification.

The approach, it must also be noted, requires a group of value propositions additional to those I have presented. Insofar as the Cambridge economists require that the economic welfare of the community be an *aggregate* of individual welfares, value judgments must be introduced to the effect that each individual contributes independently to the total welfare. These value propositions, which imply the complete measurability of the economic welfare function aside from an arbitrary origin and a scalar constant, are not necessary for the derivation of the maximum conditions, and accordingly are not essential to the analysis.[5]

The derivation of conditions of maximum economic welfare without the summation of individual utilities, by Pareto, Barone, and Mr. Lerner, is a stride forward from the Cambridge formulation. Pareto's exposition of the basis for the procedure is somewhat ambiguous. Properly stated, the argument for developing production conditions directly from (3.6) is the same as that used in developing consumption conditions. The increment Δ_i in (3.5) indicates the prefer-

3. Economic Journal, March, 1935, footnote, p. 2.
4. Cf. Robbins, The Nature and Significance of Economic Science (London, 1932); Sutton, C., Economic Journal, March, 1937.
5. Lange's discussion of utility determinateness (Review of Economic Studies, June, 1934.) errs insofar as it implies that welfare economics requires the summation of the independently measurable utilities of individuals, i.e., his second utility postulate.

ence direction of the ith individual.[6] If Δ_i is positive, the ith individual moves to a preferable position. The condition that $\Sigma\Delta_i$ be equal to zero does not assure that the *ophélimité* of each individual be a maximum, but that it be impossible to improve the position of one individual without making that of another worse. This, disregarding the misleading comparison of losses and gains, is the interpretation of Barone, and it is also the condition for a maximum used by Mr. Lerner.

But in avoiding the addition of utilities, Pareto, Barone, and Mr. Lerner also exclude the Cambridge Conditions from their analysis. None of the writers indicates his reasons for the exclusion, and I believe it has not proved an advantageous one. The first two groups of value propositions are introduced in the studies of Pareto and Barone by the use of, and the argument as to the use of, (3.6) as a basis for deriving maximum conditions, and in the analysis of Mr. Lerner by the criteria adopted for a maximum. In this respect the formulations differ little from that of the Cambridge economists. With the accompanying statements by Pareto and Barone that *the distribution of Shares* is decided on the basis of some "ethical criteria" or "rule," or with the complete exclusion of the problem by Mr. Lerner, this approach is not more conducive to an apprehension of the value content of the first two groups of maximum conditions. In the case of Mr. Lerner's study a misinterpretation does in fact appear. For in his analysis the first group of maximum conditions are advanced as objective in a sense which clearly implies that they require no value judgments for their derivation.[7]

Further, it must be emphasized, tho the point is surely an obvious one, that unless the Cambridge Conditions, or a modified form of these conditions, is introduced there is no reason in general why it is more preferable to have the other two groups of conditions satisfied than otherwise. Placing $\Sigma\Delta_i$ equal to zero does not assure that there are

6. Cf. Allen, *Economica*, May, 1932.
7. *Review of Economic Studies*, October, 1934, p. 57.

no other positions for which welfare is greater, but only that there are no other positions for which the welfare of one individual is greater without that of another being less. In general if the third group of maximum conditions is not satisfied, it is just as likely as not that any position for which $\Sigma\Delta_i$ does not equal zero will be *more* desirable than any position for which it does equal zero.

In the Pareto-Barone analysis, tho not in that of Mr. Lerner, there is reason to believe that, in a general form, the third group of maximum conditions is assumed to be satisfied. While the distribution of Shares is not specified, it is consistent with some "ethical criteria," or "rule." Whatever the rule is, it should follow that in the maximum position the marginal economic welfare "per dollar" with respect to all individuals is the same. Otherwise, in the light of that rule, some other distribution would be preferable. If this interpretation is correct, the special exposition used by Pareto and Barone to support their derivation of maximum conditions is inappropriate. In (3.6) it is true that each dollar does not express the same amount of utility in the Cambridge sense, since the value propositions of independence are not introduced. But each dollar does express the same amount of welfare. The argument used to place (3.6) equal to zero is thus not the Pareto-Barone one, but that if it were unequal to zero, a further adjustment increasing the summation would be possible, and this would directly increase welfare, *regardless* of whether the position of some individuals were improved and that of others worsened by the change.[8]

IV

I have noted elsewhere that the conditions for a maximum welfare which are presented in sections I and II are the conditions for any critical point. They are sufficient to inform us whether or not we are at the top or bottom of a hill, or at the top with respect to one variable, and the bottom with respect to another. The requirement for a

8. This argument is more fully developed in section IV, infra.

maximum position is that it be possible to reach the position from any neighboring point by a series of positive adjustments. For the determination of such a position, it is necessary to know the sign $(+, -, 0)$ of any increment of welfare.

In the welfare studies the sign of dE is specified only for limited groups of adjustments. It will be of interest to note these conditions, and the value judgments required, tho I shall not review again the formulations of the various writers.

(1) If we assume that all the conditions for a critical point are satisfied, except those relating to the distribution of the factors of production between different uses, one additional group of value judgments gives us sufficient information concerning the shape of the Economic Welfare Function to determine the sign of an increment of welfare. These value propositions are: *if all individuals except any i^{th} individual remain in positions which are indifferent to them, and if the ith individual moves to a position which is preferable to him, economic welfare increases.* If we denote a more preferable position by a positive movement of S^i, these value propositions require that

(4.1)
$$\frac{\partial E}{\partial S^i} > 0,$$

for any i. Let us write from (2.5),

(4.2) $$dE = \sum \frac{\partial E}{\partial x_i} dx_i + \frac{\partial E}{\partial y_i} dy_i + \frac{\partial E}{\partial a_i^x} da_i^x + \frac{\partial E}{\partial b_i^x} db_i^x$$
$$+ \frac{\partial E}{\partial a_i^y} da_i^y + \frac{\partial E}{\partial b_i^y} db_i^y.$$

Using the equations (1.5) through (1.10), and the notation of (3.5),

(4.3) $$dE = \omega \Sigma \Delta_i.$$

By (4.1) and the equations (1.5) through (1.10), ω must have the same sign as the price-wage rates in Δ_i. We shall take this sign as positive. Thus if the Shares are distributed equally, and if the prices and wage rates are proportionate to the marginal rates of substitution of the different kinds of commodities and types of work, economic welfare has the sign of Professor Pigou's index of the National Dividend. It will be increased by any adjustment which has as a result the movement of factors of production to a position of higher marginal value productivity.

(2) If the assumption that the Cambridge Conditions are satisfied is relaxed, (4.3) may be written in the form

(4.4) $$dE = \Sigma \omega^i \Delta_i$$

where ω^i is the marginal economic welfare per dollar with respect to the ith individual. Using the evaluation in (4.1) it follows that, for any adjustment for which no Δ_i decreases and some Δ_i increases, economic welfare will increase.

(3) Continuing to use the assumptions of (2), let us write

(4.5) $$\lambda_{ik} = \frac{\omega^i}{\omega^k},$$

and

(4.6) $$dE = \omega^k \Sigma \lambda_{ik} \Delta_i.$$

Let us introduce the value propositions: *for a given price-wage situation, and any i and k, if the Share of i is greater than that of k, a decrease in the Share of k would have to be accompanied by a larger increase in the Share of i, for economic welfare to remain unchanged.* Since it can be shown that if the Share of the ith individual increases by dm_i a concomitant decrease, $-\lambda_{ik}dm_i$, in the share of the kth will leave economic welfare unchanged,[9] these value propositions require that λ_{ik} be less than unity. It follows that, for any given adjustment, if $\Sigma \Delta_i$ is positive, and if Δ_i does not vary with m_i, or if it decreases with m_i, economic welfare will increase. In other words, if the change in the National Dividend is not counteracted by a change in its distribution, the welfare of the community will be increased, even if some Δ_i increase and others decrease.

The adjustments in (1) are those considered by Mr. Kahn;

9. This relationship follows immediately from the equations:

$$dE = \frac{\partial E}{\partial m_i} dm_i + \frac{\partial E}{\partial m_k} dm_k = \omega^i dm_i + \omega^k dm_k.$$

in (2) by Pareto, Barone, and Mr. Lerner; and in (3) by Marshall and Professor Pigou. As Professor Pigou has pointed out,[1] the sign of an increment of welfare for some adjustments is left undetermined in his analysis. To determine the sign of dE for all adjustments, all the λ's would have to be evaluated, and a similar group of value judgments for the case where prices and wages are not proportional to the marginal rates of substitution would have to be introduced. On *a priori* grounds there is no reason why more information should not be obtained, since the comparison involved in evaluating the λ's is the same as that required for the Value Propositions of Equal Shares. For some additional and fairly rough evaluations, the range of adjustments included can be extended considerably, tho an element of uncertainty is involved. Two such approximations, perhaps, are of sufficient interest to note, tho they are not introduced in the welfare studies.

(4) The assumptions of (2) are retained. Let us suppose that with respect to some individual, say the kth,

$$(4.7) \qquad \Sigma \lambda_{ik} = N$$

the sum being taken for all i. Thus ω^k is the average ω If we write

$$(4.8) \qquad a_i = \lambda_{ik} - 1; \quad \beta_i = \Delta_i - \frac{\Sigma \Delta_i}{N};$$

then

$$(4.9) \qquad dE = \omega^k (\Sigma a_i \beta_i + \Sigma \Delta_i).$$

The first term in the brackets may be regarded as an index of the distribution of the National Dividend. It follows immediately from (4.9) that (a) if Δ_i is positively correlated with λ_{ik}, dE will increase with an increase in the Dividend and conversely; (b) if the coefficient of variation of the ω's is less than one hundred per cent, that is, if the standard deviation of λ_{ik} is less than unity, and if the coefficient of variation of Δ_i is also less than one hundred per cent, dE

1. Economics of Welfare, p. 645.

will have the sign of the index of the Dividend *regardless* of changes in its distribution.[2]

To determine precisely whether the conditions enumerated are satisfied, of course, would require a complete evaluation of the λ's. But the following rough evaluations would be sufficient to assure the likelihood of the results. For (a), it must be possible to say that "on the average" the change in distribution does not affect the "poor" more than the "rich" or vice versa. For (b) it is necessary to conceive of an individual or group of individuals who are, on the whole, in an average position from the point of view of welfare, and to determine whether, for a given position, ω^i "on the average" is likely to be somewhat less than twice the marginal economic welfare per "dollar" for the average individuals, that is, less than twice ω^k. (This should be stated in terms of the average shift in Shares for which welfare remains unchanged.) If it is determined that such a position is occupied, it would be likely that if tastes did not vary greatly — that is, if the relative variation of Δ_i were not very large — dE would increase for an increase in the Dividend. Since, however, the relative variation of Δ_i would ordinarily become excessively large as $\Sigma\Delta_i$ approached zero, it would be highly uncertain, for adjustments close to the maximum, whether or not an unfavorable change in distribution would obliterate the change in the Dividend.

HARVARD UNIVERSITY

2. From (4.9),
$$dE = \omega^k(Nr_{\lambda\Delta}\sigma_\lambda\sigma_\Delta + \Sigma\Delta)$$
$$= \omega^k(Nr_{\lambda\Delta}\sigma_\lambda\sigma_\Delta/\Sigma\Delta + 1)\Sigma\Delta.$$

The proposition (a) follows immediately, and (b) is based on the fact that $r_{\lambda\Delta}$ must be less than unity.

Abram Bergson

Harvard University

Taste Differences
and Optimal Income Distribution:
A Paradox Illustrated

For purposes of normative economics, suppose that one has committed himself to a social welfare function of the familiar individualistic sort, where the community's welfare is an increasing function of the utilities of individual households. Suppose also that available supplies of consumers' goods are acquired by households in an open market at clearing prices and that the distribution of income is such as is considered optimal, i.e., social welfare would only be diminished by any redistribution. Should supplies and incomes then vary, but in a way such that each household's utility is unchanged, is one committed to consider the distribution of income that then prevails as also optimal?

In a previous essay (Bergson, 1966, pp. 78ff), the answer was found to be in the affirmative provided that tastes of different households are the same. [1] But, paradoxically, so far as tastes differ, there is actually a commitment otherwise. Even though, with the

[1] Or rather, the answer is in the affirmative if tastes are the same, and, as is likely in that case, the social welfare function is symmetric in respect of utilities of different households, with the result that in the optimum all consume the same amount of each and every good.

change in supplies and incomes, utilities of all households remain as they were initially, the distribution of income can no longer be considered optimal; and optimality can be reestablished only if income is now redistributed in such a way that benefits some households and is costly to others; in such a way, that is, that the utilities of some households increase and those of other households decrease.

In the cited essay, I proved that this is so on a general plane. It may further illuminate the intriguing matter in question if in this note I illustrate relations of interest with a specific example.

As before, it suffices to refer to a community in which there are but two individuals who consume only two commodities. Previously, though, no restrictions were imposed on the social welfare function beyond that already implied, i.e., it was required only that

$$(1) \qquad W = F\,[U^j\,(x_j,\,y_j),\,U^s\,(x_s,\,y_s)],$$

where x_j and y_j are Jones', and x_s and y_s, Smith's consumption of the two goods.

Also,

$$(2a,b) \qquad U^j = U^j\,(x_j,\,y_j);\ U^s = U^s\,(x_s,\,y_s),$$

are the utility functions of Jones and Smith and have the usual properties of such formulas. Finally, F_1 and F_2, the partial derivatives of F with respect to U^j and U^s are > 0.

I focus now on a particular variant of (1), specifically the utilitarian formula:

$$(3) \qquad W = U^j + U^s$$

Also, each household has a utility function of the CES kind, though with different coefficients reflecting the difference in their tastes, i.e.,

$$(4a,b) \qquad U^j = 2\,x_j^{\frac{1}{2}} + y_j^{\frac{1}{2}};\ U^s = x_s^{\frac{1}{2}} + 2\,y_s^{\frac{1}{2}}$$

In equilibrium then, Jones' consumption conforms to these conditions:

$$(5a) \qquad 2y_j^{\frac{1}{2}}/x_j^{\frac{1}{2}} = p/q,$$

and

(5b) $px_j + qy_j = I_j$,

where p and q are the prices of x and y, and I_j is Jones' money income. Similarly, for Smith,

(6a) $y_s^{\frac{1}{2}}/2x_s^{\frac{1}{2}} = p/q$,

and

(6b) $px_s + qy_s = I_s$.

With p and q at clearing levels, we also have,

(7a,b) $x_j + x_s = X;\ y_j + y_s = Y$,

where X and Y are the total available suppliers of the two goods.

Given (5) - (7), as well-known, the two households are on the contract curve corresponding to X and Y, and the allocation of those commodities is Pareto optimal in that sense. For an optimal distribution of income, however, a further condition must be met, namely the marginal social welfare (MSW) per dollar must be the same for the two households; i.e., for the social welfare function and utility functions considered,

(8) $1/px_j^{\frac{1}{2}} = 1/2\ px_s^{\frac{1}{2}}$.

So far as Jones and Smith are on their contract curve, that comes to the same thing as

(9) $1/2q\ y_j^{\frac{1}{2}} = 1/qy_s^{\frac{1}{2}}$

While reference is to the marginal social welfare per dollar, note that optimality necessarily requires as well that the marginal social welfare per unit of each commodity is the same for each household. Indeed, these equalities are given at once by (8) and (9) after the deletion of prices. As must always be so, then, optimality in the distribution of "real" income goes hand in hand with optimality in the distribution of money income.

Formulas (5) - (9) apply whatever the total supplies of X and Y and whatever the income distribution that is in fact deemed optimal. For present purposes, I rather arbitrarily focus on two situations in respect of supply:

$X = 5$; $Y = 5$; and $X = 250/81$ and $Y = 625/81$.

I have calculated and shown in the accompanying table pertinent magnitudes corresponding to three alternative "social states" that are then of interest:

   (A) $X = 5$; $Y = 5$; income distribution is optimal, i.e., (8) and (9) are satisfied;

   (B) $X = 250/81$; $Y = 625/81$; the utility of each household is as in (A);

   (C) $X = 250/81$; $Y = 625/81$; income distribution is optimal, i.e., (8) and (9) are satisfied.

The market for consumers' goods is in equilibrium, i.e., (5) - (7) are satisfied, in all three states.

As appears in the table, in (A), given that there is equilibrium with incomes optimally distributed, each household's utility is 5. With the new supplies available in (B) that level of utility can be maintained for both Jones and Smith, and in the equilibrium depicted that is in fact done. As a result, however, MSW per \$1 is no longer the same for the two households, so income distribution has ceased to be optimal. Hence, with the supplies available in (B), a redistribution is required if optimality is to be achieved. In (C), that redistribution has been accomplished. Income distribution, therefore, is again optimal, though Jones is now worse off and Smith better off than in (A).

As to how much the one gains and the other loses, that can be judged from the variation in utilities that is shown, each household's utility supposedly having been scaled in a manner to make it an appropriate argument in the social welfare function given by (3). But it is also of interest to see the corresponding Hicksian compensating variations: for Jones, $(+)$ 1.034, or 30.0 percent of his money income in (C); for Smith $(-)$ 1.109, or 24.5 percent of his money income in (C). I refer to the change in money income, which, with prices as in (C), would be needed to restore utility for each household to the initial level of 5.

What is the moral of this exercise? As the primers teach, where tastes differ, money incomes mean different things depending on the price structure. By the same token, in evaluating normatively alternative distributions of money income, so far as tastes do differ, account must be taken of variations in price structure. That has

EQUILIBRIUM MAGNITUDES OF VARIOUS VARIABLES IN SELECTED ALTERNATIVE SOCIAL STATES

	U	x	y	p	q	I	MSW per $1
(A) $X = 5$; $Y = 5$; income distribution optimal							
Jones	5	4	1	}1	}1	5	½
Smith	5	1	4			5	½
(B) $X = 250/81$; $Y = 625/81$; utilities as in (A)							
Jones	5	25/9	25/9	}1	}½	≅ 4.167	3/5
Smith	5	25/81	400/81			≅ 2.778	9/10
(C) $X = 250/81$; $Y = 625/81$; income distribution optimal							
Jones	≅ 4.385	200/81	125/81	}1	}(2/5)½	≅ 3.445	9/10(2)½
Smith	≅ 5.755	50/81	500/81			≅ 4.521	9/10(2)½

long been understood but the presupposition, I believe, has generally been that such an accounting for price structure changes, at least in principle, must reduce simply to allowing for such "real" gains and losses as those changes may entail for different households. The chief moral of the analysis of my previous essay, which I have illustrated here, is that that presupposition is in error. As household money incomes and the price structure vary, there necessarily are no "real" gains or losses if all household utilities are unchanged. Yet, if income were optimally distributed initially, it could not be so subsequently. A redistribution, therefore, is then still called for.

The example considered, to be sure, is rather extreme in respect of the difference in tastes envisaged. That is evident from (4a,b) and the resultant differences in consumption structure in the table. As was shown previously, however, a redistribution of income is still indicated in circumstances such as are in question so long as tastes differ at all. Moreover, while a CES function was convenient for sake of quantitative illustration, the essential result still holds for utility functions more generally. That is also true if, rather than to a utilitarian social welfare function, reference is made to any other formula of the individualistic sort, i.e., any function conforming to (1).

But in a deeper sense the analysis should not really be all that revelatory. At least, one need not be indifferent to extremes of poverty and wealth to feel that the ethical evaluation of alternative income distribution must sometimes be a rather perplexing task. The analysis that has been set forth seems only to underscore that difficulty. If despite there being no change in the utility of any household, incomes cannot be deemed to be optimally distributed in both of two situations such as are in question, one is led to wonder whether optimality could really be considered as attained in either one of them. Such doubts seem in order even though income distribution in one situation or the other, taken by itself, might be very appealing, and both situations are clearly preferable to many others. In short, we no doubt can discriminate ethically among different income distributions, but perhaps not nearly to as fine a degree as sometimes imagined.

References

- BERGSON, Abram, *Essays in Normative Economics*, Cambridge, Mass., 1966.

Journal of Public Economics 6 (1976) 171–190. © North-Holland Publishing Company

SOCIAL CHOICE AND WELFARE ECONOMICS UNDER REPRESENTATIVE GOVERNMENT

Abram BERGSON*

Harvard University, Cambridge, MA 02138, U.S.A.

Received December 1975, revised version received April 1976

In his Impossibility Theorem, Arrow demonstrated logically that certain *a priori* conditions cannot all be satisfied by a rule of social choice. Those conditions, however, are admittedly value judgments, and how ethically impelling they are remains in dispute. To appraise that matter, the theorem is properly seen in a political context, and Arrow himself has seen it so, but he focuses in effect on 'direct democracy.' Further clarification may result from reference instead to different forms of 'representative government.' The same inquiry may also illuminate another still controversial matter: the import of the theorem for welfare economics.

1. Introduction

Professor Kenneth Arrow originally published his *Social Choice and Individual Values* in 1951,[1] and the Impossibility Theorem that he elaborated there has since become rightly celebrated, but its precise import continues to be debated. In this essay, I try to clarify that matter further by viewing the theorem in an apparently rather novel perspective. Thus, I examine the application of the theorem to more or less specific political processes.

The theorem is, of course, properly seen in a political context. As Arrow is clear throughout, the 'rule' to which the theorem relates and which determines social choice, is intended to represent a political process, though, to be sure, a democratic one. Moreover, while primarily concerned to demonstrate the theorem on an abstract plane, Arrow often illustrates its meaning by reference to political institutions, particularly elections, and it is easy to see that he himself, by implication, has adumbrated the application of the theorem to *direct democracy*, where public actions tend to be determined directly by citizens through one or another voting procedure. That, however, has left open its application to *representative government*, where public actions tend to be the responsibility of public officials among whom some, with ultimate authority, are elected by and accountable to citizens generally.

*I am indebted to Professor Richard Zeckhauser for helpful comments on an earlier version.
[1]I refer, of course, to the first edition. Subsequent references, however, will be to the second edition of 1963. This differs from the first only through the addition of a new, final chapter.

Between these two broad forms of democratic government we cannot draw any sharp line, but we may be able to grasp more clearly the essential difference if we consider that Arrow's rule aggregates individual orderings of social states into a corresponding social ordering. Given the environment of feasible alternatives, the social ordering determines the corresponding social choice. That, however, is the formal nature of the rule. Politically, the rule is seen rather to register the outcome of votes that citizens cast in dependence on their individual orderings. The two forms of democratic government in question may be delineated in that light. Thus, under direct democracy, citizens tend to vote directly on social states. Under representative government, they tend rather to vote directly on public officials and are able only through such choices to record their preferences on social states.[2]

In the real world of democracy, of course, both sorts of processes are encountered, but today that appears to be true of direct democracy only infrequently. In the United States one thinks especially of the New England town meeting, though that institution has evolved in the course of time and by now sometimes appears to be more of the nature of representative government than of direct democracy.[3] In contrast, representative government prevails widely; indeed, it is often taken to exemplify democracy generally.

I have referred to Arrow's treatment of political processes. Regarding interrelations of individual and social orderings of social states, there is now a voluminous formal literature, but such writings have been largely inspired by Arrow's 1951 work, and there too, where the Impossibility Theorem is applied to a specific political system, attention seems to be focused on direct democracy rather than representative government.[4]

---

[2]In political theory, 'representative government' seems understood variously, but reference is often to political processes in which not only do public actions tend to be the responsibility of elected officials but there are among the officials some, say in a legislature, who are elected by different constituencies into which the community is divided. I hope my colleagues in political science will not be too distressed if, as is analytically convenient, I adopt a usage according to which representative government includes any and all political processes where public actions are in the hands of elected officials, whether some are elected by different constituencies or not. Indeed, as will appear, I shall even take as a form of representative government an ideal case where all public action is the responsibility of one, and only one, elected official!

[3]In the town of Belmont, Massachusetts, where I reside, a town meeting still functions but the participants are not the citizens generally but elected representatives. The town meeting assembles only periodically, but it establishes diverse committees that meet more often, while the town government also includes an elected School Committee and diverse other officials some of whom are elected.

[4]For a late survey and an extensive bibliography, see Sen (1970). Among writers attempting to deal with democratic politics on a formal plane, some focus more expressedly than others on specific political processes, and sometimes attention is directed particularly to representative government, though in such cases the Impossibility Theorem appears to be of at most only incidental concern. See, for example, Downs (1957), Buchanan and Tullock (1962) and Breton (1974). Mention should also be made of Haefele (1971), though the focus is again rather different from mine.

There can be no ground here to question the validity of the Impossibility Theorem. Any doubts about that were dispelled long ago. Formally, then, the theorem must hold for one form of government as well as the other. But opinions do still differ on the appropriateness of the well-known *a priori* conditions which Arrow imposes on the rule, and which, according to the theorem, cannot all hold. Application of the theorem to particular political processes can, I think, facilitate judgment on that basic matter. The analysis of direct democracy, even though often without explicit reference to a so-called governmental form, probably has already done so. I inquire here into the Impossibility Theorem under representative government in the hope of contributing similarly.

Although Arrow conceives of his rule as representing a political process, he has also identified it with the criterion of social welfare, the 'social welfare function,' that is employed as a standard for normative appraisal in welfare economics. That identification too has been vigorously disputed, and more recently Arrow has acknowledged that his rule might better be referred to as a 'constitution' than as a 'social welfare function,' but the difference between these two aspects has still been held to be 'largely terminological' [Arrow (1963, pp. 104–105); see also Arrow (1967, pp. 12 ff.)]. The inquiry into the Impossibility Theorem under representative government may also shed more light on the underlying conceptual issue that remains concerning the bearing of the Impossibility Theorem on welfare economics. That question, of course, is of particular interest to economists.

2. Motivation

Democratic processes in the real world tend to be notably complex, and that is only the more true of such processes where representative government prevails. We are concerned here with representative government, however, not especially for its own sake but for the further perspective that inquiry into it may provide on the larger import of the Impossibility Theorem. From that standpoint, it may not be amiss to focus, at least provisionally, on altogether simple paradigms. These differ one from another, but they have several common features. To begin with those features, both elected officials and citizens who elect them are rational in the sense that they have definite and consistent orderings of social states, at least among those states relevant to public actions [see Arrow (1963, pp. 11 ff.)]. An official's ordering may be the same as the one he would have as a private citizen. Or it may not be. Neither possibility is excluded, but in either case the ordering was made known to voters prior to the official's election. Or rather, that ordering and the orderings of competing candidates were made known to voters so that they could choose between candidates in the light of the voters' own orderings. Once in office, the victorious candidate implements his ordering in respect of those public actions with which he is concerned.

A social state is understood in an inclusive sense delineated by Arrow (1963, p. 17):

> The most precise definition . . . would be a complete description of the amount of each type of commodity in the hands of each individual, the amount of labor to be supplied by each individual, the amount of each productive resource invested in each type of productive activity, and the amounts of various types of collective activity, such as municipal services, diplomacy and its continuation by other means, and the erection of statues to famous men.

Hence, an ordering such as in question takes into account values that the person concerned may attach to 'nonmaterial' aspects as well as those of a 'material' kind.

But in respect of a public official, have I not in effect prejudged by assumption the very question that Arrow addresses? Indeed, if the Impossibility Theorem applies, is not rationality on the part of such a person precluded to begin with? The theorem would be even more remarkable than it is if that were so, but the theorem relates to a social ordering. As will appear, that may or may not come to the same thing as the ordering of any particular official or officials. True, where it does, one of the conditions that Arrow imposes on the rule, that requiring the social ordering to be definite and consistent, is necessarily satisfied. But such a result, which I believe is of very real interest, is not barred by the Impossibility Theorem. Rather, according to the theorem, the requirement of a rational social ordering and other conditions that are imposed cannot all be met simultaneously. Moreover, in those cases where the social ordering and orderings of officials coincide, rationality of the latter would seem to have little bearing one way or another on whether the other conditions are met.

Granting that the rational public official is not logically barred, he may, I think, serve us here even if he would not very often have a precise counterpart in the real world. But paradigms, to be interesting, must have at least a minimum of verisimilitude. Must we not consider, therefore, that under representative government, democratic politics are typically party politics? And is it not almost inevitable that a politician seeking office will come to be constrained by a party program which is itself neither definite nor consistent? In fact, does not the Impossibility Theorem apply, to begin with, in respect of a political party, and is not irrationality in that regard in effect shown to be altogether likely? As implied, in inquiring into the Impossibility Theorem, I focus on aggregation of orderings of citizens generally that occurs principally through elections rather than on such prior aggregation of citizens orderings as occurs within a party. But one need not rely on the Impossibility Theorem to be aware that in the real world of democratic politics a party program is not always a model of clarity or coherence. Unless at least egregious incongruities are avoided, however, a party's credibility is easily impugned, and it's ability to effectively impose its program on its members must also be weakened. In any event, rationality of the individual politician is still not precluded, and it is with the latter, rather than party rationality, that we will be primarily concerned.

Regarding a politician, however, rather than ask whether he has a definite and consistent ordering, must we not more properly ask whether he has any ordering at all? At least as revealed publicly, chiefly in election campaigns, a politician's program seems typically to be something of an amalgam of proposed measures, goals, aspirations, and rhetoric. Can that possibly be considered an ordering of social states in any meaningful sense? A politician might commit himself to an ordering not only explicitly, but, in diverse ways, implicitly. One form of commitment serves here as well as the other. And, while it would be surprising if a definite and consistent ordering of any detailed and complete sort should often clearly emerge in either way, broad and partial delineations, I suspect, are not only usual, but for voters often relatively decisive. In the interest of achieving full employment, two candidates advance rival programs, one emphasizing investment tax incentives and the other, public works. Both programs may be viewed somewhat skeptically by the electorate, but many voters may well be led to feel and stress that the first candidate will be less concerned than the second with the welfare of the unemployed and the poor. A campaign plank on automobile pollution control may be of interest less for the specific measures projected than for the indicated concern for the environment, and somehow voters may sense how that is likely to be weighed against other concerns, where choices have to be made.

A public official is also supposed here to adhere after election to the ordering on which he had campaigned as a candidate. On any realistic view, a public official must elaborate his ordering in good part after he gains office, and indeed in the very process of supporting or opposing particular public measures. In doing so, it would hardly be surprising if sometimes he should also revise his ordering, though even a fickle politician must often be constrained by concern for reelection. Such elaboration and revision, however, pose no problem here so far as they do not cause citizens to regret their votes. Note also that as long as an official does adhere after election to an ordering on which he campaigned, he is in principle not barred from resorting to 'log-rolling' and similar tactics in the interest of implementing that ordering. For our limited purposes, however, it will be just as well to abstract from such complexities.

As also indicated, the politician's ordering might or might not correspond to one that he would hold privately. I thus in no way exclude that, among our politicians, some, preoccupied with the power and prestige of public office, might find it expedient in seeking and holding such a post to commit themselves publicly to orderings rather different from those they hold privately. Our paradigms can only gain in realism at this point.

Even if public officials should seek to implement definite and consistent orderings, they need not always succeed in doing so. As one need not ponder long to see, the possibility of failure must be especially marked where the concern is with often intricate public actions. In gauging the realism of our paradigms, that too must be considered, but it should also be noted that such decision-making might be facilitated if, in the community in question, there were persons skilled in welfare economics. Such persons, we must suppose, might be helpful by clarifying intricate interrelations between broad ethical principles, orderings of social states and public measures and goals (see section 5). A corollary, though, is that in real world democracies the citizen must be concerned with a politician's competence as well as ends.

The rational citizen is no less a hypothetical construct than the rational politician, but it should be observed that I do not in any way prejudge the nature of the citizen's ordering. For present purposes, the altruist and the egoist are equally admissible. For the private citizen, implementation of a definite and consistent ordering of social states generally might be especially taxing, but I focus particularly on choices between candidates where discrimination may not be so difficult.

Actually, in assuming that each citizen has a definite and consistent ordering of social states, I have followed Arrow himself (1963, pp. 11ff.). Indeed, citizen rationality in that sense is central to his analysis, for several of the conditions he imposes on the rule are clearly only meaningful if such rationality prevails. If only on that account, therefore, such rationality had to be presupposed here.[5] A public official, however, scarcely appears in Arrow's analysis. This is understandable in view of his implied stress on direct democracy. But public officials necessarily are of cardinal concern in this essay. I have accordingly had to include them in my paradigms.

I have been considering my public officials and citizens from the standpoint of their realism, but the relation of one to the other might also be viewed normatively, and it is of interest here to do so. What is to be said, from that standpoint, of the relation that I have delineated? On the face of it, it surely is appealing. Indeed, some may feel that it is more so normatively than it is positively. In effect, the public official's ends, as given by his ordering of social states, are validated by the electorate, but he remains free to select appropriate means. Such a division of responsibility certainly appears appropriate in view of the likely difference between the official and private citizen in access to expertise.

The relation in question, however, has its limitations normatively as well as positively. Among other things, by abstracting from post-election elaboration or revision of a politician's ordering, I evidently exclude all of the informal ways by which in any real world democracy an elected official may obtain sanction for public actions between elections. I have also abstracted from the politician's role in shaping citizens' ends. Judgment on the question at issue is in any event

[5]Strictly speaking, Arrow (1963, pp. 11ff.) assumes only that the citizen has a definite and consistent ordering and for the purpose of formulating and proving the Impossibility Theorem that is all that is needed. But it is difficult to relate the theorem to specific political institutions, as he often does and as I do in this essay, without supposing that the citizen actually chooses in accord with his ordering.

best postponed. As will appear, the postulated relation between an elected official and the electorate practically assures at once that representative government will be at odds with Arrow's *a priori* conditions. As Arrow acknowledges, those conditions are value judgments, but he holds them to be ethically impelling ones. Indeed, in the debate about the appropriateness of those conditions, it is just their ethical appeal that is in question. There is thus a conflict between Arrow's values and those entailed in taking as a norm the postulated relation between an elected official and his electorate. Before committing ourselves one way or the other on that norm, therefore, we must explore further that conflict.

I noted above some writings subjecting representative government to formal analysis, though without special attention to the Impossibility Theorem. It should be observed that in these inquiries too citizens are usually taken to be rational, and, I believe, in essentially the same sense as here. As for public officials, where they are considered systematically, they do seem sometimes to bear a certain resemblance to mine, although their conduct almost inevitably turns out to be more complex than I need allow here.[6]

In more conventional political thought, inquiries into representative government appear often to be of a relatively descriptive sort, but at least since Edmund Burke such government has also been viewed normatively. It may be of interest that the relation I have delineated between an elected public official and his constituents is probably somewhat more restrictive than the one that Burke advocated. One may wonder, though, whether some division of responsibilities for ends and means such as I envisage between public officials and citizens is not often what is really intended where that so called 'free' mandate is favored. In any event, the relation I have depicted should not be confused with the alternative 'imperative' mandate, also discussed. That apparently could be relatively restrictive of both the social states sought and the means to seek them.[7]

3. Democratic One Man Rule (DOMR)

I shall now explain and apply the Impossibility Theorem to each of my paradigms in turn. For the present, I try only to be clear as to the nature of the

[6]See, for example, Downs (1957, pp. 24ff.), where a political party is taken to be a 'team of men,' all 'rational,' and hence whose 'goals can be viewed as a single, consistent preference ordering.' Apparently, reference is to an ordering relating in the first instance to the perquisites of office ('income, prestige and power'), for it is ultimately by such things that politicians are supposed to be motivated. But all public actions, including determination of an appropriate 'ideology,' are weighed accordingly. In Breton (1974, pp. 124ff.) a rather more complex motivation is envisaged for politicians, but in the upshot members of a party somehow become committed to a consistent ordering in respect of 'public policies.' The party, however, apparently campaigns on a particular mix of policies indicated by that ordering and a required prospect of election. Post-election implementation varies over time depending on the proximity of the subsequent election.

[7]For Burke's views and on political thought generally concerning the relation of a public official to his constituency, see Hoffman and Levack (1949, pp. 113ff.); Sobelewski (1968); de Grazia, Sartori and Janda (1968, pp. 461ff.).

violation that must occur of Arrow's *a priori* conditions. Implications as to the ethical appeal of the conditions and the import of the Impossibility Theorem for the criterion of social welfare in welfare economics are thus deferred. The chief of my paradigms is *Democratic One Man Rule (DOMR)*. To begin with this process: under it a single official, the President, who is elected for a fixed term by the citizens generally, is responsible for all public actions. The election is free, so voters may choose without constraint between at least two candidates. Among two candidates, majority rule prevails. If there are more than two, the outcome is determined in accord with some other conventional democratic principle.

Estoric as DOMR is, it might be viewed at least from one standpoint as, among democratic political processes, the polar opposite of direct democracy. Hence, when taken together with the latter, it embraces the whole range of democratic political processes, including those where representative government obtains. By inquiring into DOMR, therefore, and also one or two intermediate variants, we will be able, I think, to grasp essentials of interest concerning the Impossibility Theorem under representative government.

Politically construed, then, Arrow's rule is given here by DOMR. It also follows that the corresponding social ordering is simply the ordering of whoever is President at a given time. For the moment I assume that there are only two candidates for President, and that an individual's ordering as President is the same as his ordering as a private citizen. Turn now to the Impossibility Theorem. As the reader may already have sensed, representative government generally, as envisaged here, runs afoul of one of Arrow's requirements in particular, the much discussed Independence of Irrelevant Alternatives (IIA). But we are now concerned with such government as exemplified by DOMR (see above, p. 172, n. 2). That that process violates IIA is seen at once from an example. Suppose there are but three citizens, 1, 2, 3, with the following orderings for three social states, *A*, *B* and *C*.

1	2	3
A	*B*	*C*
B	*A*	*A*
C	*C*	*B*

The same three states are open as alternatives for the coming year, and the choice between them is to be made by the person then serving as President. Indeed, that is the only decision to be made by that official, for his term of office is but one year.

Of the three citizens, 1 is now President, and cannot succeed himself, but both 2 and 3 are campaigning for that office, and all three citizens, including, 1, are able to vote in the election. 1 evidently will cast his vote for 2, for while 2 will reject A, 1's first choice, he can be expected to choose B, which 1 still prefers to C. If 3 were elected, he would of course, choose C. For 1 that is the least favoured alternative.

As for 2 and 3, each presumably will vote for himself. 2, then, is elected, and B is in fact selected. Note that in 2's, and hence the social ordering, B is preferred to both A and C.

Suppose now that, of the three alternative social states, C were in fact not feasible. In that case, 1 would be bound to shift his vote to 3. With that, 3 would be elected, and A would be chosen. In the corresponding social, that is, 3's ordering, then, A is now preferred to B.

As for IIA, in Arrow's oft-quoted words (1963, p. 26), that is as follows:

Let $R_1, \ldots, R_n$ and $R'_1, \ldots, R'_n$ to be two sets of individual orderings and let $C(S)$ and $C'(S)$ be the corresponding social choice functions. If, for all individuals i and all x and y in a given environment S, $x R_i y$ if an only if $x R'_i y$, then $C(S)$ and $C'(S)$ are the same.

For Arrow, as implied, a social choice function, $C(S)$, is derived from a social ordering, and indicates the alternative or alternatives that would be chosen from any specified environment. Reference is to a functional relation in the sense that $C(S)$ 'assigns' a choice to each possible environment [Arrow (1963, p. 15)]. IIA has been subject to more than one construction, but for Arrow's purposes it clearly has the effect that the social ordering of any two alternative social states, x and y, depends only on individual orderings of those states and not at all on individual orderings of any other states.[8] Such independence might be established in either of two ways. In one, in respect of any set of three feasible alternatives, x, y and z, the social ordering of, and hence the indicated social choice between, x and y is unaffected by the exclusion of z from the feasible set, provided that individual orderings of x and y are unchanged. In the other, z remains feasible along with x and y, but its ranking in individual orderings changes. Again, the social ordering of, and the indicated social choice between, x and y remains unchanged provided individual orderings of those two states are unchanged. In elucidating IIA, Arrow stresses the first method, but independence according to the second is implied as well.

My example was constructed to show a violation of IIA according to the first method. That there is indeed such a violation is obvious. Thus, the social ordering of A and B and hence the indicated social choice between the two states depends on whether C is feasible, along with A and B. That is so even though the orderings of A and B by 1, 2 and 3 are all unchanged. But the example is easily modified to show a violation by the second method as well. Suppose, say, that C remains feasible along with A and B but that it becomes the first, instead

[8]See, for example, Arrow (1963, pp. 27–28, 98, 112).

of third, choice of 2. Individual orderings are otherwise unchanged. Then, whereas 2 was previously elected, 1 no longer has any reason to prefer him to 3, and the outcome of the election is indeterminate. Hence, while the social ordering decisively favored B over A previously, an alternative ranking in favor of A now has an equal claim to that status. Of course, C would be chosen in either case, but the fact remains that the social ordering of A and B has been affected.

While in the example only three alternative social states are open, the argument evidently is in no way contingent on options being so limited, and would still apply if instead more were available. Should the President be in office for more than one year, each social state such as figures in a citizen's ordering must be understood to represent a chronological sequence of substates that might prevail in the course of the President's tenure in office. With this, the results are again the same.

Although IIA is violated in the example, depending on the individual orderings such a violation need not occur. Thus, in the example, if 3 should prefer B to A, that would also be the social ordering of the two states regardless of whether C is feasible or not. On the other hand, another of Arrow's conditions requires that any logically possible individual orderings be admissible (see below, n. 9). Given that, a violation must always be reckoned with.

Besides IIA and the foregoing requirement, Arrow imposes on his rule two further conditions: the 'Pareto principle' and 'The condition of non-dictatorship.' Representative government as given by DOMR satisfies both of these conditions. In order to be aware that that is so in the case of the Pareto principle it suffices only to recall that according to that familiar condition, 'if $x\, p_i\, y$ for all i, then $x\, P\, y$ (in words, if every individual prefers x to y, then so does society).'[9] Obviously DOMR conforms to that requirement. That DOMR satisfies 'The condition of non-dictatorship' is also evident from the nature of that condition, which is too well known to need reproduction here.

Last but not least, the rule is supposed to yield a social ordering that is definite and consistent. Under DOMR, evidently that requirement too is met. This is so whether IIA is violated or not. DOMR is thus an initial case of the sort referred to above, where the social ordering is necessarily rational because it coincides with an official's ordering. I will have more to say later about this result.

I have been assuming that an individual has the same ordering of social states whether he is President or a private citizen. If on the contrary an individual orders social states differently depending on his status, Arrow's conditions must be reformulated to take into account the fact that for that person there are two orderings rather than one. On any plausible construction, however, DOMR must still violate IIA in much the same circumstances as in my example.

Thus, consider that case again, but suppose now that, while 2 and 3 campaign

[9]Reference is to the Impossibility Theorem as reformulated in Arrow (1963, pp. 96ff.).

on the same orderings as before, 2 does so despite his privately preferring C to both B and A. [10] The two alternative election outcomes that resulted depending on whether C is or is not available evidently still result. As for IIA, that is still violated if, as seems appropriate, the individual orderings in terms of which that condition is defined include, in the case of 2, his private rather than public ordering. Note, however, that 2's ranking of A relative to B is the same no matter which of his two orderings is considered. It follows that IIA is still violated even if that condition is defined in terms of 2's public ordering.

If we adhere to the first of the foregoing two reinterpretations of the Arrow conditions we cannot logically bar a violation of the Pareto principle, at least for low-priority social states, but as is readily seen such a violation would imply a perverse and hardly plausible disregard by an elected official of not only the private orderings of citizens generally, but his own private ordering as well. Thus, in defining the Pareto principle, it is now understood that for the politician considered as an individual citizen reference is made to his private rather than public ordering. Suppose also that all citizens other than the politician prefer x to y. Even if the politician privately should also do so, we cannot logically bar his publicly preferring y to x, but he would hardly have any incentive to do so. Hence, the social ordering given by the public ordering of a victorious politician could conceivably violate the Pareto principle, but it is hardly plausible that it should do so.

According to the alternative reinterpretation of Arrow's conditions that might be in order, in defining the Pareto principle, in the case of the politician considered as an individual citizen, we refer to his public ordering. In that case DOMR necessarily satisfies the Pareto principle. On either of the two reinterpretations of Arrow's conditions, it is also evident that 'The condition of non-dictatorship' is likewise satisfied. Evidently, under DOMR the resultant social ordering is also still definite and consistent under either reinterpretation.

If there are more than two candidates, all is essentially as before, but, as is easily seen, there could be a violation of IIA in respect of candidates comparable to that occurring in our example in respect of social states.[11] It should also be observed that successive binary choices by majority vote might not yield a consistent ordering among candidates. Here then, the so-called 'paradox of majority rule,' which Arrow has done so much to underline, does materialize, but, even in a paradigmatic world, one may perhaps wonder at the practical import of the election process in question, for successive binary choices among multiple candidates seem rarely encountered in real world political systems. In any event, as long as some candidate is somehow finally selected, any inconsistency in the ordering of candidates does not betoken here any inconsistency in

[10] 2's behaviour thus exemplifies what has been called 'implicit' log-rolling in Buchanan and Tullock (1962, pp. 134–135).

[11] As Arrow (1963, p. 27) points out, the violation might occur under the rank-order method of voting familiar in clubs. But it could also occur when, as is more usual in public elections, he outcome is determined simply by the number of first choice votes.

the social ordering of social states. The latter is again given by the ordering of the victorious candidate. This fact does not always seem to be clearly grasped.[12]

4. Variants

Before proceeding further, let us be clear as to the comparative performance, in respect of Arrow's conditions, of DOMR on the one hand, and direct democracy on the other. Arrow himself, to repeat, has by implication applied his analysis to the latter sort of process. As given by, say, a Citizens' Assembly, direct democracy might function variously depending on the precise electoral procedure employed. I shall refer to only one such procedure, which in effect is that treated by Arrow, though here too there is pair-wise choice between multiple alternatives. Thus, each citizen votes, in accord with his ordering, on alternative social states considered in pairs. With a majority vote determining the victorious state in each case, the community's social ordering is given by the implied ranking of social states generally. Actual choices are made accordingly from among social states open.

---

[12]In elucidating the paradox of majority rule, Arrow focused particularly on binary choices between alternative social states. Politically, therefore, reference is in the effect to direct democracy. That the paradox might also occur under DOMR, where there are binary choices between more than two candidates for office, is evident and need not be labored. But, it should be noted that the occurrence of the paradox under one political system is in fact closely related to its occurrence under the other. Thus, unless individual preferences are such as would produce the paradox under direct democracy, as readily seen, it could not materialize either under DOMR. On the other hand, even if the paradox would materialize under direct democracy, it need not occur under DOMR. Such a result would be bound to materialize, however, if the several candidates announced disparate first preferences for just the social states where the paradox would occur under direct democracy.

I have suggested that election by successive binary choices among more than two alternatives is a rare bird politically. Even if it is, of course, such an election process might be considered as a desideratum so far as one subscribes to IIA, for given successive binary choices that condition is necessarily satisfied. But among Arrow's *a priori* conditions, IIA is the chief one on whose desirability it is hoped this essay may shed further light. The reader should defer udgment on the normative merit of successive binary choices, therefore, until the normative merit of IIA has been considered.

Through the use of successive binary choices, I believe, one also avoids 'strategic voting,' i.e. an individual feels it expedient, even among alternatives open, to cast his vote for other than his first choice. Wherever more than two alternatives are in question, such voting may well occur. To what extent avoidance of strategic voting is, as often assumed, a desideratum, however, is an interesting question, on which more than one opinion may be permissible. But, in *Individual Choice and Social Values* (1963, p. 7), Arrow himself expressly excludes such voting from his analysis, and, intriguing as it is, I don't think there will be any serious loss if I too pass it by here.

Reference has been to DOMR, but all that has been said evidently must apply to any form of representative government, wherever there are more than two candidates for any office. That should be borne in mind in connection with the discussion below of forms of representative government other than DOMR.

In reasoning as I have above on the relation between DOMR and direct democracy regarding the paradox of majority rule, I have in effect done little more than elaborate on a conjecture by the Editor.

As Arrow makes clear, a Citizens' Assembly employing such an electoral procedure conforms to his conditions generally, but, as noted above, depending on the nature of the individual orderings, the paradox of voting might be encountered. Hence, without restriction on individual orderings, the requirement that the social ordering be definite and consistent is violated.[13] Under the indicated election procedure, then, the Citizens' Assembly differs from DOMR both in conforming to IIA and in violating the requirement that the social ordering be definite and consistent.

Our concern is primarily with representative government rather than a direct democracy, and DOMR is seen as a polar case of the former sort of system. Turning, therefore, to other forms of representative government, we focus still on the nature of the violations of Arrow's *a priori* conditions that must occur. Given the results already at hand for DOMR and direct democracy, we can, I think, be quite brief. The first of the forms of representative government now considered might be viewed as the polar opposite of DOMR. That is *Council Government*: all public actions are in the hands of a council of elected members representing constituencies. A single constituency, say, a district, might be represented by more than one council member, and there could be many candidates for any one seat, but it will suffice here to consider the simplest case where a single council member represents a given district, and is chosen by voters there from among two candidates. Election, then, is by majority vote. The council itself also acts by majority vote, the particular voting procedure employed being the same as that just described for a Citizens' Assembly. The community's social ordering and choices are determined correspondingly.

Even this very simple process might function variously. Two cases will indicate the range of possibilities. In one, there is effective party discipline. All candidates for the council are members of one or the other of two parties, each of which has a platform that is envisaged as a definite and consistent ordering of social states, to which all members adhere. If elected, a candidate also adheres to the party platform in voting in the council. In this case, so far as concerns Arrow's conditions, Council Government evidently comes to the same thing as DOMR. At least it does so if one party actually has a majority in the council (i.e. a tie is excluded). In other words, IIA is violated, so far as citizen's orderings are unrestricted, but Arrow's conditions are satisfied otherwise. Among other things, the resultant social ordering is definite and consistent.

In the other case, there is no party discipline. Each candidate, accordingly, runs on his own platform or ordering of social states, and if elected heeds only that ordering. In this case, evidently, the council in effect replicates the Citizens' Assembly, and performance in respect to Arrow's conditions is much the same as in the latter. As we saw, however, behaviour in the Citizens' Assembly conforms to IIA. In respect of the votes cast in the council by a representative of

---

[13]On the relation of the election procedure in question to Arrow's conditions generally, see Arrow (1963, pp. 46–48).

any district that is not the case. Analogously to the situation in DOMR, the district representative and the corresponding ordering might vary depending on the alternatives open. If that is true of any one representative and his ordering, it must also be true of the social ordering given by majority rule in the council. Hence, in contrast to the situation in the Citizens' Assembly, IIA is now violated.

If DOMR and Council Government are polar forms of representative government, a mix of the two should have more verisimilitude than either. Suppose, then, that there is both a council, elected and acting in the manner described, and a President, also elected in the manner described. Suppose also that all public actions require, say, the concurrence of both the council and the President. What then? Implications of interest are already fairly evident. Suffice it to say that without restriction on citizens' orderings, IIA is again violated. Should there be effective party discipline and the President and a majority of the council be of the same party, the social ordering would still be definite and consistent. Should the President and a majority of the council be of different parties, the social ordering would be definite and consistent for a limited range of social states on which the President and council concurred, while other action would in effect be blocked. Should there be no party discipline, so far as the council's actions do not result in a definite and consistent ordering, that presumably would also be so for the social ordering. 'The condition of non-dictatorship' should be satisfied throughout, and so too should the Pareto principle. Reference is, of course, to any binary comparison such as that in terms of which the principle is defined.

5. Conclusions

What follows regarding the Impossibility Theorem? No challenge to the formal validity of that theorem was intended in this essay and none has been offered. As explained, however, the *a priori* conditions that Arrow imposes on the rule are admittedly value judgments. While held by Arrow to be ethically impelling, they have been questioned, and that is true of IIA as well as the other requirements. Indeed, of all Arrow's conditions, IIA has probably proven the most controversial. There is, I think, further reason to question that requirement here.

Thus, IIA has been criticized previously chiefly because of the implied waste of ethically relevant information. To put the barest essentials in terms that I, for one, find appealing: in aggregating individual orderings for any pair of alternatives, for conformity to IIA, reference must be made only to the ranking of those alternatives, disregarding the orderings of alternatives more generally. Aggregation, however, necessarily means weighing the preferences of different citizens, and any segment of an individual's ordering, it is arguable, could signify something as to his nature, and mental and physical states, that might usefully be taken into account in determining the appropriate weight for his ordering generally, including other segments. It seems permissible, therefore, to demur at an ethical imperative that would require us, in arriving at a social ordering, to ignore such additional information.[14]

IIA might be questioned in this way on an abstract plane, without reference to whether Arrow's rule is itself seen to be a political process or a social welfare function. My analysis of representative government bears in the first instance on IIA where the rule is viewed politically. Thus, as we saw, such government comes at once in conflict with IIA. That conflict, to be sure, could possibly be regarded as ethically impugning representative government rather than IIA. Under representative government, however, the violation of IIA means that the outcome of an election, and hence the social ordering, depends on the alternative states that are open. Translated into the language of politics, that means only that the outcome of the election depends on the issues. It seems difficult to view that as an ethical deficiency of representative government.

In answering criticism of IIA, Arrow (1963, p. 110) has acknowledged that:

> The austerity imposed by this condition is perhaps stricter than necessary; in many situations, we do have information on preferences for non-feasible alternatives. It can be argued that, when available, this information should be used in social choice, and some possibilities in this direction will be briefly commented on in the following paragraphs. But, clearly social decision processes which are independent of irrelevant alternatives have a strong practical advantage. After all, every known electoral system satisfies this condition.

The last sentence appears to reflect a misapprehension, for representative government has in fact been found here to violate IIA. True, reference has been made only to very abstract paradigms, but, as readily seen, a violation might

---

[14]It is often suggested that, unless one accepts IIA, he is in effect committed to utilitarianism. It is not at all evident, however, that one need be a utilitarian in any conventional sense to wish to consider individual orderings of alternatives generally in determining the social ordering even of a limited range of alternatives. Thus, a cardinal aspect of the social state for any individual presumably is his own income share. Should the individual's ordering of alternatives generally convey information about his mental and physical state, one might wish to consider that information in determining a social ordering on income distribution. But one need not be a utilitarian in any conventional sense to do so.

True, where reference is to mental and physical states, the concern usually is with 'intensity of preferences' in some sense or other, and some would take that to be a hallmark of utilitarianism. But one might still acknowledge (as utilitarians seem reluctant to do) that value judgments are required to commensurate intensities of preferences of different persons, and indeed are also entailed in the commitment to consider such intensities to begin with. Moreover, reference to mental and physical states might be motivated by a concern for intensity of preferences, but it might also be motivated otherwise. Should some individuals be emotionally disturbed, for example, presumably one would wish to know of that in gauging appropriate income shares, and yet in the case of the persons in question it might be difficult to base one's evaluation on preference intensities in any meaningful sense. Compare Bergson (1954), reprinted in Bergson (1966); Rothenberg (1961, Ch. 6).

occur whenever, in any degree, different candidates for office are committed to different rankings of social states and voters select among them on that basis. Such circumstances cannot be infrequent in the real world.

As an ethical imperative for a political process, Arrow's requirement that the social ordering be definite and consistent has also been questioned.[15] The analysis of representative government does not seem to contribute too much on that matter one way or the other, but it is often supposed that under majority rule a social ordering will necessarily fail to be definite and consistent. Or rather, it is supposed that the social ordering will fail to do provided there is no constraint on admissible individual orderings. It should be observed, therefore, that that is in fact the case under direct democracy of the sort Arrow considered, but may or may not be so under representative government. At least, it may or may not be so under such government as depicted in our paradigms. The requirement that the social ordering be definite and consistent might be violated, for example, under Council Government without party discipline. It is not violated, however, under such government with party discipline or under DOMR.

What of welfare economics? What particularly of the seemingly inexorable conclusion of Arrow's analysis that an ethically satisfactory social welfare function is barred on purely formal grounds? What is to be said here on that still debated question is already to some extent implied, but we may usefully refer to it if we are clear first that welfare economics is envisaged essentially as a form of counselling. The counsel relates to public economic policies affecting social states and might be proffered to citizens generally, but is usually intended especially for public officials. The counsel consists of implications of some criterion of social welfare, that is, some values delimiting the 'social welfare' attaching to different social states, and hence providing a basis for ordering such states. The practitioner of welfare economics is in principle free to take any values as a point of departure, but the resulting counsel as to economic policy is not apt to be too relevant unless the values in question are held by, or can plausibly be imputed to, one or more officials concerned with the policies in question. Should the practitioner for any reason disapprove of those values, he may, of course, refrain from offering the officials any counsel at all.

All of which is surely no longer as controversial as it once was. In any event, the methodological standpoint taken, I believe, is not really at issue among those debating the import of the Impossibility Theorem for welfare economics. To come, then, to that matter, in my paradigms public officials are employed only in representative government, but all such persons have definite and consistent orderings of social states. For purposes of welfare economics, therefore, one or another such ordering evidently can serve at once to delineate the criterion of social welfare. True, so far as orderings differ among officials, the resultant

---

[15]Perhaps, however, somewhat too vigorously in Bergson (1966, p. 31). Compare Buchanan and Tullock (1962, ch. 4).

counsel might be of only limited interest to some such persons, but it should be appealing to all committed to the ordering in question.

And, depending on the form of representative government, that ordering might, of course, come to the same thing as a social ordering given by such a political process; a social ordering, that is, of the sort Arrow refers to. That is so, for example, under DOMR, if one chooses to counsel the President; for there, as we saw, the social ordering and the ordering of the President are one and the same. But then again the public officials' ordering might also differ from the corresponding social ordering. That is apt to be so, for example, under Council Government without party discipline, for there the social ordering need not correspond to the ordering of any one in particular.

But in either case, reference must be to an ordering held by some public officials. After all, it is ultimately they who make decisions, and necessarily it is only to them that counsel can meaningfully be offered to begin with. An ordering to which such persons subscribe, therefore, must serve to delineate the criterion. A social ordering subscribed to by no one in particular cannot possibly do so.

It was noted, however, that the practitioner of welfare economics is always free to offer or withhold counsel. In any case, has not Arrow in effect shown that any definite and consistent ordering that might be used to delineate the criterion must be ethically dubious? Even if practitioners are not impelled thereby to withhold counsel, must not that moral be rather troubling to them? For not a few practitioners, it clearly has been, but I have already questioned a crucial premise that underlies it, and misgivings about IIA seem only to be compounded here when it is considered that the practitioner of welfare economics privately might enthusiastically approve of an ordering in terms of which he proposes to delineate the criterion of social welfare. He might even be the more enthusiastic so far as the ordering is one held by public officials. He is nevertheless called on by the Impossibility Theorem to regard the very same ordering as ethically suspect because it supposedly reflects a faulty political process. Thus, the political process itself could be democratic in any conventional sense, but it supposedly would have to be viewed as faulty on the formal ground that it fails to conform to IIA. Such failure, moreover, would mean only that with a change in the alternatives open or in private citizens' orderings for some alternatives, the process might possibly bring to the fore officials with an ordering for alternatives generally other than the one of which the practitioner enthusiastically approves, and in terms of which he contemplates delineating the criterion.

Representative government might also violate Arrow's requirement that the social ordering be definite and consistent. So far as that too is deemed as ethically a count against representative government, imaginably it might be viewed as also flawing ethically the ordering of any public official serving in such a process. Indeed, it might be so viewed even if the public official's ordering is itself definite and consistent. But, it is difficult to consider such a basis for criticism of a public official's values as any more weighty than that turning on a

B

50

failure of the social ordering to conform to IIA. One may wonder, therefore, whether in proffering counsel a practitioner of welfare economics should really be ethically troubled on one ground any more than on the other.[16]

But here again we must consider that I have been referring to notably abstruse paradigms. In the real world, there are public officials and public officials. Moreover, some, rather than being elected, are bureaucrats serving by appointment. Is it not possible that some officials of one sort or the other might be uncommitted to any ordering, that is, that they might be 'more or less neutral ethically' and so should have as their only 'aim in life to implement the values of other citizens as given by some rule of collective decision-making'? For the counselling of such officials, I have acknowledged previously (1966, p. 38) that 'Arrow's theorem apparently contributes . . . the negative finding that no consistent social ordering could be found to serve as a criterion of social welfare . . . .' Although not stated, it was understood that the officials in question, while ethically neutral generally, wish to conform to Arrow's *a priori* conditions. It must also be on that understanding that, according to Arrow (1963, p. 107), his 'interpretation of the social choice problem agrees fully with that given by Bergson.'[17]

On that understanding, too, there is no reason now to see differently than before Arrow's formal contribution to welfare economics, but one of his conditions seems even less impelling than it did previously. Hence, the demonstration that it, together with others, cannot be fulfilled does not seem so very disconcerting. One wonders, too, whether the ethically neutral official, if he exists at all, is not to be encountered primarily under direct democracy, the now rather rare sort of democratic political process which Arrow in effect analyzes. Under the more widely prevalent alternative of representative government, an official, no matter how ethically neutral privately, surely must find it difficult ordinarily to avoid altogether a commitment as to the social ordering he will seek to implement publicly. I refer particularly to an elected official, but presumably that is also true to a degree of the bureaucrat who serves him.

It may be hoped that, through additional research, we will gain further insight into this interesting question, and also into the cognate one concerning the

---

[16]I do not wish to suggest, however, that any and all criticism of a public official's values by reference to the nature of the political process is excluded. A practitioner of welfare economics, for example, might well hesitate to counsel a dictator, even if the dictator should be a benevolent one, of whose ordering of social states the practitioner privately approves. Compare Zeckhauser (1968, pp. 61–64).

[17]Arrow was careful here to italicize the part of a lengthy quotation of mine of which he approves, and I have set forth in somewhat abridged form that passage, but it will be evident to the attentive reader that my own thinking on the criterion of social welfare has evolved somewhat from the position taken in the statement generally. Among other things, I continue to think of welfare economics as a form of counselling, but I do not hold, as I did previously, that in delineating the criterion reference must be made to the same values without regard to whether the counselling is directed to a public official or a private citizen.

nature of the more specific values of public officials in democracy.[18] Meantime, however, the presumption surely must be, as it long has been, that for purposes of welfare economics an individualistic criterion of social welfare of the well-known sort yielding a Paretian quasi-ordering of social states is likely to be widely appropriate, at least as a point of departure. It has long been very often supposed that a public official typically will wish to gauge equity in an *ad hoc* way in the light of the real income redistribution induced by any proposed public measure. No impelling reason has been found here to proceed otherwise in that regard either. There is also no bar, however, to some more definite commitment on equity where that appears suitable for the persons counselled.

In sum, the Impossibility Theorem remains formally valid, but the ethical dilemma it poses for the design of a democratic political process is perhaps less acute than has often been supposed. To say that, however, is hardly to detract from the contribution to political theory of a remarkable pioneering attempt to subject that discipline to rigorous, formal analysis. That attempt has already proven extraordinarily stimulating, and no doubt will continue to prove so in future. On the other hand, there is, I think, further reason to conclude, as I have concluded before, and others, chiefly Little (1952) and Samuelson (1967a, b), have also concluded:[19] that the Impossibility Theorem is at most only tenuously related to welfare economics. Continued affirmation otherwise can only be at the expense of confusion regarding both Arrow's real contribution and welfare economics.

[18]How to ascertain such values is an interesting problem to which Ragnar Frisch devoted a good deal of attention. On alternative methodologies that might be employed, including particularly those elaborated by Frisch, see Johansen (1974).

[19]See also Johansen (1969) and Johansen (1974).

References

Arrow, K.J., 1951 (2nd ed., 1963), Social choice and individual values (Wiley, New York).

Arrow, K.J., 1967, Public and private values, in: S. Hook, ed., Human values and economic policy (New York University Press, New York) 3–21.

Bergson, A., 1954, On the concept of social welfare, Quarterly Journal of Economics 68, 233–252.

Bergson, A., 1966, Essays in normative economics (Harvard University Press, Cambridge, MA).

Breton, A., 1974, The economic theory of representative government (Aldine, Chicago).

Buchanan, J.M. and G. Tullock, 1962, The calculus of consent (University of Michigan, Ann Arbor).

de Grazia, A., G. Sartori and K. Janda, 1968, Representation, in: International encyclopedia of the social sciences (Macmillan, New York) 13, 461–479.

Downs, A., 1957, An economic theory of democracy (Harper, New York).

Haefele, E.T., 1971, A utility theory of representative government, American Economic Review 61, no. 3 (part I), 350–367.

Hoffman, R.J.S. and P. Levack, 1949, Burke's politics: Selected writings and speeches of Edmund Burke (Knopf, New York).

Johansen, L., 1969, An examination of the relevence of Kenneth Arrow's general possibility theorem for economic planning, Economics of Planning 9, 5–42.

Johansen, L., 1974, Establishing preference functions for macroeconomic models, European Economic Review 5, 41–66.

Little, I.M.D., 1952, Social choice and individual values, Journal of Political Economy 60, 422–432.

Rothenberg, J., 1961, The measurement of social welfare (Prentice Hall, Englewood Cliffs, NJ).

Samuelson, P.A., 1967a, Forward, in: J. de V. Graaff, Theoretical welfare economics (Cambridge University Press, Cambridge) 7–8.

Samuelson, P.A., 1967b, Arrow's mathematical politics, in: S. Hook, ed., Human values and economic policy (New York University Press, New York) 41–51.

Sen, A.K., 1970, Collective choice and social welfare (Holden-Day, London).

Sobelewski, M., 1968, Elections, electors and representatives, in: J.R. Pennock and J.W. Chapman, eds., Representation.

Zeckhauser, R. and E. Shaefer, 1968, Public policy and normative economic theory, in: R. Bauer and K.J. Bergen, eds., The study of policy formation (Free Press, New York) 27–101.

Postscript

It may avoid later misunderstanding if the final sentence in the incomplete paragraph at the top of p. 43 is revised to read, "Of course, C would be chosen in either case, and, if we are to be at all realistic, we must suppose that DOMR is elaborated in some way to assure that someone—either 1 or 2—is elected. But the fact remains that the social ordering of A and B could be affected."

II
PROBLEMS OF MEASUREMENT

Real Income, Expenditure Proportionality, and Frisch's "New Methods of Measuring Marginal Utility" [1]

AN essential and at the same time dubious element in the technique of measuring marginal utility, developed by Frisch, is the substitution of one variable, the price of living, for the prices of individual commodities in the utility function. Despite the fundamental importance of this procedure to his analysis, Frisch in either his *Sur un Problème d'Économie Pure* [2] or his later and more exhaustive *New Methods of Measuring Marginal Utility* [3] nowhere advances a satisfactory explanation.

The substitution is the first step in Frisch's derivation of his new methods. Using it as basis he achieves, by an ingenious transformation, the simplification of expressing the *real* money utility—the marginal utility of real income—as a function of real income alone. And with the additional assumption that one commodity, sugar, has an independent utility, [4] he expresses marginal utility, more precisely *real* money utility, in a form which lends itself readily to statistical measurement.

Given the first step, the logic of the subsequent development cannot be challenged. But the fundamental first step is open to two serious criticisms. First, the concepts of price of living and real income, if they are to be used in theoretical work, require exact formulation. [5] While Frisch devotes some attention to the subject of index numbers in his *New Methods*, [6] his discussion is confined to the problem of making distance comparisons of real income and of the price of living; he does not give these variables the precise definition which their insertion in a utility function demands. [7] Secondly, the substitution of the single variable, price of living, for several variables in the utility function cannot be passed off as easily as it is by Frisch—as a plausible first approximation. [8] As Allen has pointed out, an assumption, rather than an approximation, is involved. [9] And the nature of this assumption must remain in doubt so long as Frisch's concepts are not strictly defined.

Fortunately, Frisch has not allowed this state of affairs to continue. In a recent and important paper, " Annual Survey of General Economic Theory : The Problem of Index Numbers," [10] he reformulates the discussion of index

---

[1] I should like to express my great indebtedness and gratitude to Professor Wassily Leontief for his encouragement and criticism in connection with the work of this paper, and to Mr. Paul Samuelson who suggested to me the likelihood of the expenditure proportionality condition stated on p. 42. [2] *Norsk Matematisk Forenings Skrifter*, Serie 1, Nr. 16, 1926.
[3] *Beiträge zur Ökonomischen Theorie.* Tübingen, 1932. Hereafter referred to as *New Methods.*
[4] The utility of that commodity thus depends only on the quantity of it consumed.
[5] It is interesting to note in this connection that Keynes, in his latest work on monetary theory, forsakes such concepts as general price level, stock of real capital, and National dividend because of their lack of precision. *The General Theory of Employment, Interest, and Money*, ch. 4.
[6] Section 9.
[7] Allen, in the course of a general consideration of Frisch's analysis, makes a similar criticism. *Economica*, May, 1933, p. 192.   [8] *New Methods*, p. 5.   [9] *Economica*, May, 1933, p. 193.
[10] *Econometrica*, January, 1936. Hereafter referred to as *Annual Survey*.

numbers which appeared in *New Methods*.[1] As a by-product of this revision the development of his technique of measuring marginal utility is clarified.

In the *Annual Survey*, Frisch carefully defines real income[2] and the two related concepts, price level and price index. He alters his derivation of a statistically feasible expression for the *real* money utility. He introduces a very useful concept, expenditure proportionality, and shows that his earlier expression for the *real* money utility assumed this condition. At the same time he generalises the earlier formula.

It is now clear that Frisch's technique of measuring marginal utility, as developed in *New Methods*, rests on two assumptions, independence and expenditure proportionality. Both of these assumptions impose restrictions upon the shape of the functions which are involved in his analysis. Consequently both limit the applicability of his technique. The generalisation in *Annual Survey* obviates the second condition. But I shall make clear in an early section of this paper that, however important it may be for the theory of index numbers, the generalised expression cannot be used to measure marginal utility. It is of considerable importance, then, to an evaluation of the practicability of Frisch's new methods that the restrictions imposed by *both* assumptions should be determined. Herein lies the chief task of this paper.

The theoretic basis of Frisch's methods of measuring marginal utility is developed from a consideration of the activities of one individual. In our discussion we shall follow Frisch in this respect. As is customary, we shall assume that the individual upon whom we focus our attention seeks to maximise the satisfaction, or utility, he derives from the consumption of goods, subject to the condition that his total expenditure is fixed and, under a previous assumption,[3] equal to his money income. We shall assume, in addition, that the individual takes the prices in the market as given so far as his purchases are concerned, and that the prices are so in fact.[4]

If we denote the amounts of the various commodities consumed by y^1, y^2, . . . y^N, the individual's utility may be expressed as a function, $U(y^1, y^2, \ldots y^N)$, of these quantities.[5] We assume, that the individual desires to maximise this function subject to the budgetary condition

(a) $$p^1y^1 + p^2y^2 + \ldots . p^Ny^N = I$$

[1] Frisch's contribution to index number theory in his *New Methods* is based on the methods of measuring marginal utility developed in the same work. The reformulation in *Annual Survey* is chiefly a response to criticisms by Allen (*Economica*, May, 1933), of both the marginal utility technique and the index number discussion.

[2] Frisch in *Econometrica* adopts the expression, real expenditure, thereby avoiding an extra assumption. I shall retain his earlier and more familiar term, real income, and will assume, therefore, that income equals expenditure.

[3] *Supra*, fn. 2, above.

[4] Frisch implicitly makes this assumption in *New Methods*. In the course of his index number discussion in *Annual Survey* (p. 14) he also considers the case where an individual is confronted with prices which depend on the amounts of his own purchases.

[5] While ordinarily it might be desirable to avoid the word utility and the expression, utility function, and use instead (say) tastes and indifference function, nothing is to be gained by such a policy here. For Frisch's assumption of independence implies that the utility function is determinate, or measurable, in the Lange sense. The arbitrariness of the function is limited to two constants, one fixing the scale of measurement and the other, the origin. For Lange's analysis, see the REVIEW OF ECONOMIC STUDIES, June, 1934.

$p^1, p^2, \ldots p^N$, the respective prices of $y^1, y^2, \ldots y^N$; and I, the individual's income, are given and in the maximising process are regarded as constants.

I

The fundamental equation which Frisch uses to measure *real* money utility is

$$\frac{w(r)}{P} = \frac{u'(x)}{h} \quad \ldots\ldots\ldots\ldots\ldots\ldots\ldots\ldots\ldots\ldots\ldots\ldots\ldots\ldots\ldots\ldots \quad (1.1)$$

Here r stands for real income; $w(r)$, the *real* money utility; P, the price of real income, or price of living; x, the amount consumed of one commodity, sugar (we use the letter x, rather than (say) y^1, to distinguish this commodity from the others); $u'(x)$,[1] the marginal utility of sugar; and h, the price of sugar (again, this corresponds to, say, p^1).

In *New Methods* Frisch derives (1.1) through an assumption and an "approximation."[2] The assumption is that sugar is an independent commodity. Thus the marginal utility of sugar may be written as a function of x alone. The "approximation" is involved in writing, the *nominal* money utility—the marginal utility of money income—as a function of I and P, i.e.

$$\omega = \omega(I, P) \quad \ldots\ldots\ldots\ldots\ldots\ldots\ldots\ldots\ldots\ldots\ldots\ldots\ldots\ldots\ldots\ldots \quad (1.2)$$

instead of expressing it as a function of I and the prices of the individual commodities, $h, p^2, \ldots p^N$, i.e.

$$\omega = \omega(h, p^2, \ldots p^N) \quad \ldots\ldots\ldots\ldots\ldots\ldots\ldots\ldots\ldots\ldots\ldots\ldots \quad (1.3)$$

The two concepts *real* money utility and *nominal* money utility derive their meaning, in Frisch's analysis, from an analogy with the marginal utility of the single commodity, sugar, measured per pound and per dollar's worth.[3] By an intuitive extension of this analogy Frisch relates the two concepts by the equation

$$w = P\omega(I, P) \quad \ldots\ldots\ldots\ldots\ldots\ldots\ldots\ldots\ldots\ldots\ldots\ldots\ldots\ldots\ldots \quad (1.4)$$

If it is assumed that ω is affected proportionately by a change in the monetary unit, w can be written in the form

$$w = w\left(\frac{I}{P}\right) = w(r) \quad [4] \quad \ldots\ldots\ldots\ldots\ldots\ldots\ldots\ldots\ldots\ldots\ldots\ldots \quad (1.5)$$

---

[1] To facilitate our later discussion I have changed slightly the form of the expression used by Frisch. In other places and for various reasons I use symbols which differ from those of Frisch. But, with one exception the alteration is quite great and no precautionary comment will be required. The exception is I, which Frisch uses in place of our U.

[2] *New Methods*, Sections 1 and 2.

[3] Ibid., pp. 12, 13.

[4] For any λ, $\omega(I, P) = \lambda\omega(\lambda I, \lambda P)$. Thus $w(I, P) = w(\lambda I, \lambda P)$. If we take $\lambda = \frac{1}{P}$ we have $w(I, P) = w(\frac{I}{P}, 1)$, and since 1 is a constant, we can write this $w(I, P) = w(\frac{I}{P})$. Frisch also gets the same result by a second method. Loc. cit., p. 14.

3*

Since in equilibrium

$$\omega = \frac{u'(x)}{h} \quad \dots\dots\dots\dots\dots\dots\dots\dots\dots\dots\dots\dots\dots\dots\dots\dots \quad (1.6)$$

equation (1.1) follows immediately.

In *Annual Survey*,[1] Frisch uses another approach. He first defines the concepts of price index, expenditure proportionality, real income, and price level.

(1) PRICE INDEX. For any price situation $h_t, p^2_t, \ldots p^N_t$, the amounts, $x_t, y^2_t, \ldots y^N_t$ of the commodities consumed will vary with income, I_t.[2] The resulting *locus* of points, $x_t, y^2_t, \ldots y^N_t$, may be called an expansion path. For each point on the t expansion path there will be associated a value of U—the utility function—and a value of I_t. Assume that along every expansion path $(t = 0, 1, 2, \ldots)$, I_t and U are monotonically related. The function

$$I = I_t(U) \quad \dots\dots\dots\dots\dots\dots\dots\dots\dots\dots\dots\dots\dots\dots \quad (1.7)$$

accordingly is single valued. Consider the ratio

$$P_{0t} = \frac{I_t(U)}{I_0(U)} \quad \dots\dots\dots\dots\dots\dots\dots\dots\dots\dots\dots\dots\dots\dots \quad (1.8)$$

This ratio expresses the relationship between the money expenditures necessary to secure equal amounts of utility in the price situations $t=t$ and $t=0$. P_{0t} is the index of the change in prices between 0 and t.

(2) EXPENDITURE PROPORTIONALITY. Ordinarily P_{0t} will vary with U. It will be different for different levels of utility, even though individual prices are constant. If for any t, P_{0t} does not depend on U, we have the condition of expenditure proportionality.

(3) REAL INCOME and PRICE LEVEL. Consider the expansion path, $t=0$. Real income along this path, the base path, may be expressed by the function $r_0(U)$, and price level by the function $P_0(U)$. These two functions must satisfy the relation

$$r_0(U) = \frac{I_0(U)}{P_0(U)} \quad \dots\dots\dots\dots\dots\dots\dots\dots\dots\dots\dots\dots\dots \quad (1.9)$$

In addition, I gather from Frisch's discussion,[3] $r_0(U)$ is subject to the restriction $r'_0(U) > 0$. Otherwise, in the general case,[4] the functions $r_0(U)$ and $P_0(U)$ are entirely arbitrary.

Along any other expansion path, $t=t$, price level is defined by the relation

$$P_t(U) = P_0(U) . P_{0t}(U) \quad \dots\dots\dots\dots\dots\dots\dots\dots\dots\dots\dots \quad (1.10)$$

and real income, by the relation

$$r_t(U) = \frac{I_t(U)}{P_t(U)} \quad \dots\dots\dots\dots\dots\dots\dots\dots\dots\dots\dots\dots\dots \quad (1.11)$$

---

[1] Sections 3, 4, and 7.
[2] This does not contradict our statement that in the maximizing process I is regarded as given. Frisch's analysis implies simply that, given the price situation, the equilibrium position $x_t, y^2_t, \ldots$ y^N_t, will depend on the level at which income is fixed. The expansion path is the *locus* of equilibrium points which correspond to different income levels.
[3] *Annual Survey*, pp. 31, 32.
[4] General case is used here in contrast with the case of expenditure proportionality. In the latter case, as we shall see, a greater restriction on the base functions is justifiable.

By substitution this equals $r_0(U)$, so we may drop the subscript and write

$$r(U) = \frac{I_t(U)}{P_t(U)} = \frac{I_0(U)}{P_0(U)} \quad \dots\dots\dots\dots\dots\dots\dots\dots\dots\dots \quad (1.12)$$

Using these concepts, Frisch derives a new expression for the relationship between the *real* money utility and the *nominal* money utility. He precisely defines *nominal* money utility as

$$\omega_t = \frac{dU}{dI_t} \quad \dots\dots\dots\dots\dots\dots\dots\dots\dots\dots\dots\dots \quad (1.13)$$

and *real* money utility as

$$w = \frac{dU}{dr} = w(r) \quad \dots\dots\dots\dots\dots\dots\dots\dots\dots\dots \quad (1.14)$$

In (1.14) U is regarded as a function of r.[1] Thus

$$\omega_t = w(r) \bigg/ \frac{dI_t}{dr} \quad \dots\dots\dots\dots\dots\dots\dots\dots\dots\dots \quad (1.15)$$

Evaluating the derivative $\dfrac{dI_t}{dr}$ by differentiating (1.12), we have [2]

$$\omega_t = w(r) \bigg/ P_t(r)\left(1 + \frac{d\log P_t(r)}{d\log r}\right) \quad \dots\dots\dots\dots\dots\dots\dots \quad (1.16)$$

It follows that equation (1.1) must also be modified. If x is assumed independent again, (1.6) still holds,[3] and we may write

$$w(r) \bigg/ P_t(r)\left(1 + \frac{d\log P_t(r)}{d\log r}\right) = \frac{u'(x)}{h} \quad \dots\dots\dots\dots\dots\dots \quad (1.17)$$

Equation (1.17) follows, I have said, "if x is assumed independent again." As a matter of fact, in *Annual Survey*, Frisch derives an expression for *real* money utility on the basis of an assumption that a subset of commodities,

---

[1] If we restrict $r_0(U)$ so that $r'_0(U) > 0$, and thus, since $r(U) = r_0(U)$, so that $r'(U) > 0$, the function $U(r)$ will be single-valued.

[2] I_t and P_t now may be regarded as functions of r, for we are so regarding U, and these variables depend upon U.

[3] If we write the equilibrium relation

$$K = \frac{u'(x)}{h} = \frac{U_{y^2}}{p^2} = \frac{U_{y^3}}{p^3} = \dots = \frac{U_{y^N}}{p^N}$$

where $U_{y^2}, U_{y^3}, \dots U_{y^N}$, are the marginal utilities of the commodities $y^2, y^3, \dots y^N$, it may be shown that

$$\omega_t = \frac{dU}{dI_t} = K$$

For,

$$\frac{dU}{dI_t} = u'(x)\frac{dx}{dI_t} + U_{y^2}\frac{dy^2}{dI_t} + \dots + U_{y^N}\frac{dy^N}{dI_t}$$

$$= K\left(h\frac{dx}{dI_t} + p^2\frac{dy^2}{dI_t} + \dots + p^N\frac{dy^N}{dI_t}\right)$$

$$= K$$

This proof is taken from Allen, *Economica*, May, 1933, p. 190. We use total, rather than partial, derivatives because the subscript t already implies that prices are held constant.

rather than one commodity, is independent.[1] This expression reduces to (1.17) when the assumption of *New Methods* is used, so without danger of misinterpretation we may regard (1.17) as the modification—for reasons which will appear immediately, the generalisation—of (1.1) developed in *Annual Survey* for the case where one commodity is assumed independent. In our discussion we shall continue to work with the latter assumption. While use of the assumption of *Annual Survey* would necessitate little change in our argument, the assumption of *New Methods* has the advantage of simplicity and also of being the one which Frisch himself has used to measure marginal utility.

The difference between Frisch's analysis in *New Methods* and in his more recent paper crystalizes in equations (1.4) and (1.16). The reason for the variance, Frisch states in *Annual Survey*, is that equation (1.4) assumes expenditure proportionality. In his words : " my original formula [(1.4)] does hold under expenditure proportionality, which was assumed in the statistical work in *New Methods*." [2]   And in reference to a more applicable form which he derives from $(1.\overline{17})$: " This is a generalisation of the isoquant method [in the *New Methods*] to the case where expenditure proportionality is not assumed." [3]

While Frisch does not elaborate these statements, the reasoning upon which they are based may be gathered quite easily from his analysis. If we adopt the convention

$$P_0(U) \equiv 1 \quad \dots\dots\dots\dots\dots\dots\dots\dots\dots\dots\dots\dots\dots\dots\dots\dots \quad (1.18)$$

it follows that

$$P_t = P_{0t} \quad \dots\dots\dots\dots\dots\dots\dots\dots\dots\dots\dots\dots\dots\dots\dots\dots \quad (1.19)$$

Thus, in the case of expenditure proportionality

$$\frac{d\log P_t}{d\log r} = \frac{d\log P_{0t}}{d\log r} = \frac{r}{P_{0t}} \cdot \frac{dP_{0t}}{dU} \cdot \frac{dU}{dr} = 0 \quad \dots\dots\dots\dots\dots\dots \quad (1.20)$$

and (1.16) reduces to (1.4).

We can turn now to the main line of our argument. It is apparent that (1.1) requires two assumptions, independence and expenditure proportionality. It is also apparent that equation (1.17) obviates the second assumption. The problems which we wish to consider, and to which we have already directed the reader's attention, are : (1) can the generalised equation (1.17) be used to measure real money utility, and if not, (2) what restrictions do Frisch's assumptions involve ? Since the importance of problem (2) depends in large part upon the answer to problem (1), it will be desirable to consider the first problem first.

---

[1] The expression (with slight changes in symbols) is

$$w(r) \Big/ P_t(r)\Big(1+\frac{d\log.P_t(r)}{d\log.r}\Big) = m(\bar{x})\Big/ H_t(\bar{x})\Big(1+\frac{d\log.H_t(\bar{x})}{d\log.\bar{x}}\Big) \quad \dots\dots\dots\dots \quad (1.\overline{17})$$

Assuming an independent subset, $x^1, x^2, \dots x^m$, the terms $\bar{x}$, $H_t(\bar{x})$, and $m_i(\bar{x})$ may be defined for this subset in the same way as r, $P_t(r)$, and $w(r)$ are defined for all commodities.
[2] *Annual Survey*, fn. p. 34.
[3] Ibid., p. 36.

II

On the face of it, though the statistical task might be overwhelming, measurement of *real* money utility by use of (1.17) would seem quite feasible theoretically. The terms on the right-hand side of (1.17) involve no new problem. And, as Frisch indicates, if some convention is adopted for $P_0(U)$, the terms on the left are subject to approximation.[1] Formally, one must agree, a series of values could be determined for the term $w(r)$ by this procedure and I should prefer to interpret Frisch's statement cited on p. 38 in this sense only.[2] For while values can be determined for $w(r)$, they can in no sense be called *measurements* of *real* money utility. The difficulty centres in the clause " if some convention is adopted for $P_0(U)$."

In order for the terms on the left-hand side of (1.17) to be statistically determinable, two decisions must be made, one as to what path shall be chosen as the zero-path or base and the other as to what function should be accepted for the price level along this path. These two decisions represent *two* elements of arbitrariness in the real income function.[3] The only restriction imposed on them by the definition of real income is that they be such that $r'(U) = r'_0(U) > 0$.

If no further limitation were imposed on the conventions adopted for the real income function, this function would be quite arbitrary in both the general case and the expenditure proportionality case. In *Annual Survey* Frisch does present an additional criterion which he believes restricts the real income function in the case of expenditure proportionality. But he grants that in the general case the function is still arbitrary. While I agree with this conclusion, for reasons which I shall indicate, I do not believe Frisch's argument is conclusive. Since the point is of considerable importance to our discussion, I shall seek further support for it.

The problem may be approached advantageously by considering the units in which real income is measured. As Frisch defines this concept the only restriction on the unit of real income for one value of U and on the relation between this unit and the unit chosen for another value of U is that the value of real income when measured in these units should increase with an increase of U. While this is the only limitation imposed by definition, it is self-evident that if it were possible to choose the units in such a way that along the path chosen as base the unit used to measure real income is the same—in kind and magnitude—for one value of U as for another, this convention ought to be adopted. This condition is both crucial and, when coupled with the implications of the real income concept as used in Frisch's analysis, restrictive. On the one hand, if the units *cannot* be the same for every value of U, there is no possible limitation on their relationship. The shape of the real income function, since it is dependent upon this relationship, must be entirely arbitrary. On the other hand, as real income is used in Frisch's analysis, this condition

---

[1] *Annual Survey*, p. 36.

[2] This interpretation is quite plausible. For Frisch's index number purposes a determination of the values of $w(r)$ in a purely formal sense is sufficient. It does not matter whether these values can be regarded as measurements of marginal utility.

[3] Only the second causes arbitrariness in the case of expenditure proportionality. *Infra*, p. 40.

leaves little freedom of choice as to the real income convention along the base path. While ordinarily identity of units could be achieved by using as the unit of real income, the unit of utility, this is out of the question in Frisch's analysis. If the concepts utility of real income and marginal utility of real income are to have any meaning it is essential that the unit in which real income is measured be independent of the unit of utility.[1] I believe I am correct in saying that the only other possibility which is meaningful[2] is that the unit used be a composite commodity made up of the individual commodities in constant proportions along the base path. If this convention can be adopted, it leads immediately to the base path real income function

$$r_0(U) = \frac{I_0(U)}{c} \dots\dots\dots\dots\dots\dots\dots\dots\dots\dots\dots\dots\dots\dots\dots\dots (2.1)$$

For, since the prices of the individual commodities are constant, and since the unit of real income for every value of U along the base path contains these commodities in constant proportions, the price level—the price of a unit of real income—is constant.[3] For convenience the magnitude of the real income unit may be chosen such that the constant c equals unity.

In the case of expenditure proportionality the convention (2.1) *can* be adopted. Not only is. it possible to select as base *one* path along which the commodities are consumed in constant proportions, but as we shall see, a necessary and sufficient condition for expenditure proportionality is that every expansion path should have this property. Thus, the first element of arbitrariness in the real income function—the choice of a price-level function—is not present. Further, in the case of expenditure proportionality, the second element of arbitrariness is not operative, aside from a scalar constant, no matter· what price-level convention is adopted. For consider the ratio

$$\frac{\bar{r}(U)}{r(U)} = \frac{r_1(U)}{r_0(U)} \dots\dots\dots\dots\dots\dots\dots\dots\dots\dots\dots\dots\dots\dots (2.2)$$

Here $\bar{r}(U)$ and $r(U)$ are the real income functions having respectively the expansion paths $t=1$ and $t=0$ as base. For a given price-level convention— any function of U—(2.2) equals the ratio of the income functions, which ratio is constant by definition in the case of expenditure proportionality.[4]

---

[1] Cf. W. Leontief, *Econometrica*, January, 1936, p. 53.

[2] There are alternatives, such as using as the unit of real income (say) a pound, irrespective of its content. But it would be impossible to derive any consistent relationship between real income and utility with such a unit. Utility does not depend on the number of pounds of goods, *per se.*

[3] Since the product of the price level and real income must equal money income for every value of U, it is proper to regard the price level as the price of a unit of real income.

[4] Frisch believes constancy of (2.2) in itself leads immediately to the convention (2.1). He states (replacing his symbols by those of this paper) : " If it is possible to formulate the convention in such a way that (2.2) becomes independent of U, and further r, respectively $\bar{r}$, a plausible expression for real expenditure, *that* particular convention ought to be adopted. In the case of income [expenditure] proportionality this leads to (2.1). Otherwise (2.1) is more or less arbitrary." [*Annual Survey*, p. 32] It is true that if the convention (2.1) is adopted in the case of expenditure proportionality (2.2) is constant. But the converse is not at all inevitable. There are an infinity of other conventions—say, $r_0(U) = I_0(U)^2$, $r_0(U) = I_0(U) \cdot U$—which lead to the same result in the case of expenditure proportionality.

In the general case there is no reason to expect that there is even one expansion path along which the commodities are consumed in constant proportions. And even if, in particular instances, there is one or more of such paths, the real income function is still arbitrary. For, while for the path (or paths) of constant proportions as base convention (2.1) is appropriate, if the base is shifted the real income function will be altered. This *must* be so in the general case.

The conclusion is clear that, while in the case of expenditure proportionality the real income function is determined to the extent of an arbitrary scalar constant, in the general case no restriction on the real income function, in addition to the *a priori* one that $r'(U) > 0$, is justifiable. The implications of this for the measurement of *real* money utility are immediate. If in the general case no further restriction can be imposed on the real income function, efforts to measure this concept on the basis of (1.17) must prove futile.

Frisch's measurements of *real* money utility in *New Methods* are based on an assumption that the only arbitrary element in this function is a proportionality factor.[1] While the absolute values of the *real* money utility function have no significance, Frisch is able to advance values for its rate of change and its *relative* rate of change (relative to a change of real income) which do possess an absolute significance.

In the general case this is no longer possible. If the real income function is restricted only as to the sign of its first derivative, any transformation $R[r(U)]$, $R'(r) > 0$, may serve as this function as well as r. Since such a transformation may alter everything but the rank or order of the real income function, the number system used for it is *only* restricted as to rank or order. The *real* money utility function is a first derivative involving r. A transformation $R[r(U)]$, $R'(r) > 0$, may alter everything but the sign of this function.[2] Accordingly the numbering system used for it is not even restricted as to rank. It need only be added that the rate of change and the relative rate of change— since the former involves a differential and the latter a derivative of the *real* money utility function—are entirely unrestricted. Under the circumstances it would be meaningless to advance any series of values as measurements of these concepts. With an appropriate transformation any other series has an equal claim to this status.

III

To simplify our discussion of the restriction imposed by the assumptions of expenditure proportionality and independence, we shall develop our argument first on the basis of a two-commodity analysis and then shall extend it, briefly, in the last section of this paper to the many-commodity case. This

---

[1] In Frisch's analysis, the admissability of all linear transformations of the utility function accounts for the arbitrary factor. But it is important to note that even if the utility function were completely determinate, Frisch's technique of measuring *real* money utility would result in the values of that function containing an unknown, though not arbitrary, proportionality factor. Cf. *New Methods*, Sections 3 and 4.

[2] Using the transformation $R[r(U)]$, $w(R) = \dfrac{w(r)}{R'(r)}$.

course, though laborious, will enable the reader to follow the argument without being distracted by the mathematical manipulations necessary to secure the generality of the many-commodity analysis. The conclusions of the two-commodity analysis, as we shall indicate, are modified in only two respects by the generalisation. To order our discussion we shall consider first the restriction imposed upon the utility function and then the restriction imposed upon the real money utility function.

IV

The condition of expenditure proportionality, as Frisch's analysis in *Annual Survey* demonstrates, is of considerable importance not only to his technique of measuring marginal utility, but for general index number theory.[1] It will be desirable, therefore, to consider separately the restriction imposed upon the utility function by the assumption of this condition.

Let us consider the slope function,[2]

$$F = F(x, y) = -\left(\frac{dy}{dx}\right)_U = \frac{U_x}{U_y} \qquad \dots\dots\dots (4.1)$$

This function is called by Hicks and Allen[3] the marginal rate of substitution of commodity y for commodity x. When the individual has attained a maximum, or equilibrium position, F equals the price ratio $\frac{h}{p}$.

We shall prove the following theorem : *a necessary and sufficient condition that P_{0t} be independent of U for any t* (the condition of expenditure proportionality) *is that F be homogeneous to the zero degree.*

First, let us prove necessity : given P_{0t} is independent of U, to prove that F is homogeneous to the zero degree. From the hypothesis, differentiating (1.8) with respect to U,

$$\frac{dP_{0t}}{dU} = \frac{I_0\frac{dI_t}{dU} - I_t\frac{dI_0}{dU}}{I^2_0} = 0 \qquad \dots\dots\dots (4.2)$$

Thus,

$$I_0\frac{dU}{dI_0} = I_t\frac{dU}{dI_t} \qquad \dots\dots\dots (4.3)$$

Consider the two points : x_0, y_0, on the zero path ; and x_t, y_t, on the t path. Suppose they are so related that

$$U(x_0, y_0) = U(x_t, y_t) \qquad \dots\dots\dots (4.4)$$

[1] In the case of expenditure proportionality the much discussed upper and lower limits for index numbers—the Laspeyre and Paasche formulae—are truly limiting. They relate to one number. In the general case this is not so. Here the Laspeyre formula is the upper limit for one index number and the Paasche formula the lower limit for another. See Frisch's discussion of the Haberler Limits. Loc. cit. p. 25.

[2] Since we are only dealing with two commodities we shall drop the superscripts from y and p.

[3] *Economica*, Feb., May, 1934. If we designate the family of curves in the x, y plane described by taking $U(x, y)$ constant at different values, the indifference *loci*, $F(x, y)$, is the slope at the point x, y of the particular indifference *locus* passing through the point x, y.

Then we can evaluate the derivatives in (4.3) at these points.[1] If we do this, and substitute for I_0 and I_t their budgetary equivalents—equation (a)—we have

$$(h_0 x_0 + p_0 y_0)\frac{U_x(x_0, y_0)}{h_0} = (h_t x_t + p_t y_t)\frac{U_x(x_t, y_t)}{h_t} \quad \dots\dots\dots\dots (4.5)$$

Since in equilibrium $\dfrac{h}{p} = \dfrac{U_x}{U_y}$, (4.5) may be stated as

$$U_x(x_0, y_0)x_0 + U_y(x_0, y_0)y_0 = U_x(x_t, y_t)x_t + U_y(x_t, y_t)y_t \quad \dots\dots (4.6)$$

Equation (4.6) must hold for every x_0, y_0 ; x_t, y_t for which (4.4) is valid. If we hold x_0, y_0 fixed, and vary t, and thus, also x_t, y_t, (4.4) describes an indifference curve—a *locus* of constant utility. Accordingly, if we take x_0, y_0 constant, (4.6) must hold as long as x_t, y_t remains on the indifference curve defined by (4.4). Let us therefore hold x_0, y_0 constant and differentiate (4.6) with respect to x_t, so varying y_t, that (4.4) holds. Since the left-hand side of (4.6) drops out, we now deal with the point x_t, y_t alone. For convenience we will omit the subscript t. Thus we have

$$0 = \left[U_{xx} + U_{xy}\left(\frac{dy}{dx}\right)_U\right]x + U_x + \left[U_{xy} + U_{yy}\left(\frac{dy}{dx}\right)_U\right]y + U_y\left(\frac{dy}{dx}\right)_U. \quad (4.7)$$

Substituting for $\left(\dfrac{dy}{dx}\right)_U$ its equivalent, $-\dfrac{U_x}{U_y}$,

$$\left(U_{xx} - U_{xy}\frac{U_x}{U_y}\right)x + \left(U_{xy} - U_{yy}\frac{U_x}{U_y}\right)y = 0 \quad \dots\dots\dots\dots\dots (4.8)$$

If we multiply through by U_y, and then divide through by $U^2 y$, (4.8) may be written

$$\left[\frac{\partial\left(\frac{U_x}{U_y}\right)}{\partial x}\right]_y x + \left[\frac{\partial\left(\frac{U_x}{U_y}\right)}{\partial y}\right]_x y = 0 \quad \dots\dots\dots\dots\dots (4.9)$$

or

$$F_x x + F_y y = 0 \quad \dots\dots\dots\dots\dots\dots (4.10)$$

From (4.10) it follows by Euler's theorem that $F(x, y)$ is homogeneous to the zero degree. Q.E.D.

Now as to the sufficiency : given F is homogeneous to the zero degree, to prove that P_{0t} is independent of U for any t. From the hypothesis we may retrace our steps from (4.10) to (4.7). Now consider the function

$$M(x, y) = U_x x + U_y y \dots\dots\dots\dots\dots\dots\dots (4.11)$$

By (4.7)

$$\left(\frac{dM}{dx}\right)_U = M_x - M_y\frac{U_x}{U_y} = 0 \quad \dots\dots\dots\dots\dots\dots (4.12)$$

Thus,

$$dM = \frac{M_x}{U_x}dU \quad \dots\dots\dots\dots\dots\dots (4.13)$$

---

[1] For the method of evaluation, see *supra*, fn. 3, p. 37.

From (4.13), when $dU = 0$, $dM = 0$: when U is constant, M is constant. Considering again the two points x_0, y_0 and x_t, y_t for which (4.4) holds, (4.6) must be true. If we evaluate the terms in (4.2) we have

$$I^2_0 \cdot \frac{dP_{0t}}{dU} = \tag{4.14}$$

$$\frac{h_t h_0}{U_x(x_t, y_t) \cdot U_x(x_0, y_0)} \left[U_x(x_0, y_0)x_0 + U_y(x_0, y_0)y_0 - U_x(x_t, y_t)x_t - U_y(x_t, y_t)y_t \right]$$

And by (4.6) the right-hand side of (4.14) equals zero. Q.E.D.

The condition that F be homogeneous to the zero degree is equivalent to the condition that all the expansion paths be straight lines through the origin. For given the homogeneity to the zero order, the slope function can be written in the form

$$F = F\left(\frac{y}{x}\right)^1 \dots \dots \dots \tag{4.15}$$

If we take a given price situation, h_t, p_t and vary I_t, the *locus* of points x_t, y_t described will be a path of constant F.[2] Accordingly, if F is constant, by (4.15) $\frac{y}{x}$ must be constant.[3] Thus the expansion path t is given by the equation

$$y = c_t x \dots \dots \dots \tag{4.16}$$

Conversely, if we are given (4.16) as the equation of the expansion path, F must be homogeneous to the zero degree. For, if F is constant for all x, y along the path (4.16)

$$F(x, y) = F(\lambda x, \lambda y) \dots \dots \dots \tag{4.17}$$

Stated in another way the homogeneity of F to the zero order is equivalent to the condition that straight lines through the origin intercept the indifference *loci* at points of constant slope.[4]

---

[1] By definition, if $F(x, y)$ is homogeneous to the zero degree $F(x, y) = F(\lambda x, \lambda y)$ for any λ. If we take $\lambda = \frac{1}{x}$ we obtain (4.15).

[2] Taking a given price situation h_t, p_t means that the price ratio $\frac{h_t}{p_t}$ is constant, and since in equilibrium, $F = \frac{h_t}{p}$, F must be constant. It may be noted here that the expansion path could be defined by constancy of the price ratio instead of constancy of the price situation. (See *Annual Survey*, p. 16). The advantage of and, I presume, Frisch's reason for using constancy of the price situation is this : while the *locus* of points x, y, in the indifference plane is unaltered by taking ah_t, ap_t, instead of h_t, p_t the third dimensional relation between I_t and U is altered, proportionally, by this procedure.

[3] If, in a particular region of the indifference plane, it is assumed that the individual can attain only one equilibrium position, $\frac{y}{x}$ must be single valued for that region.

[4] There is another interesting interpretation of the condition of expenditure proportionality. Consider the family of functions $J[U(x, y)]$. All of these functions define the same indifference *loci* ; they only differ in the third dimension. Now it may be shown—I shall leave the proof to the reader—that a necessary and sufficient condition that one member, $H(x, y)$, of the family $J[U(x, y)]$ be homogeneous to the first degree is that $F(x, y)$ be homogeneous to the first degree. This condition is thus identical with the restriction imposed on the isoquants by the marginal productivity theorem. In the third dimension, of course, the marginal productivity theorem

V

The condition of expenditure proportionality limits the shape of the indifference curves alone.   Homogeneity of the slope function leaves the third dimension—utility—unrestricted.   If to expenditure proportionality is added the assumption of independence this is no longer true.

Frisch assumes in *New Methods* that one commodity, sugar, is independent of all others.   In the two commodity case this means that both commodities are independent.   To avoid all possible misunderstanding on this account, we shall indicate in our discussion of the two-commodity case what difference in results will appear when the analysis is extended to several commodities.

If the two commodities, x and y, are independent, we can write the utility function in the form

$$U(x, y) = u(x) + v(y) \dots\dots\dots\dots\dots\dots\dots\dots\dots\dots\dots \quad (5.1)$$

Any linear transformation of this function is also admissible, but no other.[1]
From (5.1) the slope function

$$F = \frac{u'(x)}{v'(y)} \dots\dots\dots\dots\dots\dots\dots\dots\dots\dots\dots\dots \quad (5.2)$$

By (4.10)

$$\frac{u''(x)}{u'(x)}x = \frac{v''(y)}{v'(y)}y \dots\dots\dots\dots\dots\dots\dots\dots\dots\dots \quad (5.3)$$

Since x and y are independent, and since (5.3) must hold for every x and y, each side of this equation must equal a constant.   For convenience, let us write the constant as $n-1$.   We have two differential equations :

$$\frac{d\log u'(x)}{d\log x} = n-1 \dots\dots\dots\dots\dots\dots\dots\dots\dots\dots \quad (5.4)$$

$$\frac{d\log v'(y)}{d\log y} = n-1 \dots\dots\dots\dots\dots\dots\dots\dots\dots\dots \quad (5.5)$$

The solutions of these differential equations are

$$u(x) = Ax^n + k_1 \dots\dots\dots\dots\dots\dots\dots\dots\dots\dots\dots \quad (5.6)$$

$$v(y) = By^n + k_2 \dots\dots\dots\dots\dots\dots\dots\dots\dots\dots\dots \quad (5.7)$$

where A, B, k_1, and k_2 are constants.   Thus the utility function may be written

$$U(x, y) = Ax^n + By^n \dots\dots\dots\dots\dots\dots\dots\dots\dots\dots \quad (5.8)$$

For convenience we omit the k_1 and k_2, since in any case, any linear transformation of (5.8) is admissible.[2]

---

assumes that $H(x, y)$ is the production function, whereas here we assume only that another member $U(x, y)$ of the family $J[U(x, y)]$ is the utility function.   But considering only the two dimensional relations defined by the indifference curves and the isoquants, the restriction is the same.

[1] Cf. *supra*, fn. 5, p. 34.

[2] If the utility functions satisfies certain *a priori* conditions the range of possible values for the parameter n in (5.8) is considerably restricted.   If, for values of x and $y > 0$, the utility derived from x increases when x increases and the utility derived from y increases when y increases, A, B,

The logarithmic derivatives in (5.4) and (5.5) are utility elasticities, or as Frisch would designate them, utility flexibilities. It is apparent that Frisch's assumptions require that both be constant. In the many commodity case the restriction is less—only the utility flexibility for x must be constant. The many commodity analysis also involves less restriction of the function $U(x, y)$. In the place of y^n in (5.8) there appears a function of all the other commodities, which function must be homogeneous to the order n. But these two qualifications are the *only* modifications in the conclusions of the two commodity analysis necessitated by extension of the discussion to the many commodity case.

The restriction imposed upon the utility function by Frisch's assumptions is now apparent. On this basis alone there is reason to believe that the methods of measuring marginal utility developed by Frisch have a narrow range of application. But consideration of this subject may be postponed profitably until we have dealt with the relation of Frisch's assumptions to his *real* money utility function.

VI

In determining the restriction imposed upon the *real* money utility function we shall consider together Frisch's two assumptions, expenditure proportionality and independence. Since the real money utility function involves the third dimension, utility, it is fairly obvious that the condition of expenditure proportionality will leave this function unrestricted. A separate treatment of the effects of the assumption of this condition, therefore, will yield only negative results.[1]

Let us adopt the convention $P_0(U) \equiv 1$ for the price level along a base path. Thus, expressing r_0 and I_0 in terms of x_0 and y_0,

$$r_0[U(x_0, y_0)] = I_0[U(x_0, y_0)] = h_0 x_0 + p_0 y_0 \quad \ldots\ldots\ldots\ldots\ldots (6.1)$$

From (4.16)

$$r_0[U(x_0, y_0)] = (h_0 + c_0 p_0) x_0 \quad \ldots\ldots\ldots\ldots\ldots\ldots\ldots (6.2)$$

Along the base path then, real income, aside from a proportionality factor, is measured by the amount consumed of one commodity.

For another point, x_t, y_t on the expansion path $t = t$,

$$r[U(x_t, y_t)] = r_0[U(x_0, y_0)] \quad \ldots\ldots\ldots\ldots\ldots\ldots\ldots (6.3)$$

provided (4.4) is realised. From (5.8) and (4.16)

$$U(x_t, y_t) = (A + Bc_t^n) x_t^n \quad \ldots\ldots\ldots\ldots\ldots\ldots\ldots (6.4)$$

$$U(x_0, y_0) = (A + Bc_0^n) x_0^n \quad \ldots\ldots\ldots\ldots\ldots\ldots\ldots (6.5)$$

and n must have the same sign. If in addition the individual can attain a relative maximum position at any point x, y in a region of positive values of x and y, n must be < 1. Finally, if U is not constant for all values of x and y, and if for a finite linear transformation, $G(U)$, of U, $G[U(0, 0)] = 0$, n must be > 0.

[1] It is possible, with the aid of the theorem which is stated *supra*, fn. 4, p. 44, to determine the shape of the real income function from the condition of expenditure proportionality alone. But to proceed further, it is necessary to assume independence.

Thus condition (4.4) requires that

$$x_0 = \frac{(A+Bc_t{}^n)^{\frac{1}{n}}}{(A+Bc_0{}^n)^{\frac{1}{n}}}x_t \dots\dots\dots\dots\dots\dots\dots\dots\dots\dots\dots \quad (6.6)$$

By (6.2), (6.3), and (6.6),

$$r[U(x_t, y_t)] = \frac{(h_0+c_0p_0)}{(A+Bc_0{}^n)^{\frac{1}{n}}} \cdot (A+Bc_t{}^n)^{\frac{1}{n}}x_t \dots\dots\dots\dots \quad (6.7)$$

or, replacing the quotient on the right-hand side by R_0,

$$r[U(x_t, y_t)] = R_0(A+Bc_t{}^n)^{\frac{1}{n}}x_t \dots\dots\dots\dots\dots\dots\dots \quad (6.8)$$

Accordingly, real income along any path $t = t$ is measured by the amount consumed of one commodity.

While in equation (6.8) we have written r as a function of x_t and y_t, it is possible from (6.8) and (4.16) to regard x_t, and y_t, as depending upon r. Using (6.8) and (6.4) we can express utility as a function of r,

$$U(r) = \frac{r^n}{R_0{}^n} \dots\dots\dots\dots\dots\dots\dots\dots\dots\dots\dots\dots\dots\dots \quad (6.9)$$

Here R_0 is the only constant involved. It depends on the base path constants and on the constants A and B. On a *priori* grounds it may be limited to positive values,[1] but otherwise it is unrestricted.

It is possible, finally, to determine the *real* money utility function :

$$w(r) = \frac{dU}{dr} = \frac{nr^{n-1}}{R_0{}^n} \dots\dots\dots\dots\dots\dots\dots\dots\dots\dots\dots \quad (6.10)$$

While in (6.9) any linear function of $\frac{r^n}{R_0{}^n}$ is admissible as an expression for $U(r)$, the only arbitrary element in (6.10) is a scalar constant.

In his *Sur un Problème d'Économie Pure* Frisch lists five conditions which he believes the real money utility function ought to satisfy *a priori*. From a consideration of these conditions he concludes that : " La forme la plus simple que l'on puisse employer comme formule d'interpolation pour l'utilité marginale de la monnai est donc la formule."

$$w(r) = \frac{\text{constant}^{[2]}}{\log r - \log a} \dots\dots\dots\dots\dots\dots\dots\dots\dots\dots \quad (6.11)$$

Here " a " is a constant indicating the minimum of existence. In his *New Methods* also Frisch expresses a preference for (6.11) as an analytic expression for *real* money utility.[3]

The difference between (6.11) and (6.10) is evidently great. If we turn to the conditions on the basis of which Frisch deduces (6.11) the discrepancy is understandable. The first three conditions are :

(1) Il exist un nombre positif " a " (le minimum d'existence au niveau

[1] Cf. fn. 2, p. 45.
[2] P. 22. I have inserted the symbols used in the present paper.
[3] P. 31.

des prix donné P_0) tel que $w(r) > 0$ et possède des derivées de premier et second ordre pour $a < r < \infty$.

(2A) $\mathop{\text{Lim}}\limits_{r \to a} w(r) = \infty$ (2B) $\mathop{\text{Lim}}\limits_{r \to \infty} w(r) = 0$

(3) $\dfrac{dw(r)}{dr} = w'(r) < 0$ dans l'intervalle a $< r < \infty$.[1]

The relation of (6.10) to these conditions is obvious. Condition (2B) will be satisfied if $n < 1$. But as to the other conditions, all involve the constant " a." In (6.10) there is no *positive* number which could be given the properties of a minimum of existence, no *positive* critical value for r. For $n < 1$, the only critical value of r in (6.10) is *zero*.[2] If this is interpreted as a minimum of existence, the other conditions will be satisfied for $n > 0$.

The last two of Frisch's conditions relate to the logarithmic derivative of $w(r)$—the money flexibility. We have encountered this function before, though not by name. Because of the fact that the *real* money utility function is affected by an arbitrary proportionality factor, Frisch in *New Methods* turns to the rate of change and the *relative* rate of change of *real* money utility. The relative rate of change is the money flexibility. Though Frisch advances a series of values for the rate of change of real money utility,[3] his main interest in *New Methods* is to measure the *relative* rate of change—the money flexibility —for different values of income.[4]

Frisch's last two conditions are :

(4) La proportion de decroissance $-\overset{\vee}{w}(r) = -\dfrac{d\log w(r)}{d\log r}$ est plus grande que l'unité pour des valeurs de $r(>a)$ assez petites.

(5) $\mathop{\text{Lim}}\limits_{r \to \infty} \overset{\vee}{w}(r) = 0$ [5]

From (6.10) the money flexibility is

$$\overset{\vee}{w}(r) = \dfrac{r}{\dfrac{nr^{n-1}}{R_0^n}} \cdot \dfrac{n(n-1)r^{n-2}}{R_0^n} = n-1 \text{[6]} \quad \dots\dots\dots\dots\dots \quad (6.12)$$

Since n is a constant conditions (4) and (5) cannot both be satisfied. If either be valid none of the first three conditions will be satisfied.

In the light of Frisch's five conditions, all of which on *a priori* grounds seem quite reasonable, (6.10) certainly appears to be *rara avis*. But to the evidence of these conditions must be added a further and much more interesting point. By (6.12) it is apparent that, *under the assumption of independence and expenditure proportionality, the money flexibility which is the variable Frisch is mainly*

---

[1] *Sur un Problème d'Économie Pure*, p. 19.
[2] If $n \geq 1$ there is no critical value for r.
[3] *New Methods*, p. 30.
[4] For a discussion of the money flexibility, cf. loc. cit., sections 1, 2, and 3, and Allen, *Economica*, May, 1933, pp. 186, 191.
[5] *Sur un Problème d'Économie Pure*, p. 19.
[6] The value of the flexibility, it will be recalled, is the same as that for the commodity x.

interested in measuring is equal to a constant.[1][2] While in any case a question of fact is involved, I believe I am justified in saying, *a priori*, that constancy of the flexibility in itself casts considerable doubt upon the range of applicability of Frisch's new methods. When to this is added the evidence of his five conditions the usefulness of his technique is seriously open to question.

VII

To develop our analysis in the many commodity case we shall consider only three commodities. This number will be sufficient to assure the generality of our argument.

(1) *The theorem on expenditure proportionality.* Consider the two slope functions [3]

$$F = F(x, y, z) = -\left(\frac{\partial y}{\partial x}\right)_{U,z} = \frac{U_x}{U_y} \quad \dots\dots\dots\dots\dots\dots\dots\dots\dots\dots\dots\dots \quad (7.1)$$

$$G = G(x, y, z) = -\left(\frac{\partial z}{\partial x}\right)_{U,y} = \frac{U_x}{U_z} \quad \dots\dots\dots\dots\dots\dots\dots\dots\dots\dots\dots\dots \quad (7.2)$$

In equilibrium (7.1) equals $\frac{h}{p}$ and (7.2), $\frac{h}{q}$.

For the expenditure proportionality theorem we have : *a necessary and sufficient condition that P_{0t} be independent of U for any t is that F and G be homogeneous to the zero degree.*

First as to the necessity : given P_{0t} is independent of U, to prove that F and G are homogeneous to the zero degree. From the hypothesis we again have (4.3). Consider the two points : x_0, y_0, z_0 on the zero path and x_t, y_t, z_t on the t path. Suppose they are so related that

$$U(x_0, y_0, z_0) = U(x_t, y_t, z_t) \quad \dots\dots\dots\dots\dots\dots\dots\dots\dots\dots\dots\dots\dots\dots\dots\dots \quad (7.3)$$

Evaluating the derivatives and the terms I_0 and I_t in (4.3) at these points,

$$(h_0 x_0 + p_0 y_0 + q_0 z_0) \cdot \frac{U_x(x_0, y_0, z_0)}{h_0} = (h_t x_t + p_t y_t + q_t z_t)\frac{U_x(x_t, y_t, z_t)}{h_t} \quad \dots\dots\dots\dots \quad (7.4)$$

Using the equilibrium values for (7.1) and (7.2)

$$U_x(x_0, y_0, z_0)x_0 + U_y(x_0, y_0, z_0)y_0 + U_z(x_0, y_0, z_0)z_0 =$$
$$U_x(x_t, y_t, z_t)x_t + U_y(x_t, y_t, z_t)y_t + U_z(x_t, y_t, z_t)z_t \quad \dots\dots\dots\dots\dots\dots \quad (7.5)$$

Equation (7.5) is valid for all points for which (7.3) holds. Let us hold x_0, y_0, z_0, and thus U, constant. Further, let us vary t in such a way that z_t is constant. Then differentiating (7.5) with respect to x_t and for convenience dropping the subscript t,

$$0 = \left[U_{xx} + U_{xy}\left(\frac{\partial y}{\partial x}\right)_{U,z}\right]x + U_x + \left[U_{xy} + U_{yy}\left(\frac{\partial y}{\partial x}\right)_{U,z}\right]y + U_y\left(\frac{\partial y}{\partial x}\right)_{U,z} + \left[U_{xz} + U_{yz}\left(\frac{\partial y}{\partial x}\right)_{U,z}\right]z \quad (7.6)$$

Using (7.1),

$$\left(U_{xx} - U_{xy}\frac{U_x}{U_y}\right)x + \left(U_{xy} - U_{yy}\frac{U_x}{U_y}\right)y + \left(U_{xz} - U_{yz}\frac{U_x}{U_y}\right)z = 0 \quad \dots\dots\dots\dots\dots \quad (7.7)$$

If we multiply through by U_y and then divide through by $U_y{}^2$, (7.7) may be written

$$\left[\frac{\partial\left(\frac{U_x}{U_y}\right)}{\partial x}\right]_{y,z} x + \left[\frac{\partial\left(\frac{U_x}{U_y}\right)}{\partial y}\right]_{x,z} y + \left[\frac{\partial\left(\frac{U_x}{U_y}\right)}{\partial z}\right]_{x,y} z = 0 \quad \dots\dots\dots\dots\dots \quad (7.8)$$

or

$$F_x x + F_y y + F_z z = 0 \dots\dots\dots\dots\dots\dots\dots\dots\dots\dots\dots\dots\dots\dots\dots\dots\dots \quad (7.9)$$

---

[1] This has an interesting implication. Frisch, in his contribution to index number theory (*Annual Survey*, Section 7), regards the money flexibility as an indifference function. An obvious exception is the case where the logarithms of real money utility and real income are linearly related. This is true of (4.11).

[2] It hardly need be added that in this case measurement of the money flexibility is a very simple process. It is sufficient to determine its magnitude for one value of real income.

[3] To avoid the use of superscripts I have decided to use as symbols for the quantities of the three commodities x, y, z, rather than x, y^2, y^3, and as symbols for prices h, p, q rather than h, p^2, p^3. This is inconsistent with our earlier notation but at the same time is much less laborious.

In the same manner, if in (7.5) t is varied in such a way that y_t is constant, it may be shown that

$$G_x x + G_y y + G_z z = 0 \quad\dots\dots\dots\dots\dots\dots\dots\dots\dots\dots\dots\dots\dots\dots\dots\dots \text{(7.10)}$$

Equations (7.9) and (7.10) are sufficient conditions that F and G be homogeneous to the zero degree.   Q.E.D.

As to the sufficiency : given F and G are homogeneous to the zero degree, to prove that P_{0t} is independent of U.   Consider the function

$$M(x, y, z) = U_x x + U_y y + U_z z \quad\dots\dots\dots\dots\dots\dots\dots\dots\dots\dots\dots\dots\dots \text{(7.11)}$$

From the hypothesis

$$\left(\frac{\partial M}{\partial x}\right)_{U, z} = M_x - M_y \frac{U_x}{U_y} = 0 \quad\dots\dots\dots\dots\dots\dots\dots\dots\dots\dots\dots \text{(7.12)}$$

$$\left(\frac{\partial M}{\partial x}\right)_{U, y} = M_x - M_z \frac{U_x}{U_z} = 0 \quad\dots\dots\dots\dots\dots\dots\dots\dots\dots\dots\dots \text{(7.13)}$$

For, given the homogeneity of F, we can proceed immediately to equation (7.6).   Similarly, from the homogeneity of G, we can proceed to a corresponding equation.   From (7.12) and (7.13)

$$dM = \frac{M_x}{U_x} dU \quad\dots\dots\dots\dots\dots\dots\dots\dots\dots\dots\dots\dots\dots\dots\dots\dots \text{(7.14)}$$

For dU equal to zero, dM must equal zero : for U constant, M must be constant.   Consider again two points x_0, y_0, z_0 and x_t, y_t, z_t for which (7.3) holds.   Then (7.5) must be true.   The constancy of P_{0t} with respect to U follows in the same way as in the two-commodity analysis.   Q.E.D.

The homogeneity of F and G to the zero degree is equivalent again to the condition that all expansion paths are straight lines through the origin.   For given the homogeneity we can write

$$F = F\left(\frac{y}{x}, \frac{z}{x}\right) \quad\dots\dots\dots\dots\dots\dots\dots\dots\dots\dots\dots\dots\dots\dots \text{(7.15)}$$

$$G = G\left(\frac{y}{x}, \frac{z}{x}\right)^1 \quad\dots\dots\dots\dots\dots\dots\dots\dots\dots\dots\dots\dots\dots \text{(7.16)}$$

For a given price situation $h_t, p_t, q_t,$ and varying income, $I_t,$ the *locus* of points x_t, y_t, z_t will be determined by the intersection of the two surfaces F constant and G constant.   The expansion path is given by

$$y = c_t x \quad\dots\dots\dots\dots\dots\dots\dots\dots\dots\dots\dots\dots\dots\dots\dots\dots\dots\dots \text{(7.17)}$$

$$z = d_t x \quad\dots\dots\dots\dots\dots\dots\dots\dots\dots\dots\dots\dots\dots\dots\dots\dots\dots\dots \text{(7.18)}$$

which is the solution of the equations F and G constant.[2]   The converse—that F and G are homogeneous to the zero degree if (7.17) and (7.18) define the t expansion path—follows in the same manner as in the two commodity case.

(2) *Independence and the utility function.*   In the three commodity case Frisch's assumption of independence implies that the utility function may be written in the form

$$U(x, y, z) = u(x) + v(y, z) \quad\dots\dots\dots\dots\dots\dots\dots\dots\dots\dots\dots\dots \text{(7.19)}$$

Any linear function of this is also admissible.   From (7.19)

$$F = \frac{u'(x)}{v_y(y, z)} \quad\dots\dots\dots\dots\dots\dots\dots\dots\dots\dots\dots\dots\dots\dots\dots \text{(7.20)}$$

$$G = \frac{u'(x)}{v_z(y, z)} \quad\dots\dots\dots\dots\dots\dots\dots\dots\dots\dots\dots\dots\dots\dots\dots \text{(7.21)}$$

and from (7.20) and (7.9), (7.21) and (7.10)

$$\frac{u''(x)}{u'(x)} x = \frac{v_{yy}(y, z)}{v_y(y, z)} y + \frac{v_{yz}(y, z)}{v_y(y, z)} z \quad\dots\dots\dots\dots\dots\dots\dots\dots\dots \text{(7.22)}$$

$$\frac{u''(x)}{u'(x)} x = \frac{v_{yz}(y, z)}{v_z(y, z)} y + \frac{v_{zz}(y, z)}{v_z(y, z)} z \quad\dots\dots\dots\dots\dots\dots\dots\dots\dots \text{(7.23)}$$

Since x, y, and z are independent, and since (7.22) and (7.23) must hold for every value of x, y, and z, the two sides of (7.22) and (7.23)must equal a constant.   For convenience, let this

---

[1] Cf. *supra*, fn. 1, p. 44.

[2] If in a particular region of the indifference manifold, it is assumed that the individual can attain only one equilibrium position, the solution must be unique for that region.

constant be $n-1$. Equations (5.4) and (5.6) follow immediately for the function $u(x)$. As to $v(y, z)$, from the right-hand side of (7.22) and (7.23) we have

$$v_{yy}(y, z)y + v_{yz}(y, z)z = (n-1)v_y(y, z) \dots\dots\dots\dots\dots\dots\dots\dots\dots\dots\dots (7.24)$$

$$v_{yz}(y, z)y + v_{zz}(y, z)z = (n-1)v_z(y, z) \dots\dots\dots\dots\dots\dots\dots\dots\dots\dots\dots (7.25)$$

Equation (7.24), by Euler's theorem, is a sufficient condition that $v_y(y, z)$ be homogeneous to the order $(n-1)$. Similarly for (7.25) and $v_z(y, z)$.

From the homogeneity of $v_y(y, z)$ and $v_z(y, z)$ to the order $n-1$ it may be shown that there is a function $\bar{v}(y, z)$, differing from $v(y, z)$ by a constant, which is homogeneous to the order n. Consider the identities

$$v(y, z) - v(a, b) = \int_a^y v_1(\bar{y}, z)d\bar{y} + \int_b^z v_2(a, \bar{z})d\bar{z} \dots\dots\dots\dots\dots\dots\dots\dots\dots (7.26)$$

$$v(\lambda y, \lambda z) - v(\lambda a, \lambda b) = \int_{\lambda a}^{\lambda y} v_1(\bar{y}, \lambda z)d\bar{y} + \int_{\lambda b}^{\lambda z} v_2(\lambda a, \bar{z})d\bar{z} \dots\dots\dots\dots\dots (7.27)$$

In (7.27) let us change our variables to

$$\bar{y} = \lambda w \; ; \; \bar{z} = \lambda m$$

Then

$$v(\lambda y, \lambda z) - v(\lambda a, \lambda b) = \lambda \int_a^y v_1(\lambda w, \lambda z)dw + \lambda \int_b^z v_2(\lambda a, \lambda m)dm \dots\dots\dots\dots\dots (7.28)$$

Using (7.26), (7.28), and the homogeneity of $v_y(y, z)$ and $v_z(y, z)$,

$$v(\lambda y, \lambda z) - v(\lambda a, \lambda b) = \lambda^n[v(y, z) - v(a, b)] \dots\dots\dots\dots\dots\dots\dots\dots\dots (7.29)$$

This must hold for every λ, y and z, a and b. Differentiating with respect to λ, and then putting $\lambda = 1$.

$$v_y(y, z)y + v_z(y, z)z - nv(y, z) = v_1(a, b)a + v_2(a, b)b - nv(a, b) \dots\dots\dots\dots\dots (7.30)$$

Since y and z, a and b are independent, we may place both sides of (7.30) equal to a constant. for convenience nk_2. If we take

$$\bar{v}(y, z) = v(y, z) + k_2 \dots\dots\dots\dots\dots\dots\dots\dots\dots\dots\dots\dots\dots\dots\dots (7.31)$$

we have from (7.30),

$$n\bar{v}(y, z) = \bar{v}_y(y, z)y + \bar{v}_z(y, z)z \dots\dots\dots\dots\dots\dots\dots\dots\dots\dots\dots\dots (7.32)$$

By Euler's theorem this is a sufficient condition that $\bar{v}(y, z)$ is homogeneous to the order n.

In the three commodity case, from (7.32) and (5.6) we can write

$$U(x, y) = Ax^n + \bar{v}(y, z) \dots\dots\dots\dots\dots\dots\dots\dots\dots\dots\dots\dots\dots\dots (7.33)$$

For convenience we omit again the constants k_1 and k_2.[1]

(3) *The real money utility function.* Adopting the convention $P_0(U) ▰ 1$, and considering the point x_0, y_0, z_0 on the expansion path $t = 0$

$$r_0[U(x_0, y_0, z_0)] = I_0[U(x_0, y_0, z_0)] = h_0x_0 + p_0y_0 + q_0z_0 \dots\dots\dots\dots\dots (7.34)$$

From (7.17) and (7.18)

$$r_0[U(x_0, y_0, z_0)] = (h_0 + c_0p_0 + d_0q_0)x_0 \dots\dots\dots\dots\dots\dots\dots\dots\dots\dots (7.35)$$

For another point, x_t, y_t, z_t, on the expansion path $t = t$

$$r[U(x_t, y_t, z_t)] = r_0[U(x_0, y_0, z_0)] \dots\dots\dots\dots\dots\dots\dots\dots\dots\dots\dots (7.36)$$

provided (7.3) is true. By (7.17), (7.18), and (7.33)

$$U(x_t, y_t, z_t) = (A + Q_t)x_t^n \dots\dots\dots\dots\dots\dots\dots\dots\dots\dots\dots\dots\dots (7.37)$$

$$U(x_0, y_0, z_0) = (A + Q_0)x_0^n.[2] \dots\dots\dots\dots\dots\dots\dots\dots\dots\dots\dots\dots (7.38)$$

---

[1] With slight modifications in method of statement the argument of fn. 2, p. 45, concerning the range of values for the parameter n still holds.

[2] Equations (7.37) and (7.38) may be proven readily. On the expansion path $t = t$,

$$U(x_t, y_t, z_t) = Ax_t^n + \bar{v}(c_tx_t, d_tx_t)$$

Since $\bar{v}$ is homogeneous to the order n

$$\lambda^n\bar{v}(c_tx_t, d_tx_t) = \bar{v}(\lambda c_tx_t, \lambda d_tx_t) \qquad \text{[Note continued on p. 52}$$

4*

Condition (7.3) requires that

$$x_0 = \frac{(A + Q_t)^{\frac{1}{n}}}{(A + Q_0)^{\frac{1}{n}}} x_t \dots\dots\dots\dots\dots\dots\dots\dots\dots\dots\dots\dots\dots\dots\dots\dots\dots \quad (7.39)$$

By (7.35), (7.36), and (7.39)

$$r[U(x_t, y_t, z_t)] = \frac{(h_0 + c_0 p_0 + d_0 q_0)}{(A + Q_0)^{\frac{1}{n}}}(A + Q_t)^{\frac{1}{n}} x_t \dots\dots\dots\dots\dots\dots\dots\dots\dots \quad (7.40)$$

or for simplicity

$$r[U(x_t, y_t, z_t)] = R_0 (A + Q_t)^{\frac{1}{n}} x_t \dots\dots\dots\dots\dots\dots\dots\dots\dots\dots\dots\dots \quad (7.41)$$

From equations (7.17), (7.18, and (7.41) we may regard x_t, y_t, and z_t as functions of r. By (7.41) and (7.37) we can writ

$$U(r) = \frac{r^n}{R^n_0} \dots\dots\dots\dots\dots\dots\dots\dots\dots\dots\dots\dots\dots\dots\dots\dots\dots\dots\dots\dots\dots\dots \quad (7.42)$$

The *real* money utility and the money flexibility may be derived in the same way as in the two commodity case.

Cambridge, Mass.

Note continued from p. 51.]

This must hold for any λ. Taking $\lambda = \dfrac{1}{x_t}$

$$\bar{v}(c_t x_t, d_t x_t) = \bar{v}(c_t, d_t) x_t^n = Q_t x_t^n$$

Similarly for the expansion path $t = 0$.

Postscript

Since this essay appeared, Paul Samuelson has pointed out to me that in solving the differential equations (5.4) and (5.5), the case where $n = 0$ should have been treated as a special one with the solutions taking a familiar logarithmic form.

On p. 59, note 1 might be clearer if, after the first sentence, it were revised to read, "For convenience, I sometimes use elsewhere symbols which differ from Frisch's."

On Monopoly Welfare Losses

By Abram Bergson*

Are welfare losses due to monopolistic pricing apt to be consequential in an advanced economy such as that of the United States? Generations of economists have assumed that they are, but in 1954 Arnold Harberger argued that in the United States during the late 1920's, the total of such losses in manufacturing was equivalent to but "... a tenth of a percent of national income" (p. 87). Subsequently, David Schwartzman found that in the United States in 1954 welfare losses due to monopolistic pricing in industry were equivalent to "... less than $234 million, or less than 0.1 percent of the national income" (pp. 629–30). Still more recently Harvey Leibenstein, relying partly on the findings of Harberger and Schwartzman, has also argued that departures from competitive norms such as result under monopolistic pricing are likely to be relatively inconsequential. Generally, "... they hardly seem worth worrying about" (Leibenstein, p. 395).

From such findings, George Stigler was an early dissenter, and further calculations of David Kamerschen indicated that welfare losses due to monopoly pricing may be appreciably greater than Harberger and Schwartzman computed. The contention that such losses are inconsequential nevertheless has apparently gained no little currency. Perhaps that is as it should be, but the underlying methodology still does not seem to have been sufficiently explored. Some of the more basic empirical assumptions may also be more questionable than has been supposed. A brief reexamination stressing those as-

pects may facilitate appraisal of what is surely one of the more important current issues in economics.

I. Some Methodological Considerations

The evaluations of monopoly welfare losses by Harberger, Schwartzman, and Leibenstein all represent applications of consumer's surplus analysis. As such, they are in a sense rather special, for expressly or by implication, all these writers apply a well-known formula of Harold Hotelling for such surplus. Their calculations may also be viewed, however, as measurements of consumer's surplus without reference to the Hotelling formula. As a preliminary, I briefly reformulate the relevant principles, which still seem somewhat in need of clarification.

What counts for Harberger, Schwartzman, and Leibenstein is efficiency rather than equity. I assume, therefore, as is often done in similar contexts, that there is but one household in the community. The household, however, behaves competitively in purchasing consumer's goods. As will appear, the analyses being considered also assume constant costs. For present purposes it is more convenient to work with the somewhat more restrictive supposition that the community's production possibilities are linear.

As J. R. Hicks taught us long ago, consumer's surplus is susceptible to diverse constructions. The particular construction need not be a practically very important matter, but we may conveniently consider the evaluations that have been made in relation to a concept of surplus corresponding to the compensating variation as understood by Hicks (see pp. 61ff, 69ff),

* Harvard University.

853

77

i.e., the compensatory change in income needed to assure that a household's utility is unaffected by a change in price.

For Hicks, however, the compensating variation represents a change from an otherwise given income. Such a variation is properly taken to measure welfare losses or gains if income is indeed constant. Our household, however, is subject not only to changes in prices, those being the changes due to the fixing of the prices in monopolistic industries at monopolistic rather than competitive levels, but also to a concomitant variation in income. In the analysis of monopoly welfare losses, the concern is with the impact of misallocation rather than unemployment. Hence, with the prices of monopolistic products at monpolistic rather than competitive levels, resources released from monopolistic industries supposedly are reemployed in competitive ones. That is possible only if household income is higher when prices in the monopolistic industries are at monopolistic levels than when they are at competitive levels. Indeed, income must increase by the amount of monopoly profits, for only in that way will there still be sufficient income to employ all the primary factors previously employed.

In short, we are confronted with variations within a general equilibrium context. In consumer's surplus analysis the usual practice even so is to focus on partial equilibrium, but the analysis here seems facilitated if general equilibrium is put clearly to the fore, and Hicks' compensating variation is viewed accordingly.

Thus, a distinction is made between the *gross* compensating variation (*GCV*), representing the change in income needed to compensate households for some specified variation in prices, and the *net* compensating variation (*NCV*), representing the gross change, less the adjustment in income (*MIA*) required to maintain full employment in the face of such a variation in prices, i.e.,

$$(1)\qquad NCV = GCV - MIA$$

The *GCV* corresponds to what Hicks called compensating variation, but the *NCV* is of primary interest here.[1]

Of particular concern now is a rise in prices in monopolistic industries to monopolistic from competitive levels. Referring to such price changes, it suffices here if there is but a single competitive industry in the community considered. If for the moment we also assume that there is only one monopolistic industry, the price and income variations of interest may be illustrated graphically. In Figure 1, x_1 is the product of the monopolistic and x_2 the

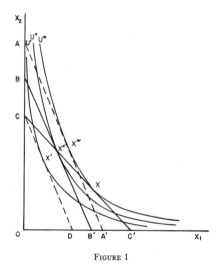

FIGURE 1

[1] For simplicity I assume throughout that monopoly price-cost ratios are unchanged under the impact of the changes in household income in question, but it is easy to see that no essentials would be affected if the ratios should vary. What counts are the monopolistic price-cost ratios when income is again at the full employment level, and the *GCV* could simply be understood as the addition to the household's initial income level that is needed to compensate for the charging of those price-cost ratios. The *MIA* is calculated as before as the difference between the two full employment income levels, one where monopolistic products are priced monopolistically and the other where they are priced competitively.

product of the competitive industry, and CC' represents, the community's production possibilities. Several of the household's indifference curves are also shown, and the point x on U''' represents the household's consumption as it would be if there were competitive pricing throughout the economy, i.e., price equals marginal costs in both the monopolistic and the competitive industries. At x' on U' the household's consumption is as it would be if under monopolistic pricing for x_1 the household's income (with x_2 as the numeraire) should be constant at the competitive level OC. With consumption at x', however, there would be unemployed resources, and that is avoided only if income rises by BC to OB, permitting consumption under monopolistic pricing for x_1 to be at x''. That point is again on the production possibilities schedule, and also on U''. The household has still suffered a welfare loss, though, as a result of monopolistic pricing for x_1. The loss is represented by the shift from U''' to U'', but this would be fully offset were there a further increase in income by AB, that would permit consumption to rise to x''' on U'''. Such consumption, of course, is not feasible, but the increase in income by AB still can serve as a hypothetical measure of the welfare loss due to monopoly.

Thus, AB represents the NCV for monopolistic pricing as that has been defined. We also have

$$(2) \qquad AB = AC - BC$$

where AC corresponds to the GCV for monopolistic pricing, and BC represents the MIA, or increase in income above the competitive level that is needed to maintain full employment under monopolistic pricing for x_1.

I have delineated the NCV in terms of the household's indifference map. Could it be calculated from a conventional Marshallian demand schedule for the

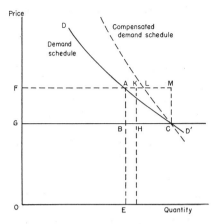

OF = MONOPOLY PRICE
OG = COMPETITIVE PRICE
FK = MONOPOLY OUTPUT AFTER ADJUSTMENT IN
    MONEY INCOME TO ASSURE FULL EMPLOYMENT

FIGURE 2

monopolized product? Subject to one proviso, it could be, for the NCV then precisely corresponds to the triangle-like area ABC in Figure 2. Here DD' represents the Marshallian demand schedule for x_1 that prevails when household income is at a level that would assure full employment under competitive pricing for x_1. Since costs are constant, such pricing means that x_1 would sell at average cost, equalling OG. Under monopoly, however, the price is increased to OF.

The proviso is the proverbial one that the income elasticity of demand for the product in question be zero. In that case, the budget points x', x'', and x''' in Figure 1 all include the same x_1 and differ only in respect of x_2. Also, the GCV, or AC in that figure, corresponds to the area ABC together with the rectangle $FABG$ in Figure, 2, for "income effects" that might distort the relation between the sum of those areas and the GCV are zero (see Hicks, pp. 68ff). It also follows that the MIA, or BC in Figure 1, corresponds to the rectangle $FABG$ in Figure 2. Given that the consumption of x_1 in x' is the same as in x'', the x_1 in x'' corresponds to FA. Hence, $FABG$ represents monopoly profits at a full employment income level, and also the addition that must be made to income if the resources released from x_1 by the introduction of monopolistic pricing there are to be fully absorbed into x_2. It also follows that the NCV, or AB in Figure 1, corresponds to the area ABC in Figure 2, which is in effect the difference between the GCV and MIA.

What if the income elasticity of demand is other than zero? As is well known, calculation of the Hicksian compensating variation from a Marshallian demand schedule in that case is subject to error. That must be so also, therefore, for the GCV, but of interest here is the NCV so we must also consider that the MIA, as just calculated, is likewise subject to error. Curiously, the errors tend to be offsetting.

Thus, suppose the monopolized product is a superior one. Then the GCV for an increase in the price of that product from the competitive to the monopolistic level now corresponds to the area that is bounded by that price change to the left of the Hicksian or compensated demand schedule, that is, the area $FLCG$ in Figure 2. That area exceeds the corresponding area, $FACG$, to the left of the Marshallian or uncompensated demand schedule, which previously represented the GCV. On the other hand, monopoly profits at a full employment income level and hence the MIA also increase, and are now represented by the area $FKHG$ in the figure, rather than the area formerly considered, $FABG$. That follows at once from the fact that FK corresponds to x_1 in x'', and is thus intermediate between x_1 in x', or FA, and x_1 in x''', or FL.

Since the monopolized product must be supposed to be absorbing a large part of the household's income, the first of these

income effects should often be rather large. Presumably that would ordinarily be true also of the second. But as indicated the two effects should also be mutually offsetting. How the NCV, now given by the area $KLCH$ (i.e., the excess of $FLCG$ over $FKHG$), compares with the area ABC, is nevertheless not an easy subject for generalization. For a superior good, however, it might be supposed that, as given by the NCV, the welfare loss would, if anything, be understated by an area such as ABC in Figure 2. Curiously that need not be so, for the error in the GCV might be more than offset by the further one in the MIA. For diverse linear demand schedules it can be shown that that is in fact the case.[2]

Proceeding more formally, we may readily extend the analysis to many monopolized products. Suppose there are n goods that are monopolized, and that a single product, $(n+1)$, is competitive. If we take that as numeraire, there are n prices, $p_1 \ldots p_n$, which vary from $p_1^c \ldots p_n^c$ to $p_1^m \ldots p_n^m$. Household income is I, and in the initial equilibrium,

---

[2] Reference is to demand schedules for the monopolized product of the form:

$$x = ap + bI + c$$

where x is the consumption of the monopolized product (for convenience, I omit subscripts at this point), p is its price, I is income, and a, b, and c are constants. This formula represents a family of Marshallian or uncompensated demand schedules, each such schedule corresponding to a given level of I. From the Slutsky equation, I derive a formula for the corresponding Hicksian or compensated demand schedules, and on this basis calculate the value of NCV corresponding to the area ABC and that corresponding to the area $KLCH$ in Figure 2 under alternative assumptions as to the uncompensated price elasticity (η_{xp}) and income elasticity (η_{xI}) of demand in the vicinity of the full employment equilibrium with monopolistic pricing for x. With $\eta_{xp}=1.5$ and $\eta_{xI}=1.0$, I find that the NCV corresponding to ABC is 1.04 and that corresponding to $KLCH$, .77 percent of household income. The corresponding measures of NCV when $\eta_{xp}=6.0$ and $\eta_{xI}=3$ are 4.17 and 3.88 percent of household income. I assume that x accounts for one-half the household budget under full employment equilibrium with monopolistic pricing for x, and that with that pricing p is 20 percent above costs.

I^c. Then the household's utility may be written as a function:

$$(3) \qquad U = U(p_1, \ldots, p_n, I)$$

Hence, the GCV is such that

$$(4) \quad U(p_1^c \ldots p_n^c, I^c)$$
$$= U(p_1^m \ldots p_n^m, I^c + GCV)$$

According to a well-known formula due mainly to Hicks (pp. 169ff), we also have

$$(5) \qquad GCV = \sum_{i=1}^{n} gcv_i$$

In (5), GCV is as before, though now changes in many prices together are being compensated for. Also, gcv_i is the gross compensating variation for the increase in the price of the ith of n monopolized products. The gcv_i for those products, however, must be determined sequentially. Thus, if they are treated in the order in which the products are numbered, then for gcv_j reference is to the income increment that would be needed to compensate for the increase in the price of the jth product when prices for all products $1 \ldots (j-1)$ have already changed and have been compensated for.[3]

---

[3] So far as it is understood that in the determination of gcv_j, previous price changes have been compensated for, this formulation seems somewhat novel. That gvc_j must be so construed, however, is seen at once when we consider that with that construction:

$$U(p_1^c, \ldots, p_j^c, \ldots, p_n^c, I^c)$$
$$= U(p_1^m, p_2^c, \ldots, p_j^c, \ldots, p_n^c, I^c + gcv_1) = \ldots$$
$$U\left(p_1^m, \ldots, p_{j-1}^m, p_j^c, \ldots, p_n^c, I^c + \sum_{i=1}^{j-1} gcv_i\right) = \ldots$$
$$= U\left(p_1^m, \ldots, p_n^m, I^c + \sum_{i=1}^{n} gcv_i\right)$$

Then,

$$U(p_1^m, \ldots, p_n^m, I^c + GCV)$$
$$= U\left(p_1^m, \ldots, p_n^m, I^c + \sum_{i=1}^{n} gcv_i\right)$$

Since utility is supposed to vary monotonically with I, (5) follows.

It also follows that GCV may still be evaluated from uncompensated demand schedules, but for each gcv_i constituting it reference, strictly speaking, must be to that uncompensated schedule for x_i conforming to the indicated determination of gcv_i. Thus, suppose the demand function for the jth product is given by

$$(6) \qquad x_j = d^j(p_1 \ldots p_j \ldots p_n, I)$$

Then gcv_j is to be calculated from the particular member of that family given by

$$(7) \quad x_j = d^j\left(p_1^m \ldots p_{j-1}^m, p_j, p_{j+1}^c \ldots p_n^c, \right.$$
$$\left. I^c + \sum_{i=1}^{j-1} gcv_i\right)$$

Each and every gcv_i as so calculated is precisely correct and all together sum to GCV if income elasticities of demand for all monopolized products are zero, but otherwise calculated gcv_i and the resulting GCV will err in one way or another. Of course, if income elasticities were zero, there would also be no need to be concerned about the precise level at which money income is held constant in each demand schedule, for example, whether at I^c or at I^c plus a sum such as appears in (7).

In order to obtain the NCV, we must deduct from GCV the MIA, the adjustment in income needed to assure full employment in the face of all price changes together. Here

$$(8) \quad MIA = \sum_{j=1}^{n} mia_j = \sum_{j=1}^{n} (p_j^m - p_j^c) x_j^m$$

where x_j^m is the consumption of x_j, when all prices of monopolized goods are at monopoly levels and income has been increased to $(I^c + MIA)$, i.e.,

$$(9) \quad x_j^m = d^j(p_1^m \ldots p_j^m \ldots p_n^m,$$
$$I^c + MIA)$$

MIA is determined in principle, along with x_j^m, from (8) together with (9) for $x_j^m, j = 1 \ldots n$.

Might we also calculate NCV as so determined simply by summing areas such as ABC in Figure 2? To calculate such areas, reference here presumbaly should be made to demand schedules corresponding to that for x_j in (7) when all prices other than p_j are at competitive levels while I corresponds to I^c, or full employment income when prices are at competitive levels. On that understanding, the answer to the question posed is in the affirmative under two conditions: (i) The income elasticity of demand for every monopolized good is zero. (ii) Cross elasticities of demand among all monopolized products are zero.

Actually, under these conditions it is immaterial at what levels prices of products other than the one considered and income are held constant in the calculation of an area such as ABC, for then all terms other than the price of the product in question drop out of the formulas for the demand for x_j in (7) and (9). The uncompensated demand schedule for any good also coincides with its compensated demand schedule. Hence for any x_i, the areas $FACG$ and $FABG$ in Figure 2 precisely correspond to gvc_j and mia_j. The difference between the aggregate of areas such as $FACG$ and the aggregate of rectangles such as $FABG$, and hence also the resulting aggregate of areas such as ABC, for all commodities, also precisely correspond to the NCV.

What if the stated conditions are not met? In that case, the aggregate of areas such as $FACG$ can only be expected to diverge from the GCV, since for any x_j such an area will differ from the gcv_j. That will be so insofar as: (i) The gcv_j is properly calculated from a demand schedule such as that in (7), where prices for products other than x_j are held constant,

some at monopolistic and some at competitive levels, and income is held constant at a level corresponding to that indicated in (7); and (ii) There are income effects of the usual sort, i.e., those manifest in a divergence between the compensated and uncompensated demand schedules for x_j. Similarly, the sum of areas such as $FABG$ can hardly be expected to correspond with the MIA as given by (8) and (9). As in the case of a single monopolized product, errors at different points may sometimes tend to be offsetting. So far as products generally are more often substitutes than complements, that, as easily seen, is apt to be so regarding errors due, on the one hand, to the difference between uncompensated and compensated demand schedules and, on the other, to the difference between the sum of rectangles such as $FABG$ and the MIA as given by (8) and (9). Nevertheless, the relation of the sum of areas such as ABC in Figure 2 to welfare losses as given by the NCV is rather complex. Without a detailed knowledge of demand functions, in all their dimensions, i.e., demand functions such as (7), we cannot really tell how nearly, if at all, the one is approached by the other.

II. The Case for Inconsequentiality

To come to Harberger, Schwartzman, and Leibenstein, their case for the inconsequentiality of welfare losses due to monopolistic pricing is too familiar to need any detailed replication here. Moreover, the chief question that I must raise about their methodology is already evident. Thus, Harberger and Schwartzman both calculate monopoly welfare losses simply by aggregating for different industries areas such as ABC in Figure 2. That is also Leibenstein's procedure, though beyond collating previous findings he limits himself to illustrative calculations. The procedure, to repeat, is also a valid one, provided that the income elasticity of demand for every monopolized product and all cross elasticities of demand among such products are zero. Otherwise, however, the procedure is subject to error at diverse points; an error, moreover, which is difficult to gauge. The practical import of the Harberger, Schwartzman, and Leibenstein findings, therefore, is obscure.

But I have considered their methodology from a more or less conventional standpoint. Is their procedure not more defensible in terms of the Hotelling formula that they apply? That seems doubtful when we consider that Hotelling derives his formula simply by disregarding higher order terms in a Taylor expansion of the utility function. As he properly explains, the formula yields "an approximate measure when deviations from the optimum system are not great" (p. 253). While Harberger, Schwartzman, and Leibenstein consider deviations from the optimum represented by varying but often sizable divergencies of prices from costs, they apparently assume that the Hotelling formula still yields a good approximation. They could be right, but it is difficult to know that without further inquiry.

According to the Hotelling formula, furthermore, welfare losses resulting from a displacement from a competitive equilibrium, and hence optimum, amount in money terms to $\frac{1}{2} \sum dp_i dx_i$. Here dp_i and dx_i are the variations in p_i and x_i that the displacement entails. The summation is taken over all goods, though if, as here, one commodity is taken as numeraire, that necessarily drops out of the formula. Note, however, that dx_i is the change in the consumption of x_i that is induced by a change not only in the price of that good but in the prices of all other goods. Supposedly income also varies in a prescribed manner.[4] Hence complex demand effects

[4] In his essay, Hotelling focuses on the impact of the introduction of excise in place of income taxes yielding

of the sort I encountered above in the calculation of the NCV are also encountered here. As already indicated, such effects are nevertheless neglected by Harberger, Schwartzman, and Leibenstein.

Finally, Hotelling takes welfare losses to be represented in money terms by the quotient dU/α, where dU is the increment in utility and α is the marginal utility of money. For variations of any magnitude, however, welfare losses as so understood are unique only if the marginal utility of money is assumed constant. That was Marshall's assumption, but he would not have made it where prices are varying for products constituting a major part of the household's budget. Constancy in the marginal utility of money also entails a further assumption of cardinal measurability of utility, which Hotelling himself apparently preferred to avoid.[5]

the same total revenue. Since what counts is money income net of income taxes, the prescribed change in money income is evidently equal to the total revenue from the excise taxes, and so corresponds precisely to the *MIA* as defined here. As it turns out, that also means that the displacement from the optimum that Hotelling considers, like the one I consider, entails a shift along a plane in which consumption at predisplacement prices is constant. In my analysis, however, that occurs because of the assumption of a linear transformation locus. I find it rather puzzling, therefore, that Hotelling, pp. 255–56, apparently considers his formula as applying even where marginal costs are variable.

[5] Might we not, however, interpret α as representing simply the marginal utility of money at some intermediate point in the range in question, and so avoid in this way the assumption of constancy of the marginal utility of money? If we may judge from a recent discussion by Harberger (1971, pp. 786ff) of a formula similar to Hotelling's, he might now argue that α in the Hotelling formula be construed in just that way. But that apparently would mean that the term

$$(\alpha/2) \sum dp_i dx_i$$

which was derived as a lower order term in a Taylor's expansion, is nevertheless to be interpreted as the remainder term. How that may be done is not clear. Moreover, it is still disconcerting that the measure of welfare losses depends on an unknown point to which reference is made within the range in question. While Harberger applies the Hotelling formula without qualification, it should be observed that Schwartzman, p.

As seen by Harberger, Schwartzman, and Leibenstein, monopoly welfare losses evidently must turn primarily on two empirical factors: price elasticities of demand and price-cost ratios for monopolized products. That is still true according to the alternative methodology that I have elaborated, though Harberger, Schwartzman, and Leibenstein refer to own price elasticities, while as seen here cross and income elasticities also matter (and in the latter case, as seen from (7) and (9), not merely through the usual sort of income effects). It should be observed, therefore, that Harberger assumes throughout a price elasticity of unity for monopolized products. In his view,

> ... one need only look at the list of industries ... considered in order to get the feeling that the elasticities in question are probably quite low. The presumption of low elasticity is further strengthened by the fact that what we envisage is not the substitution of one industry's product against all other products, but rather the substitution of one great aggregate of products ... for another aggregate. [1954, p. 79]

The assumption of a price elasticity of unity, however, was held "objectionable" by Stigler for the reason that "A monopolist does not operate where his marginal revenue is zero. . . . In any event, . . . most industries have long-run demand curves which are elastic" (p. 34). According to Schwartzman, Harberger's assumption is indeed to be thought of as applying

to an industry rather than an individual firm: "Moreover, if we are interested in the value of resource misallocation by monopolistic industries as a group, the relevant demand elasticity is less than the average of the individual industry demand elasticities" (pp. 628–29). Schwartzman assumes the price elasticity of demand is no more than 2. For purposes of illustrative calculation, Leibenstein assumes that in monopolized industries the " . . . average elasticity of demand is 1.5" (pp. 395–96).

How elastic the demand for a composite of all monopolized commodities is in respect of price is an interesting question. But for purposes of appraising monopoly welfare losses, it is also not too relevant. All monopolized products could properly be treated here as a single composite product only if the prices of all such products exceed their competitive levels by relatively the same amount. So far as the facts are otherwise, welfare losses originate not only in inordinately high monopoly prices generally, but in the variation for different products in the relation of such prices to costs. Also, what counts is variation not only between industries in any conventional sense, but between products; even between different qualities or models of the same product (for example, different models of Buicks) so far as price-cost ratios vary here as well. In principle, therefore, welfare losses must be calculated by reference to the demand for each and every such monopolistic product, quality or model as the case may be. Only in that way can all such losses be allowed for.[6]

As to how elastic demand is for one or another product, quality or model, that

---

630, notes that he is neglecting variations in the demand for a product associated with changes in equilibrium magnitudes generally, as distinct from a change in the price of that product alone. He apparently considers such variations unimportant. Leibenstein does not refer to Hotelling, but he accepts Harberger's methodology. Leibenstein, p. 396, n. 3, refers, however, to the error due to neglect of income effects originating in the divergence of uncompensated from compensated demand schedules, and concludes that such effects are apt to be negligible. He may be right but as indicated income effects are seen here to be much more complex than he thus assumes.

[6] As explained, Harberger, Schwartzman, and Leibenstein all assume constant costs. In this essay, I have fallen in with that assumption, but note that so far as costs vary even uniform monopoly price-cost ratios would not mean that monopoly prices are all in the same relation to those that would prevail under competitive pricing.

must depend on the item. Presumably it also depends on the prices of other goods and household income. That is a matter of some importance, since in the calculation of gcv_i reference is to demand schedules which vary from item to item in respect of the levels at which prices of related goods and income are held constant. Any a priori assumption must be a gross oversimplification in this sphere, but I doubt that an elasticity of unity or even of 2 can be nearly large enough to encompass the interesting range of possibilities for the purposes of a calculation such as in question.

In this connection, it is pertinent to recall the relation familiar in monopoly theory that is alluded to by Stigler:

$$(10) \qquad \eta_{xp}^i = p_i/(p_i - MC_i)$$

Here η_{xp}^i is the price elasticity of demand for the ith product, p_i is its price and MC_i, its marginal cost. No one supposes that (10) can be more than very broadly applicable to real world monoplies, but Leibenstein, for example, assumes a monopoly price-cost ratio of 1.2. It seems illuminating that with that ratio (10) would imply an elasticity of demand as high as 6. Leibenstein considers that the monopolistic price-cost ratios must in fact average less than 20 percent, but for a ratio of, say 10 percent, (10) yields an elasticity of 11. To repeat, though, (10) hardly applies exactly in practice, and it may be just as well to note here that I myself will allow later for possible divergencies from it in either direction. This assumption is in order when we consider such aspects as the limitations in a firm's knowledge of its cost and demand schedules; the fact that because of price leadership, collusion and other adaptations to oligopolistic interdependence the firm may calculate in terms of a demand schedule that is less elastic than the one relevant

here (i.e., that where prices of all other products, including even close substitutes, are unchanged), and so on.

What of the price-cost ratios? Harberger deduced these from data on profit rates for different industries. Stigler, pp. 34–35, held, however, that monopoly profits are often capitalized, and in diverse ways not always sufficiently allowed for by Harberger, with the result that the indicated price-cost ratios may often be too low. Still other forces could operate to produce the same result. As Harberger is aware, monopoly prices reflect not only monopoly profits but monopolistic advertising, but, even for the early period he considers, the resulting additional misallocation cannot be dismissed as he dismisses it simply on the ground that advertising outlays were ". . . well under 2 percent of sales for all the industries . . ." (1954, pp. 85–86) studied. The industries studied include competitive as well as monopolistic ones, so the corresponding ratio for monopolistic industries alone must be higher. What counts here, moreover, is not only average relations but their variation between industries and products.

Harberger treats intermediates as if they were consumers' goods. The relevant monopoly profits for any consumer's good, however, are not those prevailing in the industry in question, but those profits, together with the additional profits accruing on intermediate products used in that industry. That is so even though the concern is, as in the studies in question, only with misallocation between consumers' goods industries, and not with further losses due to monopolistic distortions in factor mixes. (I return to that later.) If, as a practical expedient, reference is to be made only to "direct" as distinct from "direct and indirect" monopoly profits, it should be closer to the mark to relate such profits to value-added rather than to sales, as Harberger does.

In his calculation Schwartzman seeks to determine the impact of monopoly on *U.S.* industrial prices from a comparison of ratios of sales and variable costs in similar concentrated and unconcentrated industries in the United States and Canada. In this way, the average "monopoly effect" is estimated at 8.3 percent of average variable costs. Schwartzman avowedly seeks to meet objections such as Stigler's to the Harberger calculation. To what extent he succeeds in doing so in his involved calculation is difficult to judge from his very brief exposition, and further questions such as were raised above regarding the Harberger calculation do not seem clearly disposed of. Schwartzman takes a step back from Harberger by assuming a uniform monopoly effect in all monopolized industries. He thus fails to allow for the misallocation due to variations in that effect between products. Monopoly price-cost ratios are a complex matter on which there will have to be many more studies before we can confidently narrow the possibilities.

I referred at the outset to a study of Kamerschen indicating that monopoly losses may be appreciably greater than Harberger and Schwartzman calculated. Kamerschen proceeds for the most part as Harberger did, so his findings too are difficult to construe, but he refers to profits data for a later period, 1956–57 to 1960–61. He also attempts to extend the calculations to embrace nonmanufacturing business and enterprises other than corporations, and to allow more systematically than Harberger could for capitalized monopoly profits and monopolistic distortions in costs in the form of intangible assets, royalties, and advertising expense. While intermediate products are again treated as final, however, monopoly profits are still related to sales rather than value added. Monopoly welfare losses are estimated at 1.03 to 1.87 percent of the national income depending on which of a number of variants is considered. These magnitudes, while modest, are, of course, far larger than Harberger's. They result from the assumption of a unitary elasticity of demand. Alternative calculations apparently assuming elasticities in different industries such as conform to (10) yield still much higher figures: 3.87 to 6.82 percent of national income.[7]

III. An Alternative Approach

In inquiring into the methodology of Harberger, Schwartzman, and Liebenstein, I have elaborated an alternative that is akin to theirs so far as monopoly welfare losses are still calculated from uncompensated demand schedules. But while the alternative methodology served as a basis for appraising that of Harberger, Schwartzman, and Leibenstein, it evidently must be difficult to apply when monopolized products are at all numerous. I now explore still another approach to the calculation of welfare losses due to monopoly pricing. Resting on the assumption of a special type of household indifference map, this approach can only yield hypothetical measures, but these may illuminate further what might already have been surmised: the marked sensitivity of the calculated welfare losses to the elasticity of demand for monopolized products and to the level and distribution of the monopoly price-cost ratios.

The household indifference map in question is given by equation (11):

$$(11) \quad U(x_1, \ldots, x_{n+1}) = \sum_{i=1}^{n+1} A_i x_i^{(1-1/\sigma)}$$

As before, I assume that there are $n+1$ industries producing a corresponding number of commodities, that of these industries one, $n+1$, is competitive and that all others are monopolistic. The output and

---

[7] I refer to calculations based on after-tax profits. Further calculations based on before-tax profits often yield even higher figures.

hence also the household's consumption of the ith good is x_i.

In (11), A_i is a constant, and so too is σ. If x_i stood for employment of a productive input rather than consumption, therefore, (11) would simply represent on the $x_1 \ldots x_{n+1}$ hyperplane a *CES* production function such as lately has become familiar in productivity analysis. The term σ would then represent the elasticity of substitution between any two factors, employment of all others being given.

I refer here nevertheless to consumption, but as Paul Samuelson, p. 787, has pointed out, the *CES* production function itself corresponds to a function of the same form that I derived long ago (1936, reprinted 1966) for a household's indifference map in an analysis of Ragnar Frisch's methods of measuring marginal utility. In any event, (11) may be conceived of as applying to consumption no less than to production, and for present purposes it has the distinct merit that by varying σ, now representing the elasticity of substitution between any two consumer's goods, we may allow different degrees of substitutability between products, and so ultimately for varying elasticities of demand for one or another of our monopolized goods. In the absence of empirical data on the comparative income elasticities of monopolized and competitive goods, it may be more of a virtue than a limitation of (11) that it implies unitary income elasticities of demand for all products alike.

While I shall refer to $U(x_1, \ldots, x_{n+1})$ as a utility function, our concern is only with the indifference map that the function defines. Where appropriate, utility might be envisaged as being represented by some function of $U(x_1, \ldots, x_{n+1})$, rather than by that function itself. The utility dimension, therefore, need not be representable by a linear homogeneous function such as is usually considered in productivity analysis. Even on that understanding, (11) is admittedly rather restrictive, but it still embraces an interesting range of possibilities. I use a function of the form of (11) here at the suggestion of Samuelson, who has also been helpful at other points.[8]

As before, the monopolized products, $x_1 \ldots x_n$, sell at prices $p_1 \ldots p_n$, which when fixed monopolistically have the values $p_1^m \ldots p_n^m$. The competitive good, x_{n+1}, serves as numeraire. I again designate by I^c the household's income as it would be if $x_1 \ldots x_n$ were to sell at competitive prices, $p_1^c \ldots p_n^c$, and there were no unemployment. Then

$$(12) \qquad GCV = I^* - I^c$$

where

$$(13) \quad U(p_1^m, \ldots, p_n^m, I^*) \\ = U(p_1^c, \ldots, p_n^c, I^c)$$

In other words, I^* is the income that the household would require if, when $x_1 \ldots x_n$ sell at $p_1^m \ldots p_n^m$, it is to enjoy the same utility as it would when $x_1 \ldots x_n$ sell at $p_1^c \ldots p_n^c$ and its income is I^c.

We also have

$$(14) \qquad MIA = I^m - I^c$$

where I^m is the income that the household

---

[8] As he has also pointed out to me, the usual *CES* variant of (11), i.e., the one that is linear homogeneous, might itself be properly taken as a measure of real income. Moreover, for shifts along a linear production possibility schedule such as I have been assuming and will continue to assume here, real income as so understood and the net compensating variation turn out to be essentially the same metric. Thus, I express the *NCV* below as a coefficient, the decisive term being the ratio of two magnitudes of household income, one representing the income needed to assure, under monopoly pricing in monopolistic industries, the same utility as might have been enjoyed under competitive pricing in all industries, and the other representing simply the income needed to assure full employment under monopoly pricing in monopolistic industries. That ratio, as is not difficult to see, corresponds precisely to the ratio of real income in equilibrium under competitive pricing in all industries to real income in equilibrium under monopoly pricing in monopolistic industries.

must have if employment is to continue to be full when prices are $p_1^m \ldots p_n^m$ rather than $p_1^c \ldots p_n^c$. Finally,

$$(15) \quad NCV = (I^* - I^c) - (I^m - I^c)$$
$$= I^* - I^m$$

While NCV is of interest, we may more readily relate our analysis to previous ones if I focus on a corresponding coefficient:

$$(16) \quad CNCV = (I^* - I^m)/I^m$$

In effect, this expresses the NCV as a fraction of the national income that would be produced in the full employment equilibrium under monopoly pricing.

If $x_i, i = 1 \ldots n$, is measured in units such that $p_i^c = 1$, production possibilities, which are again linear, are readily expressed in terms of a familiar formula convenient here:

$$(17) \quad \sum_{i=1}^{n+1} x_i = k$$

From (11), (16), (17) and the usual conditions for household equilibrium, it can be proven that:

$$(18) \quad CNCV = \left(\sum_{i=1}^{n+1} \gamma_i \lambda_i^{\sigma-1} \right)^{1/(\sigma-1)}$$
$$\cdot \left(\sum_{i=1}^{n+1} \gamma_i \lambda_i^{-1} \right) - 1$$

Here, for $i = 1 \ldots n$, λ_i is p_i^m when the unit of x_i is such that $p_i^c = 1$, and also represents the monopolistic price-cost ratio. The term λ_{n+1} equals unity. Also,

$$(19) \quad \gamma_i = (p_i^m x_i^m)/I^m$$

or since $p_i^m = \lambda_i$

$$(20) \quad \gamma_i = \lambda_i x_i^m/I^m$$

where x^m represents the output of x_i when $p_i, i = 1 \ldots n$ is fixed monopolistically, and there is full employment equilibrium,

i.e., income is I^m. Thus γ_i is the income share that is accounted for in such an equilibrium by the household's expenditure on x_i. A proof of (18) is given in the Appendix.

From (18), the $CNCV$ depends on: (i) γ_i, the income share devoted to x_i, $i = 1 \ldots n+1$, in the full employment equilibrium with monoply prices; (ii) λ_i, $i = 1 \ldots n$, the monopoly price-cost ratio for each and every product, it being understood that λ_{n+1}, the price-cost ratio for the competitive product, is unity; and (iii) σ the elasticity of substitution. In order to see how the $CNCV$ might vary in dependence on these parameters, let us consider first the case where there is but one monopolistic product, x_1, and the competitive product is accordingly x_2. Our parameters, then, consist simply of γ_1, λ_1, and σ. In Table 1, I show in percentages the magnitudes of the $CNCV$ indicated by alternative hypothetical values of γ_1, λ_1, and σ. In all cases, γ_1 is taken equal to 0.5, so the household divides its income equally between the monopolized and competitive products. For λ_1, the monopoly price-cost ratio, I consider three alternative values: 1.1,

TABLE 1— VALUES OF THE COEFFICIENT OF NET COMPENSATING VARIATION ($CNCV$) FOR A TWO-GOOD ECONOMY AND ALTERNATIVE λ_1 AND σ

	$CNCV$[a]		
σ	$\lambda_1 = 1.1$	$\lambda_1 = 1.2$	$\lambda_1 = 1.3$
(1)	(2)	(3)	(4)
.50	.06	.21	.43
1.00	.11	.41	.86
2.00	.23	.83	1.73
4.00	.45	1.66	3.43
8.00	.90	3.20	6.38
16.00	1.70	5.47	9.95
32.00	2.85	7.58	12.46
64.00	3.86	8.80	13.74

[a] Shown in percent.

TABLE 2—VALUES OF THE COÉFFICIENT OF NET COMPENSATING VARIATION $(CNCV)$
FOR A THREE-GOOD ECONOMY FOR ALTERNATIVE $M_m(\lambda)$, λ_1, λ_2, AND σ

	$CNCV^a$					
	$M_m(\lambda)=1.1$		$M_m(\lambda)=1.2$		$M_m(\lambda)=1.3$	
σ	$\lambda_1=1.05$ $\lambda_2=1.15$	$\lambda_1=1.05$ $\lambda_2=1.20$	$\lambda_1=1.1$ $\lambda_2=1.3$	$\lambda_1=1.1$ $\lambda_2=1.4$	$\lambda_1=1.15$ $\lambda_2=1.45$	$\lambda_1=1.15$ $\lambda_2=1.60$
	(1)	(2)	(3)	(4)	(5)	(6)
.50	.08	.10	.28	.33	.54	.62
1.00	.17	.20	.56	.70	1.11	1.29
2.00	.33	.42	1.15	1.43	2.33	2.81
4.00	.67	.88	2.43	3.18	4.98	6.48
8.00	1.41	1.97	5.15	7.39	10.43	15.09
16.00	2.93	4.46	9.82	15.10	17.93	27.08
32.00	5.36	8.46	14.34	21.85	23.38	35.01
64.00	7.50	11.54	16.94	25.47	26.21	39.03

 ^{a} Shown in percent.

1.2, and 1.3. The elasticity of substitution, σ, varies between .50 and 64.[9]

The $CNCV$ evidently varies widely in dependence on both these parameters. Thus, for $\lambda_1=1.1$, the $CNCV$ varies from less than a tenth of a percent to 3.9 percent as σ varies from .50 to 64. For $\lambda_1 = 1.2$, the corresponding variation in $CNCV$ is from two-tenths of a percent to 8.8 percent, and for $\lambda_1=1.3$, from four-tenths of a percent to 13.7 percent. For the single household economy in question, as indicated, reference in each case is in effect to the percentage relation of monopoly welfare losses to the national income. The $CNCV$ is also affected by γ_1, though often not very markedly. Interestingly, depending on σ, a deviation of γ_1 in either direction from 0.5 may raise or lower the $CNCV$.[10]

[9] Where $\sigma=1$, formula (11) gives way to the familiar Cobb-Douglas variant. In that case it is easy to show by reasoning such as is used to prove (18), that that formula is supplanted by:

$$CNVC = \left(\prod_{i=1}^{n+1} \lambda_i^{a_i} \right) \left(\sum_{i=1}^{n+1} a_i\lambda_i^{-1} \right) - 1$$

[10] For example, for $\lambda_1=1.2$, and σ taken in turn to be 2.0, 8.0, 16.0, and 46.0, I find that for $\gamma_1=.33$ the $CNVC$ has these values: .74, 3.21, 6.19 and 11.37. For

Turning to many monopolized products, from the calculations just discussed, the $CNCV$ evidently must depend on the average λ_i in monopolized industries. By merely increasing the number of monopolized products to two, we see that the $CNCV$ is also sensitive to the distribution of λ_i about their mean.

Thus, in Table 2, I assume that there are two monopolized industries, x_1 and x_2, and one competitive one, x_3. The corresponding price-cost ratios are λ_1, λ_2, and λ_3, where $\lambda_3=1$. For the weighted mean of λ_1 and λ_2, we have

$$(21) \quad M_m(\lambda) = \left(\sum_{i=1}^{n} \gamma_i\lambda_i \right) \Big/ \left(\sum_{i=1}^{n} \gamma_i \right)$$

In the table, I consider, for $n=2$, three alternative values of $M_m(\lambda)$ corresponding to the three values of λ_1 that were considered previously, that is, 1.1, 1.2, 1.3. For each $M_m(\lambda)$ I refer to two variants, one in which λ_1 and λ_2 are distributed symmetrically about their mean, and the other in which their distribution about their mean is asymmetric, with λ_2 ex-

$\gamma_1=.67$, the corresponding figures are .74, 2.56, 4.04, and 5.98.

ceeding $M_m(\lambda)$ by more than λ_1 falls short of it. The specific λ_1 and λ_2 assumed in each variant are as indicated in the table. In all cases, γ_i for the competitive good—now γ_3—is 0.5, so as with the single monopolized good considered in Table 1, the two monopolized goods account for half the household's income. For the symmetric distributions, then, $\gamma_1 = \gamma_2 = 0.25$. For the asymmetric distributions, $M_m(\lambda)$ is as assumed for $\gamma_1 = .33$ and $\gamma_2 = .17$.

With the inclusion of a second monopolized good in the economy the $CNCV$ apparently increases markedly. That is so for all the assumed $M_m(\lambda)$ and for all the symmetric distributions of λ_1 and λ_2. It is even more so if λ_1 and λ_2 are distributed asymmetrically. For example, for $\sigma = 8$, a monopoly price-cost ratio of 1.2 implied previously a $CNCV$ of 3.2 percent. With a mean price-cost ratio for the two monopolized industries of 1.2, the $CNCV$ now rises to 5.15 percent for the symmetric distribution. For the asymmetric distribution, the coefficient is still greater: 7.39 percent.

Further calculations assuming that the number of monopolistic products is indefinitely large but with price-cost ratios distributed in a more or less skew way, as might be expected, yield for a wide range of σ measures of the $CNVC$ very similar to those obtained from the asymmetric distribution in Table 2.[11]

In selecting values of parameters for evaluation of the $CNCV$, I have tried to take account of related magnitudes considered in previous analyses, though I also refer to quite other possibilities as well, though perhaps not always very realistic ones. One of the parameters considered, however, is σ, the elasticity of substitution. That is, of course, not the same thing as the elasticity of demand considered in previous analyses, but for the utility function being considered the two aspects are related by a very simple formula:[12]

$$(22) \qquad \overset{i}{\eta}_{xp} = \sigma - \gamma_i(\sigma - 1)$$

Here, η_{xp}^i, as before, is the negative of $(p_i/x_i)(\partial x_i/\partial p_i)$, the partial derivative being understood to have the usual sort of subscripts. Evidently, if $\sigma < 1$, then $\eta_{xp}^i > \sigma$, but otherwise η_{xp}^i is no greater than σ, and is in fact less than σ whenever $\sigma > 1$. The shortfall in the latter case is the greater the larger is σ and the larger is γ_i, the share of the commodity in question in the household's budget. While theoretically the divergence between η_{qp}^i and σ could thus be marked, presumably γ_i would tend to be small so far as there are many commodities. For practical purposes, therefore, η_{xp}^i should usually closely approximate σ, and my calculations may be read accordingly.

I have assumed that production possibilities are linear. That is more or less the counterpart of the assumption of constant costs made in previous analyses. Where costs are not constant but increasing, it has been held (see Harberger (1954, p. 82)) that other things equal, monopoly welfare losses will be less than where costs are constant. The appropriate translation of increasing costs here is a curvilinear production possibilities schedule that is concave from below. With such a schedule, the structural shift in outputs induced by

---

[11] The calculations assume as before that the competitive product accounts for one-half of income. The remaining half is distributed among monopolistic products on the assumption that the share of income represented by price cost ratios within a small interval $\Delta\lambda$ embracing any particular ratio λ is given by the product $\Delta\lambda$ and a linear function $\gamma(\lambda) = a\lambda + b$ which slopes downward to the right and reaches zero from above at $\lambda = h \equiv -(b/a)$. The constants a and b are evaluated so as to assure that $M_m(\lambda)$, the mean monopoly λ, corresponds to those considered previously: 1.1, 1.2, and 1.3. To cite one or two examples for $\sigma = 8.00$ the $CNCV$ for $M_m(\lambda) = 1.1$ is 1.96; for $M_m(\lambda) = 1.2$, 7.39; for $M_m(\lambda) = 1.3$, 15.19.

[12] See the Appendix.

monopoly pricing is necessarily dampened, and one might suppose that as a result monopoly welfare losses would indeed be reduced. That could be so, but I believe it need not be. I leave this matter, however, to separate inquiry. Of course, so far as there is monopoly, we cannot at all exclude that in the vicinity of the equilibrium costs will be decreasing or that production possibilities will be convex from below.

I have also assumed that the elasticity of substitution is the same between any and all pairs of goods. As seen from (22) that need not mean that the elasticity of demand is also the same for all goods, but I have tacitly assumed that monopoly price-cost ratios might vary between goods independently of their price elasticities. As indicated, (10) can hardly be expected to apply systematically, but so far as it applies at all the price-cost ratios must in some degree vary inversely with price elasticities. Given that, one surmises that losses would be less than otherwise, but I leave this, too, to separate inquiry.

VII. Conclusions

I have sought to appraise calculations indicating that welfare losses due to monopoly pricing in a country such as the United States are relatively inconsequential, and have argued that those calculations are open to question on both conceptual and empirical grounds. Under an alternative approach, which does not seem subject to conceptual limitations affecting previous calculations, the coefficient of net compensating variation, which is taken to measure monopoly welfare losses, is quite sensitive to empirical aspects which still seem unsettled, particularly, the elasticity of demand for monopolized products, and the varying magnitudes of price-cost ratios for different monopolized products, together with the shares of household income that

those products account for. While I have queried the conclusions of Harberger, Schwartzman, and Leibenstein, they have focused attention in a forceful way on an important question. That is a significant contribution in itself, from which nothing that has been said can detract.

I have joined previous writers in tacitly assuming that in the community considered, supplies of productive factors are given. No account has thus been taken of the adverse effect of monopolistic pricing on choices between leisure and work. The analysis can be extended in familiar ways to embrace such choices, however, so they seem to pose no new question of principle, though since leisure must be treated as a competitive good, its inclusion must affect the share of such goods in household income.[13]

I have also joined previous writers in focusing on welfare losses due to monopolistic pricing as that affects resource allocation as between consumer's goods. Monopolistic pricing, of course, also causes misallocation of resources at other points. Such further misallocation is properly the subject of a separate inquiry, but the calculations in question are sometimes taken to reflect monopoly welfare losses generally. Perhaps I should underscore, therefore, that whatever the losses due to misallocation between consumer goods, they are only compounded by misallocation caused by monopoly prices in other spheres, perhaps chiefly the determination of comparative factor proportions in different industries,[14] and the volume of saving and investment. Related to, but not the same thing as, misallocation due to monopoly pricing is the adverse impact of

[13] Monopolistic pricing also may have an adverse effect on effort, but at least in principle it is not difficult to extend the analysis to that aspect too.

[14] Harberger (1959) has tried to grapple with this matter, too, though reference is to distortions due to not only monopoly prices but other causes.

monopoly on the discovery and introduction of new technologies, though Schumpeter, of course, long ago made it a controversial matter whether monopoly is really always disadvantageous in this sphere. But the point being made is obvious and need not be labored: If consequential welfare losses due to monopoly are not precluded in respect of consumption structure, they hardly are so more generally.

APPENDIX

This appendix derives equations (18) and (22). To begin with (18), given (11) and that x_{n+1} is numeraire, we derive at once these equilibrium conditions for household consumption:

$$(A1) \quad U_i/U_{n+1} = (A_i/A_{n+1})(x_{n+1}/x_i)^{1/\sigma}$$
$$= p_i, \quad i = 1, \ldots, n$$

Here and elsewhere $U_i, i = 1 \ldots n+1$, represents the marginal utility of x_i. Formula (A1) holds whether prices for monopolistic products, i.e., $x_i \ldots x_n$, are at competitive or monopolistic levels. But, given our choice of units for those products, $p_i^c = 1, i = 1 \ldots n$. Hence, when prices are at competitive levels and I is such as to assure full employment at those prices, the consumption of x_i and x_{n+1} conform to the relation:

$$(A2) \quad \overset{c}{x_i} = (A_i/A_{n+1})^\sigma \overset{c}{x_{n+1}}$$

From this and (17),

$$(A3) \quad \sum_{i=1}^{n+1} (A_i/A_{n+1})^\sigma \overset{c}{x_{n+1}} = k$$

It follows that

$$(A4) \quad \overset{c}{x_{n+1}} = kA_{n+1}^\sigma \bigg/ \sum_{i=1}^{n+1} A_i^\sigma$$

and

$$(A5) \quad \overset{c}{x_i} = kA_i^\sigma \bigg/ \sum_{i=1}^{n+1} A_i^\sigma, \quad i = 1, \ldots, n$$

When prices of monopolistic products are at monopoly levels, $\lambda_1 \ldots \lambda_n$, and money income is I^m, which assures full employment

at those prices, we see by similar reasoning that the consumption of x_{n+1} is:

$$(A6) \quad \overset{m}{x_{n+1}} = kA_{n+1}^\sigma \bigg/ \sum_{i=1}^{n+1} \lambda_i^{-\sigma} A_i^\sigma$$

and of x_i,

$$(A7) \quad \overset{m}{x_i} = k\lambda_i^{-\sigma} A_i^\sigma \bigg/ \sum_{i=1}^{n+1} \lambda_i^{-\sigma} A_i^\sigma,$$
$$i = 1, \ldots, n$$

Consider now the still different equilibrium that prevails when prices of monopolistic products are at monopoly levels, but money income is at I^*, as given by (13). Proceeding again much as before, we find that consumption of x_i and x_{n+1} conform to:

$$(A8) \quad \overset{*}{x_i} = \lambda_i^{-\sigma}(A_i/A_{n+1})^\sigma \overset{*}{x_{n+1}}$$

In order to prove (18), I derive from the foregoing relations certain formulas for I^* and I^m. To refer first to I^*, we know that

$$(A9) \quad I^* = \sum_{i=1}^{n+1} \lambda_i \overset{*}{x_i}$$

Also, as seen from (13),

$$(A10) \quad U(\overset{*}{x_1}, \ldots, \overset{*}{x_{n+1}}) = U(\overset{c}{x_1}, \ldots, \overset{c}{x_{n+1}})$$

From this and (11),

$$(A11) \quad \sum_{i=1}^{n+1} A_i(\overset{*}{x_i})^{(1-1/\sigma)} = \sum_{i=1}^{n+1} A_i(\overset{c}{x_i})^{(1-1/\sigma)}$$

Using this, (A2), and (A8),

$$(A12) \quad \overset{*}{x_{n+1}} = \overset{c}{x_{n+1}} \left\{ \sum_{i=1}^{n+1} A_i^\sigma \right\}^{\sigma/(\sigma-1)}$$
$$\bigg/ \left\{ \sum_{i=1}^{n+1} \lambda_i^{1-\sigma} A_i^\sigma \right\}^{\sigma/(\sigma-1)}$$

and

$$(A13) \quad \overset{*}{x_i} = \lambda_i^{-\sigma}(A_i/A_{n+1})^\sigma \overset{c}{x_{n+1}}$$
$$\cdot \left\{ \sum_{i=1}^{n+1} A_i^\sigma \right\}^{\sigma/(\sigma-1)}$$

$$\Big/ \Big\{ \sum_{i=1}^{n+1} \lambda_i^{1-\sigma} A_i^{\sigma} \Big\}^{\sigma/(\sigma-1)}$$

From (A4), (A9), and (A13),

$$(A14) \quad I^* = k \Big\{ \sum_{i=1}^{n+1} A_i^{\sigma} \Big\}^{1/(\sigma-1)}$$

$$\Big/ \Big\{ \sum_{i=1}^{n+1} \lambda_i^{1-\sigma} A_i^{\sigma} \Big\}^{1/(\sigma-1)}$$

Turning to I^m, we have

$$(A15) \qquad I^m = \sum_{i=1}^{n+1} \lambda_i x_i^m$$

Using (A7),

$$(A16) \qquad I^m = k \Big\{ \sum_{i=1}^{n+1} \lambda_i^{1-\sigma} A_i^{\sigma} \Big\}$$

$$\Big/ \Big\{ \sum_{i=1}^{n+1} \lambda_i^{-\sigma} A_i^{\sigma} \Big\}$$

From (16), (A14), and (A16),

$$(A17) \quad CNCV =$$

$$\Big[\Big\{ \sum_{i=1}^{n+1} A_i^{\sigma} \Big\}^{1/(\sigma-1)} \Big\{ \sum_{i=1}^{n+1} \lambda_i^{-\sigma} A_i^{\sigma} \Big\}$$

$$\Big/ \Big\{ \sum_{i=1}^{n+1} \lambda_i^{1-\sigma} A_i^{\sigma} \Big\}^{\sigma/(\sigma-1)} \Big] - 1$$

From (A7) and (A16),

$$(A18) \quad \gamma_i \equiv (\lambda_i x_i^m / I^m)$$

$$= \Big(\lambda_i^{1-\sigma} A_i^{\sigma} \Big/ \sum_{i=1}^{n+1} \lambda_i^{1-\sigma} A_i^{\sigma} \Big)$$

Formula (18) follows from (A17) and (A18).

While it may have been useful to prove (18) in the foregoing manner, it should be observed that the same result can be obtained somewhat more quickly if it is considered that from (16) the *CNVC* reduces to $(I^*/I^m - 1)$. Also, as given by (11) the utility function is homogeneous. Hence, equilibrium consumption positions relating to different levels of money income but the same prices all must be on the same ray through the origin. That is true particularly of the equilib-

rium consumption positions corresponding to I^* and I^m. It also follows that the ratio I^*/I^m corresponds to the comparative consumption of any one good in the two equilibrium positions. Given that, (18) follows from (A13), (A7), (A4), and (A16).

To come to (22), from (A1),

$$(A19) \quad p_j^{\sigma}(\partial x_j/\partial p_i) - (A_j/A_{n+1})^{\sigma} \cdot (\partial x_{n+1}/\partial p_i) = 0, \qquad j \neq i,$$

and

$$(A20) \quad p_i^{\sigma}(\partial x_i/\partial p_i) - (A_i/A_{n+1})^{\sigma} \cdot (\partial x_{n+1}/\partial p_i) = - \sigma p_i^{\sigma-1} x_i$$

In these formulas, the derivatives shown are of a partial sort; with appropriate subscripts understood. Also, since

$$(A21) \qquad \sum_{i=1}^{n+1} p_i x_i = I,$$

we have

$$(A22) \qquad \sum_{j=1}^{n+1} p_j(\partial x_j/\partial p_i) = - x_i$$

From (A19), (A20), and (A22),

$$(A23) \quad (\partial x_{n+1}/\partial p_i) =$$

$$(\sigma - 1) A_{n+1}^{\sigma} x_i \Big/ \sum_{i=1}^{n+1} p_i^{1-\sigma} A_i^{\sigma}$$

And from this and (A20),

$$(A24) \quad (\partial x_i/\partial p_i) =$$

$$\Big\{ (\sigma - 1) A_i^{\sigma} x_i / p_i^{\sigma} \sum_{i=1}^{n+1} p_i^{1-\sigma} A_i^{\sigma} \Big\} - \sigma x_i/p_i$$

or

$$(A25) \qquad \eta_{xp}^{i} = \sigma - (\sigma - 1) p_i^{1-\sigma} A_i^{\sigma} \Big/ \sum_{i=1}^{n+1} p_i^{1-\sigma} A_i^{\sigma}$$

Formula (22) follows at once from (A18) for monopoly equilibrium where $\lambda_i = p_i$, but it is evident that it must hold for any other equilibrium as well, for in (A18) λ_i could be construed as well to represent any p_i, and not merely a monopolistic one.

REFERENCES

A. Bergson, "Real Income, Expenditure Proportionality and Frisch's *New Methods*," *Rev. Econ. Stud.*, Oct. 1936, *9*, 33–52.

——, *Essays in Normative Economics*, Cambridge, Mass. 1966.

A. C. Harberger, "Monopoly and Resource Allocation," *Amer. Econ. Rev. Proc.*, May 1954, *44*, 77–87.

——, "Using the Resources at Hand More Effectively," *Amer. Econ. Rev. Proc.*, May 1959, *49*, 134–46.

——, "Three Basic Postulates for Applied Welfare Economics: An Interpretive Essay," *J. Econ. Lit.*, Sept. 1971, *9*, 785–97.

J. R. Hicks, *A Revision of Demand Theory*, Oxford 1956.

H. Hotelling, "The General Welfare in Relation to Problems of Taxation and of Railway and Utility Rates," *Econometrica*, July 1938, *6*, 242–69.

D. R. Kamerschen, "Welfare Losses from Monopoly," *Western Econ. J.*, summer 1966, *4*, 221–36.

H. Leibenstein, "Allocative Efficiency vs. 'X-Efficiency'," *Amer. Econ. Rev.*, June 1966, *56*, 392–415.

P. A. Samuelson, "Using Full Duality to Show That Simultaneous Additive Direct and Indirect Utilities Implies Unitary Price Elasticity of Demand," *Econometrica*, Oct. 1965, *33*, 781–96.

D. Schwartzman, "The Burden of Monopoly," *J. Polit. Econ.*, Dec. 1960, *68*, 627–30.

G. J. Stigler, "The Statistics of Monopoly and Merger," *J. Polit. Econ.*, Feb. 1956, *64*, 33–40.

Consumer's and Producer's Surplus and General Equilibrium

Abram Bergson

In a recent essay (1973), I challenged a widely held view as to the negligible impact on welfare of monopoly pricing distortions. In the process I also elaborated on consumer's surplus analysis. As formulated, for example, in Hicks (1956), that analysis is essentially of a partial equilibrium sort. My concern was to reformulate the theory in a general equilibrium context that seemed appropriate to the measurement of monopoly welfare losses. The result also appeared to provide further perspective on pre-Hicksian, that is Marshallian consumer's surplus.

In this essay I propose to extend the analysis somewhat further. Previously I assumed a linear production possibilities schedule. For the sake of generality, I now refer to curvilinear production possibilities. The analysis will also permit a reinterpretation of pre-Hicksian consumer's surplus analysis with more explicit attention than was possible before to producer's surplus, or at least to one outstanding facet of that rather complex phenomenon.

Consumer's surplus analysis is often formulated in more or less general terms and without reference to any particular application. That might be possible here, but the analysis seems facilitated if I refer again to monopoly pricing.[1]

What is in question is the welfare loss suffered because monopolistic firms charge prices that, rather than being equal to marginal costs as under perfect competition, tend systematically to be above that level. Attention has usually been focused on monopoly pricing for final, rather than intermediate, goods. I consider here, therefore, an economy in which only consumers' goods are produced. The losses in question might fall unevenly among different income groups and so pose a question of equity, but the concern generally has been with efficiency. I will accordingly adopt the familiar device of addressing an economy in which there is but a single household that behaves as a perfect competitor in purchasing consumer's goods.

Although, consumer's surplus may be represented variously, I focus on the "compensating variation": the compensatory change in income needed to ensure that a household's utility is unaffected by a change in price (Hicks 1956, pp. 61ff, 69ff). Hicks refers, however, to the hypothetical variation from an otherwise constant money income. Such a variation is properly taken to measure a welfare loss or gain if income is actually constant. Where the concern is with the welfare loss resulting from monopoly pricing, however, attention—at least tacitly—has been focused on a particular sort of misallocation, one that occurs without any concomitant unemployment. In other words, the supposition is that any resources excluded from monopolistic industries by monopolistic pricing there are employed instead in competitive industries. In equilibrium, in the consumers' goods economy in question, the corollary is that the community fuly realizes its production possibilities both with and without monopolistic pricing in the monopolistic industries.[2] That is not apt to be possible unless our household's income changes along with prices in the monopolistic industries. At least it is apt not to be possible if, for convenience, one or another price in the competitive sector is taken as numeraire.

Consider the two-commodity economy shown in figure 2.1. Let x_1 represent the output and consumption of a monopolistic good and x_2 the output and consumption of a competitive good. The latter is the numeraire. Also shown are PP', the community's production possibility schedule, and U', U'', U''', and U'''', four of the household's indifference curves. With perfect competition in the economy generally, prices in equilibrium must equal marginal costs and are also proportional to the household's marginal utilities. The household then consumes x, and output corresponds to that budget point.

At x the household's budget constraint DK is tangent to both PP' and to one of the household's indifference curves, here shown as U''''. Furthermore, at that budget point, the price ratio, the household's marginal rate of substitution, and the community's marginal rate of transformation are all equal.

With a monopoly price charged for x_1, however, and with household income constant in terms of x_2, the good that is still produced competitively, output and consumption will be at x'. There the household's new budget constraint, DE, is again tangent to an indifference curve—in this case U'—but the economy, except by coincidence, will no longer be realizing its production possibilities. It follows that Hicks's compensating varia-

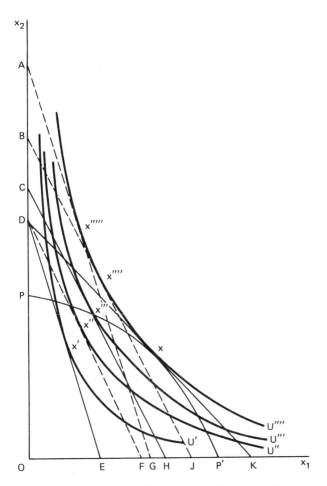

Figure 2.1 Net compensating variation for monopoly pricing.

tion, if construed as it usually is, is AD in the figure and measures the loss due to not only the misallocation occurring when production possibilities are realized but a shortfall from those possibilities. The loss due to the misallocation is alone of interest here.[3] In sum if we are to use Hicks's compensating variation, we must recast it in a way that allows the community to remain on its production possibilities schedule when prices are monopolistically instead of competitively determined. I did that in my previous article, and it was chiefly on that account that the resulting measure of loss seemed properly viewed as of a general equilibrium nature, and so to contrast with Hicks's compensating variation. The latter evidently relates to partial equilibrium. The procedure adopted before may also serve here, but, as indicated, reference previously was to a community where production possibilities are linear. With production possibilities curvilinear as in figure 2.1, the analysis must be restated.

To continue with the community shown in the figure, the measure of loss that is of interest is BC. With monopolistic pricing for x_1, we suppose that the household's income has been increased from OD to OC. On that basis the household's consumption shifts to x''', where the new budget constraint CH is tangent to another indifference curve, U'''. At x''', moreover, production possibilities are again fully realized. In other words at x''', the household's marginal rate of substitution differs from the marginal rate of transformation by just an amount corresponding to the monopolistic divergence of the price of x_1 from its marginal cost. BC, then, represents the further increment of income that would still have to be made available to the household to restore it to the initial indifference curve, U''''. With a monopolistic price charged for x_1, that would occur with the household's consumption shifting to x''''. True x'''' is beyond the range of production possibilities, but BC still can serve as a measure of the relevant loss.

I will designate the money income needed to ensure realization of production possibilities at any given prices as a 'full-employment' money income. With monopoly pricing for x_1 and income at a full-employment level, the price of x_1 (in terms of the numeraire) might conceivably be the same as when income fails to ensure that production possibilities are realized. But more likely, it would not be, and I have drawn figure 2.1 accordingly. Thus the slope of the budget constraint through x''' differs from that through x'. Recall that x' represents consumption when the household's income is as it was initially at x, but a monopoly price is charged for x_1.

Although BC is the desired measure of loss, it is obtainable as the dif-

ference between two further increments in income, *BD* and *CD*. Consider
the market basket x''. It represents the household's consumption if income
were as it was at x and a monopoly price were charged for x_1, but now
there is a monopoly price corresponding to a full-employment income
rather than the monopoly price that actually would be charged if income
remained as at x. At x'' the household experiences a level of utility U''.
BD, then, is the increment of income needed to raise the consumption to
x'''', where the household is once more experiencing its initial utility U''''.
And that increment is again Hicks's compensating variation, though now
what is compensated for is a change in the price of x_1 from the competitive
level to the monopolistic one that finally will prevail when production
possibilities are reattained. As for *CD*, that is simply the increment of
money income needed to ensure that production possibilities are in fact
reattained.

More generally, let us designate Hicks's compensating variation as the
gross compensating variation (GCV) but on the understanding that the
income variation in question is now that needed to compensate for a
change from a competitive price to the monopolistic one that would prevail when income remains at a full-employment level. The increment of
income needed to assure reattainment of production possibilities when that
monopolistic price is charged is referred to as the *money income adjustment*
(MIA), and the desired measure of loss is the *net compensation variation*
(NCV):

$$NCV = GCV - MIA. \tag{2.1}$$

Producer's surplus has diverse manifestations, but my concern is only
with one of them, though clearly it is a principal one. Suppose, for convenience, that our monopolistic product is produced by a single firm whose
marginal cost schedule is as shown in figure 2.2. Since we are interested
only in monopoly power that the firm exercises over the price of its product, I assume that prices of factor inputs do not vary as the firm varies its
employment of them. Indeed for the moment it is just as well to assume
that there is but a single variable factor employed—labor—, that the supply
of labor available to the economy generally is fixed, and that in our competitive industry the marginal and average productivity of labor are constant. Hence in terms of the numeraire, the wage rate must indeed be
constant.

In these circumstance, if our monopolistic producer charged a price
equal to marginal cost (p^c in figure 2.2), he evidently would be earning an

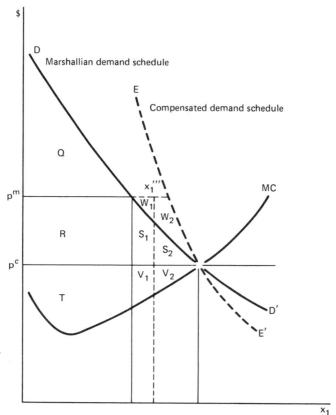

Figure 2.2 Marshallian surpluses under monopoly pricing

income in excess of his total variable costs corresponding to the area $(T + V)$, where $V = V_1 + V_2$. Such excess income is usually called *producer's economic rent*. Such rent seems always to have been understood as a form of producer's surplus, and under our assumptions it will be agreed that it is the only form that would materialize in the economy considered if the monopolist charged a price equal to marginal cost.

Suppose now that the monopolist appropriately exploits his monopoly power and charges a price above marginal cost, say p^m. Here perhaps usage in respect of the concept of economic rent varies. Such rent, it is always understood, falls by an amount equivalent to V, but some would probably hold producer's rent to rise concomitantly by the amount represented as R in the figure. That, of course, corresponds to the profit the monopolist reaps by charging a price above marginal costs. As for producer's surplus, usage here too is perhaps not fully settled, but the most usual convention clearly decrees that it still be taken to correspond to producer's economic rent, though in the inclusive sense that now embraces monopoly profits.[4] Hence producer's surplus is properly seen now as corresponding to $(R + T)$ and so as increasing by $(R - V)$.

We are interested not in producer's surplus in itself but in the welfare loss resulting from monopoly pricing. To represent that, we must also consider consumer's surplus, though now in the Marshallian way: with the monopoly's price at marginal cost, the area $(Q + R + S)$, where $S = S_1 + S_2$, and with the monopoly's charging a monopolistic price, the area Q. That means that consumer's surplus is reduced by $R + S$. In order to obtain the indicated loss of welfare—the *net surplus variation* (NSV)—we must deduct from the fall in consumer's surplus, the increase in producer's surplus:

$$NSV = (R + S) - (R - V) \qquad (2.2)$$

or

$$NSV = S + V. \qquad (2.3)$$

In this way we arrive at the proverbial textbook representation of the loss of welfare as a quasi-triangle such as that indicated in the figure. Here again, of course, the analysis is of a partial equilibrium sort, though now pre-Hicksian.

How does NSV compare with NCV as given by equation (2.1)? That is the chief question that remains to be considered, but on one further condition, the answer is simply that the two coincide. The condition is the famous one that the income elasticity of demand for the product in question be zero. In that case the budget points x'', x''' and x'''' in figure 2.1 all include the same x_1 and differ only in respect of x_2. Also the GCV in (2.1), or BD in figure 2.1, corresponds to the reduction in consumers' surplus as represented by the area $(R + S)$ in figure 2.2, for there are no income effects that might distort the relation between those two aspects (see Hicks 1956, pp. 68ff).

It also follows that MIA, or CD in figure 2.1, corresponds to the increase in producer's surplus as represented by the area $(R - V)$ in figure 2.2, for if there is still to be full employment, our household must be able to pay for the reduced output of the monopolist an amount that now includes the monopolist's profit R. The contraction of output, however, obviates the need for purchasing power by an amount V, representing the excess in the value of that output decrement over earnings of the concomitantly released labor. The latter earnings are represented geometrically by the relevant area under the marginal cost schedule. Hence V is the excess of the value of the output decrement over the value of the additional output that the released labor will produce in the competitive industry, and we have

$$NCV = (R + S) - (R - V) = NSV. \tag{2.4}$$

In short the reduction in consumer's surplus in its pre-Hicksian version comes to the same thing as our GCV. The increase in producer's surplus corresponds to MIA. The NSV that is obtained as the difference between the changes in consumer's and producer's surplus is properly viewed as the pre-Hicksian measure of welfare loss. That loss then comes to the same thing as NCV, which is obtained as the difference between GCV and MIA.

In calculating NSV, when there were no income effects, I had to consider only one demand schedule, the Marshallian one shown in figure 2.2. That schedule obtains no matter what the level of the household's income. With income effects, NSV might be calculated from either of two such schedules, one relating to a full-employment income when prices in both industries considered are at competitive levels and one relating to a full-employment income when our monopolist charges a monopoly price for his product. Although the texts are rarely explicit on the matter, NSV seems usually envisaged as reflecting a demand schedule of the latter sort, but it facilitates discussion here to refer instead to that where a full-employment income prevails with competitive pricing for the monopoly good. What has to be said about the alternative computation will be evident.

The precise correspondence of GCV and the reduction in consumer's surplus, as represented by $(R + S)$, reflects the fact that, without income effects, the Marshallian demand schedule corresponds to a compensated one associated with the initial equilibrium consumption of x_1. With income effects, those two schedules no longer coincide, and for GCV we now have

$$GCV = R + S + W, \tag{2.5}$$

where $W = W_1 + W_2$. When the Marshallian and the compensated schedules differ, as Hicks brought out, the compensating variation must be computed from the compensated schedule, and that is also true of GCV. I refer here to the compensated schedule in figure 2.2; for illustration, I assume that the monopoly good is a normal or superior one. Hence if we continue to compute the reduction in consumer's surplus as $(R + S)$, we must consider that that sum falls short of GCV by the amount W.

We must also consider, however, that the x_1 in the budget position x''' (figure 2.1) now exceeds the x_1 in the budget position x'', though it falls short of that in the budget position x''''. The indicated magnitude of x_1 is shown in figure 2.2 as x_1'''. In that case, we have

$$\text{MIA} = R + W_1 + S_1 - V_2. \tag{2.6}$$

Should the increase in producer's surplus still be taken as $(R - V)$, then, MIA exceeds that sum by $(W_1 + S_1 + V_1)$. For NCV we have

$$\text{NCV} = S_2 + W_2 + V_2, \tag{2.7}$$

and NSV, as given by (2.3), now diverges from that measure:

$$\text{NSV} = \text{NCV} + (S_1 + V_1 - W_2). \tag{2.8}$$

If we accept the Hicksian conception of consumer's surplus as reformulated here, that divergence must also be viewed as an error in NSV as a measure of welfare loss. The error, as long understood, originates in income effects. But usually attention has been focused on the bias in the Marshallian demand schedule in respect of consumer's surplus. The resultant measure of the reduction in consumer's surplus is indeed biased as far as it diverges from the GCV. But the corresponding increase in producer's surplus as calculated in the Marshallian way is also in error if it is viewed as an observation on MIA. Moreover the two sorts of error curiously tend to cancel: while the GCV is understated, so too is MIA. Recall that the latter is deducted from GCV to obtain NCV.[5]

In calculating consumer's surplus, Hicks (1956, p. 169) has held that there must always be "a sufficient background of fixed-price commodities, to serve as 'money'." In relating NSV to NCV I have not only taken x_2 as numeraire but have assumed that it is produced competitively under conditions of constant cost. Hick's requirement, therefore, has been fully met. Note, however, that there was no need to assume constant costs in defining NCV to begin with. Also in relating NSV to NCV, that assumption can be dispensed with again, but there are then two further, in some degree offsetting, sources of error in NSV viewed as an observation on NCV. Thus suppose that there are diminishing returns to labor in the competitive as well as in the monopolistic industry. Then $(R - V)$ evidently fails to allow for the additional producer's surplus generated by increased production of the numeraire good. Or rather that is so if $(R - V)$ is calculated by reference to a marginal cost schedule reflecting the wage rate prevailing when the monopolist charges a competitive price. But with the shift to a monopoly price and the transfer of labor to the competitive industry, the wage rate itself falls. Hence $(R - V)$ as so calculated also fails to allow for that reduction. For my purposes here, I continue to suppose that the monopolist acts as a competitor in hiring labor even though the wage rate ultimately varies in dependence on his price policy.

I assumed that labor is the only variable factor of production. Where there are two or more such factors, their relative prices are apt to vary as they are reallocated between monopolistic and competitive industries. Here too, therefore, the observation on MIA that is obtained from pre-Hicksian surplus analysis is affected.

In reformulating the Hicksian analysis in a general equilibrium context and in relating the result to pre-Hicksian analysis, I have considered only one monopolized product. Suppose there are many? In my previous essay I considered the question thus posed as to the welfare loss when there is monopolistic pricing for many products. While reference was to a linear production possibilities schedule, it should not be too difficult to extend the analysis to the curvilinear schedule. I will accordingly leave that to the reader.

Attention has been focused on producer's surplus accruing to an enterprise. A producer's surplus has traditionally been envisaged as possibly accruing also to suppliers of factors, but what might be said on that score too is sufficiently evident not to need laboring. A principal case in point, of course, is the surplus accruing to labor when hours vary, but as long understood that seems more properly viewed as a form of consumer's than of producer's surplus.

Although I have focused on the welfare loss due to monopoly pricing, the analysis can be extended to appraisal of welfare variations originating on other accounts.

While it has seemed of interest, at least doctrinally, to view the pre-Hicksian computation of the welfare loss due to monopoly pricing in a fresh perspective, the computation, as so viewed, is subject to error, partly of a familiar and partly of a novel sort. Moreover welfare variations often may be calculated without the kind of error that the pre-Hicksian computation provides (Bergson 1975). In the cited article, I referred only to the error in the use of the Marshallian demand schedule to gauge one or another of the Hicksian representations of benefit. But that argument applies at once to the GCV considered here, and one surmises that the pre-

Hicksian computation may also be improved insofar as it relates to the MIA, the other element figuring in a welfare variation as I have represented it.

My theme is an appropriate one for an essay in a volume honoring Abba P. Lerner. Lerner himself, in a now famous essay (1934), found it in order to apply what I have discussed as the pre-Hicksian analysis (though one somewhat different from that here) to the measurement of the welfare loss due to monopoly pricing.[6] From one standpoint, my concern here has been in part simply to update that analysis.

Notes

1. The concern here is only conceptual. Extension of the calculations of my previous paper to the case of curvilinear production possibilities is left for separate inquiry. But on that, see S. Togan, "On the Welfare Costs of Monopolistic and Average Cost Pricing," *European Economic Review* (forthcoming).

2. For simplicity, I pass by fixed coefficient production functions that might associate unemployment with realization of production possibilities.

3. May we also conclude that the loss due to the misallocation is thus overstated by Hicks's measure? One surmises that it ordinarily is, but conceivably a measure of the loss due to that misallocation alone could be even greater than Hicks's compensating variation. That would occur if, in figure 2.1, x''' were to the left of DE. On x''', see below.

4. On the concept of producer's surplus, see Currie, Murphy, and Schmitz (1971, pp. 753ff).

5. The cancellation is not complete, but in trial calculations made in connection with my previous essay, the error in the observation on MIA actually turned out to be larger than that on the GCV, so NCV on balance was understated. The calculations assume linear production possibilities, and it remains in question how the results might be affected if reference is instead to a curvilinear schedule. But these results, relating also to a linear Marshallian demand schedule for the monopolistic product (demand varies linearly with price and income), may be of interest (see table).

	Unadjusted for Income Effects			Adjusted for Income Effects		
	GCV	MIA	NCV	GCV	MIA	NCV
$N_{xp} = 1.5; N_{xI} = 1.0$	8.69	7.65	1.04	9.10	8.33	.77
$N_{xp} = 3.0; N_{xI} = 1.5$	9.38	7.29	2.09	10.11	8.33	1.78
$N_{xp} = 6.0; N_{xI} = 3.0$	10.42	6.25	4.17	12.21	8.33	3.88

On the left are the observations on GCV, MIA, and NCV indicated by variations in consumer's and producer's surplus, as determined by reference to the Marshallian demand schedule, and on the right the corresponding figures, after correction for income effects. I consider alternative cases in respect of the price (N_{xp}) and income (N_{xI}) elasticities of demand for the monopolist's product. Data on GCV, MIA, and NCV are expressed as percentages of the household's full-employment income under monopoly pricing for x_1. I assume throughout that the monopolist's price-cost ratio is 1.2, and that with x_1 so priced that good accounts for one-half of the indicated income.

6. The treatment of the welfare loss due to monopoly pricing in Lerner's 1934 essay is properly still singled out for replication in the survey on consumer's surplus of Currie, Murphy, and Schmitz (1971).

References

BERGSON, ABRAM. "On Monopoly Welfare Losses." *American Economic Review* 63 (December 1973): 853–870.

———. "A Note on Consumer's Surplus." *Journal of Economic Literature* 13 (March 1975): 38–44.

CURRIE, J. A., MURPHY, J. M., and SCHMITZ A. "The Concept of Consumer's Surplus and Its Use in Economic Analysis." *Economic Journal* 81: (December 1971): 741–799.

HICKS, J. R. *A Revision of Demand Theory.* New York: Oxford University Press, 1956.

LERNER, A. P. "The Concept of Monopoly and the Measurement of Monopoly Power." *Review of Economic Studies* 1 (June 1934): 157–175.

Journal of Public Economics 14 (1980) 31–47. © North-Holland Publishing Company

CONSUMER'S SURPLUS AND INCOME REDISTRIBUTION

Abram BERGSON*

Harvard University, Cambridge, MA 02138, USA

Received June 1979, revised version received February 1980

In reformulating consumer's surplus analysis, Hicks focused on a single household. The present essay extends the analysis to many households in a manner that seems not yet to have been explored systematically: by integrating consumer's surplus with the social welfare function. This is done in a general, as distinct from the usual partial, equilibrium context. A resulting formula, relating the community's gain from a resource reallocation in a novel way to the associated changes in volume and distribution of income, inclusive of surpluses, may facilitate applications. The analysis may also clarify some recurring issues regarding consumer's surplus.

1. Introduction

As reformulated by Hicks (1956), consumer's surplus analysis relates essentially to the behaviour of a single individual or household. Indeed, Hicks already signalled that fact by inserting the apostrophe before the final 's' in 'consumers'. On that same understanding, the punctuation has usually been retained by others who treat consumer's surplus in the Hicksian manner.[1]

Consumer's surplus nevertheless is meant to represent the benefit to a household from some change in price or prices, and any application must consider that such a change would affect many households at the same time. In normative inquiries the proverbial issue concerning interpersonal comparisons that thus arises has been dealt with in various ways, but one approach seems not yet to have been elaborated very systematically as it relates to consumer's surplus. Indeed, use of the social welfare function, with its related stress on value judgements in interpersonal comparisons, is sometimes improperly supposed to be antithetical to consumer's surplus.

In trying to repair this deficiency, I consider consumer's surplus in a general equilibrium context. For the sake of conceptual precision, that approach seems in order, although in practice the more usual partial

---

*I have benefited from the comments of anonymous referees.

[1]Marshall (1920, repr. 1936), too, treats the concept of surplus initially for a single household, but he then turns readily in a familiar way to the counterpart for consumers generally. His punctuation varies correspondingly.

equilibrium analysis no doubt has its appeal. While formally integrating the social welfare function with consumer's surplus, the analysis may serve also to allay some persistent misgivings regarding the latter.

2. From quantities to prices and incomes

I consider a community of n households, each of which acquires and spends its income in a perfectly competitive manner.[2] It suffices that the community produces only two products, X and Y, both consumers' goods. Each household spends all of its income on those goods, and derives a utility that depends only on its consumption of them, i.e.

$$U^i = U^i(x^i, y^i), \quad i = 1, \ldots, n. \tag{1}$$

U^i is supposed to be ordinally measurable and is of the conventional, well-behaved sort otherwise. Each household presumably earns income by labor, but provisionally I take working hours as fixed. Although a household's occupation is also given, it may divide its time between our two industries. The household is indifferent, however, to that allocation. Hence utility is properly represented, as in (1), as depending only on consumption. The households participate, according to their equities in the two industries, in any profits and losses realized. There can be no bar to income from ownership interests in nonlabor factors otherwise, but in our simple model such factors are best taken to be varieties of 'land' of given supply. There may also be income transfers.

In normative economics, where the social welfare function is employed, the analysis seems best construed as a form of counselling, the counsel being directed to some public official [Bergson (1976)]. Our community, therefore, must be understood to include such an official. Also, in his public actions he supposedly wishes his decisions to be consistent with some SWF of the form,

$$W = F(x^1, y^1, \ldots, x^i, y^i, \ldots, x^n, y^n). \tag{2}$$

The bundle of household consumption mixes, $x^1, y^1, \ldots, x^i, y^i, \ldots, x^n, y^n$, may be said, after Arrow (1951; 2nd edn. 1963) to represent a social state. Ideally the public official's welfare function should establish a definite ordering of all possible social states that might materialize as the bundle of consumption mixes varies; or at least of all such states within a relevant range. To what extent a public official might in fact be able and willing to commit himself to such an ordering is an interesting question. It is convenient nevertheless to suppose that the SWF is of the ideal sort. This should not be amiss if it is

---

[2]I do not exclude, however, income from equity in monopoly profits of an enterprise; see below.

understood that the public official may delineate and become meaningfully committed to such an ordering in some degree only through actual choices among limited options confronting him. As will be shown, if there is a case for consumer's surplus, it probably derives essentially from its contribution to the making of just such choices.[3]

Some delineation of the SWF in (2), however, is needed at the outset. Specifically, reference is made to what has come to be called the Bergson–Samuelson formula:

$$W = G[U^1(x^1, y^1), \ldots, U^i(x^i, y^i), \ldots, U^n(x^n, y^n)]. \tag{3}$$

Here W varies continuously with U^i, and

$$G_i > 0, \qquad i = 1, \ldots, n, \tag{4}$$

where G_i is the partial derivative of W with respect to U^i.

In addition to performing his public duties, our public official is presumably also a consumer. He supposedly, however, distinguishes between his private and public self. Privately he spends all of his personal income in accordance with some U^i, whatever that may be. Publicly he conforms to W as represented by (3). In a sense, then, he is concerned publicly with 'externalities' which do not affect his behavior as a consumer. So far as appropriate partial derivatives are nonzero, and the externalities are already manifest under (2). They necessarily prevail also under (3). To put matters in this way, however, might suggest that even in his public actions the official's perspective is a more or less private one. That surely need not be the case.[4]

In consumer's surplus analysis prices change as a result of some hypothetical resource reallocation. Where a public official is involved, the reallocation might turn on his decision on some policy issue that confronts him. Consumer's surplus analysis has multifarious applications, but especially comes into its own when variations in resource use are of a discrete sort.

[3]Even with the aid of the welfare economist, the public official's task of choosing between social states will often be a taxing one. If that is not already evident, it should become so. However, some interpretations of Arrow notwithstanding, there is no logical bar to the public official having a complete and definite ordering. Arrow has demonstrated that the public official's ordering could not be generated by a political process satisfying certain ethical postulates, but that is not at all the same thing as saying that such an ordering is impossible, or even that it could not be achieved under a political process that would be considered democratic. See Bergson (1976).

In addition to providing, if only potentially, a definite and complete ordering of social states, the SWF is assumed to have certain continuity properties of a familiar sort that will become apparent.

[4]Even a private citizen, of course, may act in accord with some SWF, such as (2) and (3), in voting or in other extra-market contexts. If he does, he too is evidently concerned with externalities. In determining on his own ordering of social states, the public official will no doubt wish to consider such evaluations by citizens generally (see below). An implied by (3), however, I pass by here externalities of the sort where one household's marginal rate of substitution between consumers' goods depends on another's consumption.

Such variations are often envisaged as occurring because of indivisibilities in factor supplies or in technologies. In our abstract model, perhaps a significant institutional change, say, imposition of competitive in place of monopolistic pricing, would be a more plausible cause.

In any event, the official must evaluate in terms of W two alternative and discretely different social states:

$$x_0^1, y_0^1, \ldots, x_0^i, y_0^i, \ldots, x_0^n, y_0^n, \tag{5}$$

representing the bundle of consumption mixes that would prevail without the reallocation; and

$$x_1^1, y_1^1, \ldots, x_1^i, y_1^i, \ldots, x_1^n, y_1^n, \tag{6}$$

representing the bundle of consumption mixes that would obtain should the decision be in favour of the reallocation. Although obviously inaccurate, we may conveniently refer to (5) as the 'initial' or '*ex ante*', and (6) correspondingly as the 'final' or '*ex post*' bundle.

The official, we assume, has indeed committed himself to (3). The economist who counsels him (presumably another consumer, or perhaps a citizen of another community) proceeds accordingly. Whatever the nature of the specific policy in question, circumstances are supposedly as usual in consumer's surplus analysis, with attention focused especially on one of our two industries, say X. If we accordingly take the price of Y as numeraire, we have to deal with two income–price situations:

$$I_0^1, \ldots, I_0^i, \ldots, I_0^n; p_0, \tag{7}$$

and

$$I_1^1, \ldots, I_1^i, \ldots, I_1^n; p_1. \tag{8}$$

Here I^i is the income of the ith household and p is the clearing price of X where each household uses its income to maximize its utility. Subscripts as before refer to initial or *ex ante* and final or *ex post* circumstances. With I^i and p as in (7), the households consume the bundle of consumption mixes in (5). Incomes and price in (8) are correspondingly related to (6).

In consumer's surplus analysis, household money income is usually taken as constant. That, however, reflects the partial equilibrium approach employed. In general equilibrium context, money income must ordinarily vary [compare Bergson (1973, 1979)]. Thus, in our simple community, rather than being constant, household money incomes vary so that resources released from (absorbed into) X, as a result of the price change, are absorbed into (released from) Y, and a new general equilibrium is established. Depending on their respective sources, moreover, the incomes of different households may vary differently. With benefits properly delineated, the changes in money incomes supersede allowance for any variations in producers' surpluses that occur in response to the reallocation. Overall, the variations in producers' surpluses may approximate the changes in money incomes, but it is the latter that count [Bergson (1979)]. Note also that the relevant change in p need not be the same as that on which attention is focused in partial equilibrium analysis. In any event, both the price and output of X under the reallocation and the changed household incomes must be consistent with each other. The two price–income situations, (7) and (8), should be seen accordingly.

We may rewrite (2) and (3) as

$$W = G[U^{*1}(I^1, p), \ldots, U^{*i}(I^i, p), \ldots, U^{*n}(I^n, p)], \tag{9}$$

or

$$W = H(I^1, \ldots, I^n, p). \tag{10}$$

The merit of the reallocation, then, turns on the comparative welfare associated with the two income–price situations referred to, in other words, on the comparative magnitudes of

$$H(I_0^1, \ldots, I_0^i, \ldots, I_0^n; p_0) \tag{11}$$

and

$$H(I_1^1, \ldots, I_1^i, \ldots, I_1^n; p_1). \tag{12}$$

In Hicksian theory, consumer's surplus takes diverse forms. Of particular interest here are: (i) the compensating variation, designated as C^i, and for the reallocation in question is given by this formula as it applies to each household:

$$U^i(I_0^i, p_0) = U^i(I_0^i + C^i, p_1), \qquad i = 1, \ldots, n; \tag{13}$$

and (ii) the equivalent variation, designated here as E^i, and given by this formula as it applies to each household:

$$U^i(I_1^i, p_1) = U^i(I_1^i + E^i, p_0); \qquad i = 1 \ldots n. \tag{14}$$

I have taken the liberty to reformulate Hicks's variations here so as to take account of the change in household incomes.

From (9), (10), (13), and (14),

$$H(I_0^1, \ldots, I_0^i, \ldots, I_0^n; p_0)$$
$$= H(I_0^1 + C^1, \ldots, I_0^i + C^i, \ldots, I_0^n + C^n; p_1), \quad (15)$$

and

$$H(I_1^1, \ldots, I_1^i, \ldots, I_1^n; p_1) = H(I_1^1 + E_1^1, \ldots, I_1^i + E^i, \ldots, I_1^n + E^n; p_0). \quad (16)$$

In evaluating the resource reallocation, then, rather than directly comparing (5) and (6), our public official evidently may proceed indirectly. He may do so in either of two ways. He may compare $I_1^1, \ldots, I_1^i, \ldots, I_1^n; p_1$, with the welfare equivalent of $I_0^1, \ldots, I_0^i, \ldots, I_0^n; p_0$, thus ordering

$$H(I_0^1 + C^1, \ldots, I_0^i + C^i, \ldots, I_0^n + C^n; p_1) \quad (17)$$

relative to

$$H(I_1^1, \ldots, I_1^i, \ldots, I^n; p_1). \quad (18)$$

Alternatively, he may compare $I_0^1, \ldots, I_0^i, \ldots, I_0^n; p_0$, with the welfare equivalent of $I_1^1, \ldots, I_1^i, \ldots, I_1^n; p_1$, thus ordering

$$H(I_0^1; \ldots, I_0^i, \ldots, I_0^n; p_0) \quad (19)$$

relative to

$$H(I_1^1 + E^1, \ldots, I_1^i + E^i, \ldots, I_1^n + E^n; p_0). \quad (20)$$

In sum, by the use of consumer's surplus analysis, it is possible to transform the comparison of bundles of household consumption mixes into one of incomes and prices; moreover, the situations that need finally to be compared are such that price is constant and household incomes alone vary. With that the public official might be able. himself to evaluate the policy issue in question, and so require no assistance from the economist who counsels him beyond that represented by the delineation of alternatives in the manner indicated. Should the official still hesitate, however, the economist can perhaps offer some limited additional guidance.

3. The indirect SWF

An indirect SWF such as (10) seems as yet to have been little analyzed. Some aspects are of particular interest here. So far as (2) and (3) provide a definite and complete ranking of alternative social states, that must also be true of (10), at least for alternative states that might be revealed by household acquisition of goods in the market, i.e. with the households always on their contract curves.

Fig. 1 shows possible contours of H for a given p. For purposes of geometric representation, our n households supposedly have contracted to only two. A single curve, such as portrayed in fig. 1, which shows alternative household income vectors (I^1, I^2) for which W is constant, has been variously designated. I shall call it an income indifference curve. Let

$$\phi^{12} = H_1/H_2. \tag{21}$$

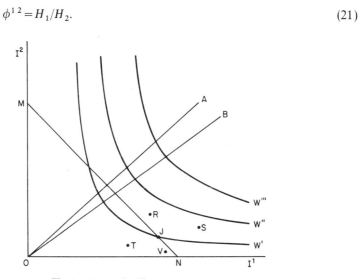

Fig. 1.   Income-indifference curves, p, given.

Here H_1 is the marginal social welfare from household 1's income and H_2 has the corresponding meaning in respect of household 2's income. Then ϕ^{12} represents the rate at which on the margin household 2's income may be substituted for household 1's income without welfare being affected. It is appropriately referred to as the marginal rate of income substitution (MRIS). In the fig. 1, the MRIS is the negative of the slope of an income-indifference curve at any point. Each income-indifference curve is shown as convex from below. This reflects the supposition that, with W constant, MRIS diminishes as I^1 increases.

Should the tastes of the two households be the same, and G be symmetric in U^1 and U^2, each curve must be symmetric about the equal income locus also shown (OA), and ϕ^{12} must be unity along that line. This evidently would also represent an optimal distribution of income in the case in question, so we are led to the obvious result that with similar tastes and a symmetric welfare function, household incomes must be equal in the optimum.

Should tastes be different, symmetricity in the welfare function becomes a somewhat elusive concept, but the counterpart of OA might then be some alternative locus, say OB, representing the departure from equality of money incomes deemed appropriate in view of the divergence in tastes. Given the difference in tastes, of course, the income-indifference curves also would be affected. Among other things, if OB is indeed an optimal locus, ϕ^{12} must now be unity alsong that locus. In fig. 1 the income-indifference curves shown conform to that requirement.[5]

I show different income-indifference curves relating to different W as not crossing each other. This is evidently appropriate if reference is to a definite ordering of social states. Although not so important here, note that as p varies each income-indifference curve is transformed into a welfare surface. For any given surface, the projection of an income-indifference curve corresponding to one p, say p_1, onto the plane corresponding to another, say p_0, must not intersect the income-indifference curve on the same welfare surface in the p_0 plane.

Income-indifference curves such as shown may be inferred from utilitarian ethical precepts, particularly the conception of social welfare as given by the famous additive variant of the B-S SWF:

$$W = \sum_i U^i(x^i, y^i). \tag{22}$$

Although not always explicitly stated, household utilities are understood to be cardinally measurable. They are also said to be 'comparable', and their addition is seen to be in order on that basis. The 'law of diminishing utility' also holds, i.e.

$$U_{11}^{*i} < 0. \tag{23}$$

Income-indifference curves that are convex from below follow at once.

[5] Even if tastes are different, might one still not be free to commit himself to equality of incomes in the optimum? For any one p, I believe one might be, but as p changes such a commitment would preclude any definite SWF. This is most easily seen if there are many commodities other than the numeraire. Suppose then that household incomes were not only equal but constant. It should be possible nevertheless to vary prices in ways such that the utilities of both households are constant. With that, it can be shown that if ϕ^{12} were initially unity, it could not remain such when tastes are different. Hence, with any given, definite SWF the equal incomes could not continue to be optimal. See Bergson (1966, pp. 78ff; 1978); and compare Bergson (1938, n. 14; 1966, p. 14), Samuelson (1947, p. 225).

Samuelson (1977) has demonstrated, however, in a stochastic context, that optimality of equal incomes would be admissible under certain conditions even though nonstochastic tastes differ. That is so even though the SWF is of the B-S sort. Reference, however, is to the additive variant which Samuelson kindly designates as Bentham–Bergson–Harsanyi.

Also, on the supposition that different households tend not to differ too much in 'sensitivity', marginal utility schedules such as those given by (23) are held to be generally similar. In terms of fig. 1, this means that the locus of optimal income distributions (OB) does not deviate much from that of equal incomes (OA).[6]

Utilitarianism, however, is not the only ethical belief that might be manifest in a preference map such as the one shown in fig. 1. For utilitarians, 'comparability' of utilities is apparently of an empirical sort. How one person's marginal utility compares with another is supposedly, at least in principle, a question to be resolved by factual inquiry. Without subscribing to such a notion, one might still become ethically committed to a B-S SWF with income-indifference curves, which, as in fig. 1, are convex from below and prescribe a more or less egalitarian income distribution as optimal. For some persons, such a commitment might have an immediate appeal that virtually defies analysis. For others, it might be deemed an appropriate expression of more basic ethical precepts such as revolve about feelings of sympathy or a concern for fairness. Here too there is no need to resort to empirical comparability of utilities; whether from feelings of sympathy or a concern for fairness, one may wish to treat similarly people in similar circumstances, but that hardly betokens that their marginal utilities from income are empirically equal. There should be no need either for additivity of satisfactions; and if not, it is just as well to forswear that too, for the implied independence assumption (MRIS between i's and j's income depends only on their earnings and on no one else's) seems of doubtful appeal. Income-difference curves such as in fig. 1 might also appear to be indicated from other standpoints; for example, because a commitment to such schedules is held to favor stability of democratic political institutions.[7]

On the other hand, some ethical beliefs might lead to preference maps rather different from that illustrated. For example, the recently much-discussed 'difference principle' of Rawls (1971) apparently requires convexity

---

[6]Among proponents of utilitarianism, 'sensitivity' seems to be different from 'tastes', but the two must be related. In any case, the proximity of OB to OA presumably requires that tastes too are not too divergent, and also that p does not assume very 'unusual' values. See footnote 5 above.

[7]To return to 'comparability', feelings of sympathy, it is true, might be viewed as involving an empathetic conflation of the satisfactions of others into one's own, and in that way as in effect commensurating the satisfactions of different persons. Such an empathetic conflation, however, while it may entail empirical inquiry, is hardly reducible to such in any conventional sense. On the other hand, should one subscribe to cardinal measurability, the conflation does provide the common dimensional unit, that has appeared so elusive, for satisfactions of different persons. This is found simply in one's own satisfactions. It is puzzling, therefore, that proponents of utilitarianism still seem to insist on empirical comparability. In order to motivate an ethical observer to wish to maximize the sum of everybody's satisfactions, the utilitarians themselves have sometimes had recourse to sympathy. Yet given the empathetic conflation that is thus required, commensuration of satisfaction already follows. On sympathy in utilitarianism see Rawls (1971, pp. 22ff, 183ff).

of the income-indifference curves of an extreme sort: the income-indifference curves degenerate into right-angles with vertices along some locus such as OB, presumably again not too far from OA. The resultant exclusion of income 'trade-offs' by Rawls's analysis has been widely noted, and for many is a decisively unappealing feature. At lower income levels, however, an approach to a Rawls-type income-indifference curve might be considered as manifesting a social commitment, now often favored, to an income minimum or 'floor'.[8]

I have referred to ethical standpoints that might be held by any individual, whether a private citizen or public official. A public official, though, presumably will also be concerned about the consistency of one or another standpoint with his retention of office.

4. Another formulation

Let us return to our public official. In dealing with the policy issue that confronts him, he may make one or other of two comparisons of income-price situations. The price of X, i.e. p, is constant in each comparison, but at different levels. In one comparison p is at its *ex ante* level, p_0, while each household's income varies from its *ex ante* level, I_0^i, to the corresponding *ex post* level, after adjustment by the equivalent variation, i.e. to $I_1^i + E^i$. In the other, p is constant at its *ex post* level, p_1, while each household's income varies from its *ex ante* level, after adjustment by the compensating variation, i.e. from $I_0^i + C^i$, to the *ex post* level, I_1^i. Let us write

$$\Delta_e^i = (I_1^i + E^i) - I_0^i; \qquad \Delta_c^i = I_1^i - (I_0^i + C^i). \qquad (24a, b)$$

I shall refer to Δ_e^i and Δ_c^i as adjusted income differences, the adjustment in question being understood as indicated.[9] Note that C^i is of the same sign as,

---

[8]Logically prior to the question of income distribution is that of 'consumers' soversignity'. As represented in (3), the B-S SWF already implies a commitment to that principle. In advancing a formula such as (3), however, Bergson (1938) sought only to formulate incisively a value judgement that tends generally to underlie normative analyses. Although not of primary concern now, a distinction still seems in order between the nature of the preferences for privately consumed goods that are finally incorporated in the SWF and the reasoning by which that matter is determined. Thus, one may join proponents of utilitarianism in normative economics in endorsing consumers' sovereignity in some more or less qualified way (making exceptions, for example, for some preferences of the emotionally disturbed) but still hesitate to reason as the utilitarians do that both the principle and the departures from it are empirically demonstratable in the light of a more ultimate commitment to consumers' utilities. The latter are understood as manifest in, but not necessarily corresponding to, preferences expressed in the market: as in the case of Pigou's famous (1932) distinction between 'desires' and 'satisfaction'.

[9]As the reader of Bergson (1973) may recognize, Δ_c^i, except for its sign, comes to the same thing as the net compensating variation referred to there. The term Δ_e^i is clearly a counterpart of Δ_c^i, and hence might properly be designated as the net equivalent variation. Adjusted income difference, however, seems to be a more suggestive designation.

and E^i is of the opposite sign from, any change in p. Relative to I_0^i, I_1^i should ordinarily vary in the direction of p. Should the household's preference be consistent, Δ_e^i and Δ_c^i must be of the same sign. This must also be the sign of the change in U^i.

Certain results follow at once. Suppose Δ_e^i is positive for all households, or positive for some and null for others. Then W increases, and the reallocation should be made. *Per contra*, W decreases and the reallocation should not be made should Δ_e^i be negative for all households, or negative for some and null for others. These results evidently would be unchanged by reference to Δ_c^i instead of Δ_e^i.

While obvious, the inferences are usefully illustrated geometrically. In fig. 1 reference is again made to variations in I^1 and I^2 (I consider again just two households) for a given p. The level of p must be appropriate to the adjusted income difference in question. Should that be Δ_e^i, reference must be to p_0, and J respresents the *ex ante* incomes, I_0^1, I_0^2. For Δ_e^i positive for both households, the situation resulting from the reallocation is equivalent for two households to incomes, $I_1^1 + E^1$, $I_1^2 + E^2$, such as at S, northeast of J. With $p = p_0$, these incomes put the community on the same welfare surface as the *ex post* incomes do when $p = p_1$. The *ex post* welfare surface necessarily is superior to the *ex ante* one, which contains *ex ante* incomes I_0^1, I_0^2, and the corresponding *ex ante* price, p_0. The *ex ante* surface on the p_0 plane has as its contour the indifference curve through J. With Δ_e^i negative for both households, the incomes $I^1 + E^1$, $I^2 + E^2$ are such as at T, southwest of J, and one sees by similar reasoning to that just employed that the *ex post* welfare surface must be inferior to the *ex ante* one. The latter again has as its contour on the p_0 plane the indifference curve through J. Should Δ_c^i be in question, the construction is quite analogous, though reference is now to $p = p_1$, and J represents *ex ante* incomes after adjustment, i.e. $I_0^1 + C^1$, $I_0^2 + C^2$. Representation of cases where Δ_e^i or Δ_c^i is positive or negative for one household and null for the other is evident.

In proceeding further, let us for the moment focus on Δ_e^i. Let

$$\Delta W = H(I_1^1 + E^1, \ldots, I_1^i + E^i, \ldots, I_1^n + E^n; p_0)$$
$$- H(I_0^1, \ldots, I_0^i, \ldots, I_0^n; p_0). \tag{25}$$

Then,[10]

$$\Delta W = \sum_i H_i \Delta_e^i. \tag{26}$$

Here H_i is evaluated at some incomes intermediate between the two levels

[10]See above, footnote 3.

represented in (25); that is, for some $\theta > 0$ and < 1, reference is to incomes

$$I_0^1 + \theta \Delta_e^1, \ldots, I_0^i + \theta \Delta_e^i, \ldots, I_0^n + \theta \Delta_e^n. \tag{27}$$

Then,

$$\Delta W = H_k \sum_i \phi^{ik} \Delta_e^i, \tag{28}$$

where ϕ^{ik} is the MRIS between income of the kth and income of the ith household; see (21). Suppose that k is an average household in the sense that the marginal social welfare per dollar of his income (H_k) is the average of the corresponding rates for all households.[11] Hence,

$$\sum_i \phi^{ik}/n = 1. \tag{29}$$

If we write

$$\alpha^i = \phi^{ik} - 1; \qquad \beta^i = \Delta_e^i - \left(\sum_i \Delta_e^i/n \right), \tag{30a, b}$$

then

$$\Delta W = H_k \left(\sum_i \alpha^i \beta^i + \sum_i \Delta_e^i \right). \tag{31}$$

The second term in the brackets represents the increase in aggregate household income resulting from the reallocation. I refer to the increase from the *ex ante* to *ex post* household incomes, after adjustment of the latter for equivalent variations; see (24a). The first term in the brackets is in effect an index of the distribution of that aggregate increment. Thus, should the increment in total income tend to go primarily to households for whom the MRIS is relatively high, $\sum_i \alpha^i \beta^i$ should be positive. Should it tend to go primarily to households for whom the MRIS is relatively low, $\sum_i \alpha^i \beta^i$ should be negative.

Since $H_k > 0$, it follows that if aggregate income increases and the increment tends to go primarily to households for whom the MRIS is relatively high, ΔW is positive and the reallocation should be made. The reverse is true in contrary circumstances. Should the change in income volume and distribution be in conflict, the outcome must depend on their comparative magnitude.

Using fig. 1 again to refer to $p = p_0$, and J again to represent the *ex ante*

[11]Compare Bergson (1938; reprinted: 1966, pp. 25ff).

incomes of the two households, the total income of the two households together would be unchanged if their earnings fell anywhere along *MN*. Points such as *R* and *S* northeast of *MN* represent, therefore, income levels for the two households that total more than *ex ante* incomes. They also represent positions in which $\sum_i \Delta_e^i > 0$. *Per contra*, points such as *V* and *T* southwest of *MN* represent reduced income totals and hence positions for which $\sum_i \Delta_e^i < 0$. The term $\sum_i \alpha^i \beta^i$ cannot literally be construed in terms of our two-household geometry, but if we fall back on (26) we see that what matters is how Δ_e^i is related to H_i. With the *ex ante* income-indifference curve as shown, that relation is favorable in the case of say *R*, but unfavorable in the case of *V*. Redistribution, therefore, compounds the gain in total income in the case of *R* and the loss of total income in the case of *V*. Welfare accordingly increases in the former and declines in the latter case.

How might one determine which circumstances obtain? The change in aggregate income is in principle an observable magnitude, and the public official, one must suppose, might often be able to evaluate for himself the redistribution that occurs. At least, he should be able to decide on its sign, for what is in question is essentially whether the redistribution is favorable or unfavorable from his normative standpoint. Provided the redistribution does not come in conflict with the change in volume, the sign of ΔW and the merit of the reallocation follow.

But might not the economist–counsellor also advise the public official on redistribution? Would that not turn simply on who benefits primarily, the 'rich' or the 'poor'? The MRIS, ϕ^{ik}, and hence α^i, must vary with income in an inverse monotonic way should the SWF be symmetric, should diminishing MRIS obtain, and should the distribution of income be suboptimal. Without symmetricity, ϕ^{ik} and α^i should still tend to vary inversely with income provided that optimality does not diverge too far from equality of incomes (i.e. in fig. 1 the departure of *OB* from *OA* is not too marked), and provided that the departure of the income distribution from optimality is at all pronounced. I refer to the relation of ϕ^{ik} and α^i to income at the point at which those coefficients are evaluated in (31). An inverse relation to *ex ante* income should also obtain, however, if the redistribution that is occurring is relatively modest, and so leaves the income distribution not too different from a distinctly suboptimal *ex ante* one, such as at *J* in fig. 1.

With ϕ^{ik} and α^i varying inversely with income, the redistribution should be desirable or undesirable depending on whether it tends to favor low- or high-income recipients. That result, strictly speaking, need not always follow, but it should often be possible to detect likely exceptions, at least with a minimum of cooperation from the public official.[12]

---

[12]In (29), the sign of $\sum_i \alpha^i \beta^i$ is necessarily that of the coefficient of correlation between ϕ^{ik} and Δ_e^i. Assuming that Δ_e^i is known to be correlated either positively or negatively with I^i, what may

I have been focusing on the equivalent variation and Δ_e^i. Should attention be directed instead to the compensating variation and Δ_c^i, as the reader may readily verify, the analysis is essentially as before. As indicated, however, reference is then to $p = p_1$, and the change in incomes in question varies correspondingly. In practice the compensating variation seems often to be favored over the equivalent variation. By analogy, Δ_c^i should be favored here over Δ_e^i. Reference to the latter nevertheless may be advantageous since *ex ante* incomes and price, which must tend to be relatively familiar, serve as a point of departure. The two approaches, of course, must yield the same result to the extent that the public official conforms to a consistent SWF.[13]

5. Conclusions

I have assumed throughout that inputs supplied by the household are constant. I leave to separate inquiry the more realistic case where such inputs are variable, but the reader is reminded that a commitment to a B-S SWF requires income distribution to take account of household preferences regarding not only consumers' goods but inputs, such as arduous labor, that the household supplies.[14]

---

be inferred as to the correlation between ϕ^{ik} and Δ_e^i? Suppose ϕ^{ik} is a linear function of I^i, i.e.

$$\phi^{ik} = AI^i + B; \quad A < 0, B > 0.$$

In that case, it follows at once that the correlation between ϕ^{ik} and Δ_e^i has the opposite sign of that between Δ_e^i and I^i. Should ϕ^{ik} vary other than linearly with I^i, that result need not follow, but it should not be too difficult through plausible 'sensitivity tests' to judge whether a contrary finding is likely in any particular case.

Note that the tendency of ϕ^{ik} to vary inversely with I^i should, *ipso facto*, become more pronounced if incomes are normalized for aspects, e.g. family size, on which the divergence between *OB* and *OA* may ultimately rest.

[13]I have considered throughout a choice between two social states. The analysis is readily extended to the case where more than two social states are in question. Specifically, what is called for is the comparison of each and every pair of alternatives. So far as the underlying social ordering is definite, the resulting pairwise rankings must conform to a consistent ordering of all alternatives together.

[14]Even with such inputs given, household preferences for them might properly be considered, at least in gauging to what extent an optimal income distribution should diverge from complete equality.

One of the principal household inputs, of course, is labor. So far as that is variable, the indicated reformulation of the analysis is of a familiar sort, with leisure being included as a consumer's good in the household's utility function. A commitment to a definite ordering of social states such as is given by the B-S SWF would also require, strictly speaking, that the household's income be redefined to exclude labor earnings. Variations in the latter then represent negatively any variations in expenditures on leisure.

The simple model on which I have focused already allows for transfers as a component of household income. These are understood, though, to be lump-sum transfers. Should transfers be otherwise, the analysis must be further restated. With labor as a variable and an income-tax on wages, for example, the price of leisure becomes the wage rate, net of taxes.

Although I have focused throughout on two consumers' goods, it goes without saying that the analysis is unchanged in all essentials if there are more than two such products.

I have sought formally to integrate consumer's surplus with the social welfare function in a general equilibrium context. The result may illuminate the extension of consumer's surplus analysis to reallocations affecting many households rather than only one.

I have referred to a marginal rate of income substitution (MRIS). That, of course, comes to essentially the same thing as the so-called 'distributional weight' that has recently been employed so often in normative inquiries where income redistribution is in question. The present analysis may usefully have reminded us, however, that such a weight, while it may be of utilitarian derivation, need not be so. As Harberger (1978) implies, there could be misunderstandings on that score. The analysis also underlines another aspect that is not always noted, namely the distributional weight is apt to depend on the price structure. The inquiry may also have clarified just what the weight is to be applied to in a general equilibrium context. It has also led, I believe, to a relatively novel disaggregation of changes in distribution and volume of income as they bear on the community's benefit. This could facilitate introduction of value judgements on income distribution and in that way normative appraisal generally.[15]

As with welfare economics generally, consumer's surplus analysis is properly seen as a form of counselling, addressed primarily to a public official. In adopting that perspective here, however, I have evaded a very pertinent question: Is consumer's surplus analysis really needed for such counselling? The question is the more in order, for redundancy has remained as a charge against consumer's surplus analysis since Hicks's reformulation. Whatever can be done with it, it is said, can as well be done without it.

What is ultimately in question apparently is the nature of the information on alternative social states that might enable a public official most readily to choose between them. That is a matter about which it is difficult to generalize. It could depend on the circumstances and perhaps even on the public official. Yet our public official's task is apt to be complex. Consumer's surplus analysis, to repeat, permits formal reduction of the alternatives dealt with to summary variations in volume and distribution of income at a given price. It would be surprising if that were not often helpful — if not indispensable.

It can only be confusing, however, to fail to recognize the affinity, pointed out by Samuelson (1947, p. 196), between consumer's surplus analysis and that other long-standing form of information processing, index number

---

[15]I have simply replicated here, however, for discrete variations the separation between volume and distribution that was made for infinitesimal changes in Bergson (1938; reprinted 1966). For discrete changes, my formula (31) seems to provide an analytically simpler and more convenient basis for inclusion of income redistribution in normative appraisal than does, say, the criterion developed for this purpose in Little (1957, pp. 103ff). By allowing for consumer's surplus, formula (31) should also permit evaluation of social gains in cases where the two-period index number comparisons relied on by Little are indecisive. See also Sen (1979, pp. 29ff).

theory. Indeed, in any two-point comparison the compensating variation is nothing other than the ideal that we seek to approximate with the Laspeyre quantity index. Similarly, the equivalent variation is nothing other than the ideal that we seek to approximate with the Paasche quantity index. Perhaps this essay should have been entitled 'Index numbers and income redistribution', but that too would be confusing.

Another objection to consumer's surplus is that there are so many different kinds of surpluses. How shall we choose among them? The compensating and equivalent variations fit neatly into the arguments of the indirect SWF. They therefore lend themselves at once to theoretically meaningful application. For purposes of benefit appraisal, they seem to merit priority.

In counselling a public official, I have assumed that it is his values that are ultimately decisive. The counsellor seeks to facilitate the formulation and implementation of the official's values, but at least *qua* economist does not endeavor to serve his own preference instead. Such a posture no longer appears as widely accepted as it once was, but the case for it that was stated long ago by Robbins (1935) is, I feel, still impelling. Should the economist find the official's preferences sharply in conflict with his own, he is, of course, free *qua* citizen to try to persuade the official otherwise and *qua* economist to seek other employment.

References

Arrow, Kenneth J., 1951, Social choice and individual values (Wiley, New York; 2nd edn, 1963).
Bergson, Abram, 1938, A reformulation of certain aspects of welfare economics, Quarterly Journal of Economics 52 (2) 310–334.
Bergson, Abram, 1966, Essays in normative economics (Harvard, Cambridge, Mass.).
Bergson, Abram, 1973, On monopoly welfare losses, American Economic Review 63 (5) 853–870.
Bergson, Abram, 1975, A note on consumer's surplus, Journal of Economic Literature 13 (1) 38–44.
Bergson, Abram, 1976, Social choice and welfare economics under representative government, Journal of Public Economics 6 (3) 171–190.
Bergson, Abram, 1978, Taste differences and optimal income distribution, in: Tullio Bagiotte and Giampero Franco, eds., Pioneering economics: International essays in honor of Giovanii Demaria (Cedam Padova).
Bergson, Abram, 1979, Consumer's and producers' surplus under general equilibrium, in: H.I. Greenfield, A.M. Levenson, W. Harmovitch and E. Rotwein, Theory for economic efficiency: Essays in honor of Abba P. Lerner (M.I.T., Cambridge, Mass.).
Harberger, Arnold C., 1978, On the use of distributional weights in social cost–benefit analysis, Journal of Political Economy 86 (2), Part 2, S87–S120.
Hicks, J.R., 1956, A revision of demand theory (Clarendon Press, Oxford).
Little, I.M.D., 1957, A critique of welfare economics, 2nd edn (Oxford, London).
Marshall, Alfred, 1920, Principles of economics, 8th edn (Macmillan, London; reprinted 1936).
Pigou, A.C., 1932, Economics of welfare, 4th edn (Macmillan, London).
Rawls, John, 1971, A theory of justice (Harvard, Cambridge, Mass.).
Robbins, Lionel, 1935, An essay on the nature and significance of economic science, 2nd edn (Macmillan, London).
Samuelson, Paul A., 1947, Foundations of economic analysis (Harvard, Cambridge, Mass.).
Samuelson, Paul A., 1948, Consumption theory in terms of revealed preference, Economica, N.S. 15 (60) 243–253.

Samuelson, Paul A., 1977, When is it ethically optimal to allocate money incomes in stipulated fractional shares, in: Natural resources, uncertainty and general equilibrium systems: Essays in memory of Rafael Lusky (Academic Press, New York).

Sen, Amartya, 1979, The welfare basis of real income comparison: A survey, Journal of Economic Literature 17 (1) 1–45.

INDEX NUMBERS AND THE COMPUTATION
OF FACTOR PRODUCTIVITY[1]

BY ABRAM BERGSON

Harvard University

For purposes of analyzing the nature and meaning of index number formulas to be used in the calculation of factor productivity, a distinction is made between intertemporal comparison of factor productivity for a single country and contemporaneous comparison of factor productivity in two different countries. In the former case, the country in question is supposed ideally to be realizing fully its production possibilities, and the concern is seen as appraisal of shifts in such possibilities over time due to the advance of technological knowledge. Following Moorsteen such an advance is taken to be represented by the change in capacity to produce a standard mix of outputs per unit of a standard mix of inputs. Any mix might be standard, but those actually realized at the times in question are of particular interest.

The index number formulas to be applied then depend on the assumed shape of the functions representing production possibilities. The conventional practice of aggregating output arithmetically and inputs geometrically, for example, is in order where production possibilities are given by an elaborated Cobb–Douglas function, but achieves only more or less approximate results otherwise. The analysis necessarily bears also on the prices at which inputs and outputs are to be valued.

For the case of contemporaneous comparison of different countries, technological knowledge is taken ideally to be the same in the countries considered. Hence the concern is to gauge differences in production efficiency, i.e., realization of production possibilities. With production capacity understood to reflect any shortfall from possibilities, and hence production inefficiency in that sense, the analysis proceeds much as before, but given the fact of inefficiency determination of suitable prices for valuation of inputs and outputs becomes relatively difficult. Alternative expedients, none entirely satisfactory, are explored.

I. INTRODUCTION

The calculation of factor productivity is by now the subject of a voluminous methodological literature, but only rarely is there any systematic treatment of a basic aspect. I refer to the problem posed by the fact that the summary data compiled for such a calculation on factor inputs and outputs take the form of index numbers. That, of course, is almost always so, at least for inputs. For output as well as inputs, the index number problem arises in an especially striking way when, as is often the case, the calculation is more or less comprehensive of the economy generally. What is in question is how properly to construct and interpret the needed index numbers. Further inquiry into this matter would seem in order.

The calculation of factor productivity, if at all inclusive in scope, represents but an extension of that of real national income. Anyone inquiring into principles of index number construction and interpretation in the case of factor productivity data, therefore, must become indebted to the classic formulation of such principles for index numbers of real national income that we owe to Hicks (1940) and Samuelson (1950). Where writers on factor productivity have considered the

[1]A revised and expanded version of Section 2, Theoretic Considerations, in Abram Bergson, "Comparative Productivity and Efficiency in the U.S.S.R. and the U.S.A.," in Alexander Eckstein, ed., *Comparison of Economic Systems*, Berkeley, California, 1971. I draw on that earlier essay with the permission of the University of California Press and of the Regents of the University of California. Work on the present version was facilitated by an award (Contract G-1525) from the National Science Foundation. I am indebted to Martin Weitzman for a critical review of an earlier version. As this essay was about to go to press, the sad news came of the untimely death of the writer whose analysis I take as a point of departure. This is not the place to try to memorialize Richard Moorsteen, but perhaps I can begin to suggest the sense of loss that all who knew him and his work must feel if I dedicate this essay to his memory.

problem of index numbers, however, use has been made of diverse approaches. Among these, I find especially illuminating one adopted in a rather neglected essay of Richard Moorsteen (1961). I myself may have been able previously (Bergson, 1961) to contribute to this sort of analysis. While drawing attention to the approach in question, this essay may carry the analysis further in some interesting ways.

Writings on factor productivity are not always explicit as to what it is that the data compiled are supposed to indicate, but the concern fairly clearly is to measure, so far as possible, the joint impact on the volume of production, relatively to the corresponding factor inputs, of variations in two related phenomena: technological knowledge, as that affects production possibilities, and production efficiency, understood as the degree of realization of such possibilities.

That is the concern whether reference is to different periods in the same community, or as is also occasionally so, to different communities at the same time. But, for obvious reasons, the two phenomena are apt to differ in relative importance depending on which sort of comparison is made. Thus, variations in technological knowledge might well be the more important variable for a single community at different times, but differences in production efficiency should often be paramount where different communities are compared at the same time. At least that should be so among communities at all modern, for technological knowledge seems to be disseminated rather rapidly among such communities.

It may not be entirely unrealistic, therefore, to focus in turn here on two ideal cases. In each, two economic situations are compared, but in the first these situations relate to two different periods for the same community. Technological knowledge varies between the two intervals, but there is no inefficiency in production in either. In the second case, reference is to two communities at one and the same time. Technological knowledge is the same in the two communities, but they differ in respect of production efficiency.

The purpose for which productivity is measured, then, also varies. Where the calculation is for one community at two different times, the concern is to gauge the increase in technological knowledge over the interval in question. Where productivity is calculated for two communities at one time, the concern is rather to appraise comparative production efficiency in the two communities.

However unrealistic, delineation of two such ideal cases is analytically convenient here. Any consequential inefficiency must pose special difficulties for the calculation of factor productivity. We need not ponder long to see that that is so, though the fact is rarely considered. It is well, therefore, to inquire first into the principles applying when there are no such difficulties, and then to consider how those principles are affected by such difficulties.

II. THE COEFFICIENT OF FACTOR PRODUCTIVITY

Turning to the comparison of two different periods for a single community where production is always fully efficient, I shall also assume for the present that in both periods the community in question produces but a single consumers' good X, the amounts of such output being X_1 in period 1 and X_2 in period 2. Similarly, only one capital good, I, is produced, and this in amounts I_1 and I_2 in the two periods.

260

For present purposes, I, is supposedly infinitely durable. Production takes place by use of a stock of the capital good amounting to K_1 in period 1 and K_2 in period 2, and a single kind of labor, L. Employment of the latter is L_1 and L_2 in the two periods.

Production possibilities in the community are, therefore, given for period 1 by the formula

$$(2.1) \qquad F^1(X, I, L, K) = 0,$$

and for period 2 by the formula

$$(2.2) \qquad F^2(X, I, L, K) = 0.$$

Thus, for any given volume of employment of the two factors, and any given output of one of the two goods, (2.1) indicates the maximum amount of the other that can be produced in period 1 with the technological knowledge available at that time. Similarly for (2.2) and period 2. Since production possibilities supposedly are always fully realized, the mixes of outputs and inputs actually experienced in 1 and 2 must also conform to (2.1) and (2.2), i.e.,

$$(2.3a,b) \qquad F^1(X_1, I_1, L_1, K_1) = 0; \quad F^2(X_2, I_2, L_2, K_2) = 0.$$

Because of the advance of technological knowledge, however, some mixes open in 2 may not be realizable in 1. It is evidently just such a change in capacity that one would wish to gauge from factor productivity data for the case considered, but it is advisable to try to delineate somewhat more precisely than is customary the nature of the change in question. Consider some mix of outputs and inputs, X^*, I^*, L^*, K^*. Let us call this the standard mix. For 1, for any $\beta_1 > 0$, there should be some $\alpha_1 > 0$, such that

$$(2.4) \qquad F^1(\alpha_1 X^*, \alpha_1 I^*, \beta_1 L^*, \beta_1 K^*) = 0.$$

Similarly for 2, for any $\beta_2 > 0$, there should be some $\alpha_2 > 0$, such that

$$(2.5) \qquad F^2(\alpha_2 X^*, \alpha_2 I^*, \beta_2 L^*, \beta_2 K^*) = 0.$$

In other words, for any multiple of the standard inputs, the community should be capable in each period of producing some multiple of the standard outputs.

Consider the ratios

$$(2.6a,b) \qquad \pi_1 = \alpha_1/\beta_1; \quad \pi_2 = \alpha_2/\beta_2.$$

The former indicates for period 1 and the latter for period 2 the volume of output per unit of inputs relative to that implied by the standrad mix. Consider now the further ratio

$$(2.7) \qquad \pi_{12} = \pi_2/\pi_1.$$

This indicates the comparative output per unit of inputs in the two periods, and hence is properly referred to as the coefficient of Factor Productivity (CFP).

The coefficient may also be written in another form of interest:

$$(2.8) \qquad \pi_{12} = (\alpha_2/\alpha_1)/(\beta_2/\beta_1).$$

261

As (2.8) underlines, while the individual period ratios, π_1 and π_2, depend on the levels of inputs and outputs in the standard mix, the CFP involves a comparison only of postulated inputs and of resultant outputs in the two periods. Only the structure of the standard mix matters, therefore, at this point.

So far as π_{12} represents relative factor productivity, it evidently also indicates the difference in capacity to produce outputs of the standard structure with inputs of the standard structure due to the difference between the two periods in technological knowledge. Thus, π_{12} varies directly with the degree to which production capacity in 2, owing to the advance of technological knowledge, has come to surpass that of 1.

That assumes, however, an absence of economies or diseconomies of scale in production. This assures that, given the standard mix, the magnitudes of π_1, π_2 and π_{12} are independent of the volume of inputs that is postulated for each period. In other words, π_1 is independent of β_1, π_2 of β_2 and π_{12} of both β_1 and β_2. With scale effects, π_{12} may still indicate the change in production capacity due to the advance of technological knowledge, but strictly speaking that presupposes that the volume of inputs considered in the two periods is the same, i.e., $\beta_1 = \beta_2$. Failing that, π_{12} depends not only on comparative technological knowledge, but on the comparative scale of inputs considered and the resulting scale economies in the two periods.[2]

Even without scale effects, reference is to inputs and outputs in each period that conform structurally to the standard mix. Conceivably, technological change might be of a neutral sort where the variation in production capacity does not depend on the structure of inputs or outputs. If technological change should be neutral in this sense, π_{12} would also be invariant of the structure of inputs and outputs, but so far as circumstances are otherwise π_{12} is relative to that structure. As reflected in production capacity, in other words, the advance of technological knowledge depends on the mix.[3]

In sum, the CFP reflects scale effects as well as technological change, but clearly it is still a metric on which we should wish to have empirical observations. So far as the coefficient depends on the standard mix, the moral must be that we should seek observations on as many mixes as possible. But note that we may take as standard one or the other of the mixes observed in the two periods, or some combination of the two. Such mixes are obviously of particular interest. How might we obtain the desired observations?

---

[2]With no scale effects, (1) and (2) are both homogeneous to the zero degree. It follows that π_1 is unaffected by a change from β_1 to $\lambda\beta_1$, for there is a corresponding change from α_1 to $\lambda\alpha_1$. Similarly, for π_2, β_2 and α_2. Note that if we take $\lambda = 1/\beta_1$, for period 1, and $\lambda = 1/\beta_2$ for period 2, π_1 and π_2 may be introduced explicitly in the production functions for the two periods:

$$(2.9a,b) \qquad F^1(\pi_1 X^*, \pi_1 I^*, L^*, K^*) = 0; \quad F^2(\pi_2 X^*, \pi_2 I^*, L^*, K^*) = 0.$$

[3]While the concept of neutral technological change is familiar in growth theory, reference is usually made to a community where only a single commodity is produced. The usage adopted here, however, seems to represent a natural extension to the case where there is more than one such commodity. Indeed, the two are closely related. Thus, it is easily seen that sufficient conditions for π_{12} to be invariant of the standard mix are: (i) F^1 and F^2 are each expressible as the sum of two separate linear homogeneous functions, one of outputs and the other of inputs; (ii) The change in technology represented by the shift from the input function of 1 to that of 2 is Hicks neutral, while the change in technology represented by the shift from the output function of 1 to that of 2 is of a similar character.

262

We owe chiefly to Moorsteen, I think, the formulation of the problem of factor productivity measurement in this plausible way. His 1961 essay, referred to above, is also illuminating on the solution, but it may be possible to offer a more complete analysis than he could in that pioneer inquiry of the specific issues that inevitably arise regarding the valuation standard or standards and the formulas to be applied in compiling the needed index numbers of inputs and outputs; and also of the relation between the resulting measures of factor productivity and the CFP for one or another mix. I turn to these questions.

III. Index Numbers of Inputs and Outputs

The needed index numbers of inputs and outputs supposedly are to be compiled from these data: (i) actual outputs and inputs during the two periods considered: X_1, I_1, L_1, K_1, and X_2, I_2, L_2, K_2; and (ii) corresponding prices p_1, q_1, w_1, r_1q_1, and p_2, q_2, w_2, r_2q_2. While q_1 and q_2 are the prices of capital goods in 1 and 2, r_1q_1 and r_2q_2 are the corresponding rental rates. In other words, the rate of interest is r_1 in 1 and r_2 in 2.

The question posed as to the valuation standard or standards to be applied in effect concerns the nature of these prices. As will appear, I fall in here with a familiar, though still not always accepted, view on that matter: ideally, the relative prices of goods produced should correspond in each period to their marginal rate of transformation. Similarly, the ratio of the wage rate to the rental for services of capital goods should correspond to the marginal rate of substitution between the two factors. The rates of transformation and substitution in the two periods are given by (2.1) and (2.2). Thus, we have

$$(3.1) \qquad \mathrm{MRT}_{XI} \equiv (F_1/F_2) = p/q,$$

and

$$(3.2) \qquad \mathrm{MRS}_{KL} \equiv (F_4/F_3) = rq/w.$$

Subscripts to F are used in the usual way to denote partial derivatives. Depending on the period, appropriate superscripts to F and subscripts to prices are understood.

Note that in the case of capital goods, (3.1) and (3.2) mean that valuation conforms to both of the two standards usually referred to: that represented by marginal cost and that represented by marginal value productivity. Thus, according to (3.1) the current output of the capital good is valued at marginal cost, or at least at a price that is the same in relation to such costs as the price for our consumers' good is to the marginal cost of that good. Similarly, with (3.2), the services of the capital good are valued as an input relatively to labor in accord with the comparative marginal productivities of the two factors.

As for the index number formulas to be applied and the relation of the resulting measures to the CFP, in inquiring into these matters we may conveniently begin with a special case: the production functions in (2.1) and (2.2) are assumed provisionally to have a specific form; particularly, (2.1) is supposed to reduce to

$$(3.3) \qquad X + AI = CL^\gamma K^{1-\gamma},$$

263

and (2.2), to

$$(3.4) \qquad X + BI = DL^{\rho}K^{1-\rho}.$$

In each period, therefore, "separability" of output and inputs obtains, and the marginal rate of transformation between the two goods is independent of the volume and structure of both inputs and outputs. That is also true of the elasticity of substitution (σ) between factors, which is everywhere equal to unity. In other words, reference is simply to a variant of the usual Cobb–Douglas function, aggregation of products, such as is assumed in the latter implicitly, being here represented explicitly.[4]

The case is illustrated in Figure 1. In 1.2 are shown the mixes of inputs observed in periods 1 and 2, g_1 and g_2, and the corresponding production isoquants, f^1f^1 and f^2f^2. Given by (3.3), f^1f^1 represents for period 1 alternative mixes of inputs yielding the same aggregate output as does g_1. Similarly for f^2f^2, though reference here is to (3.4), period 2, and g_2. In Figure 1.1 are shown the mixes of outputs observed in the two periods, G_1 and G_2, and the corresponding transformation schedules, F^1F^1 and F^2F^2. The transformation schedule F^1F^1 indicates for period 1 alternative mixes of outputs producible with the mix of inputs observed in that period or an equivalent mix. Similarly for F^2F^2, and period 2. As given by (3.3) and (3.4) both schedules are linear.

Even in the special case considered, as noted technological change is apt not to be neutral. Hence, as apparent from the figure, π_{12} depends on the standard mix. Four such mixes are of particular interest:

(i) X_2, I_2, L_2, K_2, i.e., outputs and inputs observed in 2;
(ii) X_1, I_1, L_1, K_1, i.e., outputs and inputs observed in 1;
(iii) X_2, I_2, L_1, K_1, i.e., outputs observed in 2 and inputs observed in 1;
(iv) X_1, I_1, L_2, K_2, i.e., outputs observed in 1 and inputs observed in 2.

[4] As well known, formulas such as (3.3) and (3.4) would in fact obtain if production in all industries conformed to one and the same Cobb–Douglas function, apart from the dimensional constant. That is hardly realistic, but (3.3) and (3.4) still serve here as a convenient point of departure.

As Professor Paul A. Samuelson has pointed out to me, (3.3) and (3.4) strictly speaking could not in any case fully represent production possibilities for a single community at two historically different times. Thus, in period 2 technological knowledge presumably would have increased or at least not have decreased over that in period 1, but, as is not difficult to see, while (3.4) might dominate (3.3) generally, there must be some input and output mixes for which (3.3) would be more productive than (3.4). For such mixes, therefore, (3.3), rather than being superceded by (3.4), still prevails as a representation of production possibilities.

This, however, does not preclude use of (3.3) and (3.4) here to represent production possibilities in periods 1 and 2 respectively. Rather the formulas may be so used, but simply on the understanding that for any mixes of inputs and outputs for which the implied CFP turns out to be < 1, that coefficient nevertheless has a magnitude equal to unity. As indicated, of particular interest here are the alternative mixes of inputs and outputs actually experienced in the two periods. Use of (3.3) and (3.4) to represent production possibilities in respect to those mixes rests on the foregoing understanding.

Assuming that (3.3) and (3.4) imply a CFP ≥ 1 for some mixes, for what mixes might those formulas nevertheless imply a CFP < 1? That, of course, is an empirical matter, but note that the possibility of such anomolous results arises from the variation in the production function over time in respect of the exponential coefficients for factor inputs and the constant terms relating to outputs. Also, unless such variation is very great, as readily seen, a CFP that is appreciably greater than unity for some mixes is apt to be associated with a CFP ≥ 1 for a wide range of neighboring mixes as well.

Note, that even where the implied CFP ≥ 1, (3.3) and (3.4) satisfy the first but not the second condition given in note 3, above, for π_{12} to be independent of the standard mix.

264

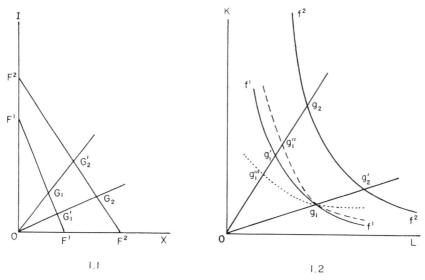

Figure 1. Output (1.1) and Input (1.2) Mixes in Periods 1 and 2

In Table 1, I show for each such standard mix the corresponding value of π_{12} as indicated by (2.8). Thus, as (2.8) requires, π_{12} is obtained for each standard mix by comparing for the two periods a relative of outputs with a relative of inputs, each of the standard structure. In the table, I also show index numbers calculated from observed prices and quantities that are supposed to correspond to the relatives of outputs and inputs conforming to (2.8). In other words, for each standard mix, by taking the ratio of the indicated index number of outputs to that of inputs, we obtain an observation on the corresponding π_{12}.

TABLE 1

CALCULATION OF π_{12} FOR ALTERNATIVE STANDARD MIXES

			Measurement in terms of observed prices and quantities	
Standard mix (1)		π_{12} (2)	Index of outputs (3)	Index of inputs[a] (4)
(i)	X_2, I_2, L_2, K_2	$\dfrac{OG_2}{OG_1'} \div \dfrac{Og_2}{Og_1'}$	$\dfrac{p_1X_2+q_1I_2}{p_1X_1+q_1I_1}$	$\dfrac{L_2^\gamma K_2^{1-\gamma}}{L_1^\gamma K_1^{1-\gamma}}$
(ii)	X_1, I_1, L_1, K_1	$\dfrac{OG_2'}{OG_1} \div \dfrac{Og_2'}{Og_1}$	$\dfrac{p_2X_2+q_2I_2}{p_2X_1+q_2I_1}$	$\dfrac{L_2^\rho K_2^{1-\rho}}{L_1^\rho K_1^{1-\rho}}$
(iii)	X_2, I_2, L_1, K_1	$\dfrac{OG_2}{OG_1'} \div \dfrac{Og_2'}{Og_1}$	$\dfrac{p_1X_2+q_1I_2}{p_1X_1+q_1I_1}$	$\dfrac{L_2^\rho K_2^{1-\rho}}{L_1^\rho K_1^{1-\rho}}$
(iv)	X_1, I_1, L_2, K_2	$\dfrac{OG_2'}{OG_1} \div \dfrac{Og_2}{Og_1'}$	$\dfrac{p_2X_2+q_2I_2}{p_2X_1+q_2I_1}$	$\dfrac{L_2^\gamma K_2^{1-\gamma}}{L_1^\gamma K_1^{1-\gamma}}$

[a] $\gamma = w_1L_1/(w_1L_1+r_1q_1K_1); \quad \rho = w_2L_2/(w_2L_2+r_2q_2K_2).$

265

130

Index number formulas, of course, are in effect procedures for aggregation. In the calculation of factor productivity, so far as aggregation is considered explicitly, reference is usually to factor inputs, and as is proper the aggregation then conforms to the nature of the production function that is assumed. Although perhaps not always clearly grasped, the same principle evidently must apply to outputs as well. Moreover, with production functions given by (3.3) and (3.4) and prices as assumed, the appropriate index number formulas clearly must be of the sorts set forth in Table 1, but the corollary may deserve underlining that while aggregation of inputs is geometric that of outputs is arithmetic. It is sometimes assumed that one and the same aggregation procedure is indicated for both inputs and outputs. Note too that with outputs or inputs observed in one period as standard, the aggregation entails use of weights that relate to the other period—prices in the case of outputs and income shares in the case of inputs. This rather paradoxical feature of the calculation also follows from the nature of the production functions considered. Indeed, given these functions, the tabulated index number formulas turn out to be ideally appropriate in the sense that the resulting measures of π_{12} correspond precisely to those indicated by (2.8). The proof is readily found and is left to the reader.[5]

To try now to be more realistic, several departures from (3.3) and (3.4) are of interest:

(i) A transformation locus is ordinarily thought to be curvilinear rather than linear. Without any knowledge of its precise shape, we may still fall back on arithmetic aggregation in compiling index numbers of comparative outputs, but the correspondence to the output relatives indicated by (2.8) is now approximate, rather than exact. If the transformation locus is curvilinear, however, it is usually thought to be concave from below. Given that, the resulting error in the calculated π_{12} is predictable; that is, as can be seen at once, the calculated π_{12} is biased in favor of the community whose price weights are used in the aggregation of output. See Table 2, col. (2).

(ii) While I have assumed unity elasticity of substitution between factors, there are reasons to think that for an isoquant such as that considered σ might well be less than unity.[6] If that is so, and σ is known, the formulas for index numbers of inputs in Table 1 should be modified accordingly. Thus, the aggregation called for in that case is simply that given by the well-known CES production function. If σ is not known, and the formulas in Table 1 are still applied, the calculated π_{12} is subject to a further bias. Specifically, relative inputs tend to be overstated for the community whose inputs are taken as a standard, and the calculated π_{12} is biased accordingly. For example, with $\sigma < 1$, and g_2 as the standard for inputs, relative inputs according to (2.8) are indicated by (Og_2/Og_1'') in Figure 2.2. The corresponding index number formula in Table 1, however, still yields the larger ratio

[5]Hint: Given formulas (3.3) and (3.4), each transformation schedule and each isoquant in question is represented by a linear homogeneous function. Along any ray, the magnitude of such a function varies proportionately with its arguments. At the same time, with product and factor prices determined as assumed, alternative mixes of outputs which have the same total value arithmetically in terms of a community's own prices must be on one and the same transformation schedule for that community. Alternative mixes of inputs which have the same total value geometrically in terms of a community's own factor shares must be on one and the same isoquant for that community.

[6]See Arrow et al. (1961); David and van de Klundert (1965); Weitzman (1970).

266

(Og_2/Og'_1).[7] It also follows that the calculated π_{12} is biased against period 2. More generally, the bias is as shown in Table 2, col. (3).

TABLE 2

BIASES IN MEASURES OF π_{12} OBTAINED FROM ALTERNATIVE INDEX NUMBER FORMULAS

Standard mix (1)	Bias due to concavity of transformation locus (2)	Bias due to less than unity elasticity of factor substitution (3)	Bias due to interdependence in production function (4)
(i) X_2, I_2, L_2, K_2	−	−	+
(ii) X_1, I_1, L_1, K_1	+	+	−
(iii) X_2, I_2, L_1, K_1	−	+	0
(iv) X_1, I_1, L_2, K_2	+	−	0

(iii) It was also assumed that for any given output mix the marginal rate of transformation does not depend on the input mix and that for any given input mix the marginal rate of substitution between factors does not depend on the output mix. Such rates and mixes are likely rather to be interdependent. To the extent that they are, the index number formulas in Table 1 may still be used to calculate π_{12} but that procedure is subject to a further error. Consider, for example, the computations where period 2 outputs and inputs, X_2, I_2, L_2, K_2, are standard. With interdependence, the output relative indicated by (2.8) is still approximated, as it was before, by the ratio (OG_2/OG'_1) in Figure 1.1, and by the corresponding index number for outputs in Table 1. The related index number formula for inputs, however, yields a relative for inputs equal to (Og_2/Og'_1) in Figure 1.2. That relative, as we saw, diverges from the measure called for by (2.8) so far as $\sigma < 1$. But even if $\sigma = 1$, the formula in question still errs, since strictly speaking the isoquant f^1f^1 relates to period 1 outputs, G_1. From this isoquant we determine g'_1, the inputs of period 2 structure which in period 1 are equivalent to that period's actual inputs g_1 in the production of G_1. What we wish to determine rather is the inputs of period 2 structure which in period 1 are equivalent to g_1 in the production of G'_1. Generally, such inputs will be on an isoquant other than f^1f^1 through g_1.

How do the inputs we wish to know, say g'''_1 compare with g'_1? A partial answer is provided by an argument due essentially to Moorsteen (1961) and Yasushi Toda (1964). Substitutions among factors which tend to make one period's factor endowment correspond structurally to that of another period should proceed more favorably to the increasing factor if the structure of output has already been modified to conform to that of the other period. While this rests on rather special

[7]With $\sigma < 1$, the marginal rate of factor substitutions is still supposed to correspond to relative factor prices at observed points. At other points, the isoquant for which $\sigma < 1$ necessarily is to the right of that for which $\sigma = 1$, as shown in Figure 1.2.

267

assumptions,[8] I show g_1''' accordingly in Figure 1.2, and have recorded in Table 2a corresponding bias in the calculated π_{12}. That bias is positive, for Og_1''' should fall short of Og_1'. Hence so far as our index number formula for inputs yields an observation on (Og_2/Og_1') it tends to overstate the volume of inputs of the standard structure that is needed in period 1 to produce a volume of outputs, OG_1', of a standard structure.

Thus far, period 2 outputs and inputs, X_2, I_2, L_2, K_2, have been taken as standard. By similar reasoning we find that, where X_1, I_1, L_1, K_1 are standard, the magnitude of π_{12} calculated from the index number formulas in Table 1 tends to be understated. Where the standard mix is a composite of outputs of one period and inputs of another, as readily seen, there is curiously no bias in the calculations due to interdependence.[9] The different biases due to interdependence are shown in Table 2, col. (4).

(iv) Formulas (3.3) and (3.4) exclude economies of scale. If there are such economies, all proceeds as before but the calculated value of π_{12} now reflects those economies as well as the advance of technological knowledge.

In considering departures from (3.3) and (3.4) I have assumed that, with outputs or inputs of one period as standard, the corresponding index number price or value weights should still relate to the other period. When production diverges from (3.3) and (3.4), we can no longer be certain that this is in order, but if we proceed as though it were, the direction of bias in the calculated π_{12} is predictable, and it may not be so otherwise. Moreover, the resultant observations, at least for

[8]In the present context, products that are relatively capital or labor intensive with one factor endowment are also that with the other; and the output structure reflects the factor endowment, in the sense that if, say, capital increases relatively to labor, the output of capital intensive products grows relatively to that of labor intensive products.

[9]Consider again the case where outputs and inputs in one period, say 2, are standard. In other words, the standard mix is X_2, I_2, L_2, K_2. By implication, in (2.8), α_2 and β_2 equal unity, while α_1 and β_1 are to be calculated. To refer first to α_1, this is implicitly given by the formula

(3.5) $$F^1(\alpha_1 X_2, \alpha_1 I_2, L_1, K_1) = 0,$$

and is estimated from the relation

(3.6) $$\alpha_1 \simeq OG_1'/OG_2 = (p_1 X_1 + q_1 I_1)/(p_1 X_2 + q_1 I_2).$$

Taking outputs in period 1 as given at the levels $\alpha_1 X_2, \alpha_1 I_2$, then, we wish also to determine β_1 so that

(3.7) $$F^1(\alpha_1 X_2, \alpha_1 I_2, \beta_1 L_2, \beta_1 K_2) = 0.$$

This is estimated from the relation

(3.8) $$\beta_1 \simeq Og_1'/Og_2 = (L_1^\gamma K_1^{1-\gamma})/(L_2^\gamma K_2^{1-\gamma}).$$

The equation on the right presupposes that $\sigma = 1$, but even if that were so, β_1 would only be approximated. Thus let us write

(3.9) $$\beta_1^* = Og_1'/Og_2.$$

Then, β_1^* is such that

(3.10) $$F^1(X_1, I_1, \beta_1^* L_2, \beta_1^* K_2),$$

and hence differs from β_1, which satisfies (3.7).

Suppose now we take as a standard outputs of one period and inputs of the other, e.g., X_2, I_2, L_1, K_1. In (2.8), then, α_2 and β_1 equal unity, and α_1 and β_2 are to be calculated. To begin with α_1, that is again given implicitly by (3.5) and estimated from (3.6). As for β_2, that is given implicitly by

(3.11) $$F^2(X_2, I_2, \beta_2 L_1, \beta_2 K_1) = 0.$$

For $\sigma = 1$, β_2 then precisely corresponds to (Og_2'/Og_1) and is measured exactly by the corresponding index number in Table 1, so there is no further error at this point.

268

output, will probably turn out to be the more accurate ones. According to the analysis of Moorsteen (1961) and my own (Bergson, 1961) already referred to, the use of price weights for the period other than that whose mix is standard must yield the more reliable observations on the change in capacity to produce the standard mix whenever the transformation locus is concave from below, or at least not very convex. Also, the "Gerschenkron effect" is supposed to hold (i.e., in the comparison of output in the two periods, period 2 is favored by the use of period 1 prices as weights), but that is very often so. Figure 1.1 illustrates such a situation.[10]

I have referred to diverse index number formulas that might be applied in the calculation of factor productivity. The chief formulas in question are of a sort very often applied in practical work, but the analysis may have clarified their rationale and limitations, together with the valuation principles that they presuppose. It still remains, however, to explore some complexities so far excluded by the simple model on which I have focused.

IV. Capital Goods Valuation

We have been considering thus far a community in which but two products, one consumers' good and one capital good, are produced, and but two inputs, labor and the capital good, employed. What if there are many products and factors rather than just two? That more realistic case was not explored by Moorsteen, and I too have passed it by previously, but evidently all is as before where there are many products and inputs. Thus, the valuation standards considered still apply in that case, and so too does the analysis of index number formulas, though these must now be adapted to the many-product, many factor case in obvious ways.

In practical work, inputs of one or another sort are customarily grouped together in a sub-aggregate as a preliminary to the calculation of the aggregate of all inputs together. Moreover, the index number formula used in the sub-aggregation usually differs from that used in the aggregation of all inputs. For example, different kinds of capital goods may be aggregated arithmetically while such goods taken together may be aggregated with other inputs geometrically. Such a procedure, of course, is usually resorted to only as a practical expedient, but it may be of interest that, as seen here, it is just one of many possible ways of translating one observed mix of inputs into another, that is taken as standard; and so may be more or less valid depending on the degree to which the translation conforms to the shape of the production function, particularly the isoquant surface that the function defines.[11]

[10]With the concavity of the transformation locus and the Gerschenkron effect, however, the alternative index numbers in alternative price weights do not constitute, as we might wish them to, limits on the change in capacity to produce the output mix of either period. See Usher (1972) and Bergson (1972, pp. 216 ff).

[11]In the light of Leontief (1947) and Solow (1955–56), it has often been supposed that the procedure in question assumes in any case that the marginal rate of substitution between any two inputs included in a sub-aggregate does not depend on the amounts of any inputs not included in the sub-aggregate. Leontief and Solow refer, however, to the conditions for collapsing variables in a production function. It should be observed that that is not quite the same thing as the problem that is germane here: how to translate one mix of inputs into another. Unless the Leontief–Solow condition is met, it is true that it becomes difficult to conceive of any sub-aggregate as an analytically distinct input, but depending on the nature of the production function, it is still imaginable that for purposes of translating one mix of inputs into another use of different index number formulas at different stages of aggregation might be appropriate.

269

For the two product, two factor case, as we saw, valuation properly is made in the familiar way where for outputs reference is to prices corresponding to their marginal rate of transformation and for inputs to prices corresponding to their marginal rate of substitution. While one of the products considered was capital, and hence also a source of inputs, the application of both standards simultaneously encounters no difficulty in principle in the simple case in question. As not always considered, however, where there is more than one capital good produced, the problem of valuation becomes somewhat more complex. Thus, the requirement for the valuation of outputs of two capital goods, I^a and I^b apparently is

(4.1) $$\text{MRT}_{ab} = q^a/q^b,$$

while that for the valuation of the corresponding inputs of services would seem to be

(4.2) $$\text{MRS}_{ab} = rq^a/rq^b = q^a/q^b$$

By implication, the relative prices of the two capital goods, q^a and q^b, must correspond at one and the same time to their marginal rate of transformation and the marginal rate of substitution between their corresponding services. Could a single set of prices conform to both conditions?

The answer is, of course, yes provided a well-known condition for dynamic efficiency is satisfied,[12] but such a requirement goes beyond the productive efficiency that has been assumed here, that is, realization of production possibilities, a purely static requirement. Hence, if we are to limit ourselves to that assumption we must consider it a possibility that $\text{MRT}_{ab} \neq \text{MRS}_{ab}$. What then? The rule is still the general one that has been applied, but it is understood that in the case of capital goods reference must be to two sets of prices: one in the valuation of outputs and the other in the valuation of inputs. To recur to an earlier formulation, the current output of capital goods is valued at marginal costs, while capital service inputs are valued proportionately to their marginal products. While reference may thus have to be made to two sets of prices for capital goods rather than one, only on that basis can the measures of factor productivity be construed as they were in the two product, two factor case.

Note that the need to refer to two sets of prices for capital goods may arise quite apart from whether any of the capital goods are new or not. In the literature on factor productivity, the issue posed for the valuation of capital goods by a divergence between their marginal cost and marginal value productivity is a familiar one, but it is usually considered in respect of situations where new capital goods are replacing old ones.

A divergence between marginal cost and marginal value productivity, however, necessarily arises also in such a situation, but in that case we are inevitably confronted too with a phenomenon that has an interest of its own, and which was also excluded from the simple model considered previously: "embodied" technological change. We in effect referred previously only to such change as was "disembodied," for the single capital good considered was available for use as an input in period 1 as well as in period 2. Over the interval considered, therefore, no new capital good embodying technological change was introduced.

[12]See Dorfman, Samuelson, Solow (1958, Ch. 12).

270

What if there are new capital goods embodying technological change? The moral here is essentially the same as that usually understood in such cases: in the case of new capital goods, we must value inputs not in accord with marginal rates of substitution, as was done previously, but in accord with marginal rates of transformation. As is not difficult to see, only in that way will the resultant measures of factor productivity indicate, as we should wish them to, a CFP reflecting embodied as well as disembodied technological progress. Note, however, that this principle applies only to new capital goods, or more precisely to the valuation of such goods relatively to old capital goods and to each other. In the case of old capital goods, valuation must still conform to marginal rates of substitution. In other words, the principle of valuation in accord with marginal value productivity still applies to inputs of the capital goods generally, but that principle is superceded by valuation at marginal cost in the case of inputs of new capital goods.[13]

New capital goods are but one example of new inputs and outputs generally, and all such inputs and outputs alike were excluded from the simple model with which we began. But what might be said here for new inputs and outputs other than capital goods should be evident, and need not be labored.

V. Contemporaneous Comparison

To come to comparative factor productivity for two communities at the same time, as explained I shall refer here again to an ideal case, though a different one from that considered previously. Thus, technological knowledge is now the same in the two communities. The communities may differ, though, in productive efficiency. In fact, it is that difference, rather than technological progress, that is now to be gauged from comparative data on factor productivity.

But may not the analysis even so proceed essentially as before? Thus, suppose 1 and 2 are seen as two different communities rather than two periods. May we not view production functions such as (2.1) and (2.2) essentially as before, but on the understanding that each formula reflects for the community concerned the alternative mixes of inputs and outputs that are open, after due allowance for inefficiency? And may we not also calculate and interpret factor productivity as before, but on the supposition that the π_{12}, on which the resultant data bear, relates to production functions as so construed?

Broadly speaking the answer in all cases, I believe, is in the affirmative, but as not often considered in writings on factor productivity appraisal of efficiency does sometimes pose novel problems. The problems, moreover, are not always very tractible, but it is well at least to be clear about them.

[13]In the case of new capital goods, then, inputs as well as outputs are to be valued at marginal cost. But the desideratum, to repeat, is that calculated factor productivity should reflect embodied as well as disembodied technological change. It should be observed, therefore, that that could also be achieved under an alternative procedure for new capital goods: valuation of both inputs and outputs in accord with marginal value productivity. The resultant representation of technological progress would differ, however, depending on which of the two approaches is employed. Thus, with valuation at marginal cost, such progress is manifest only when the new capital goods are used, while with valuation at marginal value productivity the progress is manifest when the new capital goods are produced.

On the valuation of new capital goods, while in essentials I subscribe here to a widely held view, one found for example in Denison (1957, pp. 218 ff) and Kendrick (1961, p. 35), another standpoint still seems sometimes to be taken. See, for example, Nadiri (1972, p. 133).

271

According to familiar reasoning, a community may fail to realize its theoretic production capacities, and so suffer from inefficiency in production, in three ways:

(i) Owing to wasteful practices, a production unit may not obtain from the factor inputs at its disposal as large an output as available technological knowledge permits;

(ii) Because of misallocations of factors between production units within any industrial branch, marginal returns to any factor may differ in different production units;

(iii) Because of misallocations in the economy generally, the marginal rate of substitution between factors may vary as between different branches.

An initial question concerns the nature of the production functions to be considered where there is inefficiency of the foregoing sorts. Without such inefficiency, production functions such as (2.1) and (2.2) are determined solely by available technological knowledge. We are able, therefore, to delimit the contours of such functions simply by reference to meaningful alternative hypotheses as to the nature of such knowledge. With inefficiency, the mixes of inputs and outputs that are open depend as well on the working arrangements (institutions, policies and practices) governing resource use, for it is in those arrangements that the inefficiency originates. In the circumstances it is perhaps not entirely obvious that the relevant mixes are even sufficiently determinate to be properly represented by production functions such as (2.1) and (2.2), but assuming that they are, what may be said in a general way regarding the contours of those functions?

A usual supposition is that the functions with inefficiency must be similar in shape to what they are without it. On a theoretic plane perhaps that is the only assumption to make, but transformation loci might well be more or less concave and isoquants more or less convex with inefficiency than they are without it. In fact, it is not precluded that such schedules would be radically altered. Without inefficiency, for example, technological economies of scale might result in convexity of the transformation locus, but we cannot rule out that with inefficiency, such economies would give way to diseconomies resulting in concavity of that locus. Such diseconomies might result, for example, from bureaucratic ineptness in administering large enterprises.

Given production functions such as (2.1) and (2.2), the analysis formally may indeed proceed generally as before. Thus, π_{12} is defined just as it was previously in terms of those functions, and we also obtain measurements of that coefficient by applying index number formulas such as have been set forth. The principles to be observed in selecting and interpreting those formulas are entirely the same as those considered previously.

As before, too, however, the entire exercise presupposes valuation of inputs at prices corresponding to marginal rates of substitution and of outputs at prices corresponding to marginal rates of transformation. The rates in question are those given by production functions such as (2.1) and (2.2) and so relate to the economy generally. But without inefficiency, the marginal rate of substitution thus delineated obtains for substitutions within any production unit, while the corresponding marginal rate of transformation obtains for transformations of outputs of any two production units, one producing one of the two commodities in question and the other producing the other one. These well known relations are,

272

of course, simply conditions for full efficiency, and it is their violation which results in the different sorts of waste itemized above. As it turns out, prices corresponding to rates of substitution and transformation that apply regardless of the production units affected are also identifiable with familiar behavioral norms, a feature much facilitating empirical inquiry.

With inefficiency, however, marginal rates of substitution and transformation evidently must vary depending on which production units are in question. Which of such rates are delineated by production functions such as (2.1) and (2.2) and so relate to the economy generally, therefore, must turn on the working arrangements, for it is those arrangements which determine which of all possible substitutions and transformations might actually occur in any particular instance. That is also to say that how to value inputs and outputs in factor productivity computation probably is a matter that must be dealt with in some degree in an *ad hoc* way, in the light of the working arrangements prevailing in the communities in question. Possibly the relevant valuations could be determined together with the production functions themselves, as some apparently assume, by econometric calculations. It may be illuminating, however, to consider in relation to the theoretic desiderata some specific valuation principles of an *a priori* sort that are formally similar to those applying where there is no inefficiency.

It suffices to refer at this point to but one community. Suppose that community is of the simple kind considered at the outset; that is, it produces two outputs, X and I, with two inputs, L and K, the different symbols having the same meaning as before. Alternative mixes open, with due allowance for inefficiency, are represented by:

$$(5.1) \qquad F(X, Y, L, K) = 0.$$

Just what mixes of inputs and outputs might conform to (5.1) must depend, of course, on the manner in which the two inputs are allocated between the two outputs, and within each branch, on the allocation of the inputs among and their utilization by individual production units. We must now consider such activities explicitly, but it may suffice to refer summarily to the two branches. Production of X, then, supposedly conforms to

$$(5.2) \qquad X = G(L_x, K_x),$$

and of I, to

$$(5.3) \qquad I = H(L_I, K_I).$$

In each case, there is presumably waste of types (i) and (ii) above, and so far as there is, the waste is reflected in (5.2) and (5.3), but how that waste occurs and how great it might be are not here of special concern. By implication, we focus primarily on type (iii) waste. In any actual case, of course, that type of waste might well be overshadowed by the other types, but it is, I think, the most difficult to grapple with and hence conceptually the most interesting to consider for present purposes.

To come to valuation principles, ideally we should wish again to apply prices conforming to (3.1) and (3.2), which now correspond to the inefficient (5.1) rather

273

than to (2.1) or (2.2). But owing to the inefficiency, such prices may not be directly observable, and two groups of valuation principles are to be considered provisionally as surrogates. We are supposedly able to determine prices corresponding to these principles, though that in practice might not be easy. The first group of principles constitute together what may be called the Own Factor Cost (OFC) standard of valuation. The relevant prices are designated p^0, q^0 for X and I, and w^0, for L. There are two rental charges for services of capital goods, resulting from the application of two interest rates, r_X^0 in the X industry and r_I^0 in the I industry. Among these OFC prices, w^0 is arbitrary, and serves in effect as a numéraire. For the rest, it is understood that:

(5.4a,b) $$r_X^0 q^0 / w^0 = G_2/G_1; \quad r_I^0 q^0 / w^0 = H_2/H_1.$$

Also,

(5.5a,b) $$p^0 = \frac{w^0 L_x + r_X^0 q^0 K_x}{X}; \quad q^0 = \frac{w^0 L_I + r_I^0 q^0 K_I}{I}.$$

While outputs are here priced at average cost, note that with inputs priced in accord with (5.4a,b), such prices also correspond to marginal costs provided that (5.2) and (5.3) are linear homogeneous. That, of course, follows at once from Euler's theorem.

How do OFC prices compare with those called for by (3.1) and (3.2)? From (5.2) and (5.3), we have

(5.6) $$MRT_{XI} = -\left(\frac{\Delta I}{\Delta X}\right)_{L,K} = -(H_1 \Delta L_I + H_2 \Delta K_I)/(G_1 \Delta L_x + G_2 \Delta K_x)$$

As indicated, reference is to small variations in L_X, K_X, L_I, K_I, where total employment (L) and the total stock of capital goods (K) are constant. The variations also conform to (5.1). Using (5.4a,b) and (5.5a,b), and assuming linear homogeneity,

(5.7) $$MRT_{XI} = \alpha(p^0/q^0),$$

where

(5.8) $$\alpha = -(w^0 \Delta L_I + r_I^0 q^0 \Delta K_I)/(w_X^0 \Delta L_x + r_X^0 q^0 \Delta K_x).$$

Or, for relevant variations,

(5.9) $$\alpha = (w^0 \Delta L_x + r_I^0 q^0 \Delta K_x)/(w^0 \Delta L_x + r_X^0 q^0 \Delta K_x).$$

It follows that OFC product prices correspond fully to (3.1) and hence are theoretically ideal for factor productivity computation if there is waste of types (i) and (ii), but not of type (iii). In that case $r_X^0 = r_I^0$, $\alpha = 1$, and (p^0/q^0) precisely equals MRT_{XI}. Should there be type (iii) waste, however, $r_X^0 \neq r_I^0$, $\alpha \neq 1$, and (p^0/q^0) will generally diverge from MRT_{XI}. The extent of the divergence depends on the comparative magnitudes of r_X^0 and r_I^0 and of ΔL_x and of ΔK_x. The latter terms represent the transfers of labor and capital that are called for when I is transformed into X, and possibly could differ in sign, but that seems unlikely. Hence, for any given r_X^0 and r_I^0, α ordinarily should be between two extremes: that is, between $\alpha = 1$, which results when $\Delta K_x = 0$, and means that OFC prices are

274

again ideal, and $\alpha = r_I^0/r_X^0$, which results when $\Delta L_X = 0$. It also follows that if rates of return on capital do not differ too much, p^0/q^0 should approximate 3.1 fairly closely. On the other hand, if rates of return do differ widely, p^0/q^0 could diverge appreciably from that norm, but whether and to what extent might perhaps be gauged by considering that the comparative magnitudes of ΔL_X and ΔK_X are determined in principle by (5.1) and so in effect by the working arrangements. The labor-capital ratios in the two branches in question, however, presumably might often be significant benchmarks.

To come to OFC factor prices and the marginal rate of substitution, we have from (5.2) and (5.3),

$$(5.10) \qquad \mathrm{MRS}_{KL} = -(\Delta L/\Delta K)_{X,I} = \frac{1}{\Delta K}\left(\frac{G_2}{G_1}\Delta K_X + \frac{H_2}{H_1}\Delta K_I\right).$$

Here, the variations of ΔK and ΔL and the division of ΔK between the two branches are such that X and I are constant. Also, formula (5.1) again holds. Using (5.4a,b),

$$(5.11) \qquad \mathrm{MRS}_{KL} = \frac{1}{w^0 \Delta K}(r_X^0 q \Delta K_X + r_I^0 q^0 \Delta K_I).$$

Let us designate by r^0 the average rate of interest in the economy generally, where

$$(5.12) \qquad r^0 q^0 = r_X^0 q^0 (K_X/K) + r_I^0 q^0 (K_I/K).$$

Should waste be only of types (i) and (ii) and not at all of type (iii), $r^0 = r_X^0 = r_I^0$, and

$$(5.13) \qquad \mathrm{MRS}_{KL} = r^0 q^0/w^0,$$

so OFC prices correspond to (3.2) and so are at this point again ideal, it being understood that for the needed rental rate for capital goods reference is to the rate imputable to such goods in either industry or (what is the same thing) the average of such rates for the economy generally. Suppose now there is type (iii) waste. In that case, we again have $r_X^0 \neq r_I^0$, and r^0 will ordinarily differ from either. But (5.13) still holds, and OFC prices are still ideal with the rental rate for capital goods being $r^0 q^0$ provided that the increment of capital that is supplanting labor in the economy generally is divided between the two branches proportionally to the stock already there. While such a division is hardly to be expected, if it is at all approximated, the divergence between $r^0 q^0/w^0$ and the ratio called for by (3.2) might not be very great even when $r_X^0 \neq r_I^0$. The approximation is also the closer the smaller is the discrepancy between those rates of return.

The second group of valuation principles constitute what I have referred to elsewhere in a related context (Bergson, 1961, Ch. 3) as the Adjusted Factor Cost (AFC) standard of valuation. AFC closely resembles OFC, but has an interest of its own. Let us designate the relevant prices as p^*, q^*, w^*, $r_X^* q^*$, $r_I^* q^*$ and $r^* q^*$. Then, for AFC, we have

$$(5.14\text{a,b}) \qquad r_X^* q^*/w^* = G_2/G_1; \quad r_I^* q^*/w^* = H_2/H_1$$

275

Also,

(5.15) $$r^*q^* = r_x^*q^*(K_X/K) + r_I^*q^*(K_I/K),$$

and

(5.16a,b) $$p^* = \frac{w^*L_X + r^*qK_X}{X}; \quad q^* = \frac{w^*L_I + r^*qK_I}{I}.$$

Evidently, $r^*q^*/w^* = r^0q^0/w^0$, and so has the same claim as the latter, no better and no worse, to represent MRS_{KL}. The two product price ratios p^*/q^* and p^0/q^0 also are equal if there is no type (iii) waste and capital goods rental rates, under either price system, are the same in the two branches. Otherwise, however, $p^*/q^* \neq p^0/q^0$. Thus, while both sorts of prices cover average cost, in the case of p^* and q^* a uniform charge is made for capital at an average rental rate for the whole economy. In the case of p^0 and q^0 the charge for capital varies, and corresponds in each industry to the marginal productivity of capital there. But note that the discrepancy between p^*/q^* and p^0/q^0 might be such as to make the former ratio closer to the mark. Suppose, for example, that $r_I^0 > r_X^0$. Then from (5.7) and (5.9), $\alpha > 1$, and p^0/q^0 is too small. But, as readily seen, p^*/q^* must then also be greater than p^0/q^0. Similarly, if $r_I^0 < r_X^0$, p^0/q^0 is too large, but in that case p^*/q^* is less than p^0/q^0. Of course, in either case it is still possible that p^*/q^* deviates more than p^0/q^0 from the desired price ratio.

So far I have tacitly assumed that nothing is known about the way in which working arrangements cause inefficiency. So far as such information is available, clearly we might be able either to improve on or at least gauge more definitely the biases in our surrogate principles. For example, suppose as before that (5.2) and (5.3) are linear homogeneous. Suppose also that the relative divergence between r_x^0 and r_I^0 or r_X^* and r_I^* (the latter rates, of course, come to the same thing as the former) can be expected to be more or less stable as resources are reallocated. In that case the labor-capital ratios in the two branches not only provide, as it was suggested above that they might, benchmarks for the ratio of the increment of labor to the increment of capital transferred from one branch to another when, with given factor supplies, the output mix is changed. It can be shown that the labor-capital ratios in the two branches in fact delimit the latter ratio. Though (5.2) and (5.3) are hardly likely to be of the compatible Cobb–Douglas sort which, as noted, underlie (3.3) and (3.4), it is interesting to note that, if they should be, such an increment of capital replacing labor in the economy generally would be divided between the two branches in proportion to their existing capital stocks, which is a further relation that was considered above. I leave the proofs of these propositions to the reader.[14]

What if OFC prices, i.e., p^0 and q^0 for outputs, and w^0 and r^0q^0 for inputs, or AFC prices, i.e., p^* and q^* for outputs and w^* and r^*q^* for inputs, are applied even though they may not conform to MRT_{XI} and MRS_{KL}? There is simply still

---

[14]Of course, if we know the production functions in the two branches and also the precise manner in which relative rates of return vary in the two branches, we can in principle determine (5.1) and corresponding formulas for the theoretically ideal prices conforming to (3.1) and (3.2). Even in the case of compatible Cobb–Douglas functions, however, such formulas seem to turn out to be rather complex.

276

another source of bias in the computation, in addition to those already considered. The computation would have to be construed accordingly.

I have again passed by complexities. Concerning these, suffice it to say that if there are many products and factor inputs there is a possibility that was not very meaningful previously that divergence between OFC and AFC prices and (3.1) and (3.2) might not be highly correlated with comparative levels of outputs and inputs in the two communities considered, so that the bias in resulting measures of factor productivity computation. The mode of analysis derives from a 1961 essay different products and factor inputs. Regarding embodied technological change, it should be observed that we are concerned here with the contemporaneous comparison of two communities that have the same technological knowledge. Differences in the assortment of capital goods produced, nevertheless, are not precluded, and that means that variations in embodied technologies of the sort encountered in intertemporal comparison for a single community might also be found here, but if so presumably not so frequently. In any event, the analysis of embodied technological variation elaborated for the intertemporal case applies here as well, so no further consideration of that phenomenon is needed.

I have assumed throughout that performance in both communities considered falls short of production possibilities. What if such inefficiency should prevail for one community but not the other? In the real world no community is perfectly efficient, but perhaps the inefficiency sometimes is not so consequential for purposes of calculations such as are in question. If so, all calculations may proceed as in the case where an intertemporal comparison is made for a community always realizing fully its production possibilities. Or rather, that is so where the contemporaneous valuation is in terms of prices of the community that is more or less efficient. Where valuation is in terms of prices of the other community experiencing consequential inefficiency, the problem of valuation considered in this section still arises.

VI. Conclusions

I have sought in this essay to elaborate index number theory as it applies to factor productivity computation. The mode of analysis derives from a 1961 essay of Richard Moorsteen, but it may have been possible to deal more fully than has been done previously with the central question that arises regarding the nature and meaning of measures obtained by application of different index number formulas, together with the valuation principles that they presuppose. In the process, special attention has been given to a cardinal but relatively neglected aspect: the special problem posed where the ultimate concern is to appraise variations in productive efficiency as distinct from technological knowledge.

Index number theory tends to be abstract, and that elaborated here is no exception to that rule. That means among other things that I have followed a usual practice of assuming that all economic activities in a community take place at a single point in space. The analysis, thus, abstracts from the special problem posed by transportation cost. It may be hoped that before too long it will be possible to remove this important limitation.

The mode of index number analysis that I have employed is not the only one that might be adopted in respect of factor productivity computation. Lately, use

277

has often been made of a rather different approach centering on the Divisia index. The methodological problem that is thus posed is properly the subject of a separate inquiry but in practice what is called for under the Divisia index approach is essentially the use of chained indices. It should be observed, therefore, that the analysis set forth in this essay does not preclude such calculations. The results, however, have to be interpreted in a complex way. In effect, observations are obtained on the cumulative variations in productive capacity in respect of a succession of changing standard mixes. Proponents of the Divisia index approach usually focus, moreover, on intertemporal changes in one country. That is understandable, for a chained index might be difficult to construct where reference is to contemporaneous variations between countries.[15]

References

[1] K. J. Arrow, H. B. Chenery, B. S. Minhas, and R. M. Solow, "Capital-Labor Substitution and Economic Efficiency," *Review of Economics and Statistics*, August, 1961.

[2] Abram Bergson, *The Real National Income of Soviet Russia since 1928*, Cambridge, Mass., 1961.

[3] ———, "Comparative Productivity and Efficiency in the Soviet Union and the United States," in Alexander Eckstein, ed. *Comparison of Economic Systems*, Berkeley, Calif., 1971.

[4] ———, "The Comparative National Income of the U.S.S.R. and the United States," and "Reply," in Conference on Research in Income and Wealth (D. J. Daly, ed.), *International Comparisons of Prices and Output*, New York, 1972.

[5] P. A. David and Th. van de Klundert, "Biased Efficiency Growth in the U.S.," *American Economic Review*, June, 1965.

[6] E. F. Denison, "Theoretical Aspects of Quality Change, Capital Change and Net Capital Formation," in Conference on Research in Income and Wealth (Franco Modigliani, ed.), *Problems of Capital Formation*, Princeton, New Jersey, 1957.

[7] E. Domar, "On the Measurement of Technological Change," *Economic Journal*, December, 1961.

[8] R. Dorfman, P. A. Samuelson, and R. Solow, *Linear Programming and Economic Analysis*, New York, 1958.

[9] Z. Griliches and D. Jorgenson, "The Explanation of Productivity Change," *The Review of Economic Studies*, July, 1967.

[10] ———, "Divisia Index Numbers and Productivity Measurement," *The Review of Income and Wealth*, June, 1971.

[11] J. R. Hicks, "The Valuation of Social Income," *Economica*, May, 1940.

[12] J. W. Kendrick, *Productivity Trends in the United States*, Princeton, New Jersey, 1961.

[13] W. W. Leontief, "Introduction to a Theory of the Internal Structure of Functional Relationships," *Econometrica*, October, 1947.

[14] Richard H. Moorsteen, "On Measuring Productive Potential and Relative Efficiency," *Quarterly Journal of Economics*, August, 1961.

[15] W. J. Merrilees, "The Case Against Divisia Index Numbers as a Basis in a Social Accounting System," *The Review of Income and Wealth*, March, 1971.

[16] M. I. Nadiri, "International Studies of Factor Inputs and Total Factor Productivity: A Brief Survey," *The Review of Income and Wealth*, June, 1972.

[17] P. A. Samuelson, "The Evaluation of Real National Income," *Oxford Economic Papers*, January, 1950.

[18] R. M. Solow, "The Production Function and the Theory of Capital," *The Review of Economic Studies*, 1955–56, Vol., XXIII (2).

[19] Y. Toda, "On the Consistency of Dr. Moorsteen's Efficiency Index," (Typescript), 1964.

[20] D. Usher, "Comment," in Conference on Research in Income and Wealth (D. J. Daly, ed.), *International Comparison of Prices and Output*, New York, 1972.

[21] M. L. Weitzman, "Soviet Postwar Economic Growth and Capital-Labor Substitution," *American Economic Review*, September, 1970.

[15]On Divisia indices in relation to factor productivity computation see Griliches and Jorgenson (1967, pp. 250ff); Merrilees (1971); Griliches and Jorgenson (1971). For a related approach, see Domar (1961).

278

III
PUBLIC ENTERPRISE AND SOCIALIST ECONOMICS

SOCIALIST ECONOMICS*

This survey focuses on recent theoretic studies of the economic problems of socialism and, so far as they bear on these problems, on recent inquiries in the cognate field of welfare economics. These writings, which are notably abstract, might be considered as providing a theoretic basis for the work of a Central Planning Board seeking to rationalize the planning system of a socialist state. Reference is of course to a socialist state which has not yet reached the era of unlimited abundance; in other words, one which still faces, like its capitalist predecessor, the fundamental problem of allocating scarce resources among alternative uses. In the light of whatever ends the Board serves, its task is to assure as far as practicable that the available resources are utilized to the optimum advantage. My chief aim is to appraise summarily the contributions which have been made to the solution of the Board's task.

Among the studies to be considered, of course, are the recent contributions to the debate, provoked originally by Mises' famous article,[1] as to whether socialism can work at all, and how well. By now it seems generally agreed that the argument on these questions advanced by Mises himself, at least according to one

---

* Reproduced from Howard S. Ellis, ed., *A Survey of Contemporary Economics* (Philadelphia, 1948). The essay benefited from valuable comments by Professors Frank D. Graham and Abba P. Lerner. The very dated third paragraph in the original version has been omitted.
[1] "Die Wirtschaftsrechnung im sozialistischen Gemeinwesen," *Archiv für Sozialwissenschaften*, April 1920, pp. 86–121. A translation, to which references are made in this survey, has been published in F. A. Hayek, ed., *Collectivist Economic Planning* (London, 1935).

193

interpretation, is without much force. I shall try here to arrive at an understanding as to just what has been settled and just what remains unsettled in this debate.

THE ENDS

Of the writings to be surveyed, a considerable number are concerned with one large problem: to define (in a sense that will become clear) the allocation of resources that would be an optimum. On this problem the basic works were all published some years ago. Mention is to be made particularly of the writings of Pareto[2] and Barone[3] in the field of socialist economics and of Marshall[4] and Pigou[5] in the field of welfare economics. These studies provide all the essentials of a solution to the question just posed. In more recent studies, however, much has been done to clarify and elaborate the analysis.

Marshall, Pigou, Pareto, and Barone on "ends." The definition of the optimum allocation involves, for one thing, the formulation of a scale of values, on the basis of which the alternative uses of resources are to be evaluated. In the present context this scale of values might be considered as representing the ends which the Central Planning Board serves. In order to describe the recent doctrinal developments relating to this aspect of the analysis, it is necessary to refer briefly to the formulations in the basic works just mentioned.

In the case of Marshall and Pigou, the needed scale of values is given immediately in their proverbial conception of "welfare" as the sum of the utilities of the individual households in the

---

[2] V. Pareto, *Cours d'économie politique*, II (Lausanne, 1897), pp. 90ff., 364ff.

[3] E. Barone, "Il ministerio della produzione nello stato colletivista," *Giornale degli Economisti e Rivista di Statistica*, September and October 1908, ser. 2a, pp. 267–293, 391–414. A translation has been published under the title "The Ministry of Production in the Collectivist State," in F. A. Hayek, ed. *Collectivist Economic Planning*. References made to this paper are to the translation.

[4] A. Marshall, *Principles of Economics*, 1st ed. (London, 1890); 8th ed. (London, 1920).

[5] A. C. Pigou, *Economics of Welfare*, 1st ed. (London, 1920); 4th ed. (London, 1934).

194

community.[6] For different persons of equal sensitivity the marginal utility of income supposedly is the same when incomes are equal. The optimum allocation of resources, then, is one which maximizes welfare in this sense. One condition for the attainment of the optimum is immediately apparent: incomes must be equal.

In the case of Pareto and Barone, the criterion for an optimum allocation of resources is somewhat more complex: it must be impossible by any reallocation of resources to enhance the welfare of one household without reducing that of another.[7] If a reallocation which would lead to this result were possible, it is reasoned, the resources of the community could be used to better advantage by making it; in the optimum such opportunities must already have been completely exploited.

For Pareto, this formulation had one outstanding virtue: it is possible to define the optimum allocation of resources without assuming (as Marshall did) that the welfare is the sum of the utilities of individual households. This assumption Pareto considered objectionable, on the ground that the utilities are incommensurate: "nous ne pouvons ni comparer ni sommer celles-ci, car nous ignorons le rapport des unités en lesquelles elles sont exprimées."

As Pareto and Barone recognized, however, their formulation provides a necessary but insufficient criterion for the definition of the optimum allocation. The question remains, how to decide between different allocations which make some households better off and others worse off—that is, where there is a redistribution of income. This matter Pareto disposes of simply by assuming that incomes are distributed "suivant la règle qu'il plaira d'adopter." Similarly, Barone supposes that the distribution of incomes is on the basis of some "ethical criterion."

Alternative ends. One of the recent doctrinal developments concerning ends involves the introduction into the analysis of variants of the scales of values of Marshall and Pigou, and

---

[6] For references to the pertinent passages in the works of Marshall and Pigou, see Chapter 1.

[7] This is the verbal equivalent of a mathematical criterion which Pareto introduced. Pareto himself misinterpreted his criterion; the correct interpretation given here is due to Barone.

195

Pareto and Barone. All these writers, evidently, consider the case where alternative uses of resources are evaluated on the basis of the preferences of individual households—the preferences of the households, as they see them, are to count. If such a scale of values is in operation, consumers are "sovereign." Interest has focused recently on the variants of this case that arise where the Board itself undertakes to determine, to a greater or lesser extent, what is good for consumers, and allocates resources on this basis.

An important precedent for the consideration of this variant is found in the well-known argument of Pigou that consumers do not correctly weigh their own interests in decisions on savings; that, as a result of a defective telescopic faculty, they tend to undervalue future, as compared with equivalent present, satisfactions. From this it follows at once that if consumers are sovereign in respect of questions of saving and investment, the aggregate saving will be less than is socially desirable. There is a case for disregarding consumers' preferences in this sphere.

This particular argument has recently been extended to socialist economics. Thus Dobb[8] now argues that the socialist Board must disregard consumers' preferences on the question of savings and observe instead the principle that future satisfactions be valued equally with equivalent present satisfactions. Lange[9] introduces the same postulate.

Under this assumption, as I understand it, the Board would value equally a marginal "dollar" of present and future income, provided that income is constant. To the extent that income is expected to rise as a result of the investments undertaken, presumably the marginal dollar in the future would still be valued less than in the present. This would result from the operation of the law of diminishing utility within each income period and has nothing to do with the defective telescopic faculty referred to by Pigou. Thus, in deciding on the amount of investment, the Board presumably would strike a balance between two opposing consid-

[8] M. Dobb, *Political Economy and Capitalism* (New York, 1940), pp. 298–299, 311–312.

[9] "On the Economic Theory of Socialism," in B. Lippincott, ed., *On the Economic Theory of Socialism* (Minneapolis, Minn., 1938), pp. 90ff. This is a revision of two articles which were published originally in the *Review of Economic Studies*, October 1936 and February 1937, pp. 53–71, 123–142. Unless otherwise indicated, references are to the revision.

196

erations: on the one hand, the fact just mentioned, that with a rising level of income the marginal dollar in the future would be worth less than in the present; on the other hand, the fact that by investing a marginal dollar now an agio might be earned as a result of the supposedly greater productivity of roundabout processes.

Dobb[10] envisages that under socialism there will be many other exceptions to the principle of consumers' sovereignty. He considers that consumers are to a greater or lesser extent irrational in many decisions other than that on saving; and furthermore, that in many cases (for example, education, health care), even if the consumer chooses rationally from his own point of view, his decision may not be in accord with the social interest. Dobb refers also in this same connection to goods (as, for instance, police protection) which by their very nature cannot possibly be allocated among households in accord with their individual preferences.[11]

---

[10] *Political Economy and Capitalism*, pp. 309ff. See also *idem*, "Economic Theory and the Problems of a Socialist Economy," *Economic Journal*, December 1933, pp. 588–598.

[11] One other case to which Dobb refers as indicating the need for a departure from consumers' sovereignty requires special comment. This is the case where the individual consumer's desire for a thing depends on the fact of others possessing or not possessing it. "Conspicuous consumption" is the familiar example of this sort of situation.

As Paul Samuelson observes in his *Foundations of Economic Analysis* (Cambridge, Mass., 1947), p. 224, the welfare analysis as it is usually formulated assumes that the individual's preferences depend only on the amounts of goods he consumes and not on the amounts consumed by others. In the case of "conspicuous consumption," one must restate the principle of consumers' sovereignty so that the utility of any household depends not only on the amounts of goods it consumes, but also on the amounts consumed by others.

The Board might consider, however, as Dobb implies, that because of their "conventional" character consumers' preferences in this case should be overruled. If the Board did so, there would indeed be a departure from the principle of consumers' sovereignty.

But of more interest perhaps is the fact, which Dobb does not bring out, that even if the Board determines to adhere to the principle of consumers' sovereignty in this case (where the tastes of different households are interdependent), there would be very real difficulties in implementing it. It can be shown that in a free market where consumers take prices as parameters (see below, the discussion of the distinction between consumers' sovereignty and freedom of choice), the allocation of goods as between consumers could never be an optimum one. If an effective barter

197

If a free market prevailed for consumers' goods generally, then many commodities such as are covered by the foregoing considerations presumably should be distributed communally in the form of "social services." The question of the types of goods that should be distributed in this fashion also is discussed by Dickinson.[12]

The welfare function. In another recent development, to which the writer has endeavored to contribute,[13] the concern has been to clarify the question of the number and nature of the decisions on ends required to formulate the needed scale of values. This important question is left in doubt by the various writings, both old and new, that have been cited.

From the formulation of Marshall and Pigou, and of recent writers who follow them in using the utility calculus, one might gain the impression that in reality only one such decision is involved, that is the decision to maximize "welfare." Once this decision is taken it would seem that all else is determined, that is, it remains only to settle, presumably by empirical investigation, whether consumers do or do not value future satisfactions "accurately," whether or not they are "rational" in one or another kind of choice, whether they are indeed equally "sensitive" or if not just how their "sensitivity" varies, and so on.

These, however, are rather startling implications, and it is not surprising that followers of Marshall and Pigou are in doubt as to their validity. This I take it is what Dobb[14] and Kahn[15] after him

---

market could be arranged, where consumers could trade among themselves, however, it would seem that in theory the optimum might be attained. The individual household in the former case (the free market) would disregard and in the latter case (barter) take into account the effects on its welfare of changes in the consumption pattern of other households which might be induced by its own choices.

The work of Samuelson, referred to above, unfortunately reached me too late to be taken fully into account in this essay. On a number of points, Samuelson presents a more exact formulation of the welfare analysis than hitherto has been available.

[12] H. D. Dickinson, *Economics of Socialism* (Oxford, 1939), pp. 51ff.

[13] See Chapter 1; also O. Lange, "Foundations of Welfare Economics," *Econometrica*, July-October 1942, pp. 215–228.

[14] *Economic Journal*, December 1933, p. 594.

[15] R. F. Kahn, "Some Notes on Ideal Output," *Economic Journal*, March 1935.

198

wish to convey when they express the suspicion that the welfare that is being maximized may be entirely "subjective" after all, like a "black hat in a dark room."

Pareto and Barone, as has been mentioned, are explicit that the question of income distribution must be the subject of a decision on ends. In view of their silence on the question of consumers' sovereignty, however, one inevitably is led to wonder how *this* question is settled. Uncertainty on this score is only increased by recent efforts, such as that by Hicks,[16] to establish by use of the Pareto-Barone formulation welfare principles that are in some sense "positive" or "scientific." By implication, such principles would require no decisions on ends for their derivation.

In dealing with this whole question, it has seemed useful to introduce into the analysis a welfare function, W, the value of which is understood to depend on all the variables that might be considered as affecting welfare: the amounts of each and every kind of good consumed by and service performed by each and every household, the amount of each and every kind of capital investment undertaken, and so on. The welfare function is understood initially to be entirely general in character; its shape is determined by the specific decisions on ends that are introduced into the analysis. Given the decisions on ends, the welfare function is transformed into a scale of values for the evaluation of alternative uses of resources.

On this basis, it has been argued, decisions on the following questions on ends are involved in the welfare formulations that have been outlined:

Consumers' sovereignty. According to the welfare function analysis, the question of whether and to what extent consumers will be sovereign involves one such decision or a complex of such decisions. If one understands "welfare" to *mean* that consumers are sovereign, the question is, of course, already decided when it is determined to maximize welfare; but nothing in substance is gained by this type of implicit theorizing, in which many economists seem to engage. Whether by definition or otherwise, a decision on ends must be introduced. Furthermore, differences in

[16] J. R. Hicks, "Foundations of Welfare Economics," *Economic Journal*, December 1939, pp. 696–712.

199

opinion as to consumers' "rationality," the accuracy of their evaluation of future satisfactions, etc., *are* seen as often turning at least in part on divergences in ethics and hence as not easy to resolve by empirical investigation.

If the decision is in favor of consumers' sovereignty, the welfare function may be expressed in the form,

$$W = F(U^1, U^2, U^3, \ldots). \tag{1}$$

Here U^1, U^2, U^3, etc., represent the utilities of the individual households as they see them and W, the welfare of the community, is understood to be an increasing function of these utilities. The welfare of the community, then, is constant, increases, or decreases, according to whether the utilities of the individual households are constant, increase, or decrease. If the decision is against consumers' sovereignty, the welfare function must be expressed by a formula in which the Board's own preference scales are substituted for the utility functions of the individual households.

Evidently, the formula in (1) is nothing more nor less than a generalization of the Marshall-Pigou formulation; according to the latter, W is the *sum* of the utilities U^1, U^2, U^3, etc. Also, to maximize W would satisfy the criterion of Pareto and Barone. Indeed, this function might be considered as an explicit formulation of the scale of values implicit in their criterion.

Income distribution. The analysis in question follows Pareto in holding that utilities are incommensurable,[17] and agrees with Robbins[18] that, because of this, principles of income distribution cannot be deduced from the utility calculus either by the rules of logic or by empirical demonstration. The familiar appeal (in which Lerner[19] and Lange[20] now join) that we must "assume" the

---

[17] Their incommensurability is reflected in the appearance of a dimensional constant in empirical measures of utility.

[18] L. H. Robbins, *Nature and Significance of Economic Science*, 2nd ed. (London, 1935), chap. vi; "Inter-personal Comparison of Utility," *Economic Journal*, December 1938, pp. 635–641. The latter article replies to R. F. Harrod, "Scope and Method of Economics," *Economic Journal*, September 1938.

[19] A. P. Lerner, *Economics of Control* (New York, 1944), pp. 24–25.

[20] *On the Economic Theory of Socialism*, p. 100, n. 54.

comparability of utilities in order to establish a basis for normative precepts is seen as not meeting the issue.

But all of this is regarded as saying nothing more than that here, too, a decision on ends is involved. Ends are essentially principles for the evaluation of alternatives that otherwise are incommensurable. That is why an *evaluation* is needed. Once an evaluation is made, the alternatives are indeed commensurable. Given the ethical principle according to which incomes are to be distributed, the marginal welfare per "dollar" for different households necessarily is the same *in the light of this principle* when the distribution is realized.

Interrelations in the welfare of different households. Insofar as Marshall and Pigou conceive of welfare as the sum of the utilities of different households, their formulation is seen to involve an additional decision on ends, namely, one to the effect that the interrelations in the utilities of the different households have a zero social value. The magnitude of the change in the community's welfare resulting from a change in the budget position of any one family does not depend at all on the living standards enjoyed by other households.

For purposes of analyzing the optimum allocation, however, it has been found unnecessary to refer to this special and obviously very dubious case; all propositions of interest have been deduced from the more general function in the formula given above. The demonstration of this point would seem to be one of the more interesting doctrinal gains resulting from the introduction of the welfare function into the analysis.

From this standpoint, Pareto's criticism of the Marshall-Pigou formulation is misdirected. From a purely formal point of view the objection to the Marshall-Pigou formulation is not (as Pareto implied) that incommensurate utilities are added, but that their aggregation involves a redundant and indeed dubious assumption.[21]

[21] As Samuelson makes clear (*Foundations*, pp. 224–226), the assumption of the independence of the contribution of each household to total welfare is distinct from and additional to the assumption, referred to above, n. 11, regarding the independence of the *structure of tastes* of the different households. All that independence in the latter sense implies is that each household's marginal rates of substitution depend only on the quantities

201

In the writings under review, the principle of consumers' sovereignty usually is interpreted as referring to the households' preferences not only as between consumers' goods but also as between jobs. Hence, the utility functions in the formula should be considered as representing for the different households the balance of utilities from consumption and of disutilities from work done.

It has been found convenient, following Pareto and Barone, to distinguish between the "wage" that a household earns, and its "income," which differs from the wage by the amount of a social "dividend" or "tax," as the case may be. On balance, the aggregate amount of the dividends and taxes for all households equals the aggregate amount of "profits" (including "interest" and "rent," if charged) available to the community after provision is made for capital accumulation and communal consumption. Given the wages of the different households, a decision on the dividend or tax is, in effect, a decision as to the optimum distribution of income, that is, the distribution for which the marginal welfare per "dollar" is the same for different households.

For purposes of analyzing the distribution of income in terms of these two income categories (wages and the dividend or tax) it is necessary to introduce a further assumption on ends, which is not clear in the writings under review. The assumption is that the comparative marginal welfare per dollar for different households would not be changed by a change in the composition of their budgets (including changes in work done) for which their own total utilities are unchanged.[22] This requirement, a fundamental one, assures that the decision on the distribution of income is consistent with the principle of consumers' sovereignty. As we shall see, it means in effect that differences in disutilities must be taken into account in the distribution of income.

---

of goods it consumes and not at all on the quantities consumed by other households; conceivably this condition might obtain at the same time that the household felt its total utility affected by general changes in living standards of other households.

[22] See below, p. 205.

SOCIALIST ECONOMICS

OPTIMUM CONDITIONS

Given the scale of values, the definition of the optimum allocation is formulated in these terms. In accord with familiar theoretic procedures, technical knowledge and tastes are taken as given, that is, it is assumed that they are not affected by the changes under consideration; also, the question of the resources to be allocated to research is left out of account. On this basis it is possible to derive from the given ends a series of conditions ("equations") which must be satisfied if the optimum allocation is to be achieved. The optimum conditions are sufficient in number to determine the amounts of each and every sort of goods and services allocated to each and every use (the "unknowns"). Thus, if the scale of values implied by the ends were known in complete detail (that is, if all the utility functions were known), and detailed information were available on techniques and on the stocks of resources on hand, it would be possible, at least theoretically, to solve this system of equations for the concrete values of all the unknowns.[23]

With respect to this aspect of the analysis, recent writings have been concerned chiefly to formulate explicitly the optimum conditions (which are not in every case clearly stated in the works of Marshall, Pigou, Pareto, and Barone) and to develop the analysis to deal with various complexities. These aims have been pursued by several writers, especially Lerner.[24]

For convenience, I present below a brief inventory of the more interesting optimum conditions as they have come to be formulated. That the conditions listed are indeed requirements for an

[23] As far as I know, Barone is the only writer in the field of socialist or welfare economics who has counted up and matched equations and unknowns. Much the same ground has been covered many times, however, in discussions of the determinacy of competitive equilibrium.

[24] See A. P. Lerner, "The Concept of Monopoly and the Measurement of Monopoly Power," *Review of Economic Studies*, June 1934; "Economic Theory and Socialist Economy," *Review of Economic Studies*, October 1934; "A Note on Socialist Economics," *Review of Economic Studies*, October 1936; "Statics and Dynamics in Socialist Economics," *Economic Journal*, June 1937; *Economics of Control*. Also Chapter 1 of this volume; Hicks, *Economic Journal*, December 1939; Lange, *Econometrica*, July–October 1942.

203

optimum, the reader should be able to satisfy himself without too much difficulty. My brief comments are intended only to be suggestive on this score. Except as indicated, the conditions listed are either stated or implied in one or another of the basic works to which reference has already been made.

The main conditions, then, are as follows:

(i) *The ratio of the marginal utilities (the marginal rate of substitution) for each pair of consumers' goods must be the same for all households.* If this is not the case there is always the possibility of an exchange of goods between a pair of households which would increase the utility of both, and accordingly, assuming consumers' sovereignty, would increase welfare.

(ii) *In every industry factors must be combined in a technologically optimum manner* in the sense that it is not possible technologically to dispense with any amount of any factor without a reduction in output.

(iii) *The marginal value productivity of each factor must be the same in every industry.* The "prices" at which marginal productivities are valued are understood, for the time being, to represent not market prices but merely indexes of the comparative social values of alternatives. In the case of consumers' goods, the "prices" are proportional to the common values for all households of the marginal rates of substitution. If, in terms of these prices, the marginal value productivity of a factor were larger in one industry than in another, this would mean that by a shift in resources it would be possible to realize an exchange of consumers' goods which would enhance the utilities of some or all households without any concomitant losses.

In the case of capital goods, it is supposed that the "prices" represent "present values," where the present value of any particular capital good is the discounted value of its marginal value productivity in the consumers' goods industries. The rate of discount is the rate at which the Board discounts future in comparison with present income.[25] This presupposes of course that the

---

[25] If it is assumed that the capital goods are used up fully within one accounting period, these conditions lead to a very simple relation, namely that the marginal product of an increment of a capital good employed in

204

Board has a fixed single rate of discount. One might more realistically conceive the case where the Board's rate of time preference varies with the amount of savings undertaken; or there might be multiple rates, each relating to a comparison of present income with income at some specified future date. This latter case has been treated in detail by F. P. Ramsey.[26]

(iv) *In the optimum, there must be no possibility of shifting a worker from one occupation to another to increase the value of output by more than would be required to compensate the worker for the change.* This assumes that all commodities are valued according to principles already stated and that consumers' preferences govern not only as between consumers' goods but also as between jobs.

(v) *Occupational wage differentials must correspond at one and the same time to differences in marginal value productivity and, for marginal workers, to differences in disutility.* When the marginal worker is shifted from one job to another, then, he *actually* is paid the amount that is necessary to compensate him for the change in jobs. If freedom of choice prevails, this must be the case; but it is not clear that this is desirable. The desirability of this principle of wage determination follows from the assumed ends. Given that the marginal welfare per dollar for a given household is unaffected by any change in its budget position which leaves its

---

the industry producing this capital good must equal the increment of the capital good employed plus interest on this increment. Let $A_c \Delta C$ be the marginal product of an increment of capital good in consumers' good industry A, P_A be the price of the consumers' good, A, $C_c \Delta C$ be the marginal product of the capital good in the industry producing this capital good, and P_c be the price of this capital good. It is required that

$$P_A A_c \Delta C = P_c C_c \Delta C.$$

Since $P_c = P_a A_c / (1 + r)$, it follows at once that $(1 + r)\Delta C = C_c \Delta C$. Since the marginal value productivity of capital is the same in every use, it follows also that the rate of interest earned on marginal investments of capital is the same in every use, and equal to the rate established by the Board.

[26] "A Mathematical Theory of Saving," *Economic Journal*, December 1928.

total utility unchanged, the worker must be compensated fully for any extra disutility incurred as a result of a change in jobs.[27]

(vi) *The social dividend or tax, however, must be determined independently of the workers' occupation or earnings.* This principle, advanced by Lerner,[28] also follows directly from the principle that marginal economic welfare per dollar is unaffected by any budget change which leaves the total utility of the household unchanged. Given any initial allocation of "profits," no change is called for if a marginal worker is shifted from one job to another for which the additional wage just compensates him for the extra disutility. An attempt to offset the established wage differentials by the use of the tax or dividend would be out of place. The amount of the dividend or tax might be established on any of a variety of principles: for example, it might be fixed as an equal lump sum for all households; it might be made to vary with the size of the household, and so on.

In the foregoing we have made use of the distinction, which Lange recently has clarified,[29] between "consumers' sovereignty" and "freedom of choice." Consumers' sovereignty is an "end." Freedom of choice may also be an end, in and of itself, but is also an administrative procedure. The principle of consumers' sovereignty might conceivably be accepted, while some procedure other than freedom of choice was used to ascertain consumers' preferences (statistical inquiries for instance); to distribute goods

---

[27] In theory, though hardly in practice, the possibility is not precluded that different wages be established for workers in the same occupation, workers who are not on the margin of choice between occupations being paid less than those who are. In this way, the household's "producer's surplus" would be extracted for distribution in the community at large. This in no way would conflict with the principle of consumers' sovereignty.

[28] In the original version of his essay, "On the Economic Theory of Socialism" (*Review of Economic Studies*, October 1936, pp. 64, 65), Lange assumed that the dividend should be distributed proportionately to wages. The objectionable character of Lange's solution was pointed out by Lerner in a note appended to Lange's article, and Lange has since corrected his argument. Both Lange and Lerner assume freedom of choice as well as consumers' sovereignty. As a result, it is not brought out clearly that the stated principles of wage determination and taxation follow from the principle of consumers' sovereignty alone.

[29] *On the Economic Theory of Socialism*, pp. 95–96.

among the different households (as in rationing); and to recruit workers for different jobs (conscription). Under what circumstances, if any, this might be advisable is a matter for consideration. Conceivably, also, freedom of choice might prevail without the acceptance of the principle of consumers' sovereignty. While households might be permitted to spend their incomes as they wish, at established prices, their demands might be disregarded in decisions on production.

Though it is not always made clear in the writings under review, for the purposes of defining the optimum position the assumption of consumers' sovereignty alone is sufficient. For the sake of logical clarity, the conditions are formulated here on this assumption and without regard to whether freedom of choice also prevails.

Lange has discussed also the case where consumers' sovereignty is abandoned or modified.[30] Conceptually, this case is readily dealt with. All that needs to be done is to rephrase the preceding argument to take into account the fact that the pertinent marginal rates of substitution are those decided on by the Board rather than by individual households. Thus, in terms of *these rates*, the requirement that the marginal value productivity of a factor be the same in every use still holds.

If consumers' sovereignty were abandoned, however, it is open to question whether the Board would be concerned to elaborate its preference scale with any great precision. Very possibly there would be significant ranges of choice within which the Board itself would be indifferent as to allocations. To whatever extent this is so, the optimum position is in the last analysis indeterminate.

"MARGINAL COST" VS. "AVERAGE COST"

It is an easy matter to restate the foregoing optimum conditions in terms of "costs." The total cost incurred in the production of the optimum output must be at a minimum and, in the optimum, price must equal marginal cost (costs being understood here to comprise material costs, interest, and wages). The reader may

[30] *Ibid.*, pp. 90ff.

readily verify that if the stated requirements regarding costs are met the following optimum conditions will be satisfied: the condition that the factors employed in each firm be combined in a technologically optimum manner, the condition that marginal value productivity of a factor be the same in every use, and the condition that differences in the wages of different kinds of labor equal differences in their value productivity. Conversely, it can readily be shown that if the stated requirements do not hold for all firms alike, one or another of these optimum conditions will be violated.[31]

The requirement that the total cost of producing the optimum output be a minimum means, of course, that the average cost incurred in the production of *this* output is a minimum. If there is no barrier to using at one scale of output the same combination of factors that may be used at any other, then presumably one and the same combination of factors will be the most efficient at all scales of output. We deal, then, with the case of *constant costs*. Marginal cost and average cost are constant and equal for all levels of output.

For various well-known reasons, however, the case of constant costs may not prevail in the real world. For one thing, there is the case of the so-called "fixed factors"; for another there is the case of indivisibilities in the factors employed or in the production unit (for example, bridges, railways, utilities, etc.). These two cases pose a variety of theoretic questions, which recently have been discussed in some detail by Lerner[32] and Lewis.[33] What is of concern here is that in both cases—in the former case, for the duration of the service life of the "fixed" factor; in the latter case, indefinitely—only a relative optimum combination of factors can be attained at any level of output, that is, only the amounts of factors other than those that are fixed or indivisible can be

---

[31] At this stage where no specific planning scheme is in mind, it is a matter of convention just where the line is drawn between wages and dividends or taxes. As long as *differences* in wages correspond to *differences* in marginal value productivity, all is well. For our present purposes the convention may be adopted that in some one firm and for some one occupation, wages *equal* marginal value productivity. A similar assumption is needed with respect to the prices of capital goods.

[32] *Economics of Control*, chap. xvii.

[33] W. A. Lewis, "Fixed Costs," *Economica*, November 1946.

adjusted as output varies. It is usually assumed that under these circumstances the average cost varies with output according to a familiar U-shaped pattern, and, hence, that marginal cost and average cost will be equal only at one scale of output, that for which average cost is at a minimum. In the case of indivisibilities, however, the possibility has also to be reckoned with that because of the very heavy overhead and the relatively limited importance of variable costs, average cost per unit will not follow the familiar U-shaped pattern, but instead will continue to decline for a wide range of output variations. Marginal cost may be below average cost for the entire relevant range of operations.

To repeat, the rule for the attainment of the optimum is that price must equal *marginal* cost. This principle is perfectly general: it holds regardless of the relation of marginal and average cost, regardless of whether price is above average cost and there are "profits" (as might be so in the case of "fixed factors"), or below average cost and there are losses (as might be so also in the case of "fixed factors," and very likely would be so in the case of large indivisibilities).

For this very fundamental proposition, we are indebted chiefly to Marshall and Pigou, who long ago advanced it boldly even for cases of decreasing costs. In recent years, however, the rule has had to be defended and reaffirmed on a number of occasions in the face of recurring confusion. In this connection, mention should be made of the contributions of Lerner[34] and Hotelling.[35] Both

---

[34] *Review of Economic Studies*, June 1934; *Economics of Control*, particularly chaps. xv, xvi, xvii.

Lerner takes pains to make clear that "marginal cost" must be understood as the increment of costs at *given* factor prices. Only on this understanding does the condition that price equal marginal cost correspond to the optimum conditions set forth on pp. 204ff. Only then is it assured that any factor will be equally productive in every use. Lerner's stipulation, however, requires elaboration. If variations in output that are very small in relation to the supply of factors are under consideration, then for all practical purposes factor prices will be constant anyhow, so the stipulation is not necessary. On the other hand, if there are large indivisibilities, so that the changes in output do affect factor prices, the changes in factor prices would have to be taken into account. The special problems arising when large variations in output are under consideration are discussed below in the text.

The foregoing refers to marginal variations in the output of a given production unit, as distinct from variations in output due to the opening up or shutting down of the production unit itself. For purposes of formu-

writers, Lerner with special vigor, have championed the Marshall-Pigou position against doctrinal deviations.

Part of the confusion seems to stem from the fact that the distinction is not always kept clearly in mind between the definition of the optimum allocation and the problem of realizing this optimum in practice. As Schumpeter has observed, the stated principle follows from the general logic of choice;[36] its validity does not depend at all on the possibility of devising an administrative procedure under which the optimum might be approxi-

---

lating optimum conditions, the concept of a production unit as distinct from an industry is purely conventional—except in the case of large indivisibilities, it is always possible to conceive of an industry as comprising a large number of very small production units, so that within the scale of operations of this production unit, no variations in output, whether marginal or total, have any significant effect on the prices of factors. If, however, the production units are taken to be large—let us say there is only one production unit in the industry—one more item must be added to the list of causes of a departure from constant costs, the rising supply prices of the factors. Average and marginal costs will diverge on this account even if there are no fixed factors of indivisibilities. But the optimum condition still is as before, that prices equal the marginal costs incurred at *given* factor prices.

These remarks, of course, bear directly on the controversy stirred up by Pigou, concerning the case of increasing supply price. This controversy seems no longer to be active, but it may be advisable to suggest a standpoint on the main issues. First, so far as the nature of the optimum is concerned (this seems to have been one of the questions arising), my view is as above. Second, so far as concerns the question of whether the optimum would be realized under perfect competition (this apparently was the main issue), the logic, as Pigou himself came to recognize, is overwhelmingly in favor of the affirmative as advanced by Young and Knight and against the negative originally advanced by Pigou. Regardless of whether factor prices rise with increasing output in the industry, the relevant marginal cost under perfect competition necessarily is one for which factor prices are given for any one firm. The optimum condition that price equal marginal cost *in this sense* is satisfied. Any divergence that persists in the long run between price and average cost, of course, will be absorbed by rent.

A brief review of the literature in this controversy is presented in Howard S. Ellis and William Fellner, "External Economies and Diseconomies," *American Economic Review*, September 1943.

35 Harold Hotelling, "The General Welfare in Relation to Problems of Taxation and of Railway and Utility Rates," *Econometrica*, July 1938.

36 J. A. Schumpeter, *Capitalism, Socialism, and Democracy*, 2nd ed. (New York, 1947), p. 176, n. 5. Schumpeter should have said that the principle follows from the logic of choice *and* given ends (see below, n. 44).

210

mated in practice. One important question posed by indivisibilities in the latter connection is referred to below pp. 220ff.[37]

The confusion concerning the principle of equating price and marginal cost seems to stem also from a further confusion as to the fiscal implications of the welfare principles. In particular it is often suggested that if losses are not offset by profits elsewhere, the stated principle could not be applied.[38] The optimum conditions that have been outlined, however, are fully consistent with either "profits" or "losses" for the system as a whole. The fiscal counterparts of these "profits" or "losses" are the subsidy and tax that have been mentioned. At least on a theoretic plane, a logically satisfactory fiscal device for financing the losses or disposing of the profits of the socialist economy is always at hand.

In the long run, of course, "fixed factors," too, become variable and mistakes in investments may be rectified. The rule is the same as before: price must equal marginal cost. Now, however, it is "long-run" rather than "short-run" marginal cost that is of concern. Account is to be taken of whatever increment of cost is incurred in producing an increment of output under the condition that the "fixed factors," too, are variable.

[37] Attention may be called here, however, to the article of E. F. M. Durbin, "Economic Calculus in a Planned Economy," *Economic Journal*, December 1936, which raises several practical objections to the Lerner-Hotelling condition; to Lerner's article cited in n. 24 above (*Economic Journal*, June 1937), which disposes of these objections; and finally to the recent article of R. H. Coase, "The Marginal Cost Controversy," *Economica*, August 1946, which again raises practical objections to the Lerner-Hotelling condition.

While Coase accepts the Lerner-Hotelling condition as a valid principle, he argues that in practice it might be desirable to use a multi-part price system, in which consumers are charged one price to cover overhead and another to cover marginal costs. While in the special case he considers (where the overhead actually can be imputed separately to different households) his scheme is unobjectionable, in any more typical case of indivisibility the lump sum tax scheme we have discussed, I believe, would be a preferable means of covering overhead costs.

Incidentally, under socialism this tax might be used without ill effect to offset any important unfavorable effects on income distribution such as Coase argues would result from the charging of prices below costs to some consumers. In the same way, the Board might decide to pay an extra dividend to spaghetti eaters in seasons when the price of spaghetti was abnormally high.

[38] See Durbin, *Economic Journal*, December 1936, p. 685.

211

This is to say that in practice what we have to reckon with is not a unique marginal cost for a given level of output, but a complex of marginal costs, each of which is pertinent to a particular period of time. As a longer period of time is considered, more of the "fixed factors" become variable. Because of this greater flexibility in the production process, long-run marginal cost will generally be less than short-run marginal cost. Lewis discusses in detail the complexities that would be encountered on this account in determining marginal costs in the real world.

In the case of the indivisible production unit, the stated rule has to be reformulated. If the production unit is large, its introduction may affect the structure of prices (marginal rates of substitution) and wages. The optimum conditions listed on pp. 204–206 are all formulated in terms of the prices and wages appropriate to a *given* allocation of resources. In the case of indivisibility, this is no longer possible.[39]

How is it to be decided whether or not to introduce the production unit to begin with? In place of the requirement that price equal marginal cost, one may advance here the more general requirement that the social value yielded must equal the additional social cost. But how is it possible to tell when this condition obtains?

The solution of this problem advanced by Pigou still is generally accepted. This involves the use of the dubious consumers' surplus concept,[40] and so seems methodologically objectionable, but it is hardly likely that subsequent work will overthrow Pigou's important conclusion that it might pay to introduce the production unit even though it were known in advance that losses would be incurred. Lerner presents a systematic exposition of this aspect of the problem of indivisibility.[41]

The general rule, I have said, is that price must equal marginal cost. What if prices are merely proportional to marginal cost?

[39] Cf. Lerner, *Economics of Control*, p. 176: "The indivisibility is significant when it is large enough to destroy perfect competition."

[40] A. C. Pigou, *Economics of Welfare*, 3rd ed. (London, 1929), p. 808. It should be possible to handle this question without using the consumers' surplus concept. Essentially, what is involved is an index number problem, the objective being to compare the community's real income in two different situations with different price structures.

[41] *Economics of Control*, chap. xvi.

212

Would this not suffice? In the face of a good deal of authority for the affirmative, I have argued that the correct answer is in the negative.[42] If prices are proportional but not equal to marginal costs, optimum conditions will be violated. In particular, the differences in value productivity of different types of labor will no longer equal differences in wages, and hence will not correspond to differences in disutility. A reallocation of resources, involving the shift in marginal workers from one occupation to another, would be in order.

THE CONCEPTUAL FRAMEWORK

Before going further, let us try to understand the contribution that the foregoing analysis might make to the solution of the Board's task. As I see it, what has been done is to construct a conceptual framework which might serve two purposes. On the one hand, it in effect poses for the Board a series of questions on ends, that is, on consumers' sovereignty, saving and investment, communal consumption, and income distribution. In this way the analysis might assist the Board to formulate a conceptually satisfactory scale of values to guide the economy, one that is internally consistent and, in principle at least, covers the bill. Insofar as the particular questions posed are such as the Board might be expected to deal intelligently with, this would be all to the good.

On the other hand, the analysis establishes the implications of the given ends. These implications are the optimum conditions. In this way the analysis might assist the Board to allocate resources consistently in accord with the given ends. The establishment of these implications would seem to be a prerequisite for the construction of a planning scheme which might approximate the given ends in practice. It happens that the criteria for the optimum that have been set forth are conceptually simple and, for the cases where small adjustments are possible, require for their application only facts which actually might be experienced in a given situation (the marginal rates of substitution, marginal

[42] See Chapter 8, pp. 186ff, which refers incidentally to the writings of Lerner and Dickinson on this question. Lerner, who is cited as having supported the erroneous view that proportionality is sufficient, has since corrected himself: *Economics of Control*, pp. 100ff.

213

productivities, etc.). For purposes of planning, this too is clearly all to the good.

How useful this particular framework might be, however, would depend on whether the Board would feel that the particular questions posed are the right ones for it to decide, that is, whether in this sense the underlying aim is welfare. A rather different conceptual framework might be needed if the Board's aim were, say, to build up military potential. In this case, it might be necessary at least to pose for the Board a series of questions concerning the amounts of subsidies to be allowed to particular heavy industries. If the Board took a more or less absolutistic view on such matters, it might find these questions also unsuitable: in view of the uncertainties that inevitably would surround any attempt to control output via taxes and subsidies, the Board might wish to fix directly specific goals and priorities for key industries. In the case considered, moreover, the question at issue might not be what was good for the consumers from either their point of view or the Board's, but their efficiency, which need not come to the same thing.

Conceivably, there might not be any one set of questions which was right for any length of time. We have phrased the foregoing discussion as if the decisions on ends were taken by the Board. Whether this is so, or the ends are formulated through democratic political processes, they hardly will reflect ethical considerations alone. Questions of power relations inevitably will obtrude. Probably such questions would be the more important the greater the division of opinion on ends in the community. Under certain circumstances, the Board might be compelled to do a good deal of the work of planning on an *ad hoc* basis.[43] In the light of changing political conditions, the Board might find it expedient to give a higher priority to the manufacture of farm implements on one day and to the production of automobiles on another.

What has been said as to the limitations on the relevance of the ends necessarily applies also to the optimum conditions which are

---

[43] The problems that arise for planning as a result of the existence of divisions on ends are one of the principal grounds for the argument, made familiar by F. A. Hayek, that democracy and planning are incompatible. See his *The Road to Serfdom* (Chicago, 1944), chap. v.

deduced from the ends. Any particular optimum conditions are relevant only in contexts to which the corresponding ends are relevant. Thus the proposition that the marginal value productivity of a factor must be the same in every use—it being understood that values are proportional to the marginal rates of substitution of the individual households—clearly obtains only if the principle of consumers' sovereignty prevails as an end.

Of course, if, as is often the case, the optimum conditions are formulated in more abstract terms, the context in which they are relevant is broadened correspondingly. The condition that the marginal value productivity of a factor must be the same in every use might be formulated without specification of whether the marginal rates of substitution are those of the household or of the Board. This precept for socialist economic calculation is valid, then, no matter whether the principle of consumers' sovereignty prevails or not.[44]

In saying that the analysis outlined in preceding sections poses questions on ends for the Board, we do not mean to imply that the Board would not be interested in the views that the various writers have themselves expressed on these ends. The Board

[44] It still does not follow, however, that this is a universally valid precept, or, what comes to the same thing, that it is, as often supposed, a matter of pure logic. The point is that the derivation of the optimum conditions that are listed on pp. 204-206 requires a set of valuations not yet specified, namely that a shift in any factor from one use to another does not make any difference from the point of view of welfare, except in respect of the resulting difference in the value of output. In other words, a zero social value is assigned to such phenomena as "factory smoke," differences in a worker's attitude toward different industries (as distinct from different occupations), etc. Only in this case is it rational to determine the allocation of any factor simply on the basis of a comparison of the value of output in different uses. The condition of equality of marginal value productivity, far from being universally applicable, applies only where the foregoing values prevail.

The prevalent confusion on this matter seems to have arisen in part from a tendency, for which I believe Robbins is chiefly responsible, to speak of alternative uses of a factor as if they always were alternative *indifferent* uses. Unless there are alternative *indifferent* uses, in the sense that nothing but differences in the value of output counts for welfare, there is no basis at all to speak as Robbins does of "ends" as distinct from "means." Insofar as "factory smoke," etc., have a negative social value, the optimum conditions that have been outlined must be reformulated along the familiar lines marked out by Pigou.

2 1 5

might well be glad to have the advice of economists on the basic question of ends. It might wish to hear also from sociologists, dieticians, psychiatrists, and others. Whether in offering such advice economists are acting in their capacity as *economists* or in some other capacity (which is the issue raised by Robbins[45]) is a question not necessary to debate here.

THE PROBLEM OF ADMINISTRATION

The foregoing analysis in itself provides a conceptual basis for the use of a method of successive approximations to the optimum position, at least to the extent that small adjustments are in order. On the basis of the stated criteria for the optimum allocation of resources it is readily possible to establish whether and in what respects any given allocation deviates from the optimum position. Provided it had at its disposal the necessary facts, the Board might focus attention first on one pair of alternatives and then on another, and, in the light of these criteria, try to distribute any given resources to the best advantage between each pair of alternatives in turn. There is no need even at this stage to suppose, as sometimes is suggested, that the Board would have to solve at one blow "millions of equations."[46]

That there is facing the Board any substantial administrative task is due to several facts. First, the vast stock of detailed knowledge that would be needed to decide on the myriads of alternatives that have to be dealt with is not immediately available to the Board; to the extent that it is available at all, it is scattered throughout the community—and indeed the amount of knowledge actually available will depend on the particular administrative procedure used. Second, even if such knowledge were available to the Board, it would be physically impossible for the Board within any finite period of time to decide successively on all the alternatives to be dealt with. Finally, even if the Board could specify how every sort of resource should be used, the task of controlling the execution of its directive would still remain.

[45] *Nature and Significance of Economic Science*, chap. vi.
[46] L. C. Robbins, *The Great Depression* (London, 1934), p. 151.

2 1 6

It is necessary, then, to devise a planning scheme to approximate the optimum allocation in practice. This must also take into account: the basic limitations on the knowledge and executive capacities of the Board and of any other decision-making units under it, the cost of running the planning scheme itself (some procedures might be too costly to operate), and finally the fact that "means" are also "ends." The choice of administrative procedure (for example, as between rationing and freedom of choice) cannot be made solely from the standpoint of efficiency.

A number of recent writings on socialist economics grapple with this interesting administrative problem, though without always making clear its precise nature. To these writings I now turn.

THE COMPETITION SOLUTION: MAIN FEATURES

The optimum conditions that have been devised for the case of consumers' sovereignty will be familiar to the reader of any elementary textbook on economics. With certain exceptions, they are the same as the equilibrium conditions of "perfect competition" under capitalism. The exceptions are (1) the conditions relating to income distribution and the rate of investment (insofar as this is determined without regard to the time preference of households), and (2) the case of decreasing cost, where, as the textbooks show, competition breaks down.

For well-known reasons revolving partly around the exceptions just stated, this correspondence of the optimum with the competitive equilibrium does not necessarily mean that perfect competition is itself an optimal system. The correspondence is the basis, however, for one much-discussed solution of the question in hand. This is the so-called Competitive Solution.

The correspondence of the optimum and the competitive equilibrium was noted in all the early writings to which we have referred. Indeed, this was one of the main points of Pareto and Barone. However, Pareto and Barone did not follow out this lead. The Competitive Solution is the work of a number of later writers,

217

among whom Taylor, Dickinson, and Lange are the chief contributors.[47]

The essentials of this planning scheme may readily be set forth. Reference is mainly to the very systematic exposition of Lange, and, for the moment, to the case where consumers are sovereign.

(i) All transfers of goods and services among production units and between production units and households are recorded in terms of an accounting unit, all goods being valued at established prices, and services at established wages. Both the prices and wages initially are arbitrary. In the case of transfers of goods and services between households and production units there may be a transfer of "cash."

(ii) Freedom of choice is allowed households in respect of both the work they do and the goods they consume.

(iii) Each production unit is instructed to conduct its operation in accord with two basic rules. For any given scale of output, it must seek to combine the factors of production in such a way as, at the established prices, to minimize the average cost per unit of output. Second, it must seek to fix its output at the point where the established price for its goods equals marginal cost.

(iv) The capital that is required for these purposes is made freely available to the production units at an established rate of interest, which is to be reckoned among the elements in cost.[48]

(v) On the basis of well-known theoretic arguments, it can be shown that, at the established prices, wages, and rate of interest, the aggregate demand for and supply of each and every sort of goods and services on the part of *all* households and production units is determined. There will also be some given demand for capital at the established rate of interest. One of the functions which the Board itself must perform is to adjust prices and wages from time to time in order to bring the demand for and supply of

---

[47] F. M. Taylor, "The Guidance of Production in a Socialist State," *American Economic Review*, March 1929, reprinted in B. Lippincott, ed., *On the Economic Theory of Socialism;* H. D. Dickinson, "Price Formation in a Socialist Economy," *Economic Journal*, December 1933; *idem*, *The Economics of Socialism;* Lange, in *On the Economic Theory of Socialism*. Mention is to be made also of the studies of A. P. Lerner, cited above, n. 24; and of Durbin, *Economic Journal*, December 1936.

[48] See Lange, in *On the Economic Theory of Socialism*, p. 84.

218

goods and services into line. Where the demand for a product exceeds supply (this would be evidenced in the case of goods by a depletion of stocks), the price must be raised; where supply exceeds demand (as evidenced in the case of goods by an accumulation of stocks), the price must be reduced. The Board is also supposed to determine the rate of investment. The rate of interest is fixed so that the aggregate amount of new capital demanded equals the aggregate amount of new investment that the Board wishes to have undertaken. The Board allocates the dividend, and presumably decides on the amount of resources to be devoted to communal consumption.

Under this scheme, then, socialist households, like those in a perfectly competitive capitalist system, are autonomous in respect to the acquisition of consumers' goods and sale of their services. Accordingly, they may be expected to act in agreement with the same principles in these respects as apply under competition. Likewise, under the established administrative rules, the socialist production units are called upon to act in the same way, with respect to the purchase of factors and the determination of output, as enterprises in perfect competition. Under perfect competition each enterprise is such a small element of the market that it has no power over prices and accordingly must take prices as given so far as its own decisions on production are concerned: it seeks to maximize profits at the established prices. Under the established rules, the socialist production unit would tend to do likewise.

This is as far, however, as the analogy goes. Under the Competitive Solution, the Board supplants the capitalist market as the integrator of the decisions of the households and production units. The Board rather than the market adjusts prices to bring supply and demand into line.

Lange considers that the Competitive Solution might be adapted also to the case where the Board undertakes to determine what is good for the households.[49] In this case the Board might introduce a system of taxes and subsidies on consumers' goods, to express the divergencies between its preference scale and those of

[49] *Ibid.*, pp. 90ff.

219

consumers. In other words, there might be a two-price system in the consumers' goods market, one for the purpose of distributing goods to the households and the other, based on the Board's preference scale, to guide production. Freedom of choice would still prevail, even though consumers' sovereignty had been abandoned. Alternatively, freedom of choice might be abandoned also, and consumers' goods rationed and jobs filled by assignment. For the rest, the scheme would be as above.

THE COMPETITIVE SOLUTION: AN APPRAISAL

Assuming that the socialist economic system were administered in accord with the very general principles and procedures outlined, to what extent might an optimum allocation of resources be approximated? For the moment we try only to provide a brief inventory of the more important factors which might have to be considered in forming a judgment on this central question.

Managerial controls and incentives. To begin with, there is the fundamental question of how the success of the managers of the production units is to be tested. Lange does not deal explicitly with this question. Dickinson refers to it briefly.[50]

The obvious test is profits. As Dickinson recognizes, however, this is not an altogether satisfactory criterion. For one thing, there is the case of decreasing cost due to large indivisibilities. If the scale of operations for which price equaled marginal cost were one for which price was below average cost, there would be losses, and the manager would be disinclined to engage in any additional investments, even though they might be socially desirable. The maximization of profits (or minimization of losses) in this case would lead in the long run to the restriction of output below the optimum. If profits were the test of success, managers, in order to succeed, would be compelled to violate the rules. (The case of decreasing cost, then, constitutes an exception to the statement that has been made that under the established rules the socialist like the competitive firm maximizes profits.)

Managers would be tempted to violate the rules also if their production units were large in relation to the market served by

---

[50] *The Economics of Socialism,* pp. 213–219.

220

them. In order to make a large profit they might try to take into account the effects of their actions on the Board's decisions on prices. In this case they might restrict output in much the same way as monopolists do in a capitalist economy. The Competitive Solution might not be so competitive after all.

In such cases, then, there might be no alternative but for the Board to do as Dickinson suggests: to look into the cost records of the individual production units. This, however, would raise an administrative question of some dimensions. If carried to any length, therefore, this practice would be in conflict with an essential aim of the Competitive Solution, to decentralize decision-making.

Hayek[51] seems to argue that in fact the Board would have to look into the cost records of individual firms in any and all circumstances. This will not be a "perfunctory audit," but a full-fledged study to check whether the managers have operated as efficiently as possible. This would seem to exaggerate the difficulties of the problem. Where, for example, profits might be used effectively as a control, probably much could be accomplished by tying incentives to profits and by comparing the profit records of similar firms and of one and the same firm over a period of time. A detailed examination of the costs of each and every firm would not seem to be essential.

Provided the question of controls could be disposed of satisfactorily, the question of managerial incentives probably would not present any serious difficulties. Given the possibility of fixing policy on dismissals on the one hand and on rewards on the other, it should be feasible to establish a climate in which the managers evaluate risks in whatever is considered to be the proper manner. There is no reason to suppose that they would necessarily be too venturesome or, as Hayek argues, too cautious.[52]

Errors in forecasts of managers. Lange refers to his method as a "trial-and-error" method. Dobb[53] considers that an important

[51] "Socialist Calculation: The Competitive Solution," *Economica*, May 1940, p. 141.

[52] *Ibid.*, pp. 141–142.

[53] M. Dobb, "Saving and Investment in a Socialist Economy," *Economic Journal*, December 1939, pp. 726–727.

221

source of error would be the forecasts made by individual managers concerning future market conditions. Even supposing that profits were the test of success, that there were no cases of decreasing costs, and that the managers did not seek to influence prices, they still would have to estimate the prospective behavior of prices. This is necessary for purposes of deciding on investments. Under conditions of perfect competition, managers are supposed to take prices as "given" (parameters) insofar as their own actions are concerned; but they still must form estimates of future market conditions in deciding on investments.

Errors in forecasts presumably would be the greater, the more dynamic the economy. In considering their possible magnitude under socialism, however, account must be taken of the fact that the Central Planning Board might run a comprehensive information service for the benefit of the managers. In supplying this service, the Board would presumably not hesitate to express its own opinion and sentiments on market conditions, in much the same way as central banks of capitalist countries have been doing for the markets they control.

Rigidity; undue standardization; other errors of the Board. Hayek[54] also argues that the Board itself would be unable to cope effectively with its responsibilities. For one thing, it would be impracticable for the Board to adjust prices promptly in accord with the ever-occurring changes in supply and demand. Prices will be adjusted only periodically or from time to time. For a longer or shorter period of time, then, they will not correctly measure the "true" values of alternatives. For another, the Board hardly will be able to fix in detail prices for all the infinite varieties of goods produced in a modern industrial society. Inevitably, there will be a tendency to fix prices only for broad categories of goods, with the result that on this account, also, the prices will not provide an accurate measure of alternatives in particular circumstances.

Both these deficiencies apparently would stem from two limitations on the Board's executive capacities: its limited physical powers, which restrict the number of decisions it might deal with

[54] *Economica*, May 1940, pp. 135–136.

222

effectively, and the limitations on the amount of detailed knowledge of time and place which can be placed at its disposal. Elsewhere[55] Hayek emphasizes this latter limitation. He explains that:

the sort of knowledge with which I have been concerned is knowledge of the kind which by its nature cannot enter into statistics and therefore cannot be conveyed to any central authority in statistical form. The statistics which such a central authority would have to use would have to be arrived at precisely by abstracting from minor differences between things, by lumping together, as resources of one kind, items which differ as regards location, quality, and other particulars, in a way which may be very significant for the specific decision.[56]

These remarks of Hayek's would seem to provide a wholesome antidote to the tendency among many writers on socialism to regard the Central Planning Board as a committee of supermen. In judging how important these limitations might be in practice, however, it must be considered that the Board could set up a more or less elaborate administrative apparatus just for the purpose of fixing prices. The apparatus might be broken down functionally and geographically; it might even have regional offices to take local conditions more fully into account.[57] Presumably the Board would establish general directives to guide its subordinates.

Inequality of income. Lange[58] argues that under his scheme income might be distributed on essentially equalitarian principles. While there would be differentials in wages to accord with differences in marginal value productivity, these differentials would correspond at the same time to differences in disutility. If the dividend itself were, say, equal for all households, then aside from differences in well-being due to personal variations in need, all households would in reality be equally well off. It is understood that education and training would be free for all.

[55] "The Use of Knowledge in Society," *American Economic Review*, September 1945.
[56] *Ibid.*, p. 524.
[57] This, of course, is what is actually done in the Soviet Union.
[58] In *On the Economic Theory of Socialism*, pp. 100–103.

223

Lange recognizes that this would not be so in the case of persons with unusual natural talents (artists, musicians, etc.). For these persons, payment on the basis of value productivity might lead to differences in income all out of proportion to differences in disutility. These exceptions might be more numerous than is commonly assumed—for example, what of the personnel in high-level jobs in the bureaucracy? But Lange observes correctly that in such cases a high tax might be levied without any adverse effect on the supply of these services. There would be no conflict (such as was noted above) with the principle of consumers' sovereignty.

Disparities of this sort, however, might be widespread purely as a result of dynamic factors. Workers in occupations where there is short supply might for protracted periods receive a "rent" over and above what is required to attract them into these occupations. If freedom of choice prevails, it would be out of the question to extract this rent by taxation devices. Also, as we have already observed, the equation of disutilities and value productivities holds strictly only for persons on the margin of choice between occupations. Depending on their preferences, intra-marginal workers would likewise receive a rent, which it probably would be administratively impractical to extract if freedom of choice prevailed. Thus, given freedom of choice, the departures from egalitarian principles might be much greater and more numerous than Lange envisages.

Instability; unemployment. Dobb[59] raises and answers the question as to whether under the Competitive Solution there might be any high degree of instability and large-scale unemployment of resources. He observes that a reduction in the rate of interest designed to encourage investment on the part of managers of firms might lead to a cycle of expansion and contraction: as the investments take place, there is an expansion in purchasing power, the prices for consumers' goods rise, there is a secondary increase in the demand for capital, and so on. An attempt to put an end to this process by increasing the rate of interest might lead to a cumulative movement in the opposite direction, resulting in unemployment. Dobb recognizes, however, that the Board would be able to control the volume of purchasing power directly

[59] *Economic Journal*, December 1939.

through its fiscal powers. The Board presumably would plan its policy on taxes and dividends to assure as far as possible that the volume of purchasing power in the hands of consumers was just sufficient to buy at prices covering marginal costs the volume of consumers' goods it was desirable to produce.

Errors certainly would be made here as elsewhere in the operation of the Competitive Solution. Whether these errors would be so serious as to constitute a telling point against the Competitive Solution, as Dobb implies,[60] is open to question.

Referring to socialism in general and not to any particular planning scheme, Wright[61] argues that there might be cyclic disturbances because of a tendency to overbuild the durable-goods industries. The capacity required to build up stocks of durable goods might exceed that required to maintain these stocks after they were built up. Insofar as the conclusion is that at one time or another there might be excess capacity in one or another durable goods industry, there can be no dissent from this argument. It is difficult to see, however, why this necessarily entails "waste" in any economic sense, as Wright implies. If the capacity is built up with a full knowledge of the implications, including the fact that at some future date it will be excessive, then presumably this represents an optimum use of the resources in question: the "value" of the capacity would be fully written off by the time it is released. Furthermore, it is not at all clear why the release of capacity in different industries should tend to occur merely simultaneously and thus engender a general cycle. The release of excess capacity in one industry or another might be entirely consistent with a balanced and even development of the economy as a whole. Finally, the workers released from one or another durable-goods industry would be unemployed only during the time needed to retrain them for employment elsewhere. For this reason it is difficult to see why there should be mass unemployment which Wright would expect.

Transition problems. Lange[62] seems to argue that the Competitive Solution would work not only in an established socialist society but also in the period of transition. The proviso is made

---

[60] *Ibid.*, pp. 723–726.
[61] D. M. Wright, *The Economics of Disturbance* (New York, 1947), chap. vi.
[62] *On the Economic Theory of Socialism*, pp. 121ff.

225

that the private sector of the economy must be small, that competition must reign in it, and that small-scale production must not in the long run be more expensive than large-scale production. This last condition is presumably to assure that the private small-scale enterprise can survive; why this is desirable or necessary under socialism, however, is not clear. Lange hints that political and other factors might also raise special problems for planning in the transition period.

In a more adequate treatment of this very important question, I suspect that the difficulties in applying the Competitive Solution would loom a good deal larger than Lange implies. For one thing, insofar as, in the years following the transfer of power, political considerations might have an overwhelming importance, the usefulness of the conceptual framework that has been outlined (and by the same token the usefulness of the Competitive Solution) might be seriously impaired. The reasons for this have already been stated. For another, there is the important question of the loyalty of old—and the efficiency of new—managerial personnel, which would have to be taken into account in deciding on the responsibilities to be delegated to them. This would presumably be a pressing problem in the transition period.

Schumpeter[63] argues that the political problems of transition would be more or less difficult according to whether the capitalist society from which socialism emerges is in an early or late stage of development. Thus, it is said that in a late stage of capitalist development resistance is likely to be weak and the revolution might be accomplished in an orderly manner. If we may judge from the Soviet experience, however, a most favorable moment for the socialist revolution is at an early stage of capitalist development, when the middle class still is weak and the proletariat has not yet tasted the fruits of capitalism.

But in this case, if the Soviet experience serves at all, there would be pressing economic as well as political problems to deal with after the seizure of power, and it is easy to see that on account of problems of both sorts there might be very real difficulties in the way of applying the trial-and-error Competitive

[63] *Capitalism, Socialism, and Democracy,* chap. xix.

226

Solution. Consider only the matter of high-tempo industrialization, and the rapid shifts in demand and production schedules that would be associated with this process. In such a situation, the errors involved in the operation of the Competitive Solution might well be formidable; and evidently experience could not be very helpful in rectifying them. Whether there is any alternative planning procedure that might work more effectively in such circumstances is a question that has to be considered.

In referring to the foregoing considerations under the heading of transition problems, it is not implied that there ever would be a period in which they would be entirely absent, or, at any rate, that there ever would be such a period short of the era of unlimited abundance. Lange is not explicit on this matter.

AN ALTERNATIVE APPROACH TO
SOCIALIST PLANNING

We must now consider the special case of "fixed coefficients" dealt with by Pareto and Barone: for technical reasons and regardless of their relative values, the different factors must be employed in amounts that bear a constant relationship to output.[64] In this case there is no basis for speaking of the marginal productivity of any one factor. It is necessary to formulate the analysis of the optimum conditions, as Pareto and Barone originally did, in terms of the fixed coefficients and without the use of the marginal productivity concept. With fixed coefficients, as in the case where the coefficients are variable, a scale of values is needed to decide on optimum output and the distribution of income; it turns out, however, that, for the rest, the allocation of resources is entirely a technical question.

It is easy to see that, if this case obtained, the practical work of planning might be simplified considerably. Lange[65] says that

[64] "Fixed coefficients" is itself a special case of the genus "limitational factors." Lange (*On the Economic Theory of Socialism*, p. 67, n .15; p. 94, n. 46), distinguishes two types of limitational factors, according to whether the amount of the limitational factor that must be employed is a function of output or of the amount of another factor employed. If all factors are limitational in the first sense, we have the case of fixed coefficients.

[65] *Ibid.*, p. 94, n. 46.

227

here "no prices and no cost accounting whatever are needed" in allocating resources. All is decided by considerations of technical efficiency. This is true only if, as Lange assumes, the demand for consumers' goods is in the form of fixed quotas. If demand is variable, prices and costs still would have to be taken into account in the allocation of resources among different consumers' goods industries. There would be no need, however, to rearrange production methods in the different industries in response to each and every change in the relative scarcities of the different factors of production.

If the Competitive Solution were in operation in this case, the managers of the individual production units would not have to change their production methods in response to changes in the price structure. On this account it might seem that the process of trial and error would be shortened appreciably. So far as the Competitive Solution is concerned, however, this case has an important adverse feature. If the coefficients are fixed, marginal and average costs are constant. The administrative rules established by Lange no longer provide a definite basis for managerial decisions. If prices were above marginal costs, for example, the managers would know that they should expand, but would be quite in the dark as to how much. The possibility is still open that by the manipulation of prices the Board could assure that the total output of the industry was brought in line with demand; there might be a "neutral" equilibrium such as it is supposed might be attained under capitalist perfect competition in the case of constant costs. But there would be no satisfactory basis for moving toward the equilibrium by successive approximations. As a result, the trial-and-error process might turn out to be very protracted, despite the simplification of the work of choosing between different production methods.

I turn to an alternative planning scheme which seems to be inspired in part by emphasis on this case of fixed coefficients.

The alternative planning procedure, which may be referred to as the Centralist Scheme, has been sketched only in very general terms. Under the Competitive Solution the operations of individual production units and households are integrated through a market process. Under the Centralist Scheme it is proposed that, to a greater or lesser extent, these operations be integrated

228

directly by the Board. The managers of individual production units, it is supposed, will submit to the Board the data required for this purpose. Under this scheme the process of trial and error takes place on paper rather than in the market place.

A planning scheme of this sort is suggested by Dickinson, who presents it merely as a possibly practical alternative to the Competitive Solution.[66] Dobb, however, advocates it as a preferable procedure.[67] It is in Dobb's writings that the case of fixed coefficients seems to be linked with the Centralist Scheme. Dobb emphasizes the importance of technological factors in the determination of the optimum allocation.[68]

The advocates of the Centralist Scheme, no doubt, have drawn their inspiration partly from the Soviet planning procedure, the distinguishing feature of which is a comprehensive plan that purportedly integrates the whole economy. This integration is accomplished by the so-called "Method of Balanced Estimates," by which the planned requirements of different commodities and services are checked against planned supplies.[69] Soviet economists have published very little in a theoretic vein concerning their planning system[70]—perhaps because they are too much preoccupied with practical work. From scattered writings, however, one gains the impression that they emphasize the importance of technological factors in resource allocation, and that this emphasis plays a part in their thinking about planning procedures.

It is not surprising, then, that another well-known feature of the Soviet economic system is incorporated in Dobb's program. Dobb contemplates that there might be numerous cases where the Board would overrule consumers' preferences.[71] This seems to be

---

[66] *The Economics of Socialism*, pp. 104–105. Dickinson's position on this scheme in this book seems to represent a retreat from the rather positive views he expressed earlier in *Economic Journal*, December 1933.

[67] M. Dobb, *Economic Journal*, December 1933; "A Reply," *Review of Economic Studies*, February 1935; *Economic Journal*, December 1939; *Political Economy and Capitalism*, chap. viii.

[68] See especially *Political Economy and Capitalism*, pp. 331ff.

[69] For a brief description of this procedure, see Alexander Baykov, *The Development of the Soviet Economic System* (Cambridge, Eng., 1946), chap. xx.

[70] For references to some of the Soviet sources on planning, see *ibid.*

[71] *Economic Journal*, December 1933, pp. 591ff.; *Political Economy and Capitalism*, pp. 309ff.

229

a prevailing practice in the USSR. It should be observed, however, that the Centralist Scheme itself is not tied logically to a system in which consumers' preferences are overruled or indeed tied to any particular ends. Dickinson has in mind a system designed to satisfy the demands of consumers as they see them.

The main objection to the Centralist Scheme is that it imposes an impossible administrative burden on the Board. Large-scale waste, it has been said, is inevitable if planning is on this basis. We find ourselves again confronted with the problem of solving "millions of equations."

In general, much weight would seem to attach to this objection; but the difficulties clearly are reduced in the case of fixed coefficients. Here relative prices do not make any difference for much of the work of planning. It is not necessary to suppose that the case holds strictly. To whatever extent it is approached, any technologically feasible allocation will, to that extent, approach the optimum.

So far as the Centralist Scheme is feasible, the choice between it and the Competitive Solution presumably would revolve about the nature of the ends sought and the stage of political, social, and economic development that has been reached. One might imagine, for example, that in a highly dynamic economy a Centralist allocation of investment might lead to fewer and smaller errors than a Competitive allocation. While under the Centralist Scheme the Board might err, there would seem to be a better prospect of meeting the requirements of technical consistency with respect to complementary industries. If technical rigidities are present, the chances are diminished that under the Competitive Solution the errors of individual firms would cancel out.[72] In other words, the Centralist Scheme might be able to deal more effectively than the Competitive Solution with the problem of bottlenecks and excess capacity.

To what extent does the case of fixed coefficients hold in a modern industrial society? Lange considers it to be very exceptional.[73] This is probably the view also of most "orthodox"

[72] This point was suggested to me by A. Erlich, with whom I have had many profitable discussions.
[73] In *On the Economic Theory of Socialism*, p. 94, n. 46.

economists. Lange seems to refer, however, only to situations where the case holds strictly. Clearly, it is a matter of very great interest how closely it is approximated: the more nearly it is approached, the more limited is the range within which price calculations matter. On the basis of numerous recent cost studies, [74] it would appear that, for a considerable range of short-run output variations, marginal costs for the individual firm tend to be constant. This suggests that at least in the short run the proportions are indeed fixed between labor and other variable elements in marginal costs. Mention should also be made of Leontief's study of the structure of the American economy. [75] Leontief found it practicable to assume that for broad industrial groups the production coefficients are constant. The prevailing preconception on this whole question may have to be revised as more empirical data become available.

The degree of emphasis on technological as compared with economic factors in resource allocation, by the way, might be one basis for a distinction which is now somewhat difficult to make, between the "orthodox" and "Marxian" theory of planning.

There is no need here to go into the question of the validity of the labor theory of value as a basis for socialist calculation. Mises[76] has shown clearly enough its deficiencies in this respect. What is to be noted is that there now appears to be a diversity of opinion even in Marxian circles as to the applicability of the labor theory to socialism. Indeed, it is difficult to find in any quarter unqualified support for the labor theory in this connection.

Dunayevskaya[77] and Sweezy consider that the labor theory of value does not and was not intended by Marx to apply to social-

---

[74] See the very careful evaluation of these studies issued by the Committee on Price Determination (E. S. Mason, Chairman) of the National Bureau of Economic Research, *Cost Behaviour and Price Policy* (New York, 1943), chap. v.

[75] W. Leontief, *The Structure of the American Economy, 1919–1929* (Cambridge, Mass., 1941).

[76] In Hayek, ed., *Collectivist Economic Planning*, pp. 112ff.

[77] R. Dunayevskaya, "A New Revision of Marxian Economics," *American Economic Review*, September 1944. In this article Miss Dunayevskaya comments on the much-discussed Soviet article "Some Problems in the Teaching of Political Economy," *Pod Znamenem Marksizma* (*Under the Banner of Marxism*), no. 7–8, July-August 1943. A translation of this

231

ism. On the question of what theory of value does apply, Sweezy
has taken in turn two different positions. At one time, he argued
that orthodox economics holds under socialism: "Marxian economics is essentially the economics of capitalism, while 'capitalist' economics is in a very real sense the economics of socialism."[78]
More recently, he seems to have taken the position that orthodox
economics does not apply either; he now advances in its place the
"principle of planning."[79] The nature of this principle is not
explained. Presumably the Board is to work out the logic of
choice on its own.

Dobb[80] is also difficult to classify. On the one hand, he makes
free use of orthodox value theory in the analysis of socialist
resource allocation. On the other, he seems to be unwilling to
accept the necessary implication that rent and interest must
appear as accounting categories in socialist calculation.[81] By a
well-known and very awkward adjustment for differences in the
organic composition of capital, Dobb formulates optimum conditions in terms of the labor theory.[82] It is difficult to avoid the
conclusion that in Dobb's analysis the labor theory is not so much
an analytic tool as excess baggage.

According to a recent Soviet article already cited,[83] the labor
theory of value continues to operate under socialism. As the
article explains, this represents a change in position from the view
formerly held in the USSR, according to which the labor theory
referred only to capitalism. In judging the portent of this doctri-

---

article appears in the *American Economic Review*, September 1944.
See also the comments on the article by C. Landauer, "From Marx to
Menger," *American Economic Review*, June 1944; P. A. Baran, "New
Trends in Russian Economic Thinking?" *American Economic Review*,
December 1944; O. Lange, "Marxian Economics in the Soviet Union,"
American Economic Review, March 1945; R. Dunayevskaya, "A Re-
joinder," *American Economic Review*, September 1945.

[78] P. M. Sweezy, "Economics and the Crisis of Capitalism," *Economic
Forum*, Spring 1935, p. 79.

[79] P. M. Sweezy, *The Theory of Capitalist Development* (New York, 1942),
pp. 52–54.

[80] See above, n. 67.

[81] See especially *Political Economy and Capitalism*, pp. 308–309, 326ff.

[82] *Ibid.*

[83] See above, n. 77.

nal change, however, account must be taken of the fact that here, as in so many spheres of the Soviet system, there seems to be a wide gap between theory and practice. The existence of such a gap is acknowledged in the article; it is explained that "the prices of commodities are set with certain deviations from their values, corresponding to the particular objectives of the Soviet state, and the quantity of commodities of various kinds which can be sold under the existing scale of production and the needs of society."

THE DEBATE

To come finally to Mises, there are two questions to ask: What does he say and what does he mean?

On the first question we must let Mises speak for himself:

And as soon as one gives up the conception of a freely established monetary price for goods of a higher order, rational production becomes completely impossible. Every step that takes us away from private ownership of the means of production also takes us away from rational economics . . .

The administration [of the socialist state] may know exactly what goods are most urgently needed. But in so doing, it has only found what is, in fact, but one of the two necessary prerequisites for economic calculation. In the nature of the case, however, it must dispense with the other—the valuation of the means of production . . .

Where there is no free market there is no pricing mechanism; without a pricing mechanism, there is no economic calculation . . . Exchange relations between production goods can only be established on the basis of private ownership of the means of production.[84]

As to what Mises means, there appear to be two views. According to that which seems to have gained the wider currency, Mises' contention is that without private ownership of, or (what comes to the same thing for Mises) a free market for, the means of production, the rational evaluation of these goods for the purposes of calculating costs is ruled out conceptually. With it goes any rational economic calculation. To put the matter somewhat

[84] Mises, in Hayek, ed., *Collectivist Economic Planning*, pp. 104–111. Essentially the same argument is repeated in Mises, *Socialism* (London, 1936).

233

more sharply than is customary, let us imagine a Board of Supermen, with unlimited logical faculties, with a complete scale of values for the different consumers' goods and present and future consumption, and detailed knowledge of production techniques. Even such a Board would be unable to evaluate rationally the means of production. In the absence of a free market for these goods, decisions on resource allocation in Mises' view necessarily would be on a haphazard basis.

Interpreted in this way, the argument is easily disposed of. Lange[85] and Schumpeter,[86] who favor this interpretation of Mises, point out correctly that the theory is refuted by the work of Pareto and Barone. As the analysis of these writers shows, once tastes and techniques are given, the values of the means of production can be determined unambiguously by imputation without the intervention of a market process. The Board of Supermen could decide readily how to allocate resources so as to assure the optimum welfare. It would simply have to solve the equations of Pareto and Barone.

According to the other interpretation of Mises, which has the authority of Hayek,[87] the contention is not that rational calculation is logically inconceivable under socialism but that there is no practicable way of realizing it. Imputation is theoretically possible; but, once private ownership of the means of production has been liquidated, it cannot be accomplished in practice.

Hayek's own thinking,[88] and that of Robbins,[89] seems to be along these lines. Lange, who interprets the views of Hayek and Robbins as being in reality a retreat from the original position of Mises, considers that his own analysis refutes their argument: "As we have seen, there is not the slightest reason why a trial and error procedure, similar to that in a competitive market, could not work in a socialist economy to determine the accounting prices of capital goods and of the productive resources in public owner-

---

[85] *On the Economic Theory of Socialism,* pp. 51ff.

[86] *Capitalism, Socialism, and Democracy,* chap. xvi.

[87] *Economica,* May 1940, pp. 126–127.

[88] "The Present State of the Debate," chap. v, in Hayek, ed., *Collectivist Economic Planning;* "Socialist Calculation: The Competitive Solution," *Economica,* May 1840; "The Use of Knowledge in Society," *American Economic Review,* September 1945.

[89] *The Great Depression,* p. 151.

234

ship."[90] Hayek apparently is not entirely convinced: "Whether the solution offered will appear particularly practicable, even to socialists, may perhaps be doubted."[91]

Which of these two interpretations of Mises is correct, I leave to the reader to decide. The issue between Hayek and Robbins on the one hand and Lange on the other, however, calls for further consideration.

Operationally, how is it possible to tell whether any given planning scheme is "practicable" or not? Here again, it seems necessary to deal with two different views.

According to one, expressed most clearly by Schumpeter,[92] the question is not how well or ill socialism can function, but whether a planning scheme can be devised such that it can work at all. If there is no "practicable" basis for rational calculation, the economy presumably would break down. The symptoms would be waste on a vast scale and even chaos.

If this is the test of practicability, there hardly can be any room for debate: of course, socialism can work. On this, Lange certainly is convincing. If this is the sole issue, however, one wonders whether at this stage such an elaborate theoretic demonstration is in order. After all, the Soviet planned economy has been operating for thirty years. Whatever else may be said of it, it has not broken down.

According to Hayek, the test is this:

It was not the possibility of planning as such which has been questioned, but the possibility of successful planning . . . There is no reason to expect that production would stop, or that the authorities would find difficulty in using all the available resources somehow, or even that output would be permanently lower than it had been before planning started. What we should anticipate is that output, where the use of the available resources was determined by some central authority, would be lower than if the price mechanism of a market operated freely under otherwise similar circumstances."[93]

In familiar terms, the question for Hayek is: Which is more efficient, socialism or capitalism? This, of course, is the question

[90] Lange, in *On the Economic Theory of Socialism*, p. 89.
[91] *Economica*, May 1940, p. 149.
[92] *Capitalism, Socialism, and Democracy*, p. 185.
[93] *Collectivist Economic Planning*, pp. 203–204.

235

all participants in the debate eventually come to face anyhow. As I see it, it is now the only issue outstanding. The discussion in preceding sections, it is hoped, will provide a partial basis for judgment on this important matter. For the rest, with the following few cautions, I leave this issue, too, for the reader to decide. [94]

First, in order to reach any conclusion on comparative efficiency, it is necessary to agree on the test of efficiency, that is, on the ends according to which the optimum allocation of resources is to be defined. A comparison of the total market value of the consumers' goods produced in the rival systems, such as Schumpeter proposes, [95] already implies the acceptance of the principle of consumers' sovereignty. It is necessary to decide, too, whether the egalitarian principle of distribution is one of the ends, whether consumers are to be sovereign in respect of decisions on investment, and so on.

Second, one must distinguish between blueprints of economic systems operating in hypothetical worlds and rival economic systems in the real world. There seems to be very little point, for example, in a comparison of perfect competition in a capitalist world that never existed with socialism in Russia; or, alternatively, of the Competitive Solution in an established socialist state where there is a unanimity on ends with monopolistic and unstable capitalism in the United States. We must compare ideals with ideals or facts with facts. Participants in both sides of the debate have erred in failing to observe this elementary rule.

Finally, it is necessary to bear in mind that in the real world the question of comparative efficiency cannot be divorced altogether from questions of politics. In this connection it suffices only to allude to the matter of working-class cooperation and discipline, which Schumpeter [96] rightly emphasizes, and the question of social stratification in relation to the problem of assuring the effective use of natural talents.

[94] In addition to the studies already cited, mention must be made of the very balanced study of A. C. Pigou, *Socialism versus Capitalism* (London, 1944).
[95] *Capitalism, Socialism, and Democracy*, pp. 189-190.
[96] *Ibid.*, pp. 210ff.

2 3 6

Reprinted from THE JOURNAL OF POLITICAL ECONOMY
Vol. 75, No. 5, October 1967
Copyright 1967 by The University of Chicago
Printed in U.S.A.

MARKET SOCIALISM REVISITED

ABRAM BERGSON*
Harvard University

IN THE sphere of socialist planning, this is manifestly the era of reform. The era in a sense began in the early fifties when for the first time a socialist country abandoned, for a relatively decentralized system incorporating many market-type institutions, the notably centralized and bureaucratic working arrangements that had previously been virtually sacrosanct in the socialist world. But this was for long an isolated case, and reform has now become almost the rule. While working arrangements in Yugoslavia, the venturesome country just referred to, apparently are continuing to evolve in the direction already taken, other socialist states by all accounts are also veering from "centralized planning" toward "market socialism," though probably not always as sharply

* I am most grateful to Professor Herbert A. Simon for a searching review of an earlier version, and have also benefited from comments by Professor Samuel S. Bowles and a number of other colleagues. Needless to say, however, responsibility for the views expressed is my own. A preliminary draft served as the basis of a brief talk in a session on "Convergence" that was jointly sponsored by the American Economic Association and Comparative Economics Association, December, 1966.

as has been reported. Even the U.S.S.R., the country that pioneered the earlier system, is not untouched by the strange new winds. Why are such changes being made? Will the trend toward market socialism persist? What of the possibility of further and even more basic changes in the future?

While posing these intriguing questions, for the economist recent events serve no less to draw attention to an issue long familiar in theory: the economic efficiency of market socialism. This question is also logically prior to the more topical ones just raised. Thus, in experimenting with novel working arrangements, those ultimately responsible for economic policy in the socialist world are clearly seeking greater efficiency. They are doing so with increased understanding of this desideratum and a greater willingness than they had hitherto manifested to subordinate to it conflicting concerns for ideology and politics. Though a more speculative matter than some suppose, the future evolution of socialist planning should turn in part on how efficient market socialism proves to be.

On an abstract plane, the economic

efficiency of market socialism came to the fore especially in the great theoretic debate on socialist economic rationality that was waged during the interwar period. I myself surveyed the pertinent literature in an essay first published in 1948.[1] A brief review, however, will permit me to take account of further theoretic analyses and also of further thoughts on a topic which is now increasingly important.

THE COMPETITIVE SOLUTION

As understood here, the market variety of socialism differs from that where centralized planning prevails chiefly in regard to working arrangements for determining inputs and outputs of production units. Thus, under centralized planning such inputs and outputs typically are controlled to a marked degree by superior agencies in a bureaucratic structure through use of extra-market devices, such as physical quotas. Under market socialism, determination of factor inputs and outputs typically is left to authorities immediately in charge of production units, though superior agencies may still exercise much influence through manipulation of prices and other financial instruments.

As so understood, market socialism might take very diverse forms, but in the theoretic debate on socialist economic rationality attention has been focused particularly on one of them. Moreover, while the famous Competitive Solution is notably abstract, for purposes of theoretic analysis it has the great merit that it has been elaborated relatively fully. Also, wherever appropriate it is not difficult to explore variants. In reviewing the possible efficiency of market socialism, therefore, we can do no better, I think,

than to turn again, at least initially, to the Competitive Solution.

This planning scheme is chiefly the work of the late Oskar Lange. I shall refer especially to the construction he gave to it, though it will sometimes be of interest to refer also to the work of another principal architect, H. D. Dickinson.[2] Let us recall the bare essentials: In an economy which is still pecuniary, in the sense that transfers of goods and services between agencies and persons take place at established prices, households are allowed freedom of choice in respect of the work they do and the consumers' goods they purchase with their resultant earnings.

Managers of socialist plants and industries—the former responsible primarily for current operations, the latter for larger investments, especially introduction of new plants—are allowed similarly to determine autonomously inputs of factors and corresponding outputs. In the process, however, each is supposed to observe two rules: (1) to combine factors in such a way as to assure that at the prices established for such inputs any given output is produced at a minimum cost, and (2) to fix the scale of output of any commodity produced at a point where its marginal cost equals the corresponding price.

While thus treated as "parameters" by managers as well as households, prices are fixed by the Central Planning Board (CPB). Through a trial-and-error process, the Board endeavors to adjust prices so as to assure that, for each good, supply and demand correspond. The CPB also decides on the volume of investment and fixes the rate of interest so that the requirements for new capital on the part of

[1] Bergson, 1948; to be cited hereafter as reprinted in Bergson, 1966.

[2] See Lange, 1938; Dickinson, 1939; Bergson, 1966, pp. 217 ff., and other writings cited in the latter.

managers of enterprises and industries correspond to the supply which it wishes to make available. The CPB also allocates a tax or dividend among households. In total, this corresponds to the difference between, on the one hand, the volume of investment (as this exceeds any voluntary savings) and outlays for government administration and other goods distributed communally without charge; and on the other, the sum of profits earned by enterprises, and interest and rental charges paid by them.

Except regarding investment, the system supposedly is responsive to consumers' demand. But, if for some consumers' goods the Board should wish to substitute its own preferences for those of households, it might do so simply by maintaining two prices for each such commodity, one to guide production and the other to guide their disposition to households.

THE PROBLEM OF A SUCCESS CRITERION

How efficient might the Competitive Solution be? Income distribution apart, equilibrium under the Competitive Solution is supposed generally to correspond to that under capitalist "perfect competition," and this, of course, does tend to conform to an optimum use of resources representing perfect efficiency. While such an equilibrium hardly is fully attainable anywhere in fact, proponents of the Competitive Solution consider that it might be approached relatively closely under this scheme. Moreover, externalities which would give rise to inefficiency even in the equilibrium of capitalist perfect competition, it is held, might readily be allowed for in an appropriate manner, while income distribution too can be expected to be relatively equitable. In sum, diverse sources of waste that are familiar under capitalism in the real world are largely, if not entirely, absent, and other sources that might come to prevail under socialism should not be very consequential.

In trying to judge how valid this reasoning is, we must consider that Lange nowhere provided any criterion for judging and rewarding managerial success. The rules themselves, it is true, might be viewed as such a criterion, but in order to gauge and reward success on this basis the CPB would have to probe deeply into the cost and other internal records of individual production units. This would vastly increase the CPB's responsibilities, which it is a cardinal concern of the Competitive Solution to limit. The failure to establish any practical success criterion for managers, it was held previously (Bergson, 1966, pp. 220 ff.), represents a major deficiency of the Competitive Solution and one not easily repaired. And this I still feel is a valid criticism, but the deficiency now seems, if anything, more serious than before.

To begin with, the obvious test for success is profits, and use of this standard no doubt would often induce the manager to do what is desired of him. But he might often be led to behave otherwise. Thus, if the manager seeks to maximize profits he would, of course, tend to conform to the rules provided he also behaves competitively and takes prices as data. But he might not view prices in this way whenever his production unit is large in relation to the market supplied. In such a case the individual manager might be able, through his decisions on output, to influence the CPB's decisions on prices and so find it more profitable to violate than to observe the rules. Rather than behave competitively, the manager would be led to restrict output much as a monopolist does under capitalism.

Hence, the Board, in order to assure conformity to the rules, might often have to examine internal records of production units after all.

So much was argued before, but—and this was not sufficiently taken into consideration—a test for success presumably is needed for the manager not only of a plant but also of an industry. For the latter reference to profits manifestly would be the more dubious. Thus, the manager of an industry would always have monopoly power, and if profits were the test of this success monopolistic violation of the rules might be very marked. It is sometimes suggested, however, that as he ascends a bureaucratic structure an executive tends to identify more with those at the highest level. If this is so, perhaps the manager of an industry could be counted on, to a greater degree than the manager of a plant, to conform to the rules without their being buttressed by a further success criterion. Otherwise, however, occasions where the Board would have to probe into the internal records of production units would be numerous indeed.[3]

To return to the plant manager, even if his output were not relatively large in any conventional sense, should profits be the test of success he would still be tempted to violate the rules provided either his suppliers or his customers for any reason remained more or less attached to him, even though prices were in some degree differentiated accordingly. As is rarely considered, even under socialism this must often be so. Customers who have become familiar with one plant's products, for example, might

often be reluctant to shift to another plant's products of inferior quality, even at a reduced price. Given such an attitude, it would be still more difficult to assure conformity to the rules.

Under a planning scheme such as is in question, Dickinson (1939, pp. 213–19) acknowledged that profits could not always serve as an appropriate standard for appraising and rewarding managerial success. But the alternatives he proposes, including cost reduction and output increases, clearly would also have their limitations.

Given a satisfactory test of success, managerial incentives must still be related to it appropriately. Hayek argued[4] that such a result might not be easy to achieve. In practice, managers very likely would be reluctant to take risks. This is perhaps not inevitable, but the construction of a satisfactory incentive system now appears more difficult than I envisaged it to be previously.

Suppose that profits could be taken as the test of success. Even so, the manager is properly rewarded not for profits earned but for such earnings as are attributed to his own exertions. To arrange this can never be easy wherever ownership is divorced from management, but it could be more difficult where prices are fixed not by impersonal market forces but by a CPB. Even if the manager has no monopoly power, he must, in determining investment, estimate future prices just as the competitive firm does in a capitalist market. And like the latter he must often err, but with prices fixed by the Board rather than by the market, responsibility for such error might easily become controversial.[5] Attribution of earnings to one or another manager must be further complicated when, as in the

[3] Lange (1938, p. 81) was aware that managers might influence prices by their decisions on output but apparently felt that the CPB could compel the managers to treat prices as parameters by imposing such prices as an "accounting rule." How this would impel the managers to ignore their influence was not explained.

[4] Hayek, 1940, as reprinted in Hayek, 1948, p. 199. See also Bergson, 1966, p. 221.

[5] Compare Hayek, 1948, pp. 197–98, and *infra*.

Competitive Solution, one manager introduces and another operates a new plant.[6]

The difficulties regarding the managerial success criterion that have been described must arise even if there should be no "indivisibilities" in production, but they would be compounded if such indivisibilities are present. This is by now

large overhead costs that could result, observation of Rule 2, which requires current output to be at the level where price equals marginal costs, may mean losses (see Fig. 1, where output would have to be at X'). For this reason, it might be especially difficult to establish a suitable managerial success criterion to assure conformity to Rule 2, but the rule itself could still be applied meaningfully.

Where plant capacity itself is to be varied, however, this is no longer so. Not

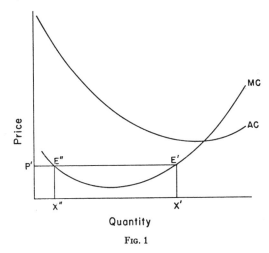

FIG. 1

familiar, but as was not made very clear in my earlier essay and perhaps is still not always understood, the further difficulties arising in the exploitation of an indivisible resource differ from those arising in its introduction. Suppose, for example, that plant capacity generally is subject to indivisibilities. Because of the

only does the variation in capacity affect price, but the effect must be considered in appraising the expansion in question. In place of Rule 2, therefore, reference must now be made to "consumers' surplus," where account is taken of the effect of the manager's decision on prices. Also, conformity to the consumers' surplus standard could not be assured through profit maximization, so use of profits as a success criterion is precluded.[7]

[6] In the Competitive Solution, profits are supposed to tend to zero, and if profits were the test of success this might be felt to be discouraging to managers but differential earnings due to differences in managerial talent presumably would persist even in the long run. Assuming such earnings could be identified and paid to the managers responsible for them, they would become wages of management. The tendency of profits otherwise to zero, therefore, should raise no further difficulty at this point.

[7] To return to the determination of the level of operation of the plant, in Fig. 1 price equals marginal cost at two levels of output rather than one, but it was tacitly assumed above that the larger output, X', would be the one sought. Unless the industry

While, as indicated, the Competitive Solution supposedly facilitates dealing with externalities generally, Lange (1938, pp. 77, 105) felt it was especially advantageous regarding external economies and diseconomies of scale of production, that is, external economies and diseconomies that are internal to the industry. In fixing output at the point where price equals marginal cost, the manager of the plant apparently considers only the costs he incurs when his output varies, but the manager of the industry is supposed to consider costs incurred by the indus-

try. Hence, gains and losses which accrue to other plants due to the actions of any one of them are taken into account "automatically."

Externalities such as are in question, however, may give rise to decreasing costs for the industry, and as Hansen (n.d., p. 179) reminds us, here too profit maximization is inappropriate. And even if the manager (in this case, of an industry rather than a plant) could be counted on to observe Rule 2, it evidently might now be difficult to approach equilibrium through a trial-and-error process, at least one of a sort applicable elsewhere.

The foregoing apart, to regard externalities as being taken into account "automatically" seems rather dubious when we consider that, whether costs are decreasing or not, proper accounting for the externalities would require the CPB to fix two prices for the product of any industry, one for the manager of a plant, which would correspond to his marginal costs, and the other for the manager of the industry, which would correspond to his marginal costs. Industry marginal costs would differ from plant marginal costs because of externalities, which somehow would have to be evaluated. The difference between the two prices, of course, would be the counterpart of the tax or subsidy which it has been urged should be established under capitalist competition in similar circumstances.

Hansen (n.d., p. 176) has also properly stressed more than I did previously the case of constant costs, for here even if the manager should seek to conform to the rules he would be in doubt how to behave, within whatever range costs are constant, whenever price equals marginal costs; and with price different from costs he would be impelled either to expand to capacity or to close down his plant. At

---

manager had erred wildly in constructing the plant to begin with, this certainly would be so, but such an error is possible. It should be observed, therefore, that X'' could also be an appropriate desideratum. Thus, suppose for simplicity that the plant in question is the only one in the industry and that the demand schedule for the industry's product passed through E''. In this case X'' might well be an appropriate output to produce in the short run. While losses are a maximum and the price would fall short even of average prime cost, the total consumers' benefits might still be large enough to warrant operating the plant rather than closing it down.

In sum, Rule 2 by itself does not suffice to determine the level of operations of the plant in question. Moreover, while the ambiguity in this rule is removed if the manager is instructed to maximize profits, or minimize losses, this precept also excludes operation at X''. To exclude such a scale of output would no doubt ordinarily be in order, but conceivably it might not be, so here again the Board would have to consider that profits might sometimes be an unsatisfactory success criterion.

While reference has been to the case of an indivisible plant, price, of course, might also equal marginal costs for two levels of output when the plant is divisible. Profits might sometimes turn out to be a defective success criterion, therefore, in the latter case as well.

Given the ambiguity of Rule 2 and the inappropriateness of profits as a success criterion, use of a trial-and-error process of the sort required in the Competitive Solution in order to induce the manager to settle at E'' would already seem precluded, but it should be observed that E'' falls in an area where marginal as well as average costs are declining. As will appear, given such decreasing costs use of such a trial-and-error process would encounter difficulties even if there were only one output for which price equals marginal cost, and the manager could be relied on to produce at this output.

some levels of operation by different managers in an industry total supply would still equal demand at the established price, but given constant costs such a situation would be difficult to approach under the Competitive Solution. While Hansen refers to the manager of a plant, constant costs would pose even more of a problem for the manager of an industry since here there is no capacity constraint. Moreover, in neither case would the difficulties be much diminished if costs should only be nearly, rather than precisely, constant. In the real world approximation to constancy must be the more usual case.

In order to grapple with the problem raised by constant costs under a planning scheme such as Lange's, Mirrlees (1966, p. 10) proposes that, in expanding capacity in response to current market conditions, the manager should be instructed to proceed cautiously. In other words, he should be required "to adjust the proposed scale of production by quite small amounts from period to period."[8] In this way, it is hoped to avoid the large errors and oscillations that otherwise might easily occur. Perhaps some such constraint on managerial behavior as is envisaged would sometimes be to the good, but in effect the manager would be required to subordinate his judgment of the market where this conflicted with the constraint, and the manager's judgment might often be nearer the mark.

I have been referring to a single-product firm or industry, but as Waelbroeck has drawn to my attention, a further related problem must arise in the case of a multiproduct firm, for transformations between products might often occur at constant rates. Hence, the Board would also find it difficult under the Competitive Solution to control satisfactorily the assortment and quality of products.

PRICE FIXING AND INCOME DISTRIBUTION

Reference has been made to the way in which the trial-and-error process of the Competitive Solution might proceed in a single industry experiencing cost variation of one or another sort. The functioning of such a process has recently been examined by Arrow and Hurwicz (n.d.) and, as is more appropriate, in respect of the economy as a whole rather than only a single industry. For a very abstract but illuminating model, it is found, not very surprisingly, that adjustments of a sort that might be called for by the Competitive Solution would tend to converge to an equilibrium provided production processes generally are subject to diminishing returns. Such adjustments may not so converge, however, if returns are constant, and difficulties regarding convergence are compounded if returns are increasing.[9]

[8] I am grateful to Mr. Mirrlees for kindly permitting me to refer to the unpublished paper cited.

[9] Arrow and Hurwicz (n.d.) assume that the community seeks to maximize welfare as given by a single function, representing the relation of utility to the aggregate consumption of different final goods by the community generally. More particularly, a "helmsman," confronted by varying shadow prices for different final goods, chooses for any set of such prices a mix of final goods which maximizes utility as so understood.

This may seem much too esoteric, but as Paul A. Samuelson (1956) has in effect shown the choices made by such a helmsman could correspond to the mix of final goods selected by different households in a competitive market, where the aggregate income of the households is continually allocated optimally among them through the use of lump sum taxes and dividends. The helmsman's choices could also be regarded as maximizing a social welfare function of the conventional individualistic sort, where social welfare varies positively with the utility of each household. By the same token, the helmsman's choices could also be viewed as corresponding to those for final goods generated by the Competitive Solution, for recall that here too households have freedom of choice in spending their incomes at established prices. Also, they apparently share in a

While convergence is of interest, as Waelbroeck has noted, of great interest too is its rapidity, for efficiency of resource use would depend on the latter (see Waelbroech, 1964, p. 22; Marschak, 1959).[10] Lange (1938, p. 89) apparently considered that under the Competitive Solution convergence would in fact be relatively rapid, but here I still find myself more in accord with Hayek (1948, pp. 187–89, 192–93) who argued that on the contrary the task of fixing prices for an entire economy, which Lange assigns to the Board, would prove formidable. Almost inevitably, the Board would find it difficult to respond quickly to continually occurring changes in supply and demand. It would also be unable to fix prices in sufficient detail to take into account almost endlessly diverse varieties of goods produced by a modern economy. Imbalances between supply and demand, therefore, might be large and persistent.

In fixing prices, the CPB admittedly might hire additional personnel. It might also establish a complex of subordinate agencies, including field offices, to assist it in its work. But such measures could be costly, and it is not clear to what extent the incongruities predicted by

---

total tax or dividend that is allocated in some manner deemed optimal.

In order to demonstrate convergence, Arrow and Hurwicz (n.d., pp. 81-82) assume that the helmsman's indifference surfaces are convex to the axes and contain no linear or planar segments. Given optimal lump-sum allocations and reallocations of the community's tax or dividend, the choices of different households taken together, I believe, would generate aggregative indifference surfaces of this sort provided the indifference surfaces of each household were shaped similarly (see Samuelson, 1956, p. 16), but it should be observed that this rules out the interesting case where the household's marginal rate of substitution between any two goods is constant for substitutions made along a given indifference surface.

[10] Strictly speaking, what really matters is the time path of convergence.

Hayek would be avoided. As the CPB expanded and proliferated agencies, it would also face a further and possibly demanding problem of directing and co-ordinating its own personnel. The Board's task in fixing prices should not be exaggerated, but its difficulties could be consequential.

They might be so even if the CPB confined itself, as Lange apparently assumed it should, to current prices. The difficulties would be greater if, as Mirrlees (1966, pp. 11 ff.) has suggested, the Board also undertook to project future prices. Probably, however, the Board, as Mirrlees argues, could predict prices for broad categories of goods more accurately than the individual enterprise. Because of the possible confusion of responsibilities, the issuance of such predictions might complicate further the task of appraising and rewarding managerial success, but perhaps such difficulties could often be avoided if it were understood that the managers need not rely on the Board's projections and would still be held accountable in any case for their own performance generally.

As indicated, Lange (1938, pp. 83–84, 99–103) considered that the Competitive Solution would not only be relatively efficient generally but quite equitable. In the absence of private ownership of productive assets, there would be no private income from such assets, which is a major source of inequity under capitalism. Also, given freedom of choice of occupation, wage differentials would tend simply to correspond to differences in disutility, and hence to be not really inequitable, while the tax or dividend might also be distributed according to some equitable criterion, such as family size. As I observed previously (Bergson, 1966, pp. 223–24), wage differentials in fact could be expected to correspond to differences in marginal utility only in equilibrium and there only for workers on the margin of choice between occupations. So far as there is disequilibrium or workers are intramarginal, their earnings have the character of rents, which by Lange's own standard would be inequitable. As Lange recognized, rents would be particularly great for persons with rare talents, though he hoped, surely rather optimistically, that these rents could be extracted by taxation without adverse effects on efficiency.

But I refer to income distribution again not to review this matter generally but to draw attention to one aspect which has tended to be neglected, I think quite improperly: managerial earnings. If profits should be a success criterion, and managers should be rewarded correspondingly, their earnings might be viewed as a kind of wage of management, and like wages generally such earnings might tend to be related to disutility. But, for managerial earnings, the relation to disutility might be particularly tenuous. Thus, from the standpoint of efficiency, the manager should receive any and all additional earnings which might result from and induce additional effort on his part. Under any likely incentive arrangements, however, an attempt to realize this principle would be bound to yield the manager rental returns, which would be difficult to absorb through taxes. Especially if the manager were talented, the resulting divergencies from disutility could be wide. Alternatively, a reluctance to sanction managerial rewards of the needed magnitude could easily be a further consequential source of inefficiency.[11]

ALTERNATIVE ARRANGEMENTS

It is time to refer to forms of market socialism other than the Competitive Solution. These are potentially infinite, but only a few are of theoretic interest, and sometimes these do not differ markedly from the Competitive Solution. They do seem to represent significant elaborations of that scheme, however, at least as it was envisaged by Lange. None was considered in my earlier essay.

Mathematical techniques.—Possible uses of these procedures in socialist planning have lately become a familiar theme. Regarding economy-wide applications which are of chief interest, reference is usually to centralized planning, and Lange himself (1938, p. 88) clearly—indeed, emphatically—envisaged no corresponding role to speak of for such procedures in market socialism. Dickinson (1939, pp. 98–105) once held, however, that under the Competitive Solution the Board might in fact be able to fix prices simply by solving pertinent equations. While Dickinson subsequently withdrew, or at least greatly qualified, this proposal, both Lange and he wrote before the age of electronic computers. Given this technology, could not the CPB, in performing its cardinal task of fixing prices, confute Hayek after all simply by using mathematical techniques? Thus, could it not in this way largely, if not entirely, avoid trial and error, or at least substitute trial and error on paper for that in practice?

The questions are in order, but, when applied on an economy-wide scale, math-

[11] Under the Competitive Solution, the taxes that must be resorted to in order to absorb rents to labor should ideally be of the lump-sum sort, but as the cited article of Samuelson (1956) has made clear, the true lump-sum tax is an even more esoteric device than has been assumed and hardly to be approached closely in practice. And this says nothing of the likely adverse political consequences of reliance on such a measure. By implication, an attempt to realize equity at this point almost inevitably would be at the expense of efficiency. (See Samuelson, 1956, pp. 8–14; also Bergson, 1966, pp. 78 ff., 186–88.)

ematical procedures are perhaps still not quite as potent as is sometimes assumed. This seems true also of such procedures in the particular economy-wide application in question. With all the progress that has been made, the use of computers still entails a cost. This could hardly be a factor in regard to calculations of any conventional sort that the Board might wish to make, but there are reasons to think it might become so should the Board seek continually to elaborate the mathematical system employed.[12]

More important, should the Board seek to employ mathematical procedures in fixing prices comprehensively and in detail, its undertaking surely could become burdensome for managers of pro-

duction units, who might be called on to predict and articulate in inordinately concrete detail the complex and ever changing constraints and opportunities that confront them, and on this basis to communicate to the Board such data on these matters as the Board would require; and for the Board itself, which promptly would have to digest such information and to communicate the results of its deliberations to the managers. The capacities of managers as well as of the Board to grapple with these tasks might often be enhanced by use of computers, but not always.

In fixing prices the CPB obviously would find it advantageous to employ mathematical techniques in some way. Thus, it should be to the good sometimes by use of such techniques to make trial calculations of a highly aggregative or selective kind, and very possibly the Board would also wish to experiment with one or another ingenious scheme, such as "the two-level planning" of Kornai (1965) and of Kornai and Liptak (1965), which seeks to combine the virtues of decentralization with those of mathematical computation. But the Board could hardly dispose entirely in such ways of a task that, at least in a modern economy, is almost infinitely complex. In fixing prices, therefore, it would still have to resort to trial and error, and in practice as well as on paper.[13]

[12] With successive elaborations of the mathematical system, such benefits as are realized might well tend to diminish. So far as additional computing costs continue to be incurred, therefore, such costs presumably could become a constraint at some point. Admittedly, a further question concerns the manner in which the costs might vary as the mathematical system is elaborated, and this unhappily is a complex matter about which it is difficult to generalize.

Costs of computing, and often also the manner of their variation, are apparently apt to depend not only on the number of equations and unknowns in the mathematical system considered but on the nature of the relations in question, particularly whether reference is to linearities or non-linearities, the nature and degree of interconnectedness of the activities represented, initial knowledge concerning the magnitudes of unknowns in the vicinity of the final solution, and the degree of novelty of initial programing work and the frequency of subsequent changes in the program adopted. In the case of a system of linear equations with random coefficients, where nothing is known of the location of the solution, machine operating time varies not with the number of unknowns but with the cube of their number; at least this is so for a given apparatus and for linear systems of a size appropriate to it. On a general plane, however, it seems difficult to say much more than this about computing costs.

But, granting the complexities, I don't think I am doing any violence to the facts in considering computing costs as a possible limitation on application of highly elaborate systems, far outside the conventional range. On this matter, I have benefited from discussions with numerous colleagues, though it is only fair to say that some feel that I am inclined to stress it unduly.

[13] As envisaged by Kornai (1965) and by Kornai and Liptak (1965), two-level planning entails decentralization of price-fixing and centralization of resource allocation, at least as between sectors. This, of course, is a quite different situation from that under the Competitive Solution, but, considered as a game, such two-level planning might possibly be employed in the context of the Competitive Solution. Thus, the Board might seek through the completion of a number of trial adjustments of a required sort to approach more readily an equilibrium when it undertook to fix prices in practice. On the other hand, I understand that under the Kornai-Liptak

In using mathematics in the manner envisaged, the CPB evidently need not infringe on the autonomy of managers regarding inputs and outputs. The Board would simply seek by applying mathematical procedures to approach equilibrium levels of prices more quickly. The procedures in question, thus, could be applied under market socialism; and it is on this understanding that they have been considered here. Indeed, within the limits of market socialism the Board might even go a step further and publish the prospective outputs, which in its calculations were found to correspond to the prices that were expected to approach equilibrium levels. Without requiring that such outputs be in any sense compulsory on managers, the Board might hope in this way to provide further guidance for the latter. Such guidance might be especially helpful in the crucial sphere of investment decisions, where as Dobb (1939, pp. 723–27) observed long ago managers must be particularly prone to error. In appraising the possible efficiency of market socialism, then, we must consider that a commitment to this system does not preclude publication of a national economic plan, even one with physical targets, and that trial and error might be abbreviated to some extent in this way.

In sum, the Board might find it in order to engage in "indicative planning," and so long as the planning remained indicative rather than imperative it

would in no way be violating the principles of market socialism (cf. Massé, 1965, pp. 265–66). Once having formulated and published a more or less detailed economic plan, however, the CPB might find it difficult to refrain from resorting to extra-market controls to enforce it, but the question posed regarding the effect of introducing such controls into market socialism is to be discussed below in a somewhat different context.

Decentralization of price fixing.—Under the Competitive Solution, the task of fixing prices must be a most difficult one for the CPB even if it should employ mathematical techniques. What, however, if price determination should be decentralized along with the determination of inputs and outputs?

As Hayek (1948, p. 186) observed, even to embrace the Competitive Solution already implies abandonment of much that was supposed to be distinctive, and hence superior, about socialism. If price fixing generally should be left to the market, this process would be carried a step further.

Nevertheless, Lange (1938, p. 78) himself envisaged that the Board would not really be responsible for any and all prices. Rather it was to leave to the market the prices of consumers' goods and labor services. Dickinson (1939, pp. 98–105) too does not always seem to have been insistent that prices be fixed by the Board. One still cannot be sure, however, that they were to be left to the market.

In any event, under market socialism decentralization of price fixing is a possibility, but assuming the Competitive Solution prevails otherwise, what can be inferred as to economic efficiency is fairly evident.

Thus, while arbitrariness on the part of the Board would be obviated, the market prices too would often diverge from

---

scheme convergence proceeds rather erratically. This could be an obstacle to the scheme's use in the manner suggested.

I have not found anywhere a systematic account of possible applications of mathematical techniques in national economic planning under market socialism, but reference may be made to the articles of Kornai (1965) and of Kornai and Liptak (1965) just referred to, to Hardt, Hoffenberg, Kaplan, and Levine (forthcoming), Marschak (1959), Neuberger (1966).

their equilibrium values. Also, the danger of monopolistic behavior referred to earlier must now increase. If there are trade unions, such behavior might not be avoided even in regard to wages, which Lange himself would have left to the market. But monopoly restrictions might tend to become pervasive if price fixing should be left to the market on any extensive scale. Perhaps such evils could be mitigated, however, if as is logical, an energetic antitrust division should be established in the Board in place of the division that was to fix prices. The possible effect on efficiency of decentralization of price fixing must be judged in the light of these diverse considerations.

Extra-market controls.—While market socialism was defined as a system in which factor inputs and outputs are *typically* determined by authorities immediately in charge of production units, reference thus far has been to forms of market socialism where factor inputs and outputs are *universally* so determined. Mirrlees (1966, pp. 18 ff.) has analyzed, however, an alternative planning scheme in which production authorities are allowed to determine factor inputs and outputs but with one notable exception. Production capacity is fixed finally by superior agencies.[14] For the individual enterprise, the pertinent superior agency might be an organization administering an industry or region. This is in itself not an essential departure from Lange, for recall that for the latter too large investment decisions are left to an industry manager. But for Mirrlees appropriate capacity levels are also imposed as quotas on the industrial or regional authority by the CPB. Price and other financial instruments, therefore, are supplanted generally in regard to production capacity.

It is perhaps in order to ask whether with such a major breach in market institutions the planning system in question should still be considered market socialism. But of more interest is the further question whether the introduction of extra-market procedures to determine capacity might be to the good, as Mirrlees apparently assumes.

This is difficult to gauge. Obviously, as Mirrlees urges, the market is not at its best in the determination of new production capacity. The Board, however, might find it difficult to do better through the imposition of quotas, for its administrative burden would be much increased. In a sense this would already be so even if the Board should engage only in indicative planning, but the errors involved in resorting to aggregation and other expedients assume quite a different aspect if the resultant targets are compulsory and not merely orientative for production authorities. One wonders too whether prices would not tend to become more dubious if the Board should no longer rely on them to bring about adjustments regarding capacity. How to arrange suitable success criteria for managers should also be no less of a problem here than in the Competitive Solution.[15]

[14] While Mirrlees refers to "scale of production," he clearly means here "production capacity."

[15] The question at issue is related to, though evidently not the same thing as, that concerning the comparative efficiency of, on the one hand, a decentralized system where extra-market controls are entirely absent, and, on the other, a centralized one, where such controls are pervasive. In his pioneer article of 1959, Marschak examines the latter problem in a highly formal way for a model embracing three decision makers. Apparently, depending on the time required for reading and writing messages and for turning from one message to another, the centralized system might be preferable to the decentralized one, at least according to one of two efficiency criteria employed.

This is clearly a plausible result, but in trying to appraise the possible merit of the two systems more realistically we must also consider a number of complexities from which Marschak understandably

THE CO-OPERATIVE VARIANT

Under the Competitive Solution, the manager of a production unit is supposed to follow certain rules, though how such behavior might be assured is an interesting question. Benjamin Ward (1958) has explored an alternative form of market socialism in which the organization of the production unit is approached rather differently. Administration is by a co-operative of workers. Assets are publicly owned, and the government levies a tax on the co-operative as a charge for their use, but otherwise all earnings, in excess of operating expenses for materials, accrue to the workers. In the simple model considered, fixed assets are non-depreciating. The co-operative firm supposedly is free to determine employment and output as it wishes.

As Ward may not consider sufficiently, such arrangements—I shall call them the Co-operative Variant—might have a favorable effect on workers' attitudes and in this way tend to increase productivity. But there is no basis otherwise to quarrel with his interesting conclusion that the firm envisaged might behave quite differently from a competitive enterprise under capitalism. Hence, the Co-operative Variant could be inherently inefficient.

To refer to a simple case of a sort considered by Ward, suppose labor is homogeneous and that net earnings are divided equally among employed work-

ers, but that more senior workers are free to vary the employment of junior ones. Also, labor is the only variable input. The more senior workers presumably will seek to determine total employment and output in such a way that average earnings per employed worker or the per worker average of sales revenue net of the government tax (which is taken to be of a lump-sum sort) are a maximum. As is readily seen, such a position is realized when

$$P \cdot MPL = \frac{PX - R}{L}. \qquad (1)$$

Here P is the going price of the product; X is output; L employment; R, the lump-sum tax, and MPL the marginal product of labor. In other words, the value of the marginal product of labor must equal average net earnings per worker. This is so because, if the value of the marginal product of labor exceeds average net earnings, it would pay the more senior workers to increase employment until this ceased to be so; and similarly if the value of the marginal product of labor falls short of average net earnings, employment would be curtailed. The equilibrium position is illustrated. See Figure 2, where at $\bar{L}$, $(PX - R)/L$ is a maximum, and equals $P \cdot MPL$. Note that here the gradients of the PX/L and R/L schedules are equal.

Depending on the comparative stocks of capital and technologies employed in different firms, then, marginal workers might produce very different value products even among firms in the same industry. Depending too on the going prices, they might also produce different value products in different industries. Such divergencies in marginal returns to employment, which might prevail even in equilibrium, necessarily would betoken inefficiency.

---

abstracts, including some that already have been mentioned, such as difficulties encountered by managers of production units in predicting and articulating pertinent constraints and opportunities and the problem of co-ordinating activities within the CPB itself.

To repeat, Marschak refers to two systems, one in which extra-market controls are absent, the other in which they are general. On the still further question regarding the comparative efficiency of market socialism and centralist planning in the real world, see below.

For any firm, output would also depend on the tax, and, as Ward points out, by varying the amount of this levy independently for different firms the government conceivably could still assure that marginal returns to labor were the same everywhere. In effect, the government would simply be taking into its budget, in addition to interest charged at some uniform rate, any and all "rents" and "windfall gains" accruing to the different firms. But such a policy would not be easy to realize in practice.

tion, the Co-operative Variant as depicted by Ward assumes that determination of prices is left to the market rather than being made the task of a CPB. The analysis thus far, however, relates to a competitive firm which takes the market price as a datum. As Ward explains, should the firm have any monopoly power it would tend to restrict output below the competitive level.

To repeat, it is assumed that, say through operation of the principle of seniority, employment in the firm may

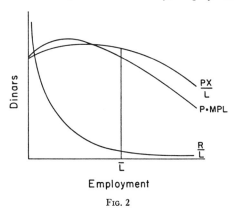

Employment

Fig. 2

Given "free entry," differences in marginal returns to labor might also be dispelled through establishment of new firms, but this could occur only in the long run.

Curiously, as the going price changes, it can be shown that the firm tends to vary its output in the contrary direction. Such a negatively sloped supply curve could be a source of economic instability, but reference is still to the case where labor is the only variable input. If, say, materials are also variable and are an important part of total cost, all is essentially as before, but the supply curve in this case might have a positive slope.

In contrast to the Competitive Solu-

be varied freely. In any more realistic case of working arrangements such as are in question, employment most likely could be varied upward more readily than downward, but, granting this, marginal returns to labor in different firms could still diverge materially. Hence the conflict between co-operation and efficiency, which Ward discovered, would still prevail.

The co-operative firm in Ward's analysis produces only one commodity. As Domar (1966) has shown, if the co-operative firm produces many products, the supply schedule for any one of them is more likely to have a positive slope than is that for all products taken together, for an increase in the price of any one product tends to cause a reallocation of inputs in its favor. Domar also elaborates Ward's model by introducing into the analysis a supply curve for co-operative labor, which apparently represents the amount of work members of the co-operative would wish to offer if their dividends were fixed at any given level. While as noted a co-operative should at least be able to increase, and hence also to refrain from increasing, its membership, Domar takes the number of members as given. The supply of labor may still vary, however, through changes in, say, working hours or outside activities. By juxtaposing the supply schedule with the schedule of average net earnings realized at different levels of employment ($[PX - R]/L$ in Fig. 2), the equilibrium level of co-operative employment is determined. As it turns out, co-operative behavior may be rather different from that envisaged by Ward, though still not necessarily the same as that of a competitive firm under capitalism.

I agree that the Domar co-operative would behave differently from Ward's, but while Domar recognizes that his "equilibrium" level of employment is not likely to be optimal for the co-operative, he is not entirely explicit as to just what is maximized in, and the determination of, the optimum. In the spirit of Ward's analysis, the co-operative presumably would seek to maximize the utility of its members, allowing for the disutility of their exertions. Given this, the co-operative's optimum must be determined in accord with members' preferences between income and leisure and their "production possibilities" in the manner illustrated (Fig. 3).

For simplicity I refer to a co-operative whose members have similar tastes and are equally skilled. In the figure, S_1,

S_2, S_3 ... represent any household's indifference curves in respect of choices between income and leisure and pp' its corresponding production possibilities. Variations in the household's employment are understood to typify variations in co-operative employment generally, while the income produced by the household is taken to be a pro rata part of the total co-operative income. With employment nil, income is negative because of the need to pay a tax

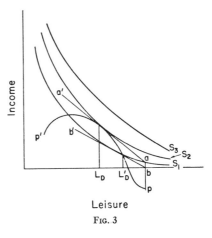

Leisure

Fig. 3

to the government. The optimum level of employment for the household, then, is at L_D, where its marginal rate of substitution between leisure and income equals the corresponding marginal rate of transformation.

As for the co-operative's equilibrium, this might properly be taken to be the same as the optimum, for the co-operative presumably would seek to realize the latter. Moreover, it could actually approach this desideratum more or less closely depending on how well the management knew the members' tastes and production possibilities. With full knowledge of these aspects, the manager might fix working hours optimally without more ado.

Domar assumes, however, that the co-operative would recruit labor through money wage offers. If it did, the equilibrium might well be at L'_D, as his analysis suggests. Here the household is induced by a wage rate corresponding to the gradient of bb' to work $(b - L'_D)$ hours, while his total wages correspond in turn to his production possibilities. As Domar is aware, however, the co-operative might still approach the optimum more closely by resorting to discrimination— in the present case, between wage rates for successive hours of work. Moreover, the optimum could also be approached simply by use of an internal tax or subsidy. Thus, in the case illustrated, the co-operative might offer the household an internal subsidy, ab, in place of the tax, bp, that is actually paid the government. The appropriate money wage rate is that corresponding to the gradient of $a'a$.

But in the Domar co-operative as in the Ward co-operative the marginal productivity of labor might still vary as between firms. This would be so whether the co-operative equilibrium is at L_D or L'_D. How a change in price of the product would affect output, however, would now depend partly on the nature of the members' preferences between income and leisure.[16]

Construed as a form of profit sharing

under socialism, the Co-operative Variant has also been examined by Kornai and Liptak (1962). Using programing methods, the authors focus particularly on the determination of the volume and structure of a firm's output under two alternative incentive schemes, one inducing maximization of profits and the other inducing maximization of the ratio of profits to sales. While implications for economic efficiency are not explored, as is readily seen co-operative behavior under the second scheme, though not the first, turns out to be fully as strange as in Ward's analysis.[17]

CONCLUSIONS

What may be concluded as to the economic efficiency of market socialism? In elaborating the Competitive Solution, Lange was concerned with how efficient market socialism might be in theory, and in appraising his scheme and exploring possible variants I have focused on the same issue. What we wish finally to know, however, is how efficient market socialism is likely to be in practice. As is still not always considered, practice here is apt to differ widely from theory, and in innumerable ways.

Suffice it to observe that market socialism has been materializing, and in the future may continue to materialize, as a successor not to capitalism but to centralist planning under socialism. For

[16] Domar (1966) calls his provocative essay "Soviet Collective Farm." For this reason, perhaps it is improper to examine the co-operative's behavior in the spirit of Ward, but note that even if the co-operative should desire only to exploit its members the optimum would still be of the sort portrayed in Fig. 3. Should the co-operative seek, for example, to limit any member to some minimum consumption standard given by, say "S_2," it could still maximize the "tax" realized from the member's activities by allowing the member to respond freely to some wage rate such as is given by the gradient of aa', and some accounting subsidy or accounting tax. In this way the member would still reach a position such as L_D.

[17] If I may revert to conventional marginal analysis, we need consider only the determination of total output. Suppose profits are maximized. Since the concern is with total profits, rather than profits per worker, and prices and wage rates are taken as data, the firm would ordinarily observe the same rules as are established for the plant under the Competitive Solution. Where the profit-sales ratio is maximized, however, output must always be fixed at the point where marginal and average costs are equal, and without regard to price. Thus, the concern is to maximize $[PX - C(X)]/PX$, where $C(X)$ represents total cost, and P and X as before represent price and output. As is readily seen, if price is given this is a maximum when $C(X)/X$ is a minimum, or $C'(X) = C(X)/X$.

this reason it surely will tend to be much combined with extra-market controls, and often with such as are not envisaged in theory. Accordingly, such controls are not very apt to serve the interests of economic efficiency.[18]

More basically, systems directors in the socialist world, as indicated above, are more understanding of and concerned with economic efficiency than they used to be, but it would be surprising if their understanding and concern should not still leave something to be desired. For this reason they may not only tolerate wasteful extramarket controls. They may also be led to adopt a relatively inefficient form of market socialism. For example, the Co-operative Variant seems distinctly less promising than the Competitive Solution, but it might still be favored if its limitations were not fully understood, or because of its ideological or political appeal.

The still limited understanding of and concern for efficiency may also affect the implementation of market socialism, whatever the form. Even should the Competitive Solution be accepted in principle, for example, one wonders whether a socialist Board would be likely soon fully to emancipate itself from Marxian skepticism of market processes and so to feel impelled to manipulate prices freely in response to changes in supply and demand; and this still says nothing of the need on the part of the Board politically to consider the "vested

interests" that might be affected by such price changes. The political concern for vested interests would be the greater if, as might be so, market socialism should be associated with some diffusion of power generally.[19] The departure from theory at this point, I believe, might be very wide.

While considering that under the Competitive Solution socialism could achieve notable efficiency, Lange (1938, p. 109) conceded that "bureaucratization of economic life" is a "real danger" in such a society. Schumpeter (1947, pp. 205 ff.) too stressed this problem. Such bureaucratization could mean many things, and in one sense what is involved presumably is the question of managerial incentives already discussed. But, given the likely pervasive importance of politics, there is further reason to wonder whether managers of bureaucratic public agencies will behave in the manner theory envisages.

Schumpeter (1947, pp. 210 ff.) also stressed, rightly, the importance of labor attitudes and discipline as a factor that might affect the economic performance of socialism. I doubt, however, that he would still consider the ability of this system to command the "moral allegiance" of the workers as conferring an advantage on it. Also, under the market variety, socialism might not be as efficacious as Schumpeter assumed in supplementing voluntary with authoritarian controls. This is because of the possible diffusion of power already referred to. The worker should become more favorably disposed to the system, however, if he were allowed to share more fully in the fruits of economic progress. Where market socialism succeeds centralized

[18] When introduced into market socialism, extra-market controls might take the form of the physical quotas which characterize centralist planning, but for practical purposes the consequences might not be very different if use should be made instead of financial instruments but in a discriminatory way. Thus authorities in charge of production units might be deprived of much of their discretion through imposition of discriminatory prices and other financial terms. Such discriminatory terms in effect violate the requirement of anonymity which Hurwicz (1960, p. 169) has established for a decentralized system.

[19] The need to consider vested interests in fixing prices presumably would arise in part because of the difficulties with lump-sum taxes already referred to (n. 11 above).

planning, perhaps he will be allowed to do so.

I have referred to market socialism as it might be in theory and practice. In Yugoslavia, however, market socialism by all accounts has in fact been approached, if not realized. How efficient is market socialism there? Relevant as it is, I cannot pursue this question here, but the Yugoslav case hardly conflicts with what I have said thus far. Indeed, at a number of points I have already had just this case in mind. Suffice it to refer to the use by superior government authorities not only of market but often (especially in regard to investment allocation) of extra-market processes for purposes of directing activities of enterprises that administer individual production units. Again, where, as often is so, prices are controlled by superior agencies, such agencies tend to postpone, or to limit, increases which manifestly might be called for by increases in demand. Last but not least, there is the famous system of workers' "self-management," with its quasi-co-operative system of labor remuneration. On an abstract plane, Ward's co-operative firm is intended, of course, to represent just this form of organization.[20]

In sum, the reader will wish to judge for himself the possible upshot for economic efficiency of the many diverse aspects that have been explored. For my part, I suspect that with all its limita-

tions market socialism, where introduced, will tend to be more efficient than centralized planning might have been in similar circumstances but not as much so as is often assumed. Even one who is favorably disposed toward market processes may feel, therefore, that the more enthusiastic proponents of market socialism will sometimes be disappointed.

We wish to compare this system not only with centralized planning but with capitalism. Lange felt that socialism could be more efficient than its great rival, but even under the Competitive Solution there are reasons to think socialism might not perform nearly as well as he assumed, and the kind of market socialism adopted in any actual case could easily be inferior to the Competitive Solution. Under centralized planning, as is widely agreed, the proverbial claims of socialists regarding the economic superiority of their system over capitalism have yet to be vindicated. One wonders whether such claims are apt to be vindicated either under market socialism, though socialist economic performance may well improve under this variant.[21]

[20] On Yugoslav planning, in addition to the previously cited article of Ward, see Ward, 1957; Neuberger, 1959; International Labor Office, 1962; Fleming and Sertic, 1962; Waterston, 1962; Economic Commission for Europe, 1965; Ward, 1965; Macesich, 1966.

[21] In pondering this weighty issue, we must of course consider that economic performance under capitalism has also been improving. Capitalism is certainly functioning far better than it did in the thirties, and there are reasons to think it may continue to improve in the future: for example, through the further development of macroeconomic forecasting procedures; the continued improvement in information available to businessmen on the state of the market and in their techniques of interpreting this information; and the further extension and improvement of accounting and other internal controls, with or without the use of computers. In order for socialism to gain on capitalism regarding efficiency, therefore, the improvement realized under the market variety of socialism might have to be not merely absolute but relative.

REFERENCES

Arrow, K. J., and Hurwicz, L. "Decentralization and Computation in Resource Allocation," in R. W. Pfouts (ed.). *Essays in Eco-* *nomics and Econometrics: A Volume in Honor of Harold Hotelling.* Chapel Hill: Univ. of N.C., n.d.

Bergson, Abram. "Socialist Economics," in Howard Ellis (ed.). *A Survey of Contemporary Economics.* Philadelphia: Blakiston Co., 1948.

———. *Essays in Normative Economics.* Cambridge, Mass.: Harvard Univ. Press, 1966.

Dickinson, H. D. *Economics of Socialism.* Oxford: Oxford Univ. Press, 1939.

Dobb, M. "Saving and Investment in a Socialist Economy," *Econ. J.,* XLIX (December, 1939), 713–28.

Domar, Evsey D. "The Soviet Collective Farm as a Producer Cooperative," *American Econ. Rev.,* LVI, No. 4 (September, 1966), 734–57.

Economic Commission for Europe. *Economic Planning in Europe.* Geneva: United Nations, 1965.

Fleming, J. M., and Sertic, V. R. "The Yugoslav Alternative," *Internat. Monetary Fund Staff Papers,* IX (July, 1962), 202–25.

Hansen, Bent. "A Note on the Rules of Behavior for Competitive Socialism," in *On Political Economy and Econometrics: Essays in Honour of Oskar Lange.* Warsaw: Polish Scientific Publishers, n.d.

Hardt, J., Hoffenberg, M., Kaplan, N., and Levine, H. S. (eds.). *Mathematics and Computers in Soviet Economic Planning.* New Haven: Yale Univ. Press, forthcoming.

Hayek, F. A. "Socialist Calculation: The Competitive Solution," *Economica,* VII, No. 26 (May, 1940), 125–49.

———. *Individualism and Economic Order.* Chicago: Univ. of Chicago Press, 1948.

Hurwicz, L. "Efficiency of Decentralized Structures," in G. Grossman (ed.). *Value and Plan.* Berkeley: Univ. of Calif. Press, 1960.

International Labor Office. *Workers' Management in Yugoslavia.* Geneva: Internat. Labor Office, 1962.

Kornai, J. "Mathematical Programming as a Tool in Drawing up the Five-Year Economic Plan," *Economics of Planning,* V, No. 3 (1965), 3–18.

Kornai, J., and Liptak, T. "A Mathematical Investigation of Some Economic Effects of Profit Sharing," *Econometrica,* XXX, No. 1 (January, 1962), 140–61.

———. "Two-Level Planning," *Econometrica,* XXXIII, No. 1 (January, 1965), 141–69.

Lange, Oskar. "On the Economic Theory of Socialism," in B. Lippincott (ed.). *On the Economic Theory of Socialism.* Minneapolis: Univ. of Minnesota Press, 1938.

Macesich, George. *The Market-Planned Economy of Yugoslavia.* Minneapolis: Univ. of Minnesota Press, 1966.

Marschak, T. "Centralization and Decentralization in Economic Organizations," *Econometrica,* XXVII, No. 3 (July, 1959), 399–430.

Massé, Pierre. "The French Plan and Economic Theory," *Econometrica,* XXXIII, No. 2 (April, 1965), 265–77.

Mirrlees, J. A. "The Price Mechanism in a Planned Economy." Unpublished paper presented at Conference on "Planning and the Market," Nice, France, August 31–September 6, 1966.

Neuberger, Egon. "The Yugoslav Investment Auctions," *Q.J.E.,* LXXIII, No. 1 (February, 1959), 88–115.

———. "Libermanism, Computopia and Visible Hand," *American Econ. Rev.,* LVI, No. 2 (May, 1966), 131–44.

Samuelson, Paul A. "Social Indifference Curves," *Q.J.E.,* LXX, No. 1 (February, 1956), 1–22.

Schumpeter, Joseph. *Capitalism, Socialism and Democracy.* 2d ed. New York: Harper & Bros., 1947.

Waelbroeck, Jean. "La grand controverse sur la planification et la theorie économique mathématique contemporaine," *Cahiers de L'ISEA,* No. 146 (February, 1964), pp. 3–24.

Ward, Benjamin. "Workers' Management in Yugoslavia," *J.P.E.,* LXV, No. 5 (October, 1957), 373–86.

———. "The Firm in Illyria: Market Syndicalism," *American Econ. Rev.,* XLVIII, No. 4 (September, 1958), 566–89.

———. "The Nationalized Firm in Yugoslavia," *American Econ. Rev.,* LV, No. 2 (May, 1965), 65–74.

Waterston, Albert. *Planning in Yugoslavia.* Baltimore: Johns Hopkins Press, 1962.

THE POLITICS OF SOCIALIST EFFICIENCY

ABRAM BERGSON*

A rarely noted feature of the long-ongoing theoretic debate on socialist economic merit is its relatively circumscribed scope. What is in question essentially is how efficient a socialist economy might be. Efficiency, moreover, is seen on both sides of the debate as a more or less technical matter. Proponents of socialism assume that the economy will be organized and administered appropriately in the light of available knowledge of economics. Except insofar as efficiency itself is a political desideratum, politics play no role whatsoever. That assumption, though not explicit, underlies the proponents' analysis throughout, and hence also their very positive view of socialist efficiency. The possibility that such superior economic performance, even if technically feasible, might in one way or another be thwarted politically is not considered.

The critics for their part do not seriously challenge this favorable presupposition of proponents. Economic affairs, it is true, are held to be threatened with politicization, but how this occurs and efficiency is affected is little explored. Rather the critics apparently prefer to meet proponents on their own ground. Accordingly, they seek to demonstrate that, even if the economy should be organized and administered as proponents suppose, efficiency will still not be nearly as great as they contend.

To limit the debate in this way has its point. The issue that is thus delineated is sharply defined. As for politics as a source of inefficiency under socialism, that is analytically a not very tractable sociological question. Or so it must have seemed to the economists, even the often notably broad-gauged ones, who have participated in the debate. Yet the political process, although often a useful corrective to markets, has frequently been a source of inefficiency in Western mixed economies. That is a familiar fact that needs no laboring. It would be surprising if the political process were not often a source of inefficiency also under socialism, where there may or may not be markets to correct. Perhaps even an economist can contribute on this theme, if only by outlining, often tentatively, the most salient aspects.

I

Socialism has come to be a protean concept. Most often, however, it is understood as a social system in which there is predominantly public ownership of the means of production. That is also the way in which socialism has generally been understood in the theoretic debate. I shall understand it so here.

Whatever the social system, a decisive feature of the political process is the underlying constitutional order. The possible variety of such arrangements is almost infinite, but two broad types are of particular interest: democracy, where under due process of law and civil liberties competing parties contend for ultimate political power; and authoritarianism, where a single part or clique is the ultimate political authority and allows no other parties lawfully to contest its status.

Of the two types, only one has thus far come into existence under socialism. For familiar reasons, which one of the participants in the debate has eloquently elaborated on in a famous tract.[1] the fact that real-world socialism is always authoritarian cannot be entirely fortuitous. Yet many proponents of socialism still sincerely aspire to it in a democratic form. Often it is that variant alone that has any appeal. I propose to suspend all doubts about the possibility of democratic socialism, and focus on that as yet quite hypothetical system. Where appropriate, however, I consider whether the experience with the authoritarian socialism of the real world might be relevant and illuminating.

In the debate on economic merit, efficiency is generally understood in the conventional way as the degree of exploitation of available opportunities to satisfy consumers' wants. Reference is made to the wants of consumers as they see them, so in effect consumers' sovereignty is supposed to prevail. The possibility has also been considered, however, that the highest authorities or (as I have referred to them elsewhere) the "system's directors" of a socialist society might themselves wish to determine what is good for consumers. There is no reason to bar such planner's preferences here, but, as Oskar Lange, himself a distinguished proponent of socialism, acknowledged, imposition of planners' preferences on any scale would be inherently undemocratic.[2]

Where consumers are sovereign efficiency reaches its maximum in the famous Pareto optimum. Public officials in a socialist economy, at least at higher administrative levels, should be concerned to approach that ideal, but that can hardly be their only concern. In the West, the motivation of politicians and bureaucrats serving them is not easily characterized summarily, but consumers' welfare must be at best only one of a variety of objectives. The diverse aims pursued, moreover, are not always exactly harmonious. That is a principal reason why governmental action is so often inimical to efficiency. We must inquire to what extent such circumstances might also prevail under socialism.

It will be asked, though, whether political aims other than consumers' welfare do not simply exemplify planners' preferences. If so, and efficiency is gauged accordingly, in the light of any and all political desiderata, the result could be rather paradoxical: depending on the political ends sought, resource allocations of almost any sort could turn out to be efficient. The further consequence is that our inquiry would become rather footless. Politics would practically be excluded by definition from being a source of inefficiency. We can avoid this not very interesting outcome, however, by adopting a plausible usage that is already more or less implied in the debate. In effect, the yardstick for gauging efficiency is provided only by consumers' preferences and by planners' preferences that, while superseding those of consumers, are isomorphic with them. Indeed, in the debate only political ends that are related in this way to consumers' preferences are designated as planners' preferences to begin with. Political ends other than those that are so related to consumers' preferences are among the causes of inefficiency. Should the system's directors value one commodity in relation to another differently from consumers, efficiency is to be appraised in that light. But should the system's directors sacrifice output, however valued, to some other kind of end, that must be considered a source of inefficiency. There is thus a conceptual basis after all for an inquiry into political sources of inefficiency.

II

Given the constitutional order, it still remains for the system's directors to organize the socialist economy. Here a basic issue concerns the comparative stress on two alternative procedures for coordinating activities of production units. Under one, to be designated bureaucratic, superior agencies in administrative structures seek to achieve such coordination through use of extra-market devices, such as physical targets and quotas. In imposing such targets and quotas, the superior agencies may consult with authorities immediately in charge of production units, but the superior agencies are the final arbiter. Under the other procedure, which I shall refer to as the market process, determination of factor inputs and outputs is left finally to authorities immediately in charge of production units. The production units are coordinated through markets. Superior agencies, however, may still exercise influence by manipulating prices and other financial instruments.

It is customary to designate as centralist planning a scheme in which the bureaucratic technique is predominant and as market socialism one where chiefly market processes prevail. The comparative stress on the two sorts of procedures has also come to be viewed as representing a difference in the degree of centralization. That is permissible, but reference is then most clearly to centralization of authority rather than information. The degree of centralization and decentralization in the latter sense may in a degree vary under each technique.

One question arises immediately: might not the choice of planning procedure itself be determined politically in a way adverse to efficiency? Logically prior to that question, however, is another as to the comparative efficiency of the alternative planning procedures. That is also a complex issue, to which there obviously can be no simple answer. But centralist planning has come to be applied almost everywhere in the socialist world, and in a notably bureaucratic form. As is by now widely understood, such planning gives rise to pervasive resource misallocations. One inevitably wonders whether a greater decentralization and use of markets might not often be economically to the good. That it might be seems to be acknowledged obliquely by the system's directors of socialist societies for they themselves complain almost ceaselessly about the performance of their economic working arrangements.

They complain and from time to time they initiate ameliorative reforms, but they continue to rely on notably bureaucratic processes. Perhaps not the least of their reasons for doing so is their own cardinal role in such planning. They would be less than human not to find that gratifying. They would be less than human, that is, not to enjoy issuing innumerable decrees and orders on economic affairs, and authoritatively monitoring their implementation. Centralist planning, as found in the socialist world, must also be inherently favorable to the continuance in office of the system's directors and their party. That too cannot be an unimportant virtue.

While centralist planning is widespread, it is not universal in the socialist world. In two countries—Yugoslavia since the early fifties and Hungary since 1968—planning has been more nearly market socialist than centralist. In respect of planning as of other matters, the USSR has by all accounts exercised a constraining influence on other socialist countries, especially in Eastern Europe. Without that, perhaps market processes would have a larger role.

Our concern, furthermore, is with democratic socialism, while the socialist world is instead authoritarian. If centralist planning predominates in that sort of world, that is hardly coincidental. But a craving for status and power is not exactly rare, even among democratic public officials in the West, and it is scarcely unknown either for efficiency to be subordinated to such impulses. Under socialism, even of a democratic sort, wholesale public ownership of the means of production could greatly favor their gratification.

No one expects the extremes of bureaucracy that are observed in the real world of socialism to be replicated or even approached should that system ever materialize in a democratic form. A proliferation of extra-market at the expense of market processes, however, could still be not the least of the drags on efficiency that emerge.

Should a concern for power and status play in this way a costly role in the design of the democratic socialist planning system, the effect could be compounded by a closely related phenomenon. Although Oskar Lange considered himself a socialist, he was far from typical of such persons in the stress he gave to markets in his famous "Competitive Solution" to the problem of socialist planning. More usual among socialists is a predisposition in favor of planning of a relatively bureaucratic sort. Such an outlook is observed even among persons who do not themselves aspire to the status and power of planners.

The predisposition towards bureaucratic planning seemingly originates variously: sometimes perhaps in no more than *Das Kapital*'s lurid passages on the malfunctioning of capitalist markets; sometimes perhaps in more reasoned beliefs in the economic merit of extra-market processes; sometimes, as with a distinguished American Marxist,[3] from a concern at the possible threat to socialism posed by the employment of capitalist-like market institutions. But, whatever its origin, the predisposition almost always is of an ideological sort whose invalidation is more or less proscribed. Even after due deflation of inflated rhetoric, it is difficult to avoid the conclusion that such an ideological posture is also a significant factor in the continued heavy reliance on extra-market planning processes in the socialist world. It would be surprising if it should not sometimes favor inordinate resort to such processes under democratic socialism as well.[4]

III

Like democratic socialism itself, then, market socialism may prove to be a rather rare phenomenon, at least, if there is to be anything more than a relatively limited stress on markets. In proceeding further, however, let us again put aside doubts, and take as a point of departure the famous model of market socialism that I referred to above: the Competitive Solution of Oskar Lange. To recall the bare essentials: households have freedom of choice of occupation and consumer's goods. Managers of publicly-owned enterprises and industry authorities also have discretion over their productive inputs and outputs, but must observe two rules: to produce any output with a least-cost input mix and to produce an output at which marginal cost equals price. The Central Planning Board (CPB) coordinates these activities by endeavouring to fix prices that will equate supply and demand for each good and service.[5]

These working arrangements are, of course, not at all a whim of Lange's. So far as households have free choice and enterprises, industry authorities and the CPB conform to the prescribed principles, markets everywhere supposedly tend to the same sort of equilibrium as prevails under competitive private enterprise. Hence, as the primers teach, if we pass by well-known complexities, resource utilization tends to be Pareto optimal, and so maximally efficient.

The system's directors who opt for Lange's Competitive Solution, though, are evidently also committing themselves to a particular theory of value: the contemporary Western one that is usually called neo-classical. The same commitment would be entailed in any form of market socialism where resource use might converge to a Pareto optimum. In a sense neo-classical value theory could also be read into centralist planning, should that system (as is conceivable) happen to be of a form allowing convergence to a Pareto optimum.

In seeking to gauge the possible impact of socialist politics on efficiency, therefore, we must consider that in practice system's directors of socialist countries in the real world seem often to have been reluctant to commit themselves to any value theory at all so far as that might inherently constrain their personal power and status. In the extreme, under Stalin, such reluctance was a corollary in economic affairs of the so-called "cult of the individual." So far as the system's directors did commit themselves to a value theory, for long the favored conception was the labor theory of value that Marx embraced. That theory nevertheless did not go unchallenged, and in the course of time some essentials of neo-classical analysis have somehow gained ascendancy. But the triumph of neo-classical theory is still by no means complete. Even for purposes of academic analysis, some concepts such as marginal utility, have yet to receive any final clearance.[6]

Here again we must not extrapolate mechanically from authoritarian socialist experience, but we must also not underestimate, even under democratic socialism, the possible grip on men's minds of a theory so central to the thought of socialism's foremost prophet. Implications of the labor theory of value for efficiency are evident and need no elaboration.

We entered the era of the electronic computer only after Oskar Lange elaborated his Competitive Solution, and mathematical planning techniques that require use of that technology are also largely a product of more recent years. The experience with these techniques under real world socialism nevertheless is not without interest here, but that is a fairly familiar story. Concerning them, therefore, I shall only say that the chief ones in question—input-output analysis and linear programming— are perhaps not quite as easily applied and as efficacious as frequently assumed in the West. As with neo-classical value theory, however, their employment manifestly has been, and in a degree must still be, impeded by their post-Marxian Western theoretic origins and resultant ideological dubiety. As with value theory of any sort, the techniques must tend also to impose constraints on the arbitrary power and status of bureaucrats. That fact too has not been favorable to their acceptance.[7]

IV

A notable feature of Lange's Competitive Solution is the apparent reconciliation of the perennially conflicting goals of equity of income distribution and efficiency. True, market processes are established for labor services, as well as for commodities, and differential wages are an inevitable corrolary. But education is supposedly free, so a principal barrier to occupational mobility in the West is removed. Given that, Lange reasons, wage differentials should tend simply to compensate for differences in "leisure, safety, agreeableness of work, etc"; in short, for differences in the disutility of different pursuits. Should socialist finances permit, citizens may receive, in addition to wages, a social dividend, but this is to be distributed independently of earnings (for example, by size of family), so there will be no adverse effect on occupational choice, and equity can be favored the more. For the rest, Lange reasons, with public ownership of the means of production, the distorting effect on equity of historically-determined inequalities in private wealth and resulting differences in marginal utility of income are also absent.

Such a reconciliation of equity and efficiency evidently presupposes a utilitarian view of income distribution, but socialists of other ethical persuasions as well might find Lange's principles appealing. As often pointed out, however, the reconciliation of equity and efficiency is in a degree only apparent. Earnings generated by a market bear at best on disutilities only of persons who are qualified to pursue one or another job. Though many workers who are incompetent for the task might be pleased to shift to a more remunerative job for less than the prevailing differential, the differential cannot be reduced on that account. Furthermore, among workers who are qualified for different tasks, market differentials will bear only on those on the margin of choice between them.

Other, intra-marginal workers will to some extent earn a rent rather than compensation for disutility. Among persons with exceptional talents, as Lange himself notes, rent-like differences in individual earnings could be especially consequential.

In the Competitive Solution, Lange provided no incentive to assure that managers of production units observe his decision-making rules. Under any likely incentives scheme, managerial earnings too could easily diverge from disutility. That is only the more likely so far as managers are risk-averse and the incentive scheme is designed to assure an appropriate managerial attitude towards risk. According to a recent analysis, the necessary rewards could be quite large.[8]

The concern of this essay is with efficiency rather than equity, but should equity be in conflict, rather than harmonious, with efficiency and should efficiency be sacrificed in consequence, that clearly would have to be considered as still another instance where politics are economically costly. Hence such a contingency is fully germane here. So far we have shown only that under the Competitive Solution there could be marked inequity, but in any practical application of that scheme, one surmises that, in one way or another, the inequity would be mitigated at the expense of efficiency.

That becomes the more evident if, as is hardly unlikely, Lange's CPB should be confronted, not with a budgetary surplus that allows a household dividend, but with a budgetary deficit that requires a household tax. In the absence of private property income, the lump-sum tax that efficiency then requires would not be as glaringly inequitable as it is usually supposed to be in the West. But given the earning disparities that have been described, a lump-sum tax hardly could be acceptable politically. The CPB would have to resort to some other source of revenue even though it is rudimentary that efficiency must suffer.

Our concern continues to be with democratic socialism, but it is at least obliquely instructive that even the authoritarian socialist systems of the real world make hardly any use of lump-sum taxes. In fact, direct taxes of any sort are generally of only limited import. The bulk of governmental fiscal needs, in excess of returns imputable to the capital of publicly-owned enterprises, have usually been met from sales taxes on consumers' goods, or what under centralist planning comes to much the same thing, inordinately high profits or state consumers' goods enterprises. Such levies are perhaps not as inequitable as might be supposed. In one case carefully researched thus far, the levies overall may be mildly progressive.[9] But, whatever the import of such levies for equity, the systems directors must find them appealing on quite another familiar account. Even under authoritarian socialism the proverbial obscurity of indirect taxes to the general public must be a virtue to political authorities.[10] Of course, indirect levies also facilitate coping with structural imbalances and, as in the West, are relatively easy to administer.

But, however egalitarian or inegalitarian tax structures may be in real world socialist societies, income differentials probably are often unduly compressed. That is especially likely in respect to managerial earnings. This is a complex and still insufficiently studied matter, which I cannot pursue here. But, whatever the facts on equity in respect of real world socialism, among socialists of almost any school, equity is avowedly a cardinal concern. Under democratic socialism a concern for equity could only be expected often to override that for efficiency. The resultant economic losses could be consequential.[11]

V

In the mixed economies of Western democracies, the political process exacts a toll of efficiency in myriad ways, but very often a decisive feature is the actual or perceived incidence of governmental action on political constituencies of concern to one or another public official. How the official acts often turns primarily on whether such constituencies will view the results favorably or unfavorably. He seemingly has little, if any, regard for economic costs to the community generally. The constituencies often have the character of more or less organized "interest groups", and depending on their capacities and tactics, the official may be especially sensitive to such bodies. He frequently must heed in some degree, however, the opinion of other groups of citizens as well. The constituencies that are advantaged by any public measure characteristically do not hesitate to claim that what is good for them is good for the community generally, or at least fully warranted as a matter of equity. For that opinion they may sometimes have some basis, but a public official may serve particular constituencies even though others in the community, with good reason, view the results rather differently.

To what extent is such constituency politics apt also to prevail and be economically costly under socialism? Concerning the politics of authoritarian socialism we are still woefully ignorant. In such a society political constituencies in any usual sense would seem almost inherently excluded. It has been argued with some plausability, however, that politically influential interest groups have emerged, if not among the population generally, then among elite strata themselves.[12] So far as that is so, through inevitable log-rolling and the like, decision-making that sacrifices efficiency must often be a corollary.

Of course, even in authoritarian regimes system's directors cannot disregard entirely public opinion. That must have been so at least minimally even under Stalin, but the resultant constraints on governmental action must be important in less repressive circumstances, where public disaffection not only can affect labor morale, but can erupt sometimes, as recently in Poland, in politically destabilizing strikes and demonstrations. So far as concerns efficiency, the result may not be too different from that where constituency politics prevails. To cite only one or two outstanding instances, by resort to extensive subsidies, food prices may be held stable in the face of rising costs; or overt price increases for consumers' goods generally may be avoided only by continuing introduction of higher-priced new and pseudo-new products. Policies of this sort, which are clearly shaped at least in part by a concern for public reactions, must often be a source of inefficiency, though under centralist planning their full impact may sometimes be rather involved.

Among socialist countries, Yugoslavia is a rather special but for our purposes particularly interesting case. Not only do the system's directors there rely heavily on market processes. In the market socialism that prevails, as noted already, industrial enterprises are organized more or less as producers' co-ops. Yugoslavia is the only socialist country where that is so. Probably not entirely by coincidence these institutions have come to prevail in a society where the political regime, though authoritarian, is by all accounts less repressive than in other socialist countries.

It is not too surprising, then, but still instructive, that phenomena suggestive of constituency politics and very likely of impaired efficiency are also pervasive. I refer to features such as the cardinal role of republican and local political entities in the establishment of new enterprises, a not unusual result being the so-called "political factory". Because of local government subsidization of losses, enterprise liquidation is a comparative rarity. Staff curtailment is reportedly very unusual and overstaffing very usual. In the permissive milieu that prevails, strikes are not infrequent and are often directed against government policy (e.g., a wage freeze). The economic effects of these phenomena are sometimes complex, but we need not probe too deeply to be aware that they must frequently betoken reduced efficiency.[13]

Although the foregoing facts about the authoritarian regimes of real world socialism are of interest, probably more relevant to constituency politics under democratic socialism is the experience in the mixed economies of the West in a particular sphere: that of publicly-owned enterprises. That is a vast topic in itself with which it is difficult to grapple briefly, but it is interesting to learn that, according to a former official in

Italian public enterprise, these actions are in order for a staff-member wishing to rise to the top: "a certain willingness to accept requests from the political world." That means among other things that a manager "should never dismiss anybody. . . . A political request to create new jobs has also played a role. . . . Once a new factory has to be built, the location is very important from a political point of view." Similar concerns are seemingly imperative once a staff-member has risen to the top.[14]

The kinds of public enterprise behavior that are in question need not always be wasteful. Should labor be in surplus, for example, employment creation can favor rather than impair efficiency. Among Western mixed economies, public enterprises one suspects are apt to be more amenable to politics in Italy than is often so elsewhere. According to two close sutdents of the subject, however, "a tour of Western Europe's nationalized firms reveals one very clear point: nationalized firms are almost always the tool of politicians."[15] That need not always mean inefficiency, but it is fairly obvious and requires no demonstration that uneconomic accommodation to political power and influence is far from a rarity anywhere.

In the West, such accommodation by public enterprise is properly seen as but an aspect of constituency politics in economic affairs generally. Under democratic socialism is not the most likely prospect simply this: that there will merely be a replication of circumstances familiar in Western mixed economy, that is with constituency politics having an impact in one case more or less comparable to that in the other? Perhaps so, but, as we have already noted in other contexts, wholesale nationalization of the means of production must greatly expand the realm within which politics could become consequential. That should be true also of constituency politics in particular. The extinction of private ownership, though, could also have something of an offsetting effect, for such ownership in a mixed economy constitutes a significant source of motivation and funding for interest groups.

I have sought to repair a deficiency in usual theoretic discussions of the comparative efficiency of socialism. Such discussions have contributed much to an understanding of the more technical economic aspects of this matter, but they have tended to neglect the role that politics might play in determining how efficient socialism might be in practice. In exploring that role, I have focused on socialism of a hypothetical and perhaps unattainable democratic sort, but have tried to take account of the experience with real world socialist societies. All of these are authoritarian.

The conclusion must be that politics could be costly indeed. True, politics also exacts a toll from efficiency in Western mixed economies, but under socialism the radical extension of public ownership must greatly increase oppoҭtunities for costly bureaucratic distortions and accommodations to constituency politics.

Under socialism, a heightened concern for equity could also cause efficiency to suffer. That, however, would be a cost that many would discount. Ideological constraints on technical options could also be a source of waste. While such constraints have obvious parallels in the West, they might well be more confining under socialism, at least where Marxian doctrinal currents are influential.

The net of all these aspects must be a matter of opinion but one wonders whether, as a source of inefficiency under socialism, politics could not be fully as consequential as the relatively technical difficulties on which attention has been focused in theoretic discussions of the comparative economic merit of socialism.

Notes

1. Friedrich A. Hayek, *The Road to Serfdom*, Chicago, Ill., 1944.

2. Lange envisages, however, that planners preferences must prevail at least in respect of choices between present and future. See Oskar Lange, "On the Economic Theory of Socialism," in B. E. Lippincott, ed., *On the Economic Theory of Socialism*, Minneapolis, Minn., 1938, pp. 84–85, 95–97.

3. Paul M. Sweezy and Charles Bettehelim, *On the Transition to Socialism*, New York, 1971.

4. To return to the two instances of market socialism that were cited above—Hungary and Yugoslavia—these differ in a cardinal respect. In Hungary, the industrial enterprise is still organized in a conventional way, with ultimate authority in the hands of managerial personnel and workers having the status essentially of wage earners. In Yugoslavia, the industrial enterprise is organized rather under the so-called system of "self-management," and at least in principle has the form of an industrial co-op, with workers possessing ultimate authority and in respect of income having the status of residual claimants. Here too a question is in order whether politics may not have dictated an economically inferior scheme in one case or the other. For my part I think it did in the case of Yugoslavia, but the comparative economic efficiency of the Yugoslav arrangements is still a controversial matter which I cannot pursue here.

5. In the case of labor services and consumers' goods, the CPB seeks to achieve the desired balance by allowing wages and prices to fluctuate freely.

6. The Soviet experience in this sphere is the best documented and, as with planning generally, has often been influential elsewhere. See Bergson, *The Economics of Soviet Planning*, New Haven, Conn., 1964, Ch. 11; Gertrude Schroeder, "The 1966–67 Soviet Industrial Price Reform," *Soviet Studies*, April 1969; Morris Bornstein, "Soviet Price Theory and Policy" and Robert W. Campbell, "Marx, Kantorovich and Novozhilov", in George R. Feiwel, ed., *New Currents in Soviet-Type Economies*, Scranton, Pa., 1968; Michael Ellman, *Soviet Planning Today*, Cambridge, 1971.

7. See note 6.

8. Abram Bergson, "Managerial Risks and Rewards in Public Enterprise", *Journal of Comparative Economics,* September 1978.

9. Franklyn D. Holzman, *Soviet Taxation,* Cambridge, Mass., 1955.

10. Obscurity, one suspects, must also be a reason why elite groups are rewarded so frequently with non-monetary privileges: access to special shops, priority for scarce housing, etc. Here too, as the primers teach, efficiency must suffer.

11. On managerial earnings under socialism in practice, see Joseph Berliner, *The Innovation Decision in Soviet Industry,* Cambridge, Mass., 1976. The rewards indicated there should be compared with those referred to in Bergson, *op cit.*

12. H. Gordon Skilling, ed., *Interest Groups in Soviet Politics,* Princeton, N.J., 1971.

13. Branko Horvat, "Yugoslav Economic Policy in the Post-War Period," *American Economic Review,* June 1971, Supplement; Stephen R. Sacks, *Entry of New Competitors in Yugoslav Market Socialism,* Berkeley, California, 1973; Joel B. Dirlam and James L. Plummer, *An Introduction to the Yugoslav Economy,* Columbus, Ohio, 1973; *The Economist,* October 28, 1978; *Radio Free Europe Research,* Vol. 3, No. 37, 14–20 September 1978.

14. Franco A. Grassini, "Government Objectives and the State Owned Enterprise," (Processed), March 1979.

15. Kenneth D. Walters and R. Joseph Monsen, "The Nationalized Firm: The Politicians' Free Lunch?", *Columbia Journal of World Business,* Spring, 1971.

THE
QUARTERLY JOURNAL
OF ECONOMICS

| Vol. LXXXVI | November 1972 | No. 4 |

OPTIMAL PRICING FOR A PUBLIC ENTERPRISE [*]

ABRAM BERGSON

INTRODUCTION

In the literature of welfare economics, the second best has lately become a cardinal theme. That is as it should be, for the problem is clearly a central one. This essay examines the second best as it arises in a classic context: In a mixed economy prices exceed marginal cost in the private sector at least in some industries. The fact of such excess is generally a datum, but the government is free to fix prices for products of enterprises that it owns and operates. According to what principles should such prices be fixed?

The government, it will be assumed, is unconstrained budgetarily: It is able simply through lump sum transfers to dispose of any profits earned, or to finance any losses suffered, by its enterprises under the price policy adopted. The analysis, thus, is complementary to previous inquiries into price fixing for public enterprises that, while excluding lump sum transfers, have assumed perfect competition in the private sector.[1]

Would it not be preferable at this stage, however, to continue to exclude lump sum transfers, while allowing for monopolistic distortions in the private sector? Such an analysis has been attempted in a very limited way.[2] But, granting that lump sum trans-

* I am grateful to Professors Paul A. Samuelson and Eytan Sheshinski for helpful advice and criticism.

1. For a recent analysis, and references to earlier writings, see Peter A. Diamond and James A. Mirrlees, "Optimal Taxation and Public Production," *American Economic Review*, LXI (March and June 1971), 8–27, 261–78.

2. R. Rees, "Second Best Rules for Public Enterprise Pricing," *Economica*, XXXV (Aug. 1968).

fers are not generally feasible, the non-lump sum transfers that can be made are also subject to constraints, at least politically. Moreover, the constraints vary over time and between countries. There is much to say, therefore, for examining determination of optimal prices assuming lump sum transfers, while leaving for separate inquiry the further question posed as to what extent a departure from such optimal prices might be in order because non-lump sum transfers actually resorted to may themselves affect efficiency adversely.[3]

While I focus on public enterprise pricing, the analysis should bear as well on related aspects of governmental policy on monopoly, for example, the degree to which an especially high monopoly price can still be considered economically dubious in a more or less monopolistic world. Indeed, the analysis, in a sense, should be more relevant to such questions than to public enterprise pricing, for governmental measures to limit monopoly power, such as antitrust action, do not pose any fiscal problem to speak of. There is no need, therefore, to be concerned about budgetary constraints such as are encountered in public enterprise pricing.

Whether reference is to public enterprise pricing or to monopoly policy, I am in effect reverting to an approach to second best price formation such as was explored very briefly long ago by Professor Meade.[4] Meade's pioneer initiative was followed by the famous critique of Professors Lipsey and Lancaster,[5] and more recently second best price formation in the absence of a budget constraint has also been analyzed by others,[6] but progress in using that approach does not yet appear comparable to that in using the alterna-

---

3. A government usually must resort to transfers in connection with not only its management of public enterprises but its provision of "public goods." For the latter, principles of public enterprise pricing such as are to be formulated are more or less inapplicable. I assume here that all transfers alike, whether connected with public enterprise management or with the provision of public goods, are of a lump sum sort. But extension of the analysis to include non-lump sum transfers that are levied at given rates need pose no problem to speak of. For example, as will become evident, non-lump sum transfers that simply take the form of sales taxes and subsidies are readily allowed for in price margins that are attributed here to monopoly.

4. J. E. Meade, *Trade and Welfare*, Vol. II (New York, 1955), ch. VIII, and *Mathematical Appendix* (New York, 1955), chs. II and III.

5. R. G. Lipsey and Kelvin Lancaster, "The General Theory of the Second Best," *Review of Economic Studies*, XXIV (Feb. 1957).

6. See especially H. A. John Green, "The Social Optimum in the Presence of Monopoly and Taxation," *Review of Economic Studies*, XXVIII (Oct. 1961). As will appear, for a special case, Green anticipates some of the results obtained in the present essay. Analysis of second best price formation along Meade's lines must also benefit from recent exchanges on the general nature of the second best problem. See P. Bohm, "On the Theory of the Second Best," *Review of Economic Studies*, XXXIV (July 1967).

tive one assuming perfect competition but excluding lump sum transfers.

Second best analysis can quickly become very involved. As is often done, I focus on an abstract model, where a single variable factor, labor, is employed in the economy generally, and leave to separate inquiry the more realistic case where there are other variable factors as well. I also follow a usual practice in assuming that labor is of a single homogeneous kind and that there is but one consuming household in the economy. But, as is not difficult to show, the analysis is readily extended to many households and also remains substantially intact where there are many kinds of labor, though some aspects of that case seem to become relatively complex.[7]

1. THE PROBLEM

Let us designate the n consumers' goods our household consumes as $x_1 \ldots x_i \ldots x_n$. The household also supplies a homogeneous kind of labor, y. For convenience, the negative of y will be designated as x_{n+1}. Since x_{n+1} increases (i.e., becomes a smaller negative) when y decreases, it may be considered as representing "leisure," though its zero point is, of course, inappropriate from that standpoint. Since labor is the only variable factor of production, x_i, $i = 1 \ldots n$, conforms to the formula

(1.1) $x_i = G^i(y_i)$,

y_i being the amount of labor devoted to the production of x_i.[8] As implied, each commodity is produced in a single production unit, though it is not precluded that a production unit even so may behave competitively.

That, moreover, is the way the household behaves in any event. Thus, the household supplies labor and acquires consumers' goods in markets and in doing so, seeks, as if it were without monopoly power, to maximize its welfare, or utility, as given by the formula

(1.2) $W = F(x)$,.

where x represents $x_1 \ldots x_i \ldots x_{n+1}$, and

(1.3) $x_{n+1} \equiv -y = -\sum_{i=1}^{n} y_i.$

7. On these variants and some others referred to later, see the expanded version of this essay that has been circulated as Discussion Paper 180, March 1971, by the Harvard Institute of Economic Research.

8. Here and elsewhere the same symbol is used to designate both an economic category, e.g., a commodity or service, and its magnitude.

While the household is indifferent as to the production units in which its labor is employed, it is able to vary, and cares about, the length of the working day. With that the economy in question is, I think, of decidedly more interest here than it would be otherwise.

The household, then, takes as parameters the prevailing prices of consumers' goods, $p_1 \ldots p_i \ldots p_n$, and the prevailing wage rate p_{n+1}. It also conforms to the requirement

(1.4) $\mathbf{px'} = I.$

I represents the household's income from other than labor services, i.e., from profits and rents earned in the private sector, and from transfers from government.

As for such nonlabor income, the household itself owns all industries except the first, that being owned and operated by the government. The ouput of that industry, however, is sold to the household just as is that of an industry it owns, and wages are paid to the household out of the proceeds for the labor services employed. Here, as in the private sector, profits and rents also accrue to the household, but as citizen rather than owner. Thus, profits and rents in the x_1 industry accrue initially to the government, which transmits them in turn to the household. As explained, the transmission is through lump sum transfers. Should the x_1 industry lose rather than make money, the household is the payer rather than the payee, but otherwise the procedure is the same.

The government may employ labor elsewhere than in the x_1 industry, but if so, such employment is taken as a datum, and y as calculated is net of it. While I includes the household's earning from such employment, those earnings are precisely offset by transfers that are required to finance the employment in question. As noted, such transfers too are taken to be of a lump sum sort.

Under familiar assumptions regarding (1.2), the household achieves its desired expenditure pattern when, subject to (1.4),

(1.5) $R^i(\mathbf{x}) \equiv F_i/F_{n+1} = p_i/p_{n+1}, \; i = 1 \ldots n.$

Here F_i is the partial derivative of F with respect to x_i, $i = 1 \ldots n$, and F_{n+1} has a corresponding meaning with respect to x_{n+1}. The term R^i, therefore, represents the marginal rate of substitution between x_i and x_{n+1}.

While as a consumer and supplier of labor, the household takes prices and the wage rate as parameters, production in the ith industry conforms to the formula.

(1.6) $p_i/p_{n+1} = m_i/G^{i\prime}(y_i),$

where m_i is the ratio of price to marginal cost prevailing in equilibrium. Moreover, privately owned industries are operated more or less monopolistically, so that $m_i \geq 1$, $i = 2 \ldots n$, it being understood that the inequality holds for some industries. Price-cost ratios vary as between industries, but, for any i, m_i is a constant in equilibrium. Monopoly, in other words, entails establishment of a given ratio of price to marginal costs, or at least one adhered to in the face of changes to be considered in equilibrium activity levels.

Formula (1.6) also applies to the first industry, but m_1 is fixed by the government. It is thus taken as a parameter, and in effect the subject of our second best analysis. For convenience, we consider the government as fixing p_1 indirectly by fixing m_1, rather than directly. Which procedure is adopted, however, is immaterial.

In sum, our economy is characterized in all essentials by a familiar sort of system of general equilibrium. Thus, from (1.4) and (1.5), the household's demand for the ith good may be viewed as a function,

(1.7) $x_i = D^i(\boldsymbol{p}, I)$, $i = 1 \ldots n+1$.

As indicated, (1.7) applies to the household's demand for leisure as well as commodities. From (1.1) and (1.6), the ith production unit supplies its output in conformity with the formula

(1.8) $x_i = S^i(\boldsymbol{p}, m_1)$,

and all production units together require labor services in conformity with the corresponding formula

(1.9) $-y = S^{n+1}(\boldsymbol{p}, m_1)$,

the negative sign being inserted for convenience. I omit $m_2 \ldots m_n$ as arguments in these supply functions, since they are taken as data. Moreover, while m_1 is inserted as such an argument in all such functions, $S^i_{m_1}$, the change in supply induced by a unit change in m_1, with $\boldsymbol{p}$ constant, is nul for $i = 2 \ldots n$. Let S^i_j be the corresponding variation induced by a unit change in p_j, $j = 1 \ldots n$. Then that too is nul for $i \neq j$, except where $i = n+1$.

Equilibrium in any ith market, then, requires that

(1.10) $D^i(\boldsymbol{p}, I) - S^i(\boldsymbol{p}, m_1) = 0$, $i = 1 \ldots n+1$.

While household money income, I, equals the community's nonlabor income, note that that is not an additional condition for equilibrium. Rather it follows from (1.10), together with (1.4). Thus, from (1.10),

(1.11) $\displaystyle\sum_{i=1}^{n+1} p_i D^i(\boldsymbol{p}, I) = \sum_{i=1}^{n+1} p_i S^i(\boldsymbol{p}, I)$.

Here the term on the right represents the community's nonlabor income, while from (1.4), that on the left corresponds to the household's money income, I.

As is usually so in a system such as is in question, one price has to be determined exogenously. Suppose that is done for the money wage rate. Then, for any given m_1, there are $n+1$ unknowns, consisting of n prices and the household's money income. For the determination of those unknowns, there are $n+1$ equations of the form of (1.10). There are also unknowns comprising the physical quantities of different goods produced and consumed, and the volume of labor services supplied and employed, but given p and I, these are determined at once by either (1.7), or (1.8) and (1.9).

While the conditions set forth thus suffice to determine an economic equilibrium, the equilibrium, of course, need not be a second best optimum, and still less does it represent a first best. For the latter, according to well-known reasoning, all is as has been described, with a vital exception: $m_i = 1$ for all i. It also follows that so far as any $m_i \neq 1$, the first best is unattained, but it should be observed that it is still not necessarily unattainable. Thus, the adverse effect of monopolistic price-cost ratios on efficiency could imaginably be fully offset by governmental action; for example, by the granting of appropriate subsidies on consumption of the products affected. A second best problem can arise, therefore, only if such compensatory action of government is excluded. [9] It is on the understanding that this is so thảt we proceed. In effect, (1.6) is, for $i>1$, a constraint that the government is unable either to violate or to vitiate. The government, however, is able to determine one variable, m_1. How should it do so?

As indicated, equilibrium magnitudes throughout the system are determined by the stated conditions for any given m_1. Hence such magnitudes should generally vary with m_1. The government supposedly, like the household, will wish to maximize W. Hence, it must determine m_1 so that

(1.12) $dW/dm_1 = 0$.

In attempting to do so, it must also be able to evaluate dW/dm_1 in a suboptimal position, for that is necessary in determining whether a given variation in m_1 is to the good or not.

Alternatively, from (1.2) and (1.5),

(1.13) $dW/\delta = \sum_{i=1}^{n+1} p_i dx_i,$

where δ is the marginal utility of money income. Hence

9. See Bohm, *Review of Economic Studies*, XXXIV (July 1967).

(1.14) $\quad \dfrac{1}{\delta} \dfrac{dW}{dm_1} = \sum_{i=1}^{n+1} p_i \dfrac{dx_i}{dm_1}.$

I shall refer to dW/δ as representing, for incremental variations, the adjusted change in the community's welfare, or simply as the change in its real income, and to the magnitude of such a change induced by a unit change in m_1, as given by (1.14), as the real income effect. On what does the sign of that effect depend? When will it vanish? Those are the questions that the government must answer, and that must be of concern here.[1]

2. The Real Income Effect and the Optimum

The following notation is to be used:

D_j^i: the change in household demand for x_i induced by a unit change in p_j.

C_j^i: the corresponding variation in household demand for x_i, induced by a compensated unit change in p_j.

D_I^i: the change in household demand for x_i induced by a unit change in I.

S_j^i; $S_{m_1}^i$: as explained on p. 523.

Turning to the questions posed, we shall differentiate (1.10) with respect to m_1, for $i = 1 \ldots n+1$. As before, p_{n+1} is taken as a datum.

Then,

(2.1) $\quad \sum_{j=1}^{n} (D_j^i - S_j^i) \dfrac{dp_j}{dm_1} + D_I^i \dfrac{dI}{dm_1} = S_{m_1}^i.$

Slutsky taught us that

(2.2) $\quad D_j^i = C_j^i - x_j D_I^i.$

Moreover, from (1.4) and (1.14),

(2.3) $\quad \dfrac{dI}{dm_1} = \sum_{j=1}^{n} x_j \dfrac{dp_j}{dm_1} + \dfrac{1}{\delta} \dfrac{dW}{dm_1}.$

---

1. It merely restates the problem again but it still is illuminating to see that, from (1.1) and (1.3), (1.14) may be reformulated as

(1.15) $\quad \dfrac{1}{\delta} \dfrac{dW}{dm_1} = p_{n+1} \sum_{i=1}^{n} (m_i - 1) \dfrac{dy_i}{dm_1}.$

Note that $(m_i - 1)$ is indicative of the gain in welfare for a unit change in employment in the ith industry. The product of that expression and dy_i/dm_1, therefore, indicates the gain in welfare in the ith industry that is induced by a unit change in m_1. It also follows that the real income effect is positive or negative or vanishes depending on whether the aggregate of such gains is plus, minus, or nul.

Using (2.2) and (2.3), we may rewrite (2.1) as

(2.4) $\sum\limits_{j=1}^{n} (C_j{}^i - S_j{}^i)\dfrac{dp_j}{dm_1} + \dfrac{D_I{}^i}{\delta}\dfrac{dW}{dm_1} = S_{m_1}{}^i.$

Recall that for $i \leqslant n$, $S_j{}^i = 0$, when $i \neq j$, and $S_m{}^i = 0$, when $i > 1$. Then, solving in a usual way, we find that

(2.5) $\dfrac{1}{\delta}\dfrac{dW}{dm_1} = (S_{m_1}{}^{n+1} \Delta_{1,\ n+1} + S_{m_1}{}^{1}\Delta_{2,\ n+1})/\Delta,$

where
(2.6)

$$
\Delta =
\begin{vmatrix}
(C_1{}^{n+1} - S_1{}^{n+1}) & (C_2{}^{n+1} - S_2{}^{n+1}) & . . & (C_n{}^{n+1} - S_n{}^{n+1}) & D_I{}^{n+1} \\
(C_1{}^{1} - S_1{}^{1}) & C_2{}^{1} & . . & C_n{}^{1} & D_I{}^{1} \\
C_1{}^{2} & (C_2{}^{2} - S_2{}^{2}) & . . & C_n{}^{2} & D_I{}^{2} \\
. & . & & . & . \\
. & . & & . & . \\
. & . & & . & . \\
C_1{}^{n} & C_2{}^{n} & . . & (C_n{}^{n} - S_n{}^{n}) & D_I{}^{n}
\end{vmatrix}
$$

Here $\Delta_{1,\ n+1}$ refers to the cofactor of $D_I{}^{n+1}$, that being the term in the first row and $n+1$th column of Δ. Similarly $\Delta_{2,\ n+1}$ refers to the cofactor of $D_I{}^1$, that being the term in the second row and $n+1$th column of Δ.[2] Formula (2.5) relates to the real income effect, but the corresponding optimum requirement evidently is

(2.7) $S_{m_1}{}^{n+1}\Delta_{1,\ n+1} + S^1{}_{m_1}\Delta_{2,\ n+1} = 0.$

Gradients of compensated demand schedules in Δ may, of course, be determined from the household's uncompensated schedules from which we started. Given such schedules, then, and also gradients of supply schedules that were assumed, (2.5) indicates the real income effect that is associated with any m_1 and the corresponding equilibrium p and I. Moreover, (2.7) serves as the equation, additional to (1.10), that is needed to determine the optimal m_1. The underlying demand and supply schedules, therefore, now serve to determine the optimal m_1 along with the equilibrium p and I.

In sum, (2.5) and (2.7) already represents in principle answers to the questions posed on p. 525. For present purposes, however, they serve rather as preliminaries to the derivation of further formulas that may, I think, be more readily construed and applied, though they necessarily resolve ultimately into essentially the same terms as (2.5) and (2.7).

Imagine that the constraints of our model may be violated.

2. This conventional sort of notation is adhered to throughout this essay.

Particularly, a good (bad) fairy allots to the economy a labor dividend (tax), which permits the amount of labor supplied by the household to diverge from the amount of labor employed in enterprises. In other words, in place of (1.3) we have the condition

$$(2.8) \qquad z = \sum_{j=1}^{n} y_j - y,$$

where z is the labor dividend (tax), and we still have $x_{n+1} \equiv -y$. Household money income, I, is viewed as including, along with profits and rents previously constituting it, the money value of the labor dividend at the prevailing wage rate. Also, if (2.8) supersedes (1.3), it is understood that (1.10) no longer holds for $i = n+1$. It follows that money income, prices other than the wage rate, and ultimately physical inputs and outputs, now depend not only on m_1 but on the labor dividend, z. The household's welfare, therefore, also depends on those two parameters, i.e., $W = H(m_1, z)$.

It is also understood, though, that z does not vary freely. Rather, two hypothetical sorts of constrained variations are envisaged:

i. The price-cost ratio for x_1, that is, m_1, is taken as a parameter, but z varies in dependence on it in such a way as to compensate for the change in m_1. In other words, z varies so that, despite the changes in m_1, welfare is constant.

ii. The foregoing assumes, as is reasonable, that $H_z \neq 0$. On the same assumption, z may also be envisaged as depending on W. Of particular interest is the variation in z that is needed to support a unit change in real income as given by (1.13), m_1 being constant.

In sum, z varies in response to the parameters, m_1 and W. As it does, so too does the economy generally. That must be borne in mind in interpreting the following terms that are to be used:

$(dz/dm_1)_F$: the variation in the labor dividend required to compensate for a unit change in m_1, W being constant;

$(dp_i/dm_1)_F$: the change in p_i induced by a unit change in m_1 that is compensated by an appropriate change in the labor dividend;

$\psi_{m_1}{}^i \equiv (dx_i/dm_1)_F$: the associated change in x_i;

$\delta(dz/dW)_{m_1}$: the variation in the labor dividend that is needed to support a unit change in real income, m_1 constant;

$\delta(dp_i/dW)_{m_1}$: the change in p_i associated with such a unit change in real income;

$\rho^i \equiv \delta(dx_i/dW)_{m_1}$: the corresponding variation in x_i.

The further formulas for the real income effect and the optimum that were referred to are as follows:

$$(2.9) \qquad \frac{1}{\delta}\frac{dW}{dm_1} = -\left(\frac{dz}{dm_1}\right)_F \bigg/ \delta\left(\frac{dz}{dW}\right)_{m_1},$$

where

$$(2.10) \qquad \left(\frac{dz}{dm_1}\right)_F = \sum_{i=1}^{n}\left(\psi^i{}_{m_1}\bigg/G^{i\prime}\right) + \psi_{m_1}{}^{n+1},$$

and

$$(2.11) \qquad \delta\left(\frac{dz}{dW}\right)_{m_1} = \sum_{i=1}^{n}\left(\rho^i\bigg/G^{i\prime}\right) + \rho^{n+1}.$$

We also find that

$$(2.12) \quad \begin{cases} (2.12a) \quad (dp_i/dm_1)_F = S_{m_1}{}^1\epsilon_{1i}/\epsilon, & i = 1 \ldots n; \\[2ex] (2.12b) \quad \psi^i{}_{m_1} = \dfrac{S^1{}_{m_1}}{\epsilon}\sum_{j=1}^{n}C_j{}^i\epsilon_{1j}, & i = 1 \ldots n+1; \end{cases}$$

and

$$(2.13) \quad \begin{cases} (2.13a) \quad \rho_i = -\dfrac{S_i{}^i}{\epsilon}\sum_{j=1}^{n}D_I{}^j\epsilon_{ji}, & i = 1 \ldots n; \\[2ex] (2.13b) \quad \rho^{n+1} = -\dfrac{1}{\epsilon}\left\{\displaystyle\sum_{j=1}^{n}\sum_{k=1}^{n}D_I{}^jC_k{}^{n+1}\epsilon_{jk} - D^{n+1}\epsilon\right\}. \end{cases}$$

Here ϵ is the minor corresponding to the cofactor of $D_I{}^{n+1}$ in Δ in (2.6), and ϵ_{ij} is the cofactor of the indicated term in ϵ.

Formulas (2.9) to (2.13) all bear on the real income effect, but the corresponding optimum requirement is evidently that

$$(2.14) \qquad (dz/dm_1)_F = 0.$$

In the optimum, then, the change in labor dividend needed to compensate for a unit change in m_1 must be nul. This is, of course, as it should be. In the optimum a unit change in m_1 must leave welfare unchanged in any case, so no compensatory change in the labor dividend is required for that result.

We also begin to sense the rationale of the additional formulas generally when we consider that the term $1/G^{i\prime}$, which appears in (2.10) and (2.11), represents the increment of labor needed to produce a marginal unit of output of x_i. In formula (2.10), then, the ratio $\psi^i{}_{m_1}/G^{i\prime}$ represents the increment of labor needed to produce the additional x_i that is induced by a compensated unit change in m_1. The term $\psi_{m_1}{}^{n+1}$ is the increment of leisure that the household is induced to consume, as a result of the same change in m_1. Hence, it is also the negative of the increment of labor that the household supplies under the impact of that change in m_1. As given by (2.10), therefore, the labor dividend induced by such a unit change in m_1 is simply the difference between, on the one hand, the aggregate of increments of labor required in all industries in response to a compensated unit change in m_1, and, on the other, the increment of labor that the household is induced to supply in response to such a unit change in m_1. Formula (2.11) is to be construed similarly, though here reference is to the change in labor dividend induced by a unit change in real income, m_1 constant; and hence also to corresponding changes in production, labor requirements, and labor supply.

From (1.6), $1/G^{i\prime}$ must also correspond to the product of the reciprocal of the price-cost ratio for x_i and the price of x_i in wage units. By implication, the magnitude of the labor dividend induced by a variation in one or another of the two parameters, m_1 and W, depends on the magnitudes of the price-cost ratios generally, and hence also on that for x_1. The latter is itself to be determined in the optimum. It also follows that the terms on the right in (2.10) and (2.11) may be viewed simply as aggregates, suitably weighted, of the reciprocals of price-cost ratios in the economy generally. On this interpretation, the provision of leisure, as is proper, is viewed as a productive activity with a price-cost ratio of unity. The final terms on the right in (2.10) and (2.11), therefore, represent the product of the reciprocal of that price-cost ratio (unity) and the corresponding weight. Further formulas set forth relate in effect to the nature of the weights for the reciprocals of the price-cost ratios that (2.10) and (2.11) established.

Turning to the proof of (2.9) to (2.13), we find that (2.10) and (2.11) follow at once from (1.1) and (2.8). As for (2.9), that can be proved in two ways. According to the first, we simply consider again that with $H_z \not\equiv 0$, z may be viewed as a function of m_1 and W, say, $z = z(m_1, W)$. Formula (2.9) follows if we differentiate z totally in respect of m_1 along a path z constant. Thus

$$(2.15) \quad 0 = \left(\frac{dz}{dm_1}\right)_W + \left(\frac{dz}{dW}\right)_{m_1}\left(\frac{dW}{dm_1}\right)_z ,$$

and

$$(2.16) \quad \frac{1}{\delta}\left(\frac{dW}{dm_1}\right)_z = -\left(\frac{dz}{dm_1}\right)_W \Big/ \delta\left(\frac{dz}{dW}\right)_{m_1}.$$

Note that $(dW/dm_1)_z$ corresponds to (dW/dm_1) in (1.14) and hence to that term in (2.9).

The second way of demonstrating (2.9) entails elaborating that formula in terms of underlying demand and supply functions, and so demonstrating that the real income effect as given by (2.9) comes to the same thing as that effect as given by (2.5). That turns out to be tedious, but the demonstration yields other formulas of interest, and may be illuminating in any event.

Recall that with (2.8) replacing (1.3), (1.10) is no longer valid for $i=n+1$. For variations of the first of the two sorts referred to above, however, that is, where welfare is constant, m_1 is again the only parameter in equilibrium. As for z, that depends on m_1, the relationship between the two being given by (2.8).

Moreover, so far as variations generally are along a path for which welfare is constant, we may rewrite (2.4) as

$$(2.17) \qquad \sum_{j=1}^{n} (C_j{}^i - S_j{}^i)\left(\frac{dp_j}{dm_1}\right)_F = S_{m_1}{}^i, \qquad\qquad i=1 \ldots n.$$

If in (2.12a) we replace i by j, that formula is obtained by solving (2.17) in a conventional way for $(dp_j/dm_1)_F$.

From (1.7), (2.2), and (2.3), since welfare is constant,

$$(2.18) \qquad \psi_{m_1}{}^i = \sum_{j=1}^{n} C_j{}^i\left(\frac{dp_j}{dm_1}\right)_F, \qquad\qquad i=1 \ldots n+1.$$

Formula (2.12b) follows from (2.12a) and (2.18).

It also follows that

$$(2.19) \qquad S_{m_1}{}^{n+1}\Delta_{1,\,n+1} + S^1{}_{m_1}\Delta_{2,\,n+1} =$$
$$-\Delta_{1,\,n+1}\left\{ \sum_{i=1}^{n} \psi^i{}_{m_1} \Big/ G^{i\prime} + \psi_{m_1}{}^{n+1} \right\}.$$

Note that, as easily shown, (2.12b) implies

$$(2.20) \qquad \psi^i{}_{m_1} = S^1{}_{m_1}S_i{}^i\epsilon_{1i}/\epsilon, \qquad\qquad i=2 \ldots n.$$

As indicated, reference is to x_i only for $i>1$, but note too that in the case of x_1, (2.12b) implies

$$(2.21) \qquad \psi^1{}_{m_1} = S^1{}_{m_1}(\epsilon + S_1{}^1\epsilon_{11})/\epsilon.$$

Also, from (1.1) and (1.6),

$$(2.22) \qquad S_{m_1}{}^{n+1}S_1{}^1 = S^1{}_{m_1}S_1{}^{n+1}.$$

The derivation of (2.19) entails use of all these relationships.

If we retrace the steps leading to (2.17) but now with W as the parameter, we arrive at once at this alternative formula:

$$(2.23) \qquad \sum_{k=1}^{n} (C_k{}^i - S_k{}^i)\left(\frac{dp_k}{dW}\right)_{m_1} = -D_I{}^i/\delta, \qquad\qquad i=1 \ldots n.$$

Solving,

$$(2.24) \qquad \delta\left(\frac{dp_k}{dW}\right)_{m_1} = -\frac{1}{\epsilon} \sum_{j=1}^{n} D_I{}^j\epsilon_{jk}.$$

Recall the derivation of (2.18). By similar reasoning,

$$(2.25) \qquad \rho^i = \delta \sum_{k=1}^{n} C_k{}^i\left(\frac{dp_k}{dW}\right)_{m_1} + D_I{}^i, \qquad\qquad i=1 \ldots n+1.$$

Using (2.24), we find that

$$(2.26) \qquad \rho^i = -\frac{1}{\epsilon} \sum_{k=1}^{n} \sum_{j=1}^{n} C_k{}^i D_I{}^j \epsilon_{jk} + D_I{}^i, \qquad\qquad i = 1 \ldots n+1.$$

Formulas (2.13a) and (2.13b) follow from (2.26) after a reversal in the order of summation. If use is made too of (1.1) and (1.6), it also follows that

$$(2.27) \qquad \Delta = \Delta_{1,\,n+1} \left\{ \sum_{i=1}^{n} \rho^i/G^{i\prime} + \rho^{n+1} \right\}.$$

Finally, (2.9) follows from (2.5), (2.19), (2.27), and (2.10) and (2.11).

3. Some Implications

What may be concluded as to the optimal m_1? Like (2.7), (2.14), when taken together with (1.10), should determine the optimal m_1, along with the equilibrium p and I that correspond to it. The relevant principles, then, turn out to be rather complex, but note that as determined by the indicated formulas the optimal m_1 is open to empirical inquiry. That is evident from an inspection of those formulas, for all terms in them are of a familiar, observable sort. But the theoretic analysis can be pushed somewhat further. To do so may shed more light on the optimum, and might also facilitate application. That seems the more likely so far as information of the sort needed for such application is usually apt to be incomplete.

To begin with, as determined by (2.14), together with (1.10), the optimal m_1 can be shown to have the interesting property that

$$(3.1) \qquad m_1 = m,$$

where

$$(3.2) \qquad 1/m = \sum_{i=2}^{n+1} \frac{p_i}{m_i} \psi^i{}_{m_1} \Big/ \sum_{i=2}^{n+1} p_i \psi^i{}_{m_1}.$$

Here m_{n+1}, the price-cost ratio for leisure, is understood, as is proper, to be unity.

From (3.2), then, m is a weighted harmonic mean of price-cost ratios for all commodities other than x_1, together with the corresponding ratio (unity) for leisure. For each good, the weight applied is the product of its price and the change in the household's consumption of that good that is induced by a compensated unit change in the price-cost ratio of x_1, that is, m_1.

Such a variation appears rather novel in theory, but evidently reference is to a counterpart for general equilibrium analysis of the term $C_1{}^i$, which indicates the impact on the demand for x_i of a compensated change in p_1 under partial equilibrium analysis. It seems fitting, therefore, to refer correspondingly to the sort of cross relation represented by $\psi^i_{m_1}$ but in order to avoid confusion, the qualification "aggregate" will be used as a prefix to make clear that reference here is to cross relations in a general equilibrium context.

Thus, in partial equilibrium analysis x_i is said to be either a net substitute for, or a net complement to, x_1, depending on whether $C_1{}^i >$ or < 0, and as being in a relation of net independence to x_1 if $C_1{}^i = 0$. Accordingly, x_i will be said here to be an aggregate net substitute or an aggregate net complement to x_1, depending on whether $\psi^i_{m_1}$ is $>$ or < 0. It will be said to be in a relation of aggregate net independence to x_1 if $\psi^i_{m_1} = 0$. While attention focuses on m_1 as a parameter, variations where some other price-cost ratio serves in that capacity are, of course, designated similarly.

From (3.2), then, m may be described as a weighted harmonic mean of price-cost ratios, the weight of each ratio being given by the product of the price of the good in question and its rate of aggregate net substitution for x_1. Also, the optimal m_1 equals m as so understood. A cardinal concern in the literature of the second best is to discover what counterpart obtains in one or another context to the rule that price equals marginal cost, which applies where the first best is achievable. Formulas (3.1) and (3.2) may be considered as representing the counterpart rule that applies here.

Formulas (3.1) and (3.2) may also be interpreted in another interesting way. Note that p_i/m_i is simply the marginal cost of x_i. Hence, from (3.1) and (3.2), the optimal price-cost ratio for the public enterprise good equals the quotient of two weighted aggregates for all other goods: one of prices and the other of marginal costs. For each good, the corresponding weight is its rate of aggregate net substitution for the public good.

Here is the proof of (3.1) and (3.2). Taken together with (2.10) and (1.6), (2.14) means that

$$(3.3) \qquad \sum_{i=1}^{n+1} (p_i/m_i)\psi^i_{m_1} = 0,$$

or

$$(3.4) \qquad 1/m_1 = - \left\{ \sum_{i=2}^{n+1} (p_i/m_i)\psi^i_{m_1} \right\} / p_1\psi^1_{m_1}.$$

For variations such as are in question,[3]

---

3. Since real income is constant,
$$(3.5) \qquad \sum_{i=1}^{n+1} F_i\psi^i_{m_1} = 0.$$
Formula (3.6) follows from this and (1.5).

(3.6) $\quad \sum\limits_{i=1}^{n+1} p_i \psi^i{}_{m_1} = 0.$

Hence

(3.7) $\quad p_1 \psi^1{}_{m_1} = - \sum\limits_{i=2}^{n+1} p_i \psi^i{}_{m_1}.$

Formulas (3.1) and (3.2) follow.

For purposes of analyzing the optimal m_1, reference may be made to its relation not only to m but to the corresponding mean for goods other than leisure, that is, to m_c, where

(3.8) $\quad 1/m_c = \sum\limits_{i=2}^{n} \dfrac{p_i \psi^i{}_{m_1}}{m_i} \bigg/ \sum\limits_{i=2}^{n} p_i \psi^i{}_{m_1}.$

From (3.1), (3.2), and (3.8), it follows at once that in the optimum

(3.9) $\quad m_1 = m_c(1+\gamma)/(1+m_c\gamma),$

where

(3.10) $\quad \gamma = p_{n+1} \psi_{m_1}{}^{n+1} \bigg/ \sum\limits_{i=2}^{n} p_i \psi_{m_1}{}^i.$

Hence γ represents the quotient of, on the one hand, the rate, in money terms, of aggregate net substitution of leisure for x_1 and, on the other, the sum of the corresponding rates for all goods other than leisure and x_1. I shall refer to γ as representing the comparative employment effect, it being understood unless otherwise indicated that reference is particularly to a compensated unit change in m_1.

Note that $\psi^i{}_{m_1}$ may differ in sign for different goods, so both m and m_c may possibly be "external" averages of the price-cost ratios. In any event, of particular interest is the relation of the optimal m_1 to m_c and to one other magnitude, unity, that is the level at which the price of x_1 equals marginal cost. What may be concluded on those matters? There are many possibilities, but I shall consider only those arising where $m_c > 0$. In Table I, I show the resulting optimal m_1 for each of a number of further cases that may then be distinguished.

Delineation of possibilities in terms of m_c and γ assumes that neither $\sum\limits_{i=2}^{n} p_i \psi^i{}_{m_1}/m_i$ nor $\sum\limits_{i=2}^{n} p_i \psi^i{}_{m_1}$ is nul. Should both expressions vanish, however, we see from (3.4) and (3.7) that the optimal m_1 is unity. Further cases where only one of the two expressions in question vanish are left to the reader.

Reference has been to different cases in respect to m_c and γ. Such cases may be expressed in turn in terms of the usage adopted

TABLE I.

THE OPTIMAL m_1 FOR ALTERNATIVE γ AND m_c

		$0 < m_c < 1$ (a)	$m_c = 1$ (b)	$m_c > 1$ (c)
(i)	$\gamma > 0$	$> m_c$; < 1	1	> 1; $< m_c$
(ii)	$\gamma = 0$	m_c	m_c	m_c
(iii)	$-1 < \gamma < 0$	$< m_c$	1	$> m_c *$
(iv)	$\gamma < -1$	$> 1 \ddagger$	1	< 1

* Provided $m_c\gamma > -1$. If $m_c\gamma < -1$, $m_1 < 0$.

\ddagger Provided $m_c\gamma < -1$. If $m_c\gamma > -1$, $m_1 < 0$.

in respect of $\psi^i{}_{m_1}$. To refer only to a few of the more interesting ones, $\psi_{m_1}{}^{n+1} \geq 0$ provided that leisure is an aggregate net substitute for x_1, or at least not an aggregate net complement to that commodity. Also, $\sum\limits_{i=2}^{n} p_i\psi^i{}_{m_1} > 0$ if commodities generally tend, in money terms, to be aggregate net substitutes for x_1. Under such circumstances, then, γ, the comparative employment effect, is necessarily positive, or at least not negative.

As for m_c, that may be written as

$$(3.11) \qquad m_c = m_{cs}(1-\beta) \Big/ \left(1 - \frac{m_{cs}}{m_{cc}}\beta\right).$$

Let us order commodities so that those numbered 2 to j are aggregate net substitutes for or in a relation of aggregate net independence to x_1 and those numbered $j+1$ to n are aggregate net complements to x_1. Then

$$(3.12a, b) \quad 1/m_{cs} = \sum_{i=2}^{j} \frac{p_i\psi^i{}_{m_1}}{m_i} \Big/ \sum_{i=2}^{j} p_i\psi^i{}_{m_1};$$

$$1/m_{cc} = \sum_{i=j+1}^{n} \frac{p_i\psi^i{}_{m_1}}{m_i} \Big/ \sum_{i=j+1}^{n} p_i\psi^i{}_{m_1},$$

and

$$(3.13) \qquad \beta = - \sum_{i=j+1}^{n} p_i\psi^i{}_{m_1} \Big/ \sum_{i=2}^{j} p_i\psi^i{}_{m_1}.$$

Suppose as before that in money terms commodities are predominantly aggregate net substitutes for x_1, so that $\beta < 1$. Suppose also that commodities that are aggregate net substitutes for x_1 tend to have price-cost ratios that are comparable to, or greater than, those of commodities that are aggregate net complements to x_1, though, if they are greater, they are not so much so, so that $(m_{cs}/m_{cc})\beta > 1$. Then $m_c \geq m_{cs}$, and the latter is of course necessarily equal to or greater than unity.

In the foregoing circumstances, then, the optimal m_1 is found in the upper right boxes of Table I, that is, in the optimum

(3.14) $1 \leqslant m_1 \leqslant m_c$.

Moreover, m_c is an internal average of m_i, $i = 2 \ldots n$. At least, it is not less than unity. Note that if $\psi_{m_1}{}^{n+1} = 0$, and leisure is in a relation of aggregate net independence to x_1, $\gamma = 0$. The optimal m_1, then, precisely equals m_c.[4]

I have inquired into the optimal m_1 associated with diverse aggregate net cross relations between goods other than x_1 and x_1 (i.e., $\psi^i{}_{m_1}$, $i = 2 \ldots n+1$). As noted (p. 535, n. 4), also relevant to the optimal m_1 is the aggregate impact on the consumption of x_1 of a compensated unit change in its own price (i.e., $\psi^1{}_{m_1}$). All these aspects may themselves usefully be subject to analysis. Particularly, four interesting theorems may be formulated in respect of them:

1. A sufficient condition for

(3.15a, b) $(dp_1/dm_1)_F > 0$; $\psi^1{}_{m_1} < 0$

is that additional applications of labor be subject to diminishing returns everywhere, or as seen from (1.6), $S_i{}^i > 0$, $i = 1 \ldots n$. With such returns, therefore, a compensated increase in m_1 not only affects, but necessarily raises, the price of x_1, while also reducing the consumption of that good.

Proof: Given diminishing returns, as is well known, ϵ must be a "Hicksian determinant"; that is,

$$(C_i{}^i - S_i{}^i) < 0, \quad \begin{vmatrix} (C_i{}^i - S_i{}^i) & C_j{}^i \\ C_i{}^j & (C_j{}^j - S_j{}^j) \end{vmatrix} > 0,$$

(3.16) $$\begin{vmatrix} (C_i{}^i - S_i{}^i) & C_j{}^i & C_k{}^i \\ C_i{}^j & (C_j{}^j - S_j{}^j) & C_k{}^j \\ C_i{}^k & C_j{}^k & (C_k{}^k - S_k{}^k) \end{vmatrix} < 0,$$

and so on for all principal minors.[5] A corollary is that $\epsilon > 0$ if n is even and $\epsilon < 0$ if n is odd.

4. Note that possibilities that are alternative to those considered are somewhat restricted. Suppose, for example, $\psi^1{}_{m_1} < 0$ so that, to fall in with the usage adopted for $\psi^i{}_{m_1}$, the aggregate impact on the consumption of x_1 of a compensated increase in its own price is negative. Then in (3.7) the summation term on the right is positive. Hence, if

$$\sum_{i=2}^{n} p_i \psi^i{}_{m_1} > 0, \text{ then } (1+\gamma) > 0.$$

I am assuming that, if there is an optimum, m_1 is such that p_1 is positive. That is to say, I pass by cases such as are noted in the table.

5. The determinant ϵ corresponds to a matrix, representing the sum of two matrices, one whose determinant is ϵ as it would be if all $S_i{}^i = 0$, and the

From (2.12a), $(dp_1/dm_1)_F$ is the product of $S^1_{m_1}$ and the ratio of the first principal minor of ϵ, that is ϵ_{11}, to ϵ. Since $S_1^1 > 0$, $S_{m_1}^1 < 0$. See (1.1), (1.6), and (1.8). From (3.16), however, ϵ_{11} and ϵ are of opposite sign, so (3.15a) holds. From (2.12b),

$$(3.17) \quad \psi_{m_1}^1 = \frac{S^1_{m_1}}{\epsilon} \begin{vmatrix} C_1^1 & C_2^1 & \cdots & C_n^1 \\ C_1^2(C_2^2 - S_2^2) & \cdots & & C_n^2 \\ \cdot & \cdot & & \cdot \\ \cdot & \cdot & & \cdot \\ \cdot & \cdot & & \cdot \\ C_1^n & C_2^n & \cdots & (C_n^n - S_n^n) \end{vmatrix}.$$

The final determinant on the right evidently corresponds to ϵ as it would be if one term in it, S_1^1, were zero. The equality of S_1^1 to zero, however, would still leave ϵ as a Hicksian determinant. Hence the final determinant on the right has the same sign as ϵ. Formula (3.15b) follows.

2. Sufficient conditions for

$$(3.18) \quad \psi^i_{m_1} \geqslant 0, \qquad\qquad i = 2 \ldots n+1,$$

that is, for all goods to be aggregate net substitutes for, or at least not aggregate net complements to, x_1, are (i) As before, $S_i^i > 0$, $i = 1 \ldots n$; (ii) All goods are net substitutes for, or at least not complements to, each other, so that $C_j^i \geqslant 0$, $i \neq j$.

Proof: From (2.20),

$$(3.19) \quad \psi^i_{m_1} = S^1_{m_1} S_i^i \epsilon_{1i}/\epsilon, \qquad\qquad i = 2 \ldots n.$$

Since ϵ is Hicksian, and all off diagonal terms in it are, by assumption, nonnegative, all the conditions of a well-known theorem of Mosak are satisfied by that determinant. It follows that the cofactor of any off-diagonal term in ϵ either has the opposite sign from ϵ or is nul.[6] That applies among other things to ϵ_{1i}. Since $S_i^i > 0$

---

other, a diagonal matrix whose diagonal elements are $(-)S_i^i$. The former matrix relates to a quadratic form that is negative definite so long as the household is in a maximum position. See I. F. Pearce, *A Contribution to Demand Analysis* (Oxford, 1964), pp. 54–57. The diagonal matrix is necessarily negative definite. It follows that the matrix for which ϵ is the determinant is itself negative definite. See Arthur S. Goldberger, *Econometric Theory* (New York, 1964), p. 38. Without applying matrix algebra, however, the same result is obtained simply by expanding ϵ and its principal minors by diagonal elements.

6. Mosak formulates his theorem for the case where all off-diagonal terms are positive, and demonstrates that cofactors of such terms must be of the same sign as a principal minor of the same order. As is evident from his proof, however, should some off-diagonal terms be zero, that means only that the cofactor of an off-diagonal term might also be zero. See Jacob L. Mosak,

and $S^1{}_{m_1} < 0$, (3.18) holds for $i = 2 \ldots n$. Since by assumption $C_j{}^{n+1} \geqq 0$, $j = 1 \ldots n$, (3.18) also follows for $i = n+1$. See (2.12b).

A corollary is that in the case considered all prices, other than p_1, rise in response to a compensated increase in m_1. See (2.12a).

3. It is now assumed that all $C_j{}^i = 0$ for $i \neq j$, except $n+1$. In other words, all commodities other than leisure are in a relation of net independence to each other. Then all commodities other than leisure are also in a relation of aggregate net independence to x_1, i.e.,

$$(3.20) \quad \psi^i{}_{m_1} = 0, \qquad\qquad i = 2 \ldots n.$$

Also $\psi^1{}_{m_1}$ and $\psi_{m_1}{}^{n+1}$ reduce to

$$(3.21\text{a, b}) \quad \psi^1{}_{m_1} = S^1{}_{m_1} C_1{}^1 / (C_1{}^1 - S_1{}^1) \, ;$$
$$\psi_{m_1}{}^{n+1} = S^1{}_{m_1} C_1{}^{n+1} / (C_1{}^1 - S_1{}^1).$$

Given the indicated assumption, these formulas follow at once from (2.12b) and (2.20).

As is well known,

$$(3.22) \quad \sum_{i=1}^{n+1} p_i C_1{}^i = 0.$$

Under the indicated assumption, therefore,

$$(3.23) \quad p_1 C_1{}^1 = -p_{n+1} C_1{}^{n+1}.$$

An evident corollary of the theorem just set forth is that this parallel relation also obtains:

$$(3.24) \quad p_1 \psi^1{}_{m_1} = -p_{n+1} \psi_{m_1}{}^{n+1}.$$

4. Reference has been to aggregate net cross relations such as obtain when m_1 varies and W is constant. What if instead m_h varies and W is constant? How in particular will the resultant $\psi^1{}_{m_h}$ compare with $\psi^h{}_{m_1}$? In general, as readily seen, aggregate net cross relations are not fully symmetric, so $\psi^1{}_{m_h} \neq \psi^h{}_{m_1}$. But, according to our fourth theorem, an interesting relation prevails between terms such as are in question. Particularly, a sufficient condition for $\psi^1{}_{m_h}$ to have the same sign as $\psi^h{}_{m_1}$ is that there be diminishing returns everywhere. With such returns, in other words, if x_h is an aggregate net substitute for x_1, x_1 is an aggregate net substitute for x_h, and so on.

Proof: From (2.20)

$$(3.25) \quad \psi^h{}_{m_1} = S^1{}_{m_1} S_h{}^h \epsilon_{1h} / \epsilon.$$

By similar reasoning, however,

$$(3.26) \quad \psi^1{}_{m_h} = S^h{}_{m_h} S_1{}^1 \epsilon_{h1} / \epsilon.$$

General Equilibrium Theory in International Trade (Bloomington, Indiana, 1944), pp. 49–51.

By assumption $S^h{}_h$ and $S_1{}^1$ are positive, and $S^1{}_{m1}$ and $S^h{}_{m_h}$ are negative. Since ϵ is symmetric, $\epsilon_{1h}=\epsilon_{h1}$. The correspondence of $\psi^1{}_{m_h}$ and $\psi^h{}_{m_1}$ in sign follows.[7]

In all four theorems, note that reference is to sufficient conditions. Corresponding necessary conditions have not been formulated, but the sufficient ones are obviously by no means necessary.

From the first two theorems, the assumed conditions assured that $\psi^i{}_{m_1}\geq0$, $i=2\ldots n+1$. The evident corollary is that m as given by (3.2) is an internal average of m_i, $i=2\ldots n+1$. Similarly, m_c as given by (3.8) is an internal average of m_i, $i=2\ldots n$. It also follows that $m\geq1$ and that $m_c\geq1$. Moreover, the comparative employment effect, γ, as given by (3.10) is nonnegative. The assumed conditions also suffice, therefore, to assure that the optimal m_1 conforms to (3.14), and on the understanding that m_c is an internal average. The assumed conditions, to repeat, are that there are diminishing returns everywhere; no goods are net complements to each other. Here again the sufficient conditions are by no means necessary.

Should the conditions of theorem 3 obtain, it follows at once from (3.1) and (3.2) that the optimal m_1 is unity; that is, the optimal price for the public enterprise equals its marginal cost.

As analyzed, the optimum m_1 depends ultimately on gradients

7. What if the dividend were in terms of some good other than labor? Would the rate of aggregate net substitution of x_h for x_1 be affected in that case? With the dividend made available in one good rather than another, the degree of aggregate net substitutability between any two goods likely would be affected. Possibly the kind of relationship would be also, though under just what circumstances is not entirely clear. Inquiry along these lines, however, seems only to underline the propriety of according priority here to labor. Thus, should the dividend be in terms of a good other than labor, goods generally are no longer necessarily aggregate net substitutes for each other even if diminishing returns are universal and there are no partial equilibrium net complements.

Reference is, as before, to a more or less monopolistic world. Should there be perfect competition, rates of aggregate net substitution are the same whatever the nature of the dividend, and whatever, too, the nature of supply schedules and partial equilibrium net cross relations. The deeper reason for that result, however, is simply that with all price-cost ratios, including that of the public enterprise, equal to unity, the equilibrium is necessarily an optimum. A small change in m_1 would then leave real income unchanged, so no dividend of any sort is needed to compensate for it.

As explained, where reference has been to a labor dividend, (1.10) has been relaxed for x_{n+1}. Reference to a dividend in terms of a good other than labor should be understood correspondingly: that is, (1.10) is relaxed for some x_i, $i\leq n$.

of demand and supply schedules. Application of the analysis may often be facilitated, however, by translation of the formulas concerned to refer to corresponding elasticities. That is readily accomplished.

Thus, from (3.2) the mean price-cost ratio may be written as

$$(3.27) \quad 1/m = \sum_{i=2}^{n+1} \frac{p_i x_i}{m_i} {}^*\psi^i{}_{m_1} \bigg/ \sum_{i=2}^{n+1} p_i x_i {}^*\psi^i{}_{m_1},$$

where ${}^*\psi^i{}_{m_1}$ represents the relative rate of change, $\frac{1}{x_i}\psi^i{}_{m_1}$. Moreover, from (2.12b),

$$(3.28) \quad {}^*\psi^i{}_{m_1} = ({}^*S^1{}_{m_1}/{}^*\epsilon) \sum_{j=1}^{n} {}^*C_j{}^i {}^*\epsilon_{1j}.$$

Here ${}^*S^1{}_{m_1} = \frac{1}{x_1}S^1{}_{m_1}$ and ${}^*\epsilon$ corresponds to ϵ, except that all gradients of demand and supply are replaced by corresponding elasticities. Also, ${}^*C_j{}^i$ is an elasticity corresponding to $C_j{}^i$. Hence, the mean price-cost ratio, which the optimal m_1 equals, is now seen to be a weighted harmonic mean of price-cost ratios where the weight of each ratio is the product of the value of consumption involved and the corresponding relative rate of aggregate net substitution. The latter is expressed in turn in terms of the conventional partial equilibrium elasticities of net substitution and elasticities of supply of goods generally.

The mean price-cost ratio for goods other than leisure, m_c, and the comparative employment effect may be reformulated similarly.

As explained, the optimal m_1 is determined in principle by (2.14) when that formula is taken together with (1.10). That is also true, therefore, of (3.1), which is derived from (2.14). In practical work, however, it is often expedient to assume that pertinent demand and supply elasticities are constant within a relevant range. With such an assumption here, (3.1) suffices by itself to determine the optimal m_1, and there is no longer any need to refer to (1.10). As for the pertinent elasticities, those are evidently the ones needed to complete (3.27) and (3.28).

4. THE SIGN OF THE REAL INCOME EFFECT

Formula (2.14) for the optimum was derived from (2.9), for the real income effect. As so determined, the real income effect too must be a matter for empirical inquiry, but of particular interest is the sign of that effect. Further analysis may be illuminating on that aspect.

From (2.9) to (2.11) and (1.6)

$$(4.1) \quad \frac{1}{\delta} \frac{dW}{dm_1} = - \left\{ \sum_{i=1}^{n+1} \frac{p_i}{m_i} \psi^i_{m_1} \right\} \Big/ \left\{ \sum_{i=1}^{n+1} \frac{p_i}{m_i} \rho^i \right\}.$$

Hence,

$$(4.2) \quad \frac{1}{\delta} \frac{dW}{dm_1} = -p_1 \psi^1_{m_1} \left(\frac{1}{m_1} - \frac{1}{m} \right) \Big/ M,$$

where m is as in (3.2) and

$$(4.3) \quad M = \sum_{i=1}^{n+1} \frac{p_i}{m_i} \rho^i.$$

We have already examined $\psi^1_{m_1}$. If diminishing returns prevail everywhere, that term is negative. Presumably that value also often obtains otherwise, though it need not do so. We have also explored the term m. If $\psi^1_{m_1} < 0$, then real income varies positively with m_1 when $m_1 < m$, and negatively with m_1 when $m_1 > m$. Or, rather, that is so provided $M > 0$. Otherwise, the real income effect is negative when $m_1 < m$ and positive when $m_1 > m$. In any event, what of the sign of M?

The term ρ^i in M represents the change in consumption of x_i that is induced by a unit change in real income. The price-cost ratio for x_1, that is m_1, is constant along with price-cost ratios generally. Prices, however, vary along with output and costs as real income varies. Like $\psi^i_{m_1}$, therefore, ρ^i relates to general equilibrium variations, but just as $\psi^i_{m_1}$ had its counterpart $C_1{}^i$ in partial equilibrium analysis, so ρ^i has such a counterpart in the form of $D_1{}^i$. Accordingly, similar usage to the one adopted for $\psi^i_{m_1}$ seems in order here. Thus, in partial equilibrium analysis a good x_i is characterized as superior, inferior, or independent of income depending on whether $D_1{}^i > 0, < 0$, or $= 0$. I shall refer to a good x_1 as being aggregatively superior, inferior, or independent of income depending on whether $\rho^i > 0, < 0$, or $= 0$.

The term M is simply the sum of ρ^i for all goods, including leisure. For each rate of change, output is valued at the corresponding ratio of price to the price-cost ratio, which is to say at the corresponding money cost per unit. It follows that M is positive or negative depending on whether, with such a valuation, goods tend to be primarily aggregatively superior or aggregatively inferior. Imaginably neither tendency might predominate, so that $M = 0$, though in that case the real income effect is indeterminate.

Note that $\rho^i \geqslant 0$, $i = 1 \ldots n+1$, under conditions postulated in theorem 2, p. 536, provided also that all goods are superior, or at least none is inferior, i.e., $D_i{}^i \geqslant 0$, $i = 1 \ldots n$. This follows from (2.13) if ϵ_{jk} is of opposite sign to ϵ. The latter relation follows from the Mosak theorem referred to in connection with theorem 2. It should be observed that the assumed conditions are sufficient, but not necessary for $\rho^i \geqslant 0$, $i = 1 \ldots n+1$. Under the postulated conditions, though, M is necessarily nonnegative.

Note, too that from (1.13)

$$(4.4) \qquad \sum_{i=1}^{n+1} p_i \rho^i = 1.$$

Hence, with each good valued at its prevailing price, the total of all variations in consumption induced by a unit change in real income is not only positive but unity. Unless there are many aggregatively inferior goods with price-cost ratios that are especially low relative to those for goods generally, therefore, the presumption must be that M is positive.

Reference has been to the sign of M in any suboptimal position. If, as has been assumed, (3.1) and (3.2) define a single global optimum rather than many local optima, one is led to suppose that $M > 0$ in any event. The second order maximum conditions that are in question, however, are left to separate inquiry.

As before, relevant formulas are readily translated in terms of elasticities. From (4.3)

$$(4.5) \qquad M = \sum_{i=1}^{n+1} (p_i x_i / m_i)^* \rho^i,$$

where

$$(4.6) \qquad {}^*\rho^i = \rho^i / x_i.$$

Then with M as in (4.5) and m as in (3.27), the real income effect is completely translated in terms of elasticities when we write it as

$$(4.7) \qquad \frac{1}{\delta} \frac{dW}{dm_1} = -p_1 x_1 {}^* \psi_1{}^1 \left(\frac{1}{m_1} - \frac{1}{m} \right) / M.$$

The term ρ^i, as given by (2.13), is translated in terms of elasticities of demand and supply in much the same way as $\psi^i_{m_1}$, as given by (2.12b), was so translated.

Conclusions

Even for the rudimentary economy considered, our inquiry has been lengthy. A brief summary may help bring essentials into focus.

The second best price for a public enterprise in a more or less monopolistic world, it is found, must conform to these formulas:

$$(3.1; 3.2) \quad 1/m_1 = 1/m \equiv \sum_{i=2}^{n+1} \frac{p_i}{m_i} \psi^i{}_{m_1} \bigg/ \sum_{i=2}^{n+1} p_i \psi^i{}_{m_1}.$$

Here m_1 is the optimal ratio of the price of the public enterprise's product to its marginal cost, and m, as indicated, is a weighted harmonic mean of corresponding price-cost ratios of all other goods. Among the goods in question is leisure, for which the price-cost ratio is unity.

The weight for each price-cost ratio is given by the product of the price of the good in question (p_i), and the corresponding rate of aggregate net substitution of that good for the public enterprise product $(\psi^i{}_{m_1})$.

The rate of aggregate net substitution is a rather novel concept. Essentially, commodity x_j is an aggregate net substitute for commodity x_i provided that a unit increase in m_i, the price-cost ratio of x_i, increases the consumption of x_j (i.e., $\psi^j{}_{m_i} > 0$). Reference is to the impact of a unit increase in m_i in a general equilibrium context where prices generally vary in response to the change in m_i, but welfare is held constant through variations in a hypothetical labor dividend. Should a unit increase in m_i induce a reduction in consumption of x_j (i.e., $\psi^j{}_{m_i} < 0$), x_j is said to be an aggregate net complement to x_i. If the consumption of x_j is unaffected (i.e., $\psi^j{}_{m_i} = 0$), x_j is in a relation of aggregate net independence to x_i.

On that understanding, the rate of aggregate net substitution between different goods and the public enterprise good is given by further formulas derived. As it turns out, the rate of aggregate net substitution of any good for the public enterprise good resolves into conventional rates of net substitution among goods generally, such as are familiar in partial equilibrium analysis, together with gradients of supply schedules for different products.

As so determined, rates of aggregate net substitution for the public enterprise good must be a matter for empirical inquiry, but a delineation of hypothetical cases may have illuminated the more interesting possibilities. Of particular interest, though obviously ideal, is the case where all goods are net substitutes for each other in the partial equilibrium sense and production everywhere is subject to diminishing returns. In those circumstances, all goods are also aggregate net substitutes for the public enterprise good. Given (3.1, 3.2), the further implication is that the second best price of the public enterprise good must exceed marginal cost, but relatively by less than m_c, an average of price-cost ratios similar to m, but relating to goods other than leisure. That, moreover, is an internal (rather than external) average, which it need not be always.

The results are unchanged if there should be occasional instances of net independence among goods, including leisure, but should leisure be in a relation of net independence to goods generally, it would also be in a relation of aggregate net independence to the public enterprise good. In that case, the optimal m_1 precisely corresponds to m_c, the average price-cost ratio for goods other than leisure.[8] On the other hand, should all commodities other than leisure be in a relation of net independence to each other, all such commodities are also in a relation of aggregate net independence to the public enterprise good. It also follows that the optimal m_1 is unity. The optimal price of the public enterprise good equals its marginal cost.

As implied, the second best price-cost ratio for the public enterprise good conceivably could also be above m_c. That must be so, for example, if all other goods, except leisure, are aggregate net substitutes for the public good, and leisure is an aggregate net complement for the public good. Moreover, sufficient, though not necessary, conditions for the rates of aggregate net substitutions to be as assumed are that there be diminishing returns everywhere, and that commodities generally be net substitutes for each other and net complements for leisure in the partial equilibrium sense.

A recurring concern in second best literature is to discover a rule corresponding to the classic first best principle that price equals marginal cost. Formulas (3.1; 3.2) might be viewed as such a rule for the problem considered.

While attention has been focused on the optimal m_1 a further concern is the appraisal of a change in m_1 in a suboptimal position. Evaluation of such a change is necessary, of course, to determine how to approach the optimum from a suboptimal position. For this purpose further formulas, (4.1) and (4.2), are derived for the "real income effect" of a change in m_1. That effect turns on the relation of m_1 and m, and also on further aspects, including aggre-

8. In the foregoing I have in effect restated somewhat the pertinent theorem set forth on pp. 536ff, to distinguish cases where relations of substitutability or complementarity prevail from those where such relations are rather ones of independence. The propositions set forth, however, follow at once from the previous analysis.

gative income effects for different goods. Those effects, like the aggregate net cross relations in (3.1; 3.2), relate to variations within a general equilibrium context.

It has been tacitly assumed that labor everywhere is subject to variable returns. If that is not so, analysis proceeds most readily if it is supposed not to be so anywhere. In other words, labor input coefficients are constant in all industries. In that case, our main formulas still apply, but further formulas are strikingly simplified. Among other things, ψ^i_{m1} reduces simply to the corresponding partial equilibrium rate of net substitution between x_i and the public good, i.e., $C_1{}^i$. Rather, it reduces to that apart from a proportionality factor reflecting the fact that the parameter in one case is m_1 and in the over p_1.[9]

While but a single industry, x_1, has been assumed to be publicly owned, should another industry, say x_2, be publicly owned as well, all is as before except that there is an additional optimum condition for m_2 entirely comparable to that derived for m_1, and correspondingly a second real income effect representing the impact on welfare of a change in m_2. That too is comparable to the one where m_1 is the parameter.

I have also assumed that in equilibrium monopolistic price margins are constant. That is not highly realistic, but for present purposes it perhaps would not be too far from the mark to suppose that, where not constant, such margins vary with the level of output. If so, the analysis should not, I think, require any essential change on account of varying price margins. The varying price margins then would serve simply to compound or dampen the varying supply price that is considered in any event.

HARVARD UNIVERSITY

9. The proportionality factor, of course, cancels in (3.1) and (3.2). The resultant formula for the optimum was derived previously by H. A. John Green in the article cited above, p. 520, n. 6. I refer particularly to Green's formulas (111.1), (111.2), and (111.3). Those formulas come to the same thing as mine for the optimum in the case of constant coefficients, though because of Green's further assumptions on units of measurement that may not seem at all the case.

JOURNAL OF COMPARATIVE ECONOMICS **2**, 211–225 (1978)

Managerial Risks and Rewards in Public Enterprises[1]

ABRAM BERGSON

Department of Economics, Harvard University
Cambridge, Massachusetts 02138

Received August 1977; revised January 1978

A. **Bergson**—Managerial Risks and Rewards in Public Enterprises

This essay explores a twofold problem: from the standpoint of the community, what is the appropriate attitude for managers of a public enterprise to have toward decisions with uncertain outcomes; and what is implied for the managerial rewards or penalties that are required to induce managers to adopt that attitude. Taking a theorem of Arrow's as a point of departure, the essay argues that managers should be induced to maximize expected benefit. With the aid of "career" and "bonus" functions, implications for managerial rewards and penalties are explored under alternative assumptions as to the nature of managerial utility function. *J. Comp. Econ.*, Sept. 1978, 2(3), pp. 211–225. Harvard University, Cambridge, Massachusetts.

Journal of Economic Literature Classification Numbers: 052, 614, 512, 020.

I

Inducement of an appropriate attitude toward risks on the part of public-enterprise management became a subject of discussion during the interwar years in the ongoing debate on socialist economic rationality. In his celebrated essay of 1920 on that theme, von Mises already expressed doubts that managers of a public enterprise could be counted on to exercise a necessary initiative. At least they could not be counted on to do so if managerial rewards are constrained ideologically in a manner that socialism supposedly requires.[2]

Addressing himself more specifically to risk bearing, Hayek (1935, reprinted in 1948, pp. 173ff; 1940, reprinted in 1948, p. 199) reasoned similarly, but stressed not so much ideological constraints on rewards for

---

[1] I have benefited much from discussions with Martin Weitzman, Stephen Shavell, and Richard Zeckhauser and have also been aided by comments of the editor and unidentified readers.

[2] A translation from the original German was published in 1935. See especially pp. 116ff.

success as the incentive "to prefer the safe to the risky enterprise" that is provided by the possible loss of the manager's post in case of failure.

In the interwar debate, von Mises and Hayek, of course, were both among the skeptically inclined on the possibilities of socialist economic rationality. Among those taking a favorable view of that matter, Lange (1938) curiously had hardly anything to say on the problem of managerial risk taking. But, then, in the seminal essay in question Lange also hardly deals with managerial motivation in the absence of risk. Dickinson (1939, pp. 213ff), however, acknowledged that an improper managerial attitude toward risk taking could be a source of difficulty, but with suitably calibrated bonuses managers supposedly "would have an incentive to experiment and improve the service and yet would be made to feel the consequences of imprudent and extravagant ventures." Bonuses varying over a range from one half to a little more than 100% of the base salary were felt to suffice. Dickinson apparently considered such rewards as not precluded ideologically.

So the matter stood when the interwar debate was reviewed in Bergson (1948; reprinted in 1966). There I argue that: "Given the possibility of fixing policy on dismissals on the one hand and on rewards on the other, it should be feasible to establish a climate in which the managers evaluate risks in whatever is considered to be the proper manner. There is no reason to suppose that they would necessarily be too venturesome or, as Hayek argues, too cautious." As to what is a "proper manner," taking as a point of departure a theorem of Arrow (1970, reprinted 1971), Bergson (1976) argues that public-enterprise managers should be induced to maximize "expected economic returns." For risk-averse managers "whose careers as well as earnings depend on success," however, it is conjectured that the indicated rewards for success might have to be large.

II

And that still seems right as far as it goes, but, on the important question at issue, it may be in order to try to go somewhat further. To begin with, let us consider again the question of what, from the standpoint of the community, is the appropriate attitude of public-enterprise managers toward risk. As before, I take as a point of departure the theorem of Arrow just referred to.

This theorem holds that a public investment with an uncertain outcome is to be evaluated simply in terms of its expected return. That is so though the return accrues ultimately to citizens, many or all of whom are risk-averse. While reference is to a single public investment, the principle should apply equally to public-enterprise actions generally in any period. All such actions alike must be of concern here. While Arrow addresses a public investment, given his focus on the evaluation of risk, he is able to limit his analysis to a single time period. For the most part, that is also possible here, though time cannot be ignored altogether.

Arrow's result follows logically only under ideal conditions: essentially all citizens have identical utility functions of the Morgenstern–von Neumann sort, and incomes represented by identically distributed random variables. Also, all share equally in gains and losses of public enterprise, such gains and losses being statistically independent of the incomes of households from other sources. The theorem then becomes valid in the limit as the number of citizens approaches infinity.

Still, as Arrow points out, circumstances should often be such that, even though the limit is not reached and the indicated conditions are not fully met, evaluation in terms of expected return is apt to be sufficiently near the mark. Among other things, gains and losses from the actions of any particular public enterprise will often be sufficiently small relatively to the community's income and sufficiently widely dispersed among households to represent only a very limited variation in the income of any single household.[3] I focus here on circumstances in which Arrow's theorem is applicable, but for clarity we must distinguish between public-enterprise managers and the entire community, aside from managers. The managers may have to be offered, as a material incentive, an inordinately large share of the benefit from their actions. Moreover, if we single out managers in this way, we may as well allow their utility functions to differ from those of citizens generally.

Also, if resource allocation is to be Pareto efficient, Arrow's theorem supposedly must hold: public-enterprise managers must maximize expected returns. I refer to Pareto efficiency of the stochastic sort relating to expected utilities. From that standpoint, however, once managers are recognized as a distinct entity, a curious corollary is that full efficiency is apt to be very difficult to achieve. At least, that is so if managers are risk-averse maximizers of their own expected utilities, as they are usually assumed to be. It is conceivable, nevertheless, that a manager in choosing among alternatives with uncertain outcomes might be instructed always to accord priority to one yielding a higher over one yielding a lower expected benefit to the community. Conceivably also, he might do so without having his status or income depend in any way on his choice.

If these conditions were met, not only would managerial behavior conform to Arrow's theorem; efficiency would also be achieved in another sphere relevant here: the allocation of risk bearing between the community and the manager. Under the stated conditions, the community bears all the risk and the manager none. According to familiar reasoning, with the

[3] For a somewhat different view of the practical import of Arrow's theorem, see Foldes and Rees (1977).

manager risk-averse and the community risk-neutral, such a result is indeed efficient (compare with Arrow, 1971, pp. 257–258). In the language of insurance theory, the manager who acts faithfully in accord with his instructions poses no "moral hazard." In comparison with any alternative arrangement, then, both he and the community gain if the community fully "insures" him against risk.

Should such circumstances actually prevail, the problem of inducing an appropriate managerial attitude toward risk evidently would also have been fully resolved. But critics of socialism will hardly feel that their strictures have been so easily disposed of, and properly so. I shall assume, therefore, that managers do experience some material penalties and *pari passu* must be offered some material rewards depending on their performance. Given these assumptions, inefficiency is in a sense unavoidable, but we can still fruitfully inquire how material penalties and rewards might be arranged so as to induce managers to behave as Arrow's theorem requires. Should such a desideratum be achieved, it might still be possible to improve on the results by providing additional "insurance" for managers, but I suspect that such gains are apt to be relatively limited, at least for the community. In any event, I leave that matter to separate inquiry.[4]

Granting the inherent limitation on what can be attained, efficiency is

---

[4] It can be shown that the desideratum on which I focus does not provide a sufficient basis for delineating a Pareto optimum, even subject to the "institutional constraint" given by the need to provide material penalties and rewards to control managerial behavior. To improve on the results obtained here, however, the community or the Central Planning Board (CPB) that acts for it, I believe, would require information on probabilities and benefits constituting the alternatives open in any particular case. With such information on any scale, the question arises why the CPB should delegate choice of alternatives to managers to begin with. In any event, as will appear, I assume that the CPB substantially delegates to managers assessment of probabilities and benefits as well as choices between alternatives (refer to Section III). I refer to improvements on results obtained within the general framework of the model to be explored. That framework entails among other things that the manager's income depends on the benefit he produces but not on the social state in which the benefit is produced. In practice, managerial rewards almost inevitably depend in some degree on the social state (e.g., dismissal for losses may or may not occur depending on "extenuating circumstances"). In any case, that would seem to be a way in which managerial risk bearing might be reduced to the advantage of both the managers and the community generally. Adaptation of my incentive arrangements in this manner, however, would presumably require some extension in the CPB's knowledge of probabilities and benefits. I also abstract from any variation in managerial effort and hence from any consideration of that aspect in determining managerial rewards. Here, too, there should be opportunities for mutual gain for the manager and the community generally from additional "insurance" of the manager against risks. Again, the CPB would require additional information, though now on managerial effort. In another context, Steven Shavell is currently exploring the problem of the use of rewards to control behavior where effort is a variable. He was good enough to let me see a late draft of a paper that he is writing on this subject.

still, as in Arrow, the desideratum. Given Arrow's assumed requirement that all households be identical, however, equity is necessarily achieved along with efficiency, so his principle is valid from that standpoint as well. With managers having special utility functions and receiving special rewards, we no longer can assume such a felicitous conjuncture of efficiency and equity. By exploring efficiency, however, we may be able to clarify the inevitable question of the extent to which that objective might come in conflict with equity.

It would be overly pedantic not to refer sometimes, as I have already done, to the "community," where the community, aside from managers, is intended. On the other hand, we may here and there have in mind the entire community, including managers, or at least the Central Planning Board (CPB) acting for it, but that should be sufficiently clear from the context and will not need laboring.

III

We may now restate our problem: during any given period, managers of a public enterprise must contemplate that diverse social states may prevail with diverse probabilities. Following conventional usage in the analysis of choice under uncertainty (compare Hirshleifer, 1970, pp. 216–217), I assume that the social state (e.g., good or bad weather) and its associated probability are beyond managerial control. Depending on the managers' decisions on variables that may be more or less subject to their discretion (e.g., inputs, outputs, prices), the enterprise may be made to yield differing benefits to the community in any particular social state, but the benefit actually occurring from any given decisions is still uncertain so far as it depends also on the social state.

For any public enterprise, then, the problem is how to share between managerial personnel and the community generally the benefits produced so that, in choices among alternatives with uncertain outcomes, managerial personnel may be induced to maximize expected benefits to the community. For their part, the managers are only interested in their own expected utilities, and must be induced to maximize expected benefit to the community by penalties and rewards which depend on the benefit produced.

So stated, the problem is simply a variant of the classic "principal-and-agent" situation of stochastic choice theory and has a familiar and fairly obvious kind of solution. By briefly working through the matter, however, I will be able to highlight novel aspects of particular interest here.

I assume for simplicity that managerial personnel in the public enterprise considered are all alike. All, therefore, receive for their services the same wage, w. Through its operations during any given period, the enterprise realizes benefits with a money value, B, and payment of w to a manager is premised on $B = B_0$. Should B vary from that magnitude, each manager receives, in addition to w, a bonus conforming to a bonus function,

$$b = b(B); b'(B) \geq 0, \tag{1}$$

where

$$b(B_0) = 0. \tag{2}$$

The magnitude of B is net of appropriate charges for resource inputs, including managerial wages, but not of bonuses. On the other hand, both wages, and bonuses include any share of B that might accrue to managers *qua* citizens, i.e., w and b are net of "taxes" and gross of any corresponding "dividends." Although B accrues to the community as a whole, it is expressed here per capita of managerial personnel in the enterprise considered.

So far as their current earnings depend on benefits produced, our managers already acquire a material interest in the enterprise's performance, but if we are to be at all realistic we must consider that their careers generally could be affected. Such a relation is apt to be complex, but it may suffice to suppose that under the prevailing personnel policies, managers know that the wage they will receive in the next period will have a present value conforming to the formula

$$c = c(B); \qquad c'(B) \geq 0, \tag{3}$$

where B is this year's benefits. Or, rather, c represents the difference in present values of two wage levels: the one that will be received next year depending on B, and the one that would be received next year if B were equal to B_0. Hence,

$$c(B_0) = 0. \tag{4}$$

In gauging the impact of their current performance managers look no further ahead than one period.

Little seems lost analytically if, for convenience, we assume that our managers gauge the impact on their next year's income of a difference between B and B_0 solely in terms of wages and without regard to possible bonuses.[5] A difference in careers may also mean for a manager differences in effort and status. I abstract from any resultant utilities and disutilities. The formula $c(B)$ will be called a career function, and c, a career value. Although B depends on the social state, the analysis is further facilitated if we assume that both the bonus and career values depend only on the magnitude of B and not on the social state in which B materializes.[6]

Although (1) and (3) are formally similar, they supposedly reflect rather different forces. In seeking to induce managers of any particular public

[5] See Footnote 7.
[6] See Footnote 4.

enterprise to behave in an appropriate manner, the community, it is understood, may adapt the bonus function to the circumstances of that enterprise. Among other things, it may even take account of the nature of the utility function of the management of the enterprise in question. In the process, the community also considers the career function, but that is assumed to reflect the structure of job descriptions and base salaries in the economy more generally. Depending on their performance, managers in one enterprise may be advanced or demoted to another; they may even cease to be managers. But the resultant rewards or penalties depend on the qualifications established for different tasks and the associated base salaries in all enterprises together.

With these suppositions, our divergence from reality often becomes glaring, but the distinction made between the two sorts of rewards is, I believe, essentially valid and significant. It seems in order, therefore, to accord a rather different status to the two functions. While the bonus function is a formula to be determined, the career function is more or less parametric in character.

We may write a manager's utility function, then, as

$$U = U(I), \tag{5}$$

where I, the manager's income or consumption, is obtained as

$$I = w + b + c. \tag{6}$$

The utility function in (5), like those of citizens generally, is of the Morgenstern–von Neumann sort, and hence determinate up to a linear transformation. Since b and c depend on B, I does also, but I follow Arrow in assuming that U depends only on consumption, and not on the social state in which the consumption is experienced.

Of the total benefit produced by the enterprise, the community, apart from the managers, derives an amount $\bar{B}$, where

$$\bar{B} = B - b. \tag{7}$$

This is on the supposition that c, prior to its reduction to present value, corresponds to an expected difference in a manager's contribution to future output. Since it will be earned next year, from the standpoint of the community it is properly chargeable against next year's benefits. It is not to be viewed as either an addition to or a charge against benefits accruing currently to the community, apart from managers.[7]

---

[7] The supposition seems more plausible than otherwise so far as c refers to the next period's wages, as distinct from bonuses. In any event, although properly a charge against next year's rather than this year's benefits, c is evidently in no sense "free" from the community's standpoint. Note, however, that an asymmetry such as results this year between additions to rewards to managers and deductions from benefits to the community

Coming to the problem posed, managers must in effect choose among alternative "prospects" for their enterprise for the period in question. Each prospect reflects a complex of decisions regarding activities of the enterprise during that period and consists of a resulting vector of benefits. Each element in the vector corresponds to the social state in which the particular benefit materializes and has a probability that attaches to that social state. In reaching a decision, managers maximize their expected utilities, or, as is more convenient here, their expected gain in utility over what they would experience if they were just to earn w. Thus, consider

$$y = E[U(I) - U(w)]. \tag{8}$$

Here b and c and hence I vary with B over the n social states that are to be reckoned with. Reference is to the variation associated with a particular prospect. Hence y represents the expected gain in utility from that prospect. Among the prospects open to managers, they are assumed to choose the one for which y is a maximum. If more than one prospect yields a maximum y, managers choose any one of those prospects.

Consider now

$$z = E[B - b], \tag{9}$$

where B varies as before and b varies with it over the relevant social states. I refer again to a particular prospect. Then z represents the expected benefit to the community, aside from managers, in the enterprise in question, from that prospect. The desideratum, therefore, is that managers, in choosing a prospect that maximizes y, will be induced by the rewards offered them to choose at the same time one that maximizes z.

A necessary and sufficient condition that this desideratum be achieved is that for any social state and its associated probability

$$U(I) - U(w) = \alpha(B - b) + \beta. \tag{10}$$

Here α is a positive constant. From (2), (4), (6), and (10),

$$\beta = -\alpha B_0, \tag{11}$$

so (10) means that

$$U(I) - U(w) = \alpha(B - B_0 - b). \tag{12}$$

---

generally would occur in any case, but for the fact that I abstract from utilities and disutilities associated with career differences in status and effort. By the same token, c might be regarded here as in part a surrogate for such career differences. To represent status and effort as a component of money income, and an argument in the utility functions, however, we must suppose that the marginal rate of substitution between status and effort, on the one hand, and other consumption, on the other is a single, constant magnitude. I have assumed that in appraising the career effect of current performance managers look ahead only one period. All things considered, it may be just as well to suppose that that is also the horizon of the community generally.

Formulas (10) and (12) are examples of the well-known "similarity" relation of stochastic choice theory.[8] That the equality that they establish is sufficient to assure the desired coincidence of the two maxima in question is evident once it is understood, as seems proper here, that in evaluating expected benefits the community accepts managerial judgments on the outcomes of and probabilities to be attached to different social states.[9] Given that and (10), the ranking of all relevant prospects in terms of expected managerial utilities and expected benefits to the community must be the same. Coincidence of maxima from the two standpoints follows at once.

The necessity of (10) should also be fairly evident. At least, that appears so if reference is made to a continuum of prospects rather than to just a limited set of discrete alternatives. A formal proof, however, does not seem readily available in the relevant literature. In the addendum, therefore, I provide such a proof. For completeness I prove sufficiency as well as necessity.

IV

Considered together with (2), (4), and (6), Eq. (12) is to be viewed as constraining admissible pairs of bonus and career functions. In trying to grasp the nature of the constraint, it is helpful to see (12) in this form:

$$I = U^{-1}[\alpha(B - B_0 - b) - U(w)]. \tag{13}$$

Note that $U(w)$ is a constant. Hence, when efficiently scaled, managerial income should vary with a linear function of net benefits (as they exceed B_0) in a manner given simply by the inverse of the manager's utility function.

This might be pursued further, but of more interest than total managerial income is the relation of its two variable constituents, the bonus and career value. Turning to that, we see at once from Eq. (12) that with either the bonus or career function given, the other schedule is determined. While (12) constrains $b(B)$ and $c(B)$ only implicitly, an explicit solution is assured by our assumption throughout that $U'(I) > 0$.

We must consider that $U(I)$ is subject to linear transformations, but should there be such transformation in (12), only the constant fixing the utility unit (as distinct from that fixing the origin) matters. For any such representation of managerial utility, (12) must hold for some α. As for α, apart from being positive, this constant is arbitrary; but with $c(B)$ given, one is free to specify $b(B)$ only for one value of $B \neq B_0$. With that, α is

[8] See Ross (1973, 1974).

[9] Reference is to outcomes and probabilities that are in question in "day-to-day" managerial decision making. The community presumably must to some extent form its own opinion of outcomes and probabilities in determining, for any period, the level of expected benefits to which w is to be pegged.

determined and so too is $b(B)$ for all other B. The situation is similar for $c(B)$ if $b(B)$ is given.

I propose to illustrate these relations by reference to three managerial utility functions:

$$U(I) = \log I; \qquad U(I) = I^{1/2}; \qquad U(I) = I. \qquad (14a,b,c)$$

Let us designate by ρ the manager's relative risk aversion, that being understood in the usual way, i.e.,

$$\rho = -(I/U')U''. \qquad (15)$$

Then, for (14a) $\rho = 1$. That sort of utility function is identified especially with Bernoulli. If relative risk aversion is taken as a constant, Arrow (1971, pp. 90ff) has argued a priori in favor of unity as that constant. Of course, one might expect relative risk aversion to vary in some degree with income. In (14b) and (14c), we have two examples of utility functions where $\rho \neq 1$. For (14b), $\rho = \frac{1}{2}$; so there is still relative risk aversion but not as much as in the Bernoulli case. For (14c), $\rho = 0$, and the individual is risk-neutral.

For reasons indicated, I take the career function as a datum over the relevant range and explore implications of alternative career values for the bonus function. I take w as a numéraire and scale benefits so that $B_0 = 0$. As explained above, even with $c(B)$ given, in order to determine α, and hence bonuses generally, we must specify b for some nonzero value of B. I assume that bonuses remain null when $(B = -10)$, that is, when "losses" per member of the managerial staff are 10 times the managerial wage (w). Three alternative values of c are postulated when losses are of that magnitude: $-.1$; $-.3$; and $-.5$. In other words, with losses of the indicated magnitude, a manager considers the adverse effect on his career as having a present-value equivalent to a reduction in his wage by 10%, or 30%, or 50%, as the case may be.

For each value of c, given the utility function, there is a corresponding α. We are now able to determine $b(B)$ generally by specifying $c(B)$ for nonnegative values of B. Two rather extreme specifications are considered for $c(B)$ for $B \geq 0$. On the one hand, $c(B) = 0$, on the other, $c(B) = \phi B$, where ϕ is given by the assumption concerning c when $B = -10$. In the former case, then, the career function is asymmetric with respect to losses and benefits: the manager's career suffers when there are losses but there is no corresponding gain whatever when benefits are positive. In the latter case, the career function is symmetric and the manager's career prospects stand to improve when there are positive benefits, indeed to an extent proportional to the benefits.

The benefit-maximizing bonuses corresponding to each of these assumptions (expressed as a multiple of the managerial wage) are shown in Table 1.

TABLE 1

INDICATED BONUSES (b) FOR ALTERNATIVE BENEFITS (B) UNDER SPECIFIED ASSUMPTION

B	Case I: $c(-10) = -.1$		Case II: $c(-10) = -.3$		Case III: $c(-10) = -.5$	
	$c(B) = 0$, for $B \geq 0$	$c(B) = B/100$ for $B \geq 0$	$c(B) = 0$ for $B \geq 0$	$c(B) = 3B/100$ for $B \geq 0$	$c(B) = 0$ for $B \geq 0$	$c(B) = B/20$ for $B \geq 0$
	Relative risk aversion of unity					
10	.11	.01	.41	.12	.88	.44
20	.23	.03	.97	.41	2.39	1.58
30	.36	.07	1.74	.92	4.75	3.69
	Relative risk aversion of one half					
10	.10	0^a	.34	.05	.61	.15
20	.21	.02	.73	.15	1.39	.47
30	.33	.03	1.16	.30	2.28	.93
	Risk neutrality					
10	.10	0	.29	0	.48	0
20	.20	0	.58	0	.96	0
30	.30	0	.87	0	1.43	0

[a] .005 before rounding.

The chief results are perhaps not very surprising: bonuses are very sensitive to the shape of the career function as well as to relative risk aversion. Thus, should the manager with unity relative risk aversion find that his career suffers little from even sizable losses (Case I), even modest bonuses might suffice to induce the desired attitude towards risk. The bonuses are especially modest if the career function is symmetric. For a benefit per manager of 30 times his wage, a bonus of 36% of the wage would suffice if there were no favorable impact on the manager's career, and of but 7% if there were a favorable impact commensurate with the unfavorable impact where losses are incurred.

Should the manager's career be much damaged by losses (Case III), however, the needed bonuses might have to be quite large. For a benefit per manager of 30 times his wage, the bonus would have to be 4.75 times his wage, in case the career function were asymmetric. But even if the career function were symmetric, his bonus would still have to be 3.69 times his wage.

With relative risk aversion of one half, should the manager's career be little damaged by losses, the bonuses continue as before to be comparatively modest, and the difference in relative risk aversion hardly matters. If the manager's career is more significantly affected by losses, however, bonuses, while again large, tend to be decidedly smaller than before. Where the career effect of losses is greatest (Case III), for example, the required bonuses could be as little as one fourth of those indicated previously.

With risk neutrality, where the career function is symmetric with respect to positive and negative benefits, bonuses, of course, are zero, for the career values alone fully assure the desired managerial attitude toward risk. Where the career function is asymmetric, however, bonuses are still needed of a magnitude commensurate with the adverse career values when there are losses. Even when such adverse career values are large, however, the required bonuses tend to be distinctly smaller than in the cases involving risk aversion.

In trying to judge the import of these relations, it should be noted that if in a meaningful sense managerial personnel should constitute, say, 1% of all employees, and should such persons be earning wages (apart from bonuses) of two times the average wage, a benefit per manager of as much as 30 times the managerial wage (the highest B considered in Table 1) would mean that total benefits would come to nearly 60% of the wage bill— probably an unusually large but not entirely improbable figure.

I have determined α throughout on the assumption that $b(B)$, which is zero when $B = 0$, remains so for $B = -10$. Conceivably bonuses could be negative over a relevant range of losses, but the implications of such a scheme are readily inferred from the examples that have been given.

The utility functions assumed are all subject to linear transformations, but for reasons indicated such transformations would not affect my results.

V

I conclude that there is no logical bar to incentive for public-enterprise managers that will induce them to take an attitude toward risk that is appropriate from the standpoint of the community. Further analysis here, thus, seems to corroborate the more optimistically inclined on that long-debated issue. Nevertheless the rewards for success that are needed to assure a proper evaluation of risky ventures apparently might turn out to be rather large. Should there be any pronounced ideological commitments to equality, therefore, these could be a serious stumbling block to assuring an appropriate managerial attitude. The familiar contention that appropriate managerial risk taking might come in conflict with accepted precepts of equity is also borne out.

But are not inordinately large rewards needed mainly because I assume a relatively punitive policy with respect to dismissals and promotion where managerial results are disappointing? Could not inordinate bonuses be avoided by commitment to a less harsh regime? Very likely they could, but such a policy could be costly if it entailed a disregard of experience and hence of resulting reasonable expectations as to future managerial performance. Opportunity to manipulate the career function is obviously greater when that is done throughout the economy, rather than just for a single enterprise, but this manipulation must be kept within bounds if salaries are to be related at all to productivity. In practice, the "career function" must to some extent be judgmental and discretionary, although it cannot be entirely so.

On the other hand, the "bonus function" must also be kept within bounds in practice, so much so that one may wonder whether here, too, there might not be difficulties in realizing theoretical imperatives. While negative bonuses might sometimes be called for, to impose them might be inexpedient. Whatever the theoretic requirements, bonuses might have to exceed some threshold magnitude in order to be effective at all.

Assuring an appropriate managerial attitude toward risk can also be expected to encounter practical difficulties of a more substantial sort. The whole endeavor can make sense only if there is to begin with a satisfactory way to measure benefits that managerial decisions might yield to the community in different social states. Depending on the working arrangements for determining resource use generally, achieving that result could be difficult. But that is a familiar theme and does not seem special to risky actions, so there is no reason to expatiate on it here.

Of particular concern where there is risk, however, is the degree of managerial risk aversion. It is rather awkward, therefore, that required rewards could vary markedly depending on that aspect. By implication, arranging a suitable system of managerial compensation might require a good deal of empirical inquiry into the variety of managerial utility functions.

In writings through the years on managerial attitudes toward risk in a public enterprise reference seems generally to have been to public enterprise in a socialist economy; that is one where such an enterprise predominates in the economy generally. I have tacitly oriented this essay similarly, but essentially all that has been said, I think, still applies if reference is instead to a public enterprise in a mixed economy, where privately owned enterprises are still pervasive. Possibly, though, equity would not then be quite the constraint that it is apt to be under socialism. If so, that might much facilitate achieving a suitable managerial attitude towards risk in a public enterprise. On the other hand, public policy on dismissals and promotions then can only partially determine a managerial career function, for in a mixed economy that must depend also on opportunities in private enterprise. With the career function thus constrained, arranging for a suitable managerial attitude toward risk to that extent might require even greater stress on bonuses in a mixed than in a socialist economy.

ADDENDUM

The purpose of this addendum is to demonstrate the proposition associated with Eq. (10), where options for the enterprise are such that, for any social state, the benefit realized varies continuously among alternatives available. More precisely, we postulate that the enterprise is confronted with "benefit possibilities" given by

$$F(B_1, B_2, \ldots, B_i, \ldots, B_n) = 0, \tag{16}$$

where B_i is the benefit realized in the ith social state ($i = 1, \ldots, n$) and varies continuously. Also F is a continuous function and has continuous first- and second-order derivatives. Managers act so as to maximize y, as given in (8), subject to (16) and what is to be demonstrated is that (10) is a necessary and sufficient condition for the resulting equilibrium of the enterprise to be such that z, as given by (9), will also be a maximum, subject to (16).

If y is a maximum subject to (16), it is readily shown that for any two social states j and k,

$$\frac{\pi_j{}^j U'({}^j b' + {}^j c')}{\pi_k{}^k U'({}^k b' + {}^k c')} = \frac{F_j}{F_k}, \tag{17}$$

where U', b', and c' are the derivatives of the corresponding variables with respect to B. Also, π_j and π_k are probabilities for the social states j and k; a superscript to the left of a symbol means that the variable in question is valued at B for the corresponding social state. Similarly, with z a maximum, subject to (16) we have for any two social states j and k,

$$\frac{\pi_j(1 - {}^j b')}{\pi_k(1 - {}^k b')} = \frac{F_j}{F_k}. \tag{18}$$

The sufficiency of (10) then follows at once, since (10) is supposed to hold for any social state. Given that and (17), we obtain (18) by differentiating (10) with respect to B for social states j and k in turn. As for necessity, we now start with (17) and (18) so

$$\frac{{}^j U'({}^j b' + {}^j c')}{{}^k U'({}^k b' + {}^k c')} = \frac{(1 - {}^j b')}{(1 - {}^k b')}. \tag{19}$$

We are free here to treat B_k as a constant and B_j as a variable. If we do, we have

$$^j U'({}^j b' + {}^j c') = \alpha(1 - {}^j b'). \tag{20}$$

Integrating, and bearing in mind that (20) holds for any j, we have

$$U(I) = \alpha(B - b) + \kappa, \tag{21}$$

Evaluating at $B = B_0$, we obtain (10) in the more specific form of (12). In (21) α is properly written, as (12) requires, without a subscript for the social state, because from (20) the constant is independent of the social state.

REFERENCES

Arrow, Kenneth J., and Lind, Robert C., "Uncertainty and the Evaluation of Public Investments." *Amer. Econ. Rev.* **60**, 3:364–378, June 1970.

Arrow, Kenneth J., *Essays in the Theory of Risk Bearing*. Chicago, Ill.: Markham, 1971.

Bergson, Abram, "Socialist Economics." In Howard S. Ellis, ed., *A Survey of Contemporary Economics*. Philadelphia: Blakiston, 1948.

Bergson, Abram, *Essays in Normative Economics*. Cambridge, Mass.: Harvard Univ. Press, 1966.

Bergson, Abram, "Entrepreneurship and Profits under Socialism: The Soviet Experience." Mimeo., 1976. In Bergson, *Productivity and the Social System*.

Bergson, Abram, *Productivity and the Social System*. Cambridge, Mass.: Harvard Univ. Press, 1978.

Dickinson, Henry D., *Economics of Socialism*. London/New York: Oxford Univ. Press, 1939.

Foldes, L. P., and Rees, R., "A note on the Arrow–Lind Theorem." *Amer. Econ. Rev.* **67**, 2:188–193, March 1977.

Hayek, Friedrich A., ed., *Collectivist Economic Planning*. London: Routledge, 1935.

Hayek, Friedrich A., "The Present State of the Debate." In F. A. Hayek, ed., *Collectivist Economic Planning*. London: Routledge, 1935.

Hayek, Friedrich A., "Socialist Calculation: the Competitive Solution." *Economica* N.S. **7**, 2:125–149, May 1940.

Hirshleifer, Jack, *Investment, Interest, and Capital*. Englewood Cliffs, N. J.: Prentice–Hall, 1970.

Lange, Oskar, "On the Economic Theory of Socialism." In Benjamin E. Lippincott, ed., *On the Economic Theory of Socialism*. Minneapolis: Univ. of Minnesota Press, 1938.

von Mises, Ludwig, "Economic Calculation in the Socialist Commonwealth." In F. A. Hayek, ed., *Collectivist Economic Planning*. London: Routledge, 1935.

Ross, Stephen A., "The Economic Theory of Agency: The Principal's Problem." *Amer. Econ. Rev.* **63**, 2:134–139, May 1973.

Ross, Stephen A., "On the Economic Theory of Agency and the Principal of Similarity." In M. S. Balch, D. L. McFadden, and S. Y. Wu, eds., *Essays on Economic Behaviour under Uncertainty*. Amsterdam: North Holland, 1974.

IV
PRICES, INCOME, AND EMPLOYMENT

PRICES, WAGES, AND INCOME THEORY

By Abram Bergson

I

It is, I believe, a major shortcoming of current income theory that it is developed by the treatment of special, and often highly restrictive, cases of price behavior. The assumption of Professor Pigou in his recent contribution to this subject[1] is unique, but the procedure is illustrative. The entire analysis is developed under the assumption that the elasticities of demand for consumption goods and investment goods depend respectively on the amounts of consumption goods and investment goods supplied.[2] Conceivably the multiplication of such studies as this will enable us ultimately to ascribe determinacy to an important sector of the real world. Where, as in the case of Bissell's study,[3] an effort is made to select for analysis likely limiting cases of price behavior, the prospect is by no means discouraging. Nevertheless, this is at best an awkward approach; and where such a conjectural subject as price policy is treated uneasiness as to the significance of the conclusions derived must persist.

It is idle to hope that the varieties of price policies prevailing in the modern capitalist economy ever will be embraced in any single formulation. A greater generality than has been achieved so far, however, is not precluded. In the present essay a formulation of short-run price-determining conditions is presented, which has the merit of embracing not only the special cases which have been studied thus far in income theory, but also certain interesting additional possibilities as well. With the aid of this formulation, a fresh attack will be made on the vexatious problem of the effect of a change in money wages on real income and employment.

II

We may consider first the behavior of prices in some one industry, which, as occasion demands, may be conceived of alternatively as an industry producing a final consumption good, or a final investment good, or an intermediate good for use in either of the first two industries. For the moment a desired generality may be attained by assuming, after Professor Pigou, that price behavior within each of the sectors distinguished is uniform. The industry studied is understood to consist of firms producing either a homogeneous commodity, or a group of close substitutes, the relative prices of which may be relied

[1] A. C. Pigou, *Employment and Equilibrium*, London, 1941.

[2] *Ibid.*, p. 46.

[3] R. M. Bissell, Jr., "Price and Wage Policies and the Theory of Employment," Econometrica, Vol. 8, July, 1940, pp. 199–239.

275

on not to change substantially under the impact of the events to be investigated. The upshot of the analysis is affected little if it is assumed that the cost structures of all firms in the industry (if there are more than one) are identical.

It is proposed that for the purpose of developing income theory the price (p) at which a given output (x) will be maintained in the short run in the industry studied be taken as a function,

$$(1) \qquad\qquad p = P(x, v),$$

where v is the increment of cost per unit of labor input associated with a marginal application of labor. If labor were the only variable factor, the latter term would be equal to the wage rate. The proposed price function, thus, is simply a variant of the supply function familiar to price theory. Price is taken as the dependent variable and the prices of all variable factors which affect short-run supply price are summed in a single expression, incremental cost per unit of labor input.

What is novel, however, is the suggestion that the function be applied to monopolistic as well as to competitive prices. In view of the omission of reference to the demand for the industry's product, novelty would seem to be all that might be claimed for this proposal. But the departure from contemporary price theory is less startling than it appears. Either as a datum, or as a magnitude which varies with one or the other of the variables included explicitly in the price function, the elasticity of demand confronting (say) a representative producer may be taken into account in the proposed formulation. Excepting Harrod's suggestive analysis,[4] no more consideration than this has yet been accorded the elasticity of demand in income theory.

Clearly the price function cannot describe all monopolistic price variations. The price advance posted by a particular firm at the conclusion of an intensive advertising campaign, for instance, can be represented only as a shift in the price function, and, so too, must be treated the price reduction initiated by a firm in the face of an improvement in a competitor's product. The examples easily are multiplied, and together they doubtless comprise an important category of price variation. To abstract such behavior from the analysis, as to pass by any interesting segment of reality, is surely a lamentable expedient. But what is of special concern to income theory is the adjustment of prices to shifts in cost and demand schedules which affect all business firms similarly. In this restricted context it does not seem presumptuous to claim that the price formulation advanced is a likely first approximation to an annoyingly complex reality.

[4] See below, p. 277.

Harrod's proposition that the elasticity of demand confronting business firms diminishes as the community's real income increases[5] suggests at once, however, the desirability of inserting a third variable, real income, in the price function. Harrod's argument that consumers' spending habits are more firmly entrenched against relative price changes at high than at low income levels, indeed, is highly plausible. But the implications of this phenomenon for the elasticity of demand confronting any one firm are by no means translucent. If account is taken of a fact which Harrod neglects, that with increases in income consumers in any one income bracket tend to shift their purchases to brands and qualities of goods formerly purchased by the consumers who have now shifted to an even higher income bracket, it seems quite possible that the producer of any one product will be confronted by customers who are no more nor less price conscious than the previous ones.[6] The possibility that changes in real income have some consistent and substantial over-all effect on the elasticities of demand confronting individual producers is not to be disposed of so easily. But, even if Harrod's principle were valid, the inclusion of real income in the price function would be warranted in the present context only if the individual producers varied their price margins significantly on account of changes in this variable even though their own output and that of other producers in the same industry were constant. While an effort to reckon with such changes in the elasticity of demand as Harrod posits is presumed of the individual producers by price theory, I must confess great doubt as to the prevalence of such behavior in practice.[7]

[5] R. F. Harrod, *The Trade Cycle*, Oxford, 1936, pp. 17 ff.

[6] This is to be distinguished from the objection that Pigou has raised against Harrod's principle. Pigou (*op. cit.*, pp. 46 ff.) observes that, with a rise in real income, the community will devote a larger part of its expenditures to luxuries, the demand for which is more elastic than that for necessities. In consequence, the *representative* elasticity of demand may increase even though the elasticity of demand confronting individual producers diminishes. This seems a valid criticism, and yet I must confess an iconoclastic doubt on one point: that in general the demand for luxuries is more elastic than that for necessities. While for any one consumer this proposition is probably unassailable, it must be reckoned that what are luxuries to one income group may be necessities to another. I should question, for example, whether the demand for champagne is more elastic than the demand for beer.

[7] By identifying changes in the output of a representative producer of consumer's goods with changes in real income, Professor Pigou (*op. cit.*, p. 46) excludes at the outset of his analysis the possibility that real income will have an independent influence on the producer's price margin. This procedure, however, seems to me quite confusing, and entirely vulnerable to the criticism which Samuelson has levied against it ("Professor Pigou's *Employment and Equilibrium*," *American Economic Review*, September, 1941).

It is not necessary here, nor is it my purpose, to stage an assault on current price theory. But it is trite to observe that the gap between the price calculus and reality often is distressingly wide. What has enamored me especially of the price formulation that has been advanced is that it embraces a wide variety of plausible behavior patterns, without there being any necessary implication that these patterns in some sense are loci of maximum positions.

III

If in the particular industry studied the ratio of material to labor costs varies when output changes, the incremental cost per unit of labor input, v in the price function, will be partially dependent on the level of output. The analysis is facilitated, however, and at the same time the variety of price patterns embraced by the price function is increased, if it is assumed that the over-all proportion of material to labor costs approximates that in a marginal increment of resources.[8] The price function, in this case, may be characterized by two elasticities. One, which corresponds to the elasticity (or flexibility) of the supply function of price theory, indicates the percentage change in price that will be associated with a unit percentage change in output, incremental cost per unit of labor input being given. The other which is novel, indicates the percentage change in price which will be associated with a unit percentage change in incremental cost per unit of labor input, output being given. These two elasticities may be designated η_{px} and ρ_{pv}, respectively.

The so-called flexibility of prices is understood variously. But where it is measured by the reaction of prices to such a variety of forces as (say) are operating in the downswing of a business cycle, it should be clear, price flexibility depends on the values of the two elasticities that have been defined. The two elasticities isolate those attributes of the price function which are of special concern to us here. It is convenient, then, to use them as a basis for cataloguing the more plausible types of price behavior which the price function describes. Taking the value of the price-cost elasticity as the primary criterion, the following classes of price reaction patterns may be distinguished:

[8] Where this assumption is not valid the price function, in its present form, cannot embrace cases where price is fixed as a percentage of average variable cost or of average total cost per unit of output (see below, pp. 279, and 280). The prices of elements in variable costs which do not vary proportionately with labor in these cases must be inserted separately in the price function, and additional elasticities must then be defined to characterize the function. The conclusions of the present study, however, are not altered when this more complex function is employed.

$$\text{(i)} \quad \rho_{pv} = 1.$$

In the case of a perfectly competitive market the price function assumes the specific form given by the equilibrium condition that price equal marginal cost.[9] Accordingly, for any given output, the equilibrium price must change proportionately to any change in the incremental cost per unit of labor input, and the price-cost elasticity is unity.[10] The price-output elasticity equals the elasticity of the marginal-cost schedule, (γ).

The same reaction patterns, evidently, must appear under conditions of monopolistic competition wherever individual firms establish prices at a constant percentage margin over marginal cost. In terms of current price theory such producers reckon with a constant elasticity of demand in establishing their prices.[11] If, as is not unlikely the price margin over marginal cost increases with the level of operations, ρ_{pv} still will equal unity, but η_{px} will be greater than γ. The elasticity ρ_{pv} will approximate unity also if price is established at a constant or varying percentage margin over average variable cost. If the price margin is constant η_{px} will be less than γ, unless the marginal-cost schedule is also constant, in which case both elasticities will equal zero and prices will be rigid with respect to output variations.

$$\text{(ii)} \quad \rho_{pv} = 0.$$

It is conceivable, though I have been unable to think of such a case, that the price-cost elasticity be equal to zero, and yet the price-output elasticity be unequal to zero. Situations where both elasticities are zero, however, are not rare. They constitute the cases of complete price rigidity.

Such cases easily are embraced by the price function, but they are a source of some embarrassment to price theory. If the demand for an industry's product is inelastic, a reluctance on the part of individual firms to cut prices under any circumstances is quite understandable.

[9] That is,

$$p = v \frac{dl}{dx},$$

where l is the amount of labor employed, and in the short run may be taken as a unique function of output.

[10] Under conditions of perfect competition, this is to say, output is a zeroth-degree homogeneous function of prices and wages.

[11] The short-run maximum condition for a monopolistic competitor may be written

$$p \left(1 - \frac{1}{e_{px}} \right) = v \frac{dl}{dx},$$

where e_{px} is the elasticity of demand confronting the producer.

But to explain their failure to raise prices when (say) wages increase, or even their failure to set prices at a higher level at the outset, one must resort to such considerations as the fear of political intervention, potential competition, inertia, and collective frustration, i.e., each firm fails to raise its price for fear that others will not follow.[12] Under none of these circumstances may the individual producers be described as equating marginal revenue and marginal cost.

$$\text{(iii) } 0 < \rho_{pv} < 1.$$

Perhaps the bulk of the cases of this category are cases where prices are established as a percentage of the average total cost per unit of output. Here the price-cost elasticity must be between zero and unity, its actual value depending on the proportion of variable to total costs. If the price margin does not vary with output, the price-output elasticity is less than the elasticity of the marginal-cost schedule, and, if the firm is producing less than the least-cost output, it is negative. Where the price margin is taken as a percentage of average cost at some "normal" or "average" level of production—probably a usual case—, the price-output elasticity is zero and prices are rigid with respect to output variations.

A public-utility price formula designed to assure a constant rate of return on invested capital at any level of operations is in effect equivalent to the application of a percentage price margin which declines with increases in output. The price-output elasticity is negative when less than the least-cost output is produced, and positive but less than γ when the output exceeds that level.[13] If the price formula is one which assures a given rate of return on invested capital at a "normal" level of operations, the results are the same as in the case where the price margin is taken as some percentage of average cost at "normal" output.

A fixed absolute-price margin is equivalent to a relative margin which rises with output up to the point of least cost and declines thereafter.

$$\text{(iv) } \rho_{pv} < 0; \; \rho_{pv} > 1.$$

In particular circumstances a change in variable cost might be associated with a more than proportionate change in price. The change in cost, for example, might provide the occasion for a large price change that had been contemplated in any case. But such instances would seem to be very special. A negative price-cost elasticity is highly improbable.

[12] See P. M. Sweezy, "Demand Under Conditions of Oligopoly," *Journal of Political Economy*, August, 1939.

[13] Costs must be defined here, however, as including the rate of return allowed on invested capital.

IV

The relation of the price behavior studied in income theory to that embraced by the price function is readily stated. Below are tabulated, in terms of the two price elasticities, the price reactions studied in Keynes' *General Theory* and in those contributions to income theory which incorporate variations from the Keynesian case. Only the more recent of Pigou's two contributions is referred to.

Keynes: $\rho_{pv} = 1$ (taken as an approximation), $\eta_{px} > 0$ (implicit in assumption that real wages decline with increases in output and employment).[14]

Hicks: $\rho_{pv} = 1$, $\eta_{px} = \gamma$ (perfect competition).[15]

Douglas: $\rho_{pv} = 1$, $\eta_{px} = \gamma$ (perfect competition); $\rho_{pv} = 0$, $\eta_{px} = 0$.[16]

Bissell: $\rho_{pv} = 1$, $\eta_{px} = \gamma$; $\rho_{pv} = 0$, $\eta_{px} = 0$; and one case where $0 < \rho_{pv} < 1$ and $\eta_{px} < \gamma$.[17]

Pigou: $\rho_{pv} = 1$, $\eta_{px} > -1$.[18]

A number of alternative hypotheses as to the behavior of the prices of the ultimate factors of production, labor, and land, have been analyzed by Lerner, but his assumption as to the reaction of the prices of final goods to the variations of these parameters is the same as that of Keynes.[19] The behavior of prices is not a primary concern of Lange, but apparently his analysis of the optimum propensity to consume is restricted to the case of perfect competition.[20] Harrod's principle of diminishing elasticity of demand is distinctly novel, but beyond this, I believe, no departure from the Keynesian case is intended.[21]

[14] J. M. Keynes, *General Theory of Employment, Interest and Money*, New York, 1936. While it has been suggested that in the Keynesian analysis $\eta_{px} = \gamma$, I have been able to find no clear support for this interpretation in the *General Theory*. The use of wage units, if rigorously interpreted, requires that $\eta_{px} = 0$.

[15] J. R. Hicks, "Mr. Keynes and the Classics: A Suggested Interpretation," ECONOMETRICA, Vol. 5, April, 1937, pp. 147–159.

[16] P. H. Douglas, "The Effect of Wage Increases Upon Employment," *American Economic Review, Supplement*, March, 1939. Douglas also explores the general case of monopolistic competition without committing himself to any definite assumption as to price behavior.

[17] R. H. Bissell, Jr., *op. cit.* In the third case referred to, prices are assumed to move by the same *absolute* amount as marginal cost. Bissell, however, mistakenly argues that this will be the case when the elasticity of demand is constant.

[18] A. C. Pigou, *op. cit.* The condition that $\eta_{px} > -1$ is implied in Pigou's requirement that the value of investment varies positively with the amount of labor demanded or supplied for investment.

[19] A. P. Lerner, "The Relation of Wage Policies and Price Policies," *American Economic Review, Supplement*, March, 1939.

[20] Oskar Lange, "The Rate of Interest and the Optimum Propensity to Consume," *Economica*, February, 1938.

[21] See R. F. Harrod, *op. cit.*, pp. 75 ff.

V

In the real world, it must be reckoned, the different cases of price behavior that have been delineated are not mutually exclusive, but exist side by side in a bewildering variety of market situations. If income theory is to maintain at least a macroscopic communion with this complex reality, resort to the not altogether satisfactory device of index numbers to measure changes in prices and production in the different industrial sectors studied is unavoidable.[22] In the present analysis the incremental cost per unit of labor input also must be taken as an average for all final-consumption-goods industries, for all final-investment-goods industries, and—if materials are recognized, as they should be, as an element in marginal cost—for the industries which supply these industries with materials.

Whether a price function relating such entities is more or less stable than one relating the price, output, and costs in an individual industry is open to question. But at least two interesting propositions concerning the aggregative function inspire confidence. From what has been said already, it would appear that for most market situations the price-cost elasticity is not less than zero nor greater than unity. A negative price-output elasticity, furthermore, is *rara avis*, while a positive one is usual. It is plausible, then, that the aggregative price-cost elasticity has a value between zero and one and that the aggregative price-output elasticity is positive.

The two elasticities, of course, are not likely to be the same in the consumption-goods, investment-goods, and materials industries. Their variation is of much import for income analysis, and it is an advantage of the present formulation that the implications of this phenomenon may be explored. Equality of at least the price-cost elasticity of investment goods and consumption goods is assumed in all the analyses referred to in Section IV.[23]

VI

It would be tempting to take the price-cost elasticity as indicating

---

[22] Income analyses are not always explicit on the relative price behavior in different industries, but some such assumption as that of Professor Pigou is usually implied. Professor Pigou (*op. cit.*, pp. 42–43) assumes that the relative prices and quantities of all consumption goods and of all investment goods are constant. Bissell, however, includes in his study a suggestive section on relative price changes and substitution effects.

[23] Douglas (*op. cit.*, pp. 150 ff.), in seeking to extend his analysis to monopolistic markets, refers briefly to the possibility that the response of prices to cost changes in the consumption-goods industries will differ from that in the capital-goods industries. The studies of Bissell and Lerner contain suggestive material on the effect of differences in price reactions in different sectors of the economy.

not only the response of prices to a change in variable costs, but also, when a correction is made for the extent of the impact of a wage change on variable costs, the response of prices to a change in wages. Considered as a group, however, the industries producing materials evidently must supply their own needs for these goods. Accordingly a change in wages will have not only a direct effect on variable costs and hence on the price of materials, but also a series of indirect effects, as variable costs are affected by the change in the price of materials. If the wage change is over-all, the prices of final goods, too, will be affected not only directly, but indirectly via the change in the price of materials associated with the change in wages. The net result is that prices in each sector are more sensitive to wage changes than the corrected price-cost elasticity would indicate.

It facilitates much the development of income theory to introduce into the analysis a price-wage elasticity, $\bar{\rho}_{pw}$, which incorporates the indirect as well as direct effects of wage variations on prices, output being given. Using the subscripts, m, c, and i, to denote that the variables referred to pertain respectively to the materials, consumption-goods, and investment-goods industries, it may readily be shown that

$$(2) \qquad \bar{\rho}_{p_m w} = k_m \rho_{p_m v_m} / (1 + k_m - \rho_{p_m v_m}),$$

$$(3) \qquad \bar{\rho}_{p_c w} = \frac{k_c}{1 + k_c} \rho_{p_c v_c} + \frac{1}{1 + k_c} \rho_{p_c v_c} \bar{\rho}_{p_m w},$$

and

$$(4) \qquad \bar{\rho}_{p_i w} = \frac{k_i}{1 + k_i} \rho_{p_i v_i} + \frac{1}{1 + k_i} \rho_{p_i v_i} \bar{\rho}_{p_m w}.$$

Here k denotes the proportion of labor to material costs in a marginal increment of resources used in the industry group concerned. The indirect effect of the over-all wage change on the prices of the final goods is isolated in the second term on the right-hand side of (3) and (4).

It is evident at once that, even though wages are not the only element in variable costs, if $\rho_{p_m v_m}$ is unity, $\bar{\rho}_{p_m w}$ must also be unity. When the effect of a change in the price of materials on variable costs in the materials industries is reckoned with, the equilibrium price, for a given output, ultimately must change proportionately to a change in wages. If at the same time $\rho_{p_c v_c}$ or $\rho_{p_i v_i}$ is also unity, the price-wage elasticity in the corresponding sector likewise must be unity. An over-all wage change, through its effect on material prices, causes a proportionate change in the price of consumption goods or in the price of investment goods as the case may be.

If $\rho_{p_m v_m}$ is less than unity but positive, $\bar{\rho}_{p_m w}$ must not only be within these limits, but less than $\rho_{p_m v_m}$. A less-than-unity $\rho_{p_c v_c}$ or $\rho_{p_i v_i}$ has the same implication with respect to the price-wage elasticity in the industrial sector concerned, and if $\rho_{p_m v_m}$ is less than unity at the same time, the disparity between $\rho_{p_c v_c}$ and $\bar{p}_{p_c w}$, or between $\rho_{p_i v_i}$ and $\bar{p}_{p_i w}$, is all the greater.

Analogous to the indirect effect on prices of an over-all change in wages is the effect on prices, via its impact on the price of materials, of a change in output in any one of the industry groups studied. Using $\bar{\eta}_{px}$, with appropriate subscripts, to designate the price-output elasticity which incorporates the total effect on prices of a variation in output in a particular industry group, wages being given, it may be shown that

(5)
$$\bar{\eta}_{p_m x_m} = \frac{\eta_{p_m x_m}}{1 - \dfrac{1}{1 + k_m} \rho_{p_m v_m}},$$

(6)
$$\bar{\eta}_{p_c x_c} = \eta_{p_c x_c} + \frac{1}{1 + k_c} \rho_{p_c x_c} \bar{\eta}_{p_m x_m} \alpha_{mc},$$

and

(7)
$$\bar{\eta}_{p_i x_i} = \eta_{p_i x_i} + \frac{1}{1 + k_i} \rho_{p_i v_i} \bar{\eta}_{p_m x_m} \alpha_{mi}.$$

The elasticity α, with appropriate subscripts, indicates the percentage increase in materials required to produce a given percentage increase in consumption goods or investment goods as the case may be.

It is evident from (5) that $\bar{\eta}_{p_m x_m}$ will be large relatively to $\eta_{p_m x_m}$ the larger is the price-cost elasticity and the smaller the proportion of labor to material costs in the materials industries. The indirect effect on prices of a variation in output in the consumption- and investment-goods industries is segregated in the second term on the right-hand side of (3) and (4). Its magnitude in each case varies directly with the value of $\bar{\eta}_{p_m x_m}$ and with the proportion of material to labor costs and the value of the primary price-cost elasticity in the industry group concerned.

The foregoing assumes, of course, that the same materials are used in the consumption-goods and investment-goods industries. To the extent that the materials used by the two final-goods sectors differ— and it will simplify the ensuing exposition to assume that they are entirely distinct—, the elasticities $\bar{p}_{p_m w}$ and $\bar{\eta}_{p_m x_m}$ must be understood to have different values in (3) and (4) from those which they have in (6) and (7).[24]

[24] To the extent that the final-goods sectors do draw on the same industries for materials, it is necessary to reckon with the possibility that a change in the

VII

The problem referred to at the outset of this essay, of the effect of an over-all wage change on real income and employment, affords an interesting context in which to apply the price formulation that has been elucidated. Attention will be confined here to the case where, through appropriate bank action with respect to the supply of money, the interest rate is held constant. It is on the effect of a wage change under this circumstance that controversy recently has centered.

It will be assumed provisionally, following Hicks, that the community's propensities to save and invest each depend on two variables, the level of income and the rate of interest. For a constant rate of interest, then, the propensities may be expressed as functions of income alone. If the analysis is not to be prejudiced at the outset to the special case where all prices change proportionately to wages, however, it is necessary to forsake both Keynes's wage units and Hicks's monetary units. The propensities and income are understood here to be expressed in physical terms. The real saving which the community desires to realize (money saving divided by the price of final consumption goods) is taken as a function, $S(y)$, and the real investment which the community desires to realize (money value of investment divided by the price of final investment goods) as a function, $I(y)$, of the community's real income, y (money income divided by the price of final consumption goods). In equilibrium, then,

$$(9) \qquad\qquad p_c S(y) = p_i I(y).$$

The community's propensity to consume, $C(y)$, also is understood to be expressed in physical units. In equilibrium x_c, the amount of consumers' goods produced, must equal $C(y)$. In the present context it should be pardonable to assume that the community's stock of capital goods is perfectly durable. Hence x_i, the amount of final investment goods produced, must equal $I(y)$.

Given these conditions and the determinants of prices already formulated, it is an easy matter to establish the relation between changes in money wages and in the community's real income. If we denote the

---

output of investment goods will affect the price of consumption goods, via the price of materials, even though the output of consumption goods is unchanged, and that a change in the output of consumption goods similarly will affect the price of investment goods. These two price effects are measured respectively by the two cross elasticities:

$$(8a) \qquad\qquad \bar{\eta}_{p_c x_i} = \frac{1}{1 + k_c}\, \rho_{p_c v_c} \bar{\eta}_{p_m x_m} \alpha_{mi};$$

$$(8b) \qquad\qquad \bar{\eta}_{p_i x_c} = \frac{1}{1 + k_i}\, \rho_{p_i v_i} \bar{\eta}_{p_m x_m} \alpha_{mc}.$$

percentage change in real income associated with a unit percentage change in wages as the elasticity ϵ_{yw} it may be shown that

(10)
$$\epsilon_{yw} = -\frac{\bar{p}_{p_cw} - \bar{p}_{p_iw}}{\Delta},$$

where

(11)
$$\Delta = (\bar{\eta}_{p_cx_c}\kappa_{Cy} - \bar{\eta}_{p_ix_i}\kappa_{Iy}) + (\kappa_{Sy} - \kappa_{Iy}).$$

Here κ_{Cy} is the elasticity of the propensity to consume and denotes the percentage change in consumption that will be associated with a unit percentage change in real income. κ_{Iy} and κ_{Sy} are respectively the elasticity of the propensity to invest and the elasticity of the propensity to save.[25]

In (11), the terms $\bar{\eta}_{p_cx_c}\kappa_{Sy}$ and $\bar{\eta}_{p_ix_i}\kappa_{Iy}$ indicate respectively the percentage change in p_c and the percentage change in p_i that will be associated with a unit percentage change in y, for a given wage level. Accordingly Δ may be abbreviated as

(12)
$$\Delta = (\bar{\eta}_{p_cy} - \bar{\eta}_{p_iy}) + (\kappa_{Sy} - \kappa_{Iy}).\text{[26]}$$

Something might be learned as to the sign of this expression by inspection. But if the equilibrium under consideration is stable, it may be proven, Δ must be positive.[27] A positive Δ is the equivalent, in the

[25] Since in the present context the prices p_c and p_i are ultimately functions of y and w alone, it is clear that equation (9) defines implicitly the relation between these two variables. The explicit relation in (10), with Δ expressed in the form of (12), thus might be perceived at once.

In detail, the determinants of the system from which equation (10) is derived are as follows: (i) one price equation of the form of equation (1) for each of the economic sectors that have been distinguished—the materials industries, the final-investment-goods industries, and the final-consumption-goods industries; (ii) equation (9), together with the further conditions that $x_c = C(y)$ and $x_i = I(y)$; (iii) three equations, one for each of the economic sectors distinguished, of the form $v = a(w+bp_m)$, where the constants a and b may differ in the different sectors (the constant a may be regarded as allowing for interest on working capital, and b indicates the amount of materials associated with a unit of labor in a marginal increment of resources); (iv) a final equation expressing the amount of materials produced, x_m, as a function of x_c and x_i, i.e., $x_m = F(x_c) + G(x_i)$.

[26] If the cross effects referred to in footnote 24 are reckoned with, equation (11) takes the form:

(13)
$$\bar{\Delta} = (\bar{\eta}_{p_cx_c}\kappa_{Sy} + \bar{\eta}_{p_cx_i}\kappa_{Iy}) - (\bar{\eta}_{p_ix_i}\kappa_{Iy} + \bar{\eta}_{p_ix_c}\kappa_{Sy}) + (\kappa_{Sy} - \kappa_{Iy}).$$

This also reduces to (12), however, and the argument advanced in the text and in footnote 27 concerning the sign of Δ applies also to the sign of $\bar{\Delta}$.

[27] Stability was investigated under the following dynamic postulates: (a) the equilibrium saving $S(y)$ and the equilibrium prices are realized instantaneously, but the level of investment, $I(y)$, is intended investment and coincides with

present context, of the stability condition that the sum of the marginal propensity to consume and the marginal propensity to invest, in monetary units, must be less than one, which has been derived by Samuelson with respect to a Keynesian system in which variations in the ratio p_c/p_i are not explicitly recognized.[28] If the price ratio is constant, the requirement of a positive Δ reduces to the condition that the sum of the marginal propensities to consume and invest, in physical units, weighted respectively by p_c and p_i, be less than one.

From (10) the Keynesian proposition that a change in money wages will not affect real income evidently requires that the price-wage elasticities in the consumption-goods industries and in the investment-goods industries be equal. This condition, clearly, is satisfied in the case of perfect competition where both elasticities equal unity. But it could also be satisfied under monopolistic conditions, even if the price-wage elasticities were less than unity, provided prices were equally responsive to wage changes in the consumption-goods and investment-goods industries. It is not required either that the relative prices of consumption and investment goods be the same under all circumstances. Variations in relative prices with changes in real income are entirely admissible.

That the responses of price to changes in wages in the two sectors are the same, or proximate, in the real world, however, would be a hardy assumption. The sign and the extent of the difference in the price-wage elasticities is not to be settled here. But there is substantial evidence that the degree of concentration in industries which produce goods that are designed primarily for investment is markedly greater than in industries producing goods designed primarily for consumption.[29] When it is reckoned also that the demand for investment goods

---

$(p_c/p_i)S(y)$ only in equilibrium; and (b) the time derivative of money income is a function, with positive derivative and zero equilibrium value, of the difference $[p_i\ I(y) - p_c\ S(y)]$. These postulates are essentially the same as those used by Samuelson ("The Stability of Equilibrium," ECONOMETRICA, Vol. 9, April, 1941, pp. 115 ff.) in examining the stability of a Keynesian system in which variations of relative prices are not explicitly recognized. Except in the highly unlikely case that $\bar{\eta}_{p_c y} < -1$, stability of the system studied here requires that $\Delta > 0$. An $\bar{\eta}_{p_c y} < -1$ also must be excluded if the assumption regarding the time derivative of money income is to be valid. If real income is substituted for money income in the time derivative, Δ still must be positive for a stable equilibrium.

[28] Samuelson, op. cit.

[29] See TNEC Monograph No. 27, The Structure of American Industry, Washington, 1941, pp. 303–312, and particularly the comparative data on p. 311 on the degree of concentration in industries producing goods of which the consumer is the ultimate user and in industries producing goods of which the producer is the ultimate user. Only manufacturing industry is included in the study.

is predominantly a joint demand, and perhaps more often than not in-elastic, a greater over-all rigidity in the prices of such goods, not only with respect to output changes but changes in wages, is entirely plausible. If this argument is valid and the price-wage elasticity in the investment-goods industries is significantly less than in the consumption-goods industries, a change in money wages necessarily will have an inverse effect on real income. Provided there are unemployed workers who are willing to accept employment at the lowered money wages, a cut in money wages, as the "classical economists" argued, must result in an increase in aggregate real income. If employment in the consumption industries were slack and marginal costs approximately constant, however, and if furthermore there were a close approach to perfect competition in these industries, the reduction in money wages and increase in real income might not be associated with any significant reduction in real wages. If $\bar{\eta}_{p_c y}$ is positive and large, real wages must also be reduced.

Since in the case under consideration both the physical volume of consumption and investment depend only on the level of real income, and since the amount of materials used depends on the amounts of these goods produced, the volume of employment in the community may be expressed as a single valued-function, $L(y)$, of the level of real income. Accordingly the elasticity of demand for labor has the value

$$(14) \qquad\qquad \epsilon_{Lw} = \epsilon_{Ly} \cdot \epsilon_{yw},$$

where ϵ_{Ly} is the elasticity of the employment function, $L(y)$, and is positive.

VIII

Hicks's generalization of the Keynesian propensities has received a merited currency. But in the present context, where prices do not necessarily change proportionately to wages, the expression of the propensities to save and invest as functions of real income and the rate of interest alone obviously is not an altogether satisfactory device. The determination of saving and investment under these conditions warrants a separate inquiry. There is no formal obstacle, however, to the extension of the analysis to more general cases. If, as it should be, the propensity to save is expressed as a function not only of aggregate real income, but also of the share of real income accruing to workers, the real-income–money-wage elasticity depends not only on the relative magnitude of the price-wage elasticities, but also on the extent to which, for a given level of real income, a change in money wages will affect aggregate real wages and hence real saving. These two elements, however, should be of opposite sign. The possibility that an increase in money wages, by stimulating consumption, will increase real income and employment is thus admissible. The possibility becomes the more remote, however, the more nearly the price-wage elasticity in the consumption-goods industries approximates unity. It must be reckoned, furthermore, that a narrowing price-wage margin may discourage investment at the same time that it stimulates consumption. Recognition of this additional possibility in the analysis requires that the real wage rate, at least, should be included as a variable in the investment function.

The concept of a substitution effect is yet to be adequately explored. But to the extent that it refers to shifts in the employment of labor and other factors at a given level of real income, the substitution effect of a change in money wages on employment is neglected in Section VI. While changes in relative prices are incorporated in the analysis, employment is taken to be uniquely related to production, and hence to real income. Disregard of substitution effect is permissible, and I believe inevitable, in the study of short-run equilibrium. Nevertheless to the extent that they occur it is evident that they must contribute in the long run to the establishment of an inverse relation between money wages and employment, through not necessarily between money wages and real income.

The University of Texas

PRICE FLEXIBILITY AND THE LEVEL OF INCOME

ABRAM BERGSON
University of Texas

As it affects the community's propensities to save and invest, so will a price-cut in any sector of the economy affect total real income. The observation is trite, but the systematic analysis of this interesting effect, in the light of recent developments in income theory, has not yet been undertaken. This essay, it is hoped, will provide the necessary tools for the project.

The problem may be approached by considering an illuminating but probably quite unrealistic case. Suppose the producers of investment goods voluntarily reduce their prices, having been persuaded, (say) by reading the Brookings Institution study, *Industrial Price Policies and Economic Progress,*[1] that their profits ultimately will be enhanced thereby. That the producers might be disappointed—the authors of the Brookings study themselves would grant the possibility—need not for the moment concern us. What is of immediate interest is the community's gain.

It is convenient and probably not remote from fact to assume that our enlightened producers execute their price reduction in a community in which the supply of money is highly elastic, and hence, in which interest rates do not change significantly under the impact of the events studied.[2] Then the facts on which the impact of the price cut will depend can be discerned at once.

Presumably, the reduction in prices will affect directly the demand for investment goods. That the effect will be positive, if interest rates are unchanged, is not implausible, but it suffices to observe here that unless the increase in demand is at least proportionate to the price cut, the money value of investment will be reduced. Subject to the same proviso, then, the community's investment activities will absorb less saving after the price cut than before, and saving will have to be curtailed. Apparently, unless the producers of consumption goods also are proselytized by the Brookings study, the price cut will have the paradoxical effect of reducing the community's real income. To suggest that if real income did

---

[1] Edwin G. Nourse and Horace B. Drury, *Industrial Price Policies and Economic Progress* (Brookings Institution, Washington, D.C., 1938).

[2] The consideration of alternative banking policies is a task which it seems unwise to assume in this initial effort, but such a task should prove laborious rather than difficult.

increase, this in itself might induce an increased volume of investment is not in point. If the demand for investment were not stimulated sufficiently by the price cut alone, the increase in real income would not occur.

The reduction in the price of investment goods, however, also affects at once the distribution of income. Even if the demand for investment goods did not respond at all to the price cut, could not the consequent reduction in entrepreneurial income cause the necessary reduction in saving? The answer, of course, is yes—*provided* that the producers of investment goods reduce their saving by the full amount of their loss. Even in this extreme although, perhaps in the shortest run, not unlikely case, however, both the community's money income and, if the price of consumption goods is unchanged, its real income are reduced. The burden is borne entirely by the adventurous, and not very abstemious, producers of investment goods. If the producers reduce their expenditures on consumption goods as well as their saving, the burden to that extent will be shifted to other members of the community.

Provided the demand for investment goods responds at all to the price cut, employment, and hence the wage bill, as well as entrepreneurial income, will be altered. The question remains whether in this circumstance, at least, real income would not increase, even if the value of investment declined. The answer is neither unique nor simple. The *impact* of the price cut, of course, would depend on whether the change in total income as well as the change in its distribution resulted in a greater decline in the saving which the community desired to realize than in investment. Ultimately, however, real income would increase only if the redistribution of income alone were sufficient to reduce saving more than the price cut reduced investment.

II

The possibility that a reduction in the price of investment goods, even though it stimulates demand, might depress real income is one for which I believe current literature on price theory leaves the reader quite unprepared. The determinants of the result obviously have relevance much beyond the limited context in which they have been revealed. To define them exactly, then, should be profitable. At the same time, an expression for the magnitude of the effect of the price reduction on real income may readily be derived.

For convenience, let us assume at first that the community's saving in real terms depends on the amount of real income, but not on its distribution. Saving in real terms (S) and real income (Y) are understood here to be respectively money saving and money income, each divided by the price of consumption goods (p).[3] The propensity of the community to save, then, may be expressed as a function, $S(Y)$. The producers of consumption goods are assumed for the moment to be so remote from the Brookings' influence as to maintain their prices constant despite the changes in demand that occur. The community's real investment (I)— money value of investment divided by the price of investment goods (q)—may be taken, then, to depend in the short run on the level of the community's real income and on the price of investment goods; i.e., real investment is a function $I(Y, q)$. Interest rates, it will be recalled, are assumed constant, and so, we shall assume, are wage rates.[4]

In terms of these categories the condition for an equilibrium income, that the saving and investment which the community desires to realize should in fact be realized, takes the form

$$p \cdot S(Y) = q \cdot I(Y,q). \tag{1}$$

The price of consumption goods being given, this condition alone is evidently sufficient to determine the relation between changes in the price of investment goods and changes in real income.

If we denote as E_{Yq} the percentage change in real income that will be associated with a unit percentage change[5] in the price of investment goods, it may readily be shown that

$$E_{Yq} = \frac{1 + K_{Iq}}{\Delta}, \tag{2}$$

where

$$\Delta = K_{SY} - K_{IY}, \tag{3}$$

and other terms are defined as follows. K_{Iq} is the percentage change in real investment that is associated with a unit percentage change in q, real income being given. Hence K_{Iq} is the negative of the elasticity of demand for investment goods.[6] The terms K_{SY} and K_{IY} are simply the elasticities of the propensities to save and invest, and indicate respectively the

[3] The Keynesian wage units are discarded advisedly, for they are appropriate only if all prices are assumed to change proportionately to wages.

[4] Incorporation of the price of investment goods in the investment function, thus, is a generalization of the Hicks formulation. See J. R. Hicks, "Mr. Keynes and the Classics: A Suggested Interpretation," *Econometrica,* v (April, 1937).

[5] The sign of E_{Yq} and of other elasticities is understood to be that given them when the unit percentage change of the independent variable is positive.

[6] This implicitly assumes, however, that I is gross rather than net investment. For the purposes of this essay, "investment" will in fact be understood in this sense, and accordingly "saving" will be understood as gross saving.

percentage change in saving and in investment that will be associated with a unit percentage change in real income, q being given.

For the equilibrium that condition (1) defines to be stable, it may be proven, Δ must be positive.[7] It follows at once that real income will increase, when the price of investment goods is cut, only if the elasticity of demand for investment goods is greater than unity ($K_{Iq} < -1$).

This conclusion is unaffected if account is taken of the possibility that changes in the demand for consumption goods, associated with changes in real income, will induce the producers of these goods to alter their prices. But the change in consumption-goods prices would dampen whatever change in real income was stimulated by the reduction in investment-goods prices.[8] If, for example, the price of consumption goods varied markedly with changes in demand, the stimulating or depressing effect of the reduction in investment-goods prices would be largely reflected in changes in money income rather than in real income. Unless the elasticity of supply of consumption goods were zero,[9] however, the impact of the price cut necessarily would fall in part on real income.

For present purposes the dependence of saving on the distribution of income is accounted for adequately if we introduce into the saving function a second variable, the real wage bill (M). The condition for an equilibrium income, then takes the form

$$p \cdot S(Y,M) = q \cdot I(Y,q), \tag{5}$$

where

$$M = \frac{w}{p}L, \tag{6}$$

and p, again, is taken to be constant. The number of workers employed (L) may be regarded, in the short run, as depending only on the amounts of consumption goods and investment goods produced.[10]

---

[7] Except that the prices in (2) had to be taken as parameters rather than as determined variables, the dynamic postulates under which stability was investigated are the same as those stated in my "Prices, Wages and Income Theory," *Econometrica*, x (July–October, 1942), p. 286, footnote 27.

[8] The denominator of (2) takes the form

$$\Delta = (1 - K_{Ip}) N_{pC} K_{CY} + K_{SY} - K_{IY} \tag{4}$$

where K_{Ip} is the percentage change in the demand for real investment associated with a unit percentage change in p, Y and q being given; N_{pC} is the elasticity of the supply function $p(C)$; and K_{CY} is the elasticity of the propensity to consume.

[9] And hence N_{pC} in (4) is infinite.

[10] Thus

$$L = F(C) + G(I) \tag{7}$$

These conditions suffice to determine the relation between the price of investment goods and real income. In terms of the two elasticities, K_{Iq} and K_{IY}, and of others yet to be defined, E_{Yq} has the value,

$$E_{Yq} = \frac{1 + K_{Iq} - K_{SM} R_{Lq}}{\Delta} \tag{8}$$

where

$$\Delta = K_{SY} - K_{IY} + K_{SM} R_{LY}. \tag{9}$$

The term K_{SY} is now taken to indicate the response of saving to changes in real income, when the real wage bill is given, while the percentage change in saving associated with a unit percentage change in the real wage bill, total real income given, is represented by the elasticity K_{SM}. The term R_{Lq} indicates the percentage change in total employment that will be associated with a unit percentage change in the price of investment goods, the contribution to changes in employment of changes in real income attendant on the price change being neglected, while R_{LY} indicates the percentage change in total employment that will be associated with a unit percentage change in real income, q being constant.[11]

Again, if the equilibrium that is defined is stable, Δ is positive.[12] Whether a reduction in the price of investment goods will increase or reduce real income, then, depends on the elasticity of demand for investment goods, and on the responsiveness of saving to a change in the price of investment goods, real income being given. The elasticity R_{Lq} in (8) is negative. Its value is directly dependent on the value of K_{Iq}, and in absolute terms is probably less than the latter. For ordinarily—even allowing for the interaction of employment and consumption *via* changes in the distribution of income—a given percentage change in the price of investment goods could not be expected to stimulate directly as large a

[11] Specifically,

$$R_{Lq} = \frac{R_{LI} \cdot K_{Iq}}{1 - R_{LC} \cdot K_{CM}}.$$

Here R_{LI} and R_{LC} are the partial elasticities of the employment function in (7), and K_{CM} is the consumption elasticity corresponding to the savings elasticity K_{SM}. If employment in the investment-goods and consumption-goods industries varied proportionally with output, the terms R_{LI} and R_{LC} would equal the proportion of the working force employed in the investment-goods and in the consumption-goods industries, respectively. If, at the same time, to take an extreme case, K_{CM} were equal to unity, R_{Lq} would equal K_{Iq}. Since in fact K_{CM} should be distinctly less than unity, R_{Lq} might be expected to be less than K_{Iq}.

The elasticity R_{LY} may be expressed in terms of the same elasticities as R_{Lq}, the numerator in (10) being replaced by the expression $(R_{LC} K_{CY} + R_{LI} K_{IY})$.

[12] Stability was investigated under the same dynamic postulates as are referred to in footnote 7.

percentage change in total employment as in real investment.[13] The elasticity K_{SM} is also negative, but, in absolute terms, it might well be greater than unity. This is especially likely in a period of depression, when the extraction of a given percentage increment in the wage bill from all other income might be expected to cause a relatively large change in the much reduced savings of the community.[14] What is essential, however, if a reduction in the price of investment goods is to stimulate real income when the demand for investment goods is inelastic, is that the absolute value of K_{SM} be greater than the amount by which the reciprocal of K_{Iq}, in absolute terms, exceeds unity. If investment were quite unresponsive to a price cut, as it well might be in a depression, even a relatively large value of K_{SM} would be inadequate. The price cut would reduce real income.

If changes in demand induce the producers of consumption goods to alter their prices, the impact on real income of a cut in the price of investment goods again will be dampened. Here, however, the induced change in the price of consumption goods will affect the direction as well as the magnitude of the impact,[15] and the effect will be in the opposite direction to that of the induced change in employment. An increase in the price of consumption goods, in response to an increase in demand, would offset in some measure the favorable effect on the distribution of income of the cut in the price of investment goods. At the same time, if the increase were marked, the community's *money* saving at a given level of *real* income might be greater rather than less than before.

III

If the producers of consumption goods rather than of investment goods were the ones who spontaneously cut their prices, the response of the demand for investment goods again would be a critical element in the

---

[13] See footnote 11. The indirect effect of the price cut on employment *via* the change in real income induced by the price cut, and hence in consumption and investment induced by this change in real income, is not taken into account by R_{Lq}.

[14] If we denote all other income than wages as N, then

$$K_{SM} = \frac{W}{S} \left[\left(\frac{\partial S}{\partial M} \right)_N - \left(\frac{\partial S}{\partial N} \right)_M \right]. \tag{11}$$

Thus, K_{SM} is the difference between the marginal propensity to save of wage earners and of all other income recipients, multiplied by the ratio of the wage bill to total saving.

[15] The variation in the price of consumption goods necessitates the introduction of additional terms in both the numerator and the denominator of the fraction on the right-hand side of (8). The explanation of these terms is a larger task than may be assumed here, but it should be observed that unless the demand for investment were exceedingly sensitive to changes in the price of consumption goods, the net contribution to both the numerator and denominator would be positive.

outcome. In this case, however, unless the price cut *reduced* the demand for investment goods, real income would increase. Analysis, which will not be developed here, discloses that, for a given price of investment goods, the reduction in demand at least would have to be more than proportionate to the price cut to cause a decline of real income. The elements on which the outcome will depend should be apparent.

IV

While the price behavior that has been analyzed here is highly fictitious, the forces revealed are set in motion by price changes in the real world. Price reductions in response to cost reductions, or in response to public pressure or the threat of government intervention, all can be analyzed in terms of the elements that have been described. If the cost reduction were due to a wage cut, however, the stimulating effect of the price reduction on the distribution of income probably would be obliterated. If the price reduction were made under duress, the response of investment doubtless would be less favorable than if the price reduction were voluntary.

That a reduction in the prices of investment goods, or, more realistically, of goods used primarily for investment might cause a decline in real income, is a possibility that must be reckoned with in the real world as well as in our fictitious one. Programs that urge the reduction of investment-goods prices as a recovery measure hardly are discredited on this account, but their merit is in question. That the producer who maintains prices in a depression in the face of an inelastic demand is acting contrary to the public interest is not self-evident.

ERRATA

References are to the present pagination.

Page 49, line 9: *Insert* so *after* do

Page 59, formula (1.3): *Insert I as an additional argument on right-hand side*

Page 109, line 19: *Delete* and

Page 111, line 24: *Delete* is

Page 138, formula (5.1): *For Y read I*

Page 142, line 8: *For* computation. The mode of analysis derives from a 1961 essay *read* might not be commensurate with distortions in valuations of

Page 209, after entry for Lange, Oskar: *Insert* Macesich, George. *Yugoslavia: The Theory and Practice of Development Planning,* Charlottesville: University of Virginia Press, 1964.

Page 209, the entry that followed that for Lange, Oskar: *For* Macesich, George. *read* Pejovich, Svetozar.

Page 242, line 13: *For* over *read* other

Page 270, last two lines of text: *For* (3) and (4) *read* (3) and (6) *and for* (6) and (7) *read* (4) and (7)

PERMISSIONS

The essays included in this volume are listed chronologically below. I also indicate in each case the holder or holders of the corresponding copyright. I wish to thank the latter for permission to reprint.

"Real Income, Expenditure Proportionality, and Frisch's 'New Methods of Measuring Marginal Utility,'" *Review of Economic Studies,* Vol. IV, No. 1 (October 1936): *Review of Economic Studies*, pp. 33–52.

"A Reformulation of Certain Aspects of Welfare Economics," *The Quarterly Journal of Economics,* Vol. LII, No. 2 (February 1938): John Wiley & Sons, pp. 310–334.

"Prices, Wages, and Income Theory," *Econometrica,* Vol. X, Nos. 3–4 (July–October 1942): Econometric Society, pp. 275–289.

"Price Flexibility and the Level of Income," *The Review of Economic Statistics,*" Vol. XXV, No. 1 (February 1943): North-Holland Publishing Co, pp. 2–5.

"Socialist Economics," in H. Ellis, ed., *A Survey of Contemporary Economics,* Philadelphia, Blakeston, 1948: Richard D. Irwin, Inc. and the President and Fellows of Harvard College, pp. 193–236.

"Market Socialism Revisited," *The Journal of Political Economy,* Vol. LXXV, No. 5 (October 1967): University of Chicago, pp. 655–673.

"Optimal Pricing for a Public Enterprise," *The Quarterly Journal of Economics.* Vol. LXXXVI, No. 4 (November 1972): John Wiley & Sons, pp. 519–544.

"On Monopoly Welfare Losses", *The American Economic Review,* Vol. LXIII, No. 5.(December 1973): The American Economic Association, pp. 853–870.

"Index Numbers and the Computation of Factor Productivity," *The Review of Income and Wealth,* Series 21, No. 3 (September 1975): International Association for Research in Income and Wealth, pp. 259–278.

"Social Choice and Welfare Economics under Representative Government," *Journal of Public Economics,* Vol. VI, No 3 (October 1976): North-Holland Publishing Co., pp. 171–190.

"Taste Differences and Optimal Income Distribution: A Paradox Illustrated," in T. Bagiotti and G. Franco, eds., *Pioneering Economics.*

Essays in Honor of Giovanni Demaria, Padova, Cedam, 1978: CEDAM, pp. 81–86.

"Managerial Risks and Rewards in Public Enterprises," *Journal of Comparative Economics,* Vol. II, No. 3 (September 1978): Academic Press, pp. 211–225.

"Consumer's and Producer's Surplus and General Equilibrium," in H. Greenfield et al., *Theory for Economic Efficiency. Essays in Honor of Abba P. Lerner,* Cambridge, MA, MIT Press, 1979: The Massachusetts Institute of Technology, pp. 12–23.

"Consumer's Surplus and Income Redistribution," *Journal of Public Economics,* Vol. XIV, No. 1 (August 1980): North-Holland Publishing Co., pp. 31–47.

"The Politics of Socialist Efficiency," *The American Economist,* Vol. XXIV, No. 2 (Fall 1980): the author, pp. 5–11.

INDEX

price-output elasticity and, 272, 274, 276

price-wage elasticity and, 276, 279–281

public-utility price formula and, 272

savings elasticity and, 278

supply function elasticity and, 270

Independence of Irrelevant Alternatives, Arrow's condition of, 41–44, 45n12, 47–48, 50

Index number formulas, 128–134, 137

Index number theory, 66, 73n1, 121–122, 124, 274. *See also* Frisch, Ragnar, *New Methods*

Indivisibilities

and Competitive Solution, 174, 195

and marginal cost pricing, 161–166 passim

Interdependence of household welfare, 155–156

Investment goods, 274–286 passim

Kahn, R. F., 3nn2,3, 10–11n5, 13n7, 17nn3,4,5, 18, 21, 152–153

and distribution of money incomes, 14–15n9

Kamerschen, David, 77, 86

Kaplan, N., 200–201n13

Kendrick, J. W., 136n13

Keynes, J. M., 57n5, 273, 277, 278–279n27, 284n3

Knight, Frank, 163–164n34

Kornai, János, 200

Labor theory of value, 185–187

Lancaster, Kelvin, 224

Landauer, C., 185–186n77

Lange, Oscar, 14n9, 21n5, 58n5, 152n13, 157n24, 199, 202, 208, 211, 221n2, 250, 273

on Competitive Solution, 172–181 passim, 193, 194, 196–201 passim, 207, 214–217

on Consumers' Sovereignty, 150, 160–161

on fixed coefficients, 181–182, 184–185

on Mises, 188–189

on socialist distribution of income, 154, 199

Laspeyre formula for index numbers, 66n1

Laspeyre quantity index, 122

Leibenstein, Harvey, 77, 82–86 passim, 91

Leontief, Wassily, 57n1, 134n11, 185

Leontief-Solow conditions, 134n11

Lerner, Abba P., 3n3, 10–11n5, 13n7, 14n9, 19–22, 105, 106n6, 147n, 273, 274n23

on socialist economics, 154, 157, 160, 162–166 passim, 167n42

Lerner Conditions, 9–10

Levine, H. S., 200–201n13

Lewis, W. A., 162, 166

Lipsey, R. G., 224

Liptak, T., 200

Little, I. M. D., 121n15

Macesich, George, 208n20

Managers under socialism

errors in forecasts of, 175–177, 194, 201

incentives for, 174–175, 194, 198–199, 207, 217, 250–257 passim

risk taking of, 249–250, 252, 257–261

success criteria for, 193–199 passim

Marginal utility, 58–59, 66

Frisch's measure of, 87

Marginal versus average cost and economic optimum, 161–167

Marschak, Jacob L., 198, 200–201n13, 202–203n15

theorem of, 240, 245

Marshall, Alfred, 3nn2,3, 10–11n5, 13n7, 14–15n9, 17–18, 95, 100–104 passim, 105n5, 148–156, 163–164

demand schedule of, 79–80

Marx, Karl

and labor theory of value, 185–187, 215

and market processes, 207

Massé, Pierre, 201

Mathematical planning techniques, 215–216

under socialism, 199–201